Talking Matters

Research on Talk and Communication of International Teaching Assistants

Edited by Greta Gorsuch

Stillwater, Oklahoma
U.S.A.

NEW FORUMS PRESS INC.

Published in the United States of America
by New Forums Press, Inc.1018 S. Lewis St.
Stillwater, OK 74074
www.newforums.com

Copyright © 2015 by New Forums Press, Inc.

All rights reserved. No part of this publication may be reproduced or transmitted in any form or by any means, electronic or mechanical, including photocopy, or any information storage or retrieval system, without permission in writing from the publisher.

Library of Congress Cataloging-in-Publication Data Pending

This book may be ordered in bulk quantities at discount from New Forums Press, Inc., P.O. Box 876, Stillwater, OK 74076 [Federal I.D. No. 73 1123239]. Printed in the United States of America.

ISBN 10: 1-58107-284-8
ISBN 13: 978-1-58107-284-6

Table of Contents

Introduction: International Teaching Assistants Learning to Talk in Academic Departments..........................*vii*
By Greta Gorsuch, Texas Tech University

What Academic Departments and ITA Programs Need to Do ....*xix*

Contributors, Reviewers, and Acknowledgements ....*xxvii*

Part One: ITAs' Talk in and out of Classrooms 1

Spoken Parentheticals in Instructional Discourse in STEM and Non-STEM Disciplines: The Interaction of the Prosodic, Ideational, and Interpersonal Resources in Signaling Information Structure..3
By Tammy Slater, John Levis, and Greta Muller Levis, Iowa State University

Achieving Successful Instructional Interaction in a Chemistry Laboratory: Participant Perspectives 33
By Barbara Gourlay, Brown University

Interaction and Discourse Markers in the ITA-led Physics Laboratory 75
By Stephen Daniel Looney, Pennsylvania State University

>Classroom Learning Material: The Location and Function of *Okay* and *So* Worksheet 105

Judgments of Non-standard Segmental Sounds and International Teaching Assistants' Spoken Proficiency Levels..109
By Jiyon Im, Suwon High Tech High School and John Levis, Iowa State University

Cohesion and Perceived Proficiency in ITA Oral
   Communication across Engineering and the Sciences 139
   By Jennifer Haan, University of Dayton

   >Classroom Learning Material: Sample Lab Procedure 161

   >Classroom Learning Material: Schema for Explanation
   Plus Example 162

**Part Two: University Community Entry and Creating
   Contexts for ITAs' Talk and Participation 167**

Communication Enhancement Through Positive Contact
   Activities Between International Teaching Assistants s
   and U.S. Undergraduate Students 169
   *By Okim Kang and Meghan Moran, Northern
   Arizona University*

ITAs' Perceptions of ITA Teaching and Training: The
   Importance of Ongoing and Contextualized Training
   and Mentoring Programs 203
   By Diana Trebing, Saginaw Valley State University

A Study of International Teaching Assistant Recruitment
   Practices in Academic Departments 239
   *By Dale T. Griffee and Greta Gorsuch,
   Texas Tech University*

Working with International Graduate Students as New
   Instructors in a Chemistry Department During a
   Department-specific Summer Orientation 263
   *By Matthew Miller, Ronald Hirko, Kevin Sackreiter,
   and Madelyn Francis, South Dakota State University*

Supporting International Teaching Assistants: A
   Benchmarking Study of Administrative
   and Organizational Structures 287
   *By Karen Brinkley-Etzkorn, Ferlin McGaskey, Laurie Knox, and
   Taimi Olsen, University of Tennessee at Knoxville*

Part Three: ITAs, Tests, and Language Politics 311

Native and Non-native English Speaking ITA
 Performance Test Raters: Do They Rate ITA Candidates
 Differently? 313
 By Jeremy Ray Gevara, Pennsylvania State University;
 Greta Gorsuch, Texas Tech University;
 Hasan Almekdash, Texas Tech University;
 Wei Jiang, Texas A & M University

Index 347

Introduction: International Teaching Assistants Learning to Talk in Academic Departments

By Greta Gorsuch, Texas Tech University

When I arrived in the U.S. after many years abroad to take a new job as an assistant professor, I was almost casually told that I would be running a "summer workshop" for international teaching assistants (ITAs). "If their English isn't good enough at the end of the workshop, they can take the summer workshop again next year," I was told. This was a stupendous under-conceptualization of the situation on so many levels, and needless to say, my early years of academic life in the U.S. were frantic while I pursued survival and growth as an English as a second language (ESL) teacher and applied linguistics researcher.

At first, I had to learn what ITAs were. In terms of my own school I learned that ITAs were Indian, Chinese, Korean, Turkish, Jordanian, Taiwanese, etc. international students who had been admitted to graduate study at Texas Tech and were to be supported as instructors of undergraduate-level classes and labs in biology, chemistry, physics, and math. The number of ITAs at my school has increased as part of an institution-wide drive to increase student enrollments to 40,000 by the year 2020 (Cook, 2013), and we now actively work with 160+ ITAs per year.

As time passed I developed three strategies to learn how

to plan for and direct the summer workshop, which quickly became a full-year program. I still use the three strategies now. First, set aside all curriculum and assessment structures being used when I arrived, and re-create them using more theoretically motivated instruction, materials, tests, and testing procedures. This process is continuing, and we are currently using Version 9 of our teaching simulation performance test (see contribution by Jeremy Gevara, Greta Gorsuch, Hasan Almekdash and Wei Jiang, this volume). Second, find out as much as I can about ITAs as learners in as many contexts as I can. I have done this by reading, interviewing and observing ITAs, audio recording classes (the biology lab with live rats was a real doozy), and asking ITAs what they thought. Third, get into contact with whoever will talk to me about their work with ITAs, whether they are ITA educators; applied linguists; administrators; or faculty members in math, chemistry, biology, or art departments. *Talking Matters: Research on Talk and Communication of International Teaching Assistants* focuses on the third strategy, in which contributors present their research about ITAs' talk in U.S. university classrooms with an unexpected audience in mind: Faculty members and staff in academic departments. Why them? Because I think we have something to offer, and because I do not think that ITA educators are alone in the venture of supporting ITAs in their roles as instructors of undergraduate content.

Most importantly, in order for ITA programs to survive, we need the support of the academic departments in which ITAs teach, and in which U.S. undergraduates learn. There are signals that student support programs, such as remedial reading, writing, and math programs for U.S. undergraduates are being shortsightedly cut because they are seen as "obstacles to progress" to students' timely graduation (Mangan, 2013). Given the slowness of critical aspects of ITAs' second language development (Gorsuch, 2014), there must be some individuals in academic departments and university administration, and even among ITAs themselves, who think that ITA preparation courses are an obstacle to timely degree completion. Perhaps they think that ITAs will learn to talk in English and teach in English simply by being in the U.S. (incorrect), and by observing teaching done by senior faculty members, which is not a model that works well for American TAs, much less ITAs. Therefore, a major audience for this book is faculty members and staff in academic departments who take a different view and see the need to work with ITAs and their talk in sustained ways over time. This book is designed to inform and facilitate their work, and to create an accessible knowledge base portraying how ITA educators describe and think about ITAs' talk, and how they try to expand ITAs' resources to talk and teach in English.

In this report I will present a context for ITA education, and then will make a case for what I think ought to be a central purpose for our mutual work with ITAs: Planning programs and cultivating in-department conditions to develop ITAs' procedural knowledge for talking and teaching in English. In other words, learning to do by doing.

Background on International Teaching Assistants (ITAs) and Institutional Support

Thirty years ago, as the number of ITAs assigned to teach required undergraduate classes in the U.S. began to increase, the ITAs' lack of ability to use English to talk and teach in classrooms brought noises of protest from students and parents, and legislation mandating language assessment for ITAs at universities (Hoekje & Linnell 1994; Thomas & Monoson 1991). The ITA program I was running was an early response to this movement and was, and still is, an ESL program (Texas Tech University, 2013). Nationally, 300,430 international graduate students were enrolled in U.S. universities in 2011-2012, and 164,394 were supported by those schools, likely many of them as teaching assistants (The Institute of International Education, 2013). 90% of them came from countries in which English is not widely or consistently used for official, social, or educational purposes (The Institute of International Education, 2013). The overall trend of growth in ITA numbers and an increasing salience of ITAs' contributions to undergraduates' educational experiences are mirrored in Canada (Kim & Kubota, 2012). The website of the ITA Interest Section of TESOL (Teachers of English to Speakers of Other Languages), a large international professional ESL organization, has links to 57 ITA programs in the U.S. (ITA Interest Section, 2013).

Universities have responded to ITAs' needs in other ways,

including department-specific efforts (see Mestenhauser, 1988; Weimer, Svinicki, & Bauer, 1989) and also university-wide programs orchestrated by teaching specialists in now-familiar "teaching and learning centers" (Gorsuch, 2006; see also Smock & Menges, 1985; Wulff, Nyquist, & Abbott, 1991). North Carolina State University has a Certificate of Accomplishment in Teaching which, in order to attain it, ITAs and TAs have to take multiple, accumulated short courses and workshops. A positive correlation between ITAs and TAs taking teaching development courses and workshops, and a willingness to innovate in the classroom, has been convincingly established (Ferzli, Morant, Honeycutt, Warren, Fenn, & Burns-Williams, 2012).

There is much to recommend these approaches. Department-specific training would demonstrate to ITAs that learning how to teach is valued by the department. If workshops were designed with authentic practice teaching or guided teaching, and principled feedback and debriefing, such workshops would help ITAs gain access to opportunities for procedural knowledge growth. Valued teaching practices specific to the discipline, *and the talk that goes with them*, can be cultivated (see contribution by Matthew Miller, Ronald Hirko, Kevin Sackreiter, and Madelyn Francis, this volume). At this time, it would be fair to say that all of the approaches described here probably coexist in many universities with varying degrees of intentionality and interconnection. Contributors to this volume Karen Brinkley-Etzkorn, Ferlin McGaskey, and Taimi Olsen provide current and generalizable information on ITA support structures in universities. More to the point, they provide a basis for evaluating how intentional and interconnected ITA support programs are within institutions.

Those Who Work in ITA Programs, and Fields of Knowledge and Inquiry They Draw From

ITA educators employed in ITA programs are ESL instructors (Gorsuch, 2012), and can also be applied linguists (e.g., Hahn, 2004), intercultural communication specialists (e.g., La Rocco, 2012), and conversation analysis specialists, which is a sub-field of sociology (see the contribution in this book from Stephen

Looney, and also Chiang, 2009). There are small (but encouraging) numbers of faculty members in the sciences and humanities who design and run programs for ITAs. There are two bedrock constructs that underlie the areas of knowledge that most of these groups draw on to build and run ITA courses: 1. Communicative competence, and 2. An intermarriage of language, teaching, and culture.

Communicative competence. Communicative competence refers to a second language learners' ability to use the forms of a language (vocabulary, grammar, pronunciation) accurately *and appropriately* in different social contexts (Bachman & Palmer, 1996; Munby, 1978). In other words, ITAs, who are second language *learners*, need to use a difficult-to-learn second language system to listen to and talk with bosses, colleagues, and students; in classrooms as students and as teachers; in offices; and in society. These different contexts represent at-first-unfamiliar educational and social cultures for ITAs. Even ITAs who have "good English" do not necessarily know how to *use* English appropriately or effectively in these new contexts. Communicative competence includes components such as textual competence that are used by ITA educators to plan second language curricula, lessons, and tests. Textual competence, for example, has to do with how well a learner knows and uses well-known and taken-for-granted "scripts" in a language, such as how topics are started and ended in talk, or how concepts such as "energy" are explained to undergraduates (e.g., Levis, Levis Muller, & Slater, 2012). ITA educators are, by and large, concerned with understanding and describing second language *use* in academic contexts, and finding ways to develop ITAs' communicative competence in those contexts. The contributions by Stephen Looney and Jennifer Haan are but two examples of this type of inquiry to be found in this volume.

Language, teaching, and culture. Language, teaching, and culture are seen as comprising the needs of ITAs (Civickly & Muchisky, 1991; Hoekje & Williams, 1994). This trilogy guides the curricula of most ITA programs (see Gorsuch, 2012 for empirical evidence of this; see also Kaufman & Brownworth, 2006). For ITA educators, language, teaching, and culture have deep theoretical and practical connections. In terms of *language and teaching* for instance, many ITA educators focus on ITAs' talk as teachers, employing teaching simulations, and authentic classroom dialogs and recordings for instruction and assessment of ITAs' talk (Gorsuch, 2012; Gorsuch, Meyers, Pickering, & Griffee, 2013; Halleck & Moder, 1995). Applied linguists such as Levis et al (2012) pointed out that a lack of second language resources interacts in significant ways with the effectiveness of ITAs' teaching talk used to explain fundamental science concepts. They suggested areas needing explicit ESL instruction based on their findings, which were later applied to a suggested course of second language learning tasks (Gorsuch, forthcoming) aimed specifically at improving ITAs' teaching talk in English.

In terms of *language and culture*, at least one ITA program has used theoretical understandings from sociolinguistics to explore "the various contextualization cues ([speech]rhythm, intonation, lexicon) that contribute to miscommunication between speakers from different cultures" (Tapper & Kidder, 2006, p. 17; Tyler & Davies, 1990). The ITA program at the University of Florida uses a curriculum model based on these research findings where ITAs are given supervised teaching duties, are video-recorded by ITA program staff, and then given feedback on their talk and communicative competence.

Debates over language, teaching, and culture. There has arisen some debate as to which of the three components to emphasize more, and how to combine them. In a distinct departure from the concerns of many ESL-oriented ITA educators, a core emphasis on "language" has been questioned with various commentators arguing for more emphasis on teaching (e.g., LoCastro & Tapper, 2006; Kim & Kubota, 2012;) or culture (e.g., Kang & Rubin, 2012) for ITA support. This seems to come partly out of a resistance to viewing ITAs as linguistically deficient. Is it not the case that the undergraduates who ITAs teach, have just as great a role and responsibility in classroom communication? Do they not have just as much learning to do as ITAs? Applied linguists and intercultural specialists such as Okim Kang have a point— U.S. undergraduates are responsible to adjust to ITAs' talk, as ITAs are to adjust to talking and teaching in classroom cultures new to them. There are principled and practical ways to increase contact between U.S. undergraduates and ITAs through shared talk and problem-solving which will have positive effects on

ITAs' *and* undergraduates' intercultural competence (see Okim Kang's and Meghan Moran's contribution in this volume).

Nonetheless, ITAs' ability to talk in English and use it to teach is a pervasive subtext that cannot be discounted, and this is the chosen mantle of many ITA educators, including me. Learning to talk fluently and reasonably accurately in any second language is a slow, time-consuming process--just imagine a native English speaker learning how to lecture on physics in Chinese or Italian (Gorsuch, 2014; see also Lennon, 2000). This is particularly true with key features of pronunciation ITAs need to learn how to use while talking in classrooms so they can emphasize key information in their talk, and show engagement with students and enthusiasm about the course content (Gorsuch, forthcoming). For ITAs to learn how to teach, or to access teaching experience gained in their home countries, they have to develop procedural knowledge, or "how to perform things" in their second language, which is English (Chiang, 2009, p. 464). As Kim (2001) argues, one main means of cultural adaptation "occurs in and through communication," which is, again, in English, the second language. This then leads us to the importance of working with ITAs and their talk from the point of view of procedural knowledge development.

What Procedural Knowledge is, Why ITAs Need It, and Why ITA Programs Alone Cannot Give It

"Procedural knowledge" is "how to perform things" (Chiang, 2009, p. 464). This type of knowledge is different from "propositional knowledge" which is "factual knowledge about the world" (Chiang, 2009, p. 464). I think that on some areas of ITA need, ITA programs end up offering propositional knowledge at the expense of opportunities to develop procedural knowledge. The main reason is that ITA educators are caught up in a contradiction, both in terms of teaching and in terms of educational cultures. We are, more often than not, language learning specialists but not content specialists in science, math, or history. We work with advanced second language learners who work in academic areas we are not completely familiar with. Working with ITAs from 20 - 25 different academic departments, we do not necessarily know what teaching talk is valued, even though we care deeply about it.

We have limited time to work with ITAs (usually three hours per week for up to two semesters; see descriptions of ITA program curricula, Gorsuch, 2012). We may find it easier and more time-efficient to reduce culture and teaching to presenting "norms" of undergraduate behavior to ITAs through reading assignments or lectures on "good teaching practices," which assumes ITAs do not already know good teaching practices. This would build ITAs' propositional knowledge but would not give ITAs opportunities to learn how to use talk to negotiate cultural differences in the classroom ("Yes, I know you work until late at night but I still want you to come to class on time." Or "You look confused. You don't get my example of a torch? You use a different word for that? Ah, flashlight.") or handle undergraduates' questions in a way that result in learning ("You have questions about your lab report grade? Bring over the lab report grading criteria and tell me on which criteria you think you should be graded higher on.").

Gaining procedural knowledge requires ITAs getting experience doing things. Thus, procedural knowledge to talk and teach in English requires ITAs talking and teaching in English. This may seem self-evident and something not requiring theories to demonstrate it. Yet theories point out the "how" part, which we need to know in order to create more effective ITA support. There are two theoretical areas that strongly point to the role of experience doing things to attain desired expertise. One, self-efficacy, is from psychology, and a second, practice, comes from applied linguistics and second language learning. The theories have high usability for ITA support personnel from any background.

Self-efficacy. Self-efficacy "is an ability construct…that refers to individual's beliefs about their capabilities to perform well" (Graham & Weiner, 1995, p. 74). Self-efficacy is not naïve self-confidence. Self-efficacy is based on learners' accumulating experiences of growing success doing tasks, such as verbally reviewing or re-teaching a concept to undergraduates under guidance from a faculty member. Thus when an ITA is asked to perform a new task in English, such as being the sole leader of a review session on to-be-tested science concepts, he or she makes a self-judgment about what he or she knows how to do, and organizes and executes "courses of action required to attain designated performances" (Snow, Corno, & Jackson, 1995, p. 277). In other words, ITAs need to have experiences talking in classrooms in order to mentally plan, prepare, and self-evaluate other future target tasks they must do in English.

Self-efficacy, then, suggests that ITAs (or any novice teachers, including native English speaking TAs) be given clear tasks they are to do, and preparation time for doing them. It does not take a lot of time for an ITA educator or ITA mentor to talk through a just-completed teaching task with an ITA. Sample mentoring questions would be:

- What do you think went well? How do you know?
- What have you done before in the classroom or office hours that helped you prepare?
- What do you want to change? How do you want to go about changing it?
- What do you want to try next? What do you need to do to prepare?
- What do you need from me?

Practice. Practice may seem like a commonplace term, but in the field of second language learning, "practice" refers to cognitive processes that transform declarative (or propositional) knowledge into procedural knowledge (DeKeyser, 2007a). Most second language (L2) learners take classes in high school or college (such as German, French, or Japanese courses for American students in the U.S., or English or Thai courses for Chinese students in China) where declarative knowledge is built up in the form of lessons on grammar and vocabulary. Generally, L2 courses are scheduled the same as content courses such as history or math, at perhaps three times a week for 14 weeks, which is not sufficient to practice what is learned in authentic, communicative ways to the point declarative knowledge (propositional knowledge) becomes proceduralized. In other words, most L2 learners know *about* the second language (even though grammar and vocabulary is only a part of communicative competence), but they do not know *how to do* the L2. This may be true even after four or five years of study. Certainly, many ITAs come to the U.S. unable to use English to talk and teach (Gorsuch, 2011).

ESL programs in China are largely unaware of future Chinese ITAs' communication needs as teachers overseas (Gorsuch, 2011).

How U.S. undergraduates' study abroad is like ITAs being in the U.S. DeKeyser (2007b) described what may happen with propositional and procedural knowledge in the second language in U.S. university students who study an L2 abroad. His commentary is eerily apt for describing the cognitive experiences of ITAs in the U.S. American students studying abroad in say, France, certainly have more opportunities to use some of the French they previously learned in the U.S. This is accomplished in study abroad during homestays and through other contacts in ordinary French society. U.S. students' talk in French improves in fluency ("smoothness") with longer utterances, which suggests some automatization of some of their propositional knowledge of French. This means that this part of their knowledge has become easier to access so it can be used in real-time speech conditions.

Unfortunately, there is little evidence that the same learners improve in grammatical range (DeKeyser, 2007b), suggesting a lack of conceptual richness in the students' talk. DeKeyser (2007b, p. 213) explained: "when students begin their stays overseas, they are so overwhelmed by the communicative demands on them that they try to skip the proceduralization stage" and they simply learn to use some memorized phrases and chunks more automatically. Learners are working hard to talk with their French homestay families but "that leaves them no time to draw on their hard-to-access declarative [propositional] knowledge" (p. 213). Without ways to access, and re-access, *and re-access* declarative knowledge at the same time it is being used and practiced, L2 knowledge cannot become proceduralized. Thus learners tend to talk and perform at levels below what they are capable of and may get stuck there. DeKeyser also questions how much L2 practice overseas study learners actually get, suggesting that the homesick students actually seek out their classmates to use English with (p. 212). There are many anecdotal reports that ITAs in the U.S., seeking social and emotional support, create Chinese or Korean or Turkish speaking communities and use very little English (Gorsuch, 2012).

What is relevant to ITAs, ITA programs, and academic departments in terms of practice, is DeKeyser's recommendation that by all means L2 learners (ITAs) should have practice opportunities (which academic departments can do more to provide), but with an eye to helping learners retrieve and review declarative (propositional) knowledge through debriefing sessions (p. 219) and continuing instruction in the second language (which ITA programs can do). This would contribute to ITAs' procedural knowledge growth, their ability to "do" English pursuant to target tasks. Practice alone is not enough. Figure 1 below shows a model of how this might work in North American universities:

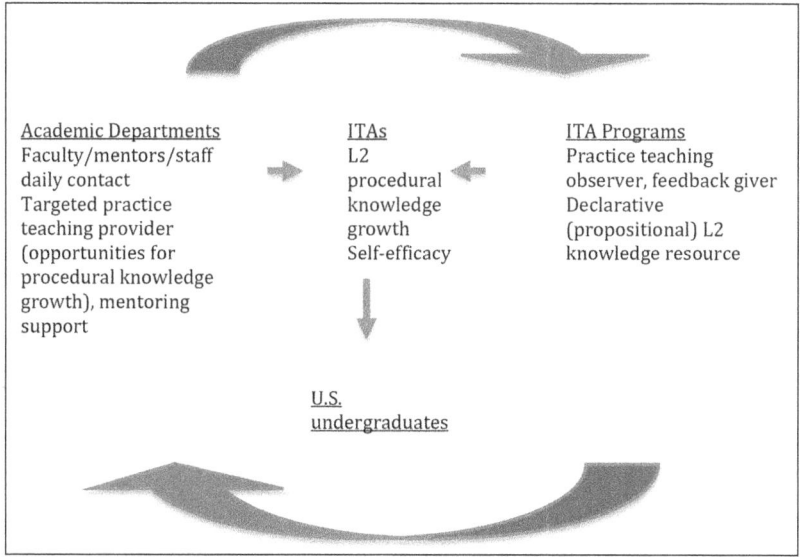

Figure 1. Existing and proposed relationships between academic departments, ITA programs, ITAs, and undergraduates.

Existing Relationships Which can be Enhanced

The small arrows in Figure 1 depict existing relationships between academic departments, ITAs, undergraduates, and ITA programs. Firstly, we know that academic departments provide teaching opportunities for ITAs--the ITAs were admitted to graduate school with the assumption they would be eventually supported as instructors of undergraduate math or science classes (see contribution by Dale Griffee and Greta Gorsuch, this volume). It is likely these teaching opportunities have an effect on ITAs' L2 learning and self-efficacy by offering experience using English talk in department-specific target tasks (giving an assignment, explaining a lab procedure, etc.). Admittedly, this assumption remains under-researched. For instance, if mentors in the departments do not offer consistent feedback or otherwise let ITAs know what they have accomplished and what still needs work, ITAs cannot develop self-efficacy with a realistic self-understanding of what they do that works well. These self-understandings are needed as building blocks with which to plan performances on new tasks. Conversations with ITAs already teaching suggest that at least some departments do not offer feedback (Gorsuch & Sokolowski, 2007).

Secondly, we know that ITA programs have an effect on ITAs' L2 learning and, possibly, self-efficacy, by offering non-specific teaching simulation tasks. Certainly, there is much discussion among ITA educators on good ways to give feedback to ITAs for their teaching simulation tasks, which we can take only on trust as being somewhat relevant to department-specific task targets. But this again is an under-researched area. Is our feedback to ITAs focused consistently on the same English talk and classroom communication issues, session after session? ITA programs can offer explicit instruction and/or advice on language forms, such as appropriate phrases for calling class to order or to change topics, examples for concepts undergraduates would be familiar with, and specific pronunciation strategies to show engagement and interest. If DeKeyser is right, ITA programs ought to focus on ways for ITAs to access, and re-access, their declarative knowledge in the context of practice.

Thirdly and finally, we know that ITAs have an effect on the learning of undergraduate students.

Two Proposed Relationships

The two large curved arrows at the top and bottom of the model in Figure 1 are proposed relationships which may enhance existing relationships to optimize ITAs' procedural knowledge growth to use English to teach: 1. ITA programs need to seek academic departments' cooperation in setting up regular practice teaching opportunities for ITAs who still need work on their English, and 2. Academic departments need to seek the cooperation of ITA programs to observe ITAs' teaching in the departments and offer consistent feedback and instruction designed to proceduralize ITAs' L2 and teaching knowledge.

There are challenges. Many academic departments may be unwilling to hand off ITAs with shaky English to already-overworked senior TAs, ITAs, and other instructional staff. Most instructors find it challenging enough to teach their own classes at the level of professionalism and skill they desire. They may wish to focus on undergraduates' learning and getting decent student evaluations. Imagine then having a senior faculty member say, "Here's a new person, don't know how good her English is, have her teach some review sessions." It takes extra thought and planning to include another instructor in a lesson. It may turn out alright, and mostly it has done in my 14 years of observations, but what if the new ITA bombs, or cannot teach the last minute? And there is a case to be made for allowing only *higher-level*, almost-but-not-quite-there ITA candidates to do practice teaching in their departments. ITAs who come to the U.S. with very low English levels may not have sufficient automaticity to even have social conversations. It would be a cruelty to make them stand up and stammer in front of a classroom full of 18 and 19 year old undergraduates.

What Academic Departments and ITA Programs Need to Do

For the model in Figure 1 to work, the following is needed from academic departments:
1. Academic departments should find ways to reward and recognize instructional staff who take ITAs into their classrooms as guest teachers (see Appendix for an example letter).
2. Academic departments should decide and disseminate their preferences for practice teaching arrangements. These could include considerations of: How many times a week an ITA should attend a practice teaching class; What sorts of target talking tasks ITAs should build up to; Ensuring the ITA feels a sense of responsibility to

teach when the hosting instructor wants him or her to teach; How much advance notice an ITA should have on the teaching topic; and Whether or not ITAs should write up a lesson plan for the hosting instructor's perusal prior to teaching.
3. Academic departments need to include in their general mindset that ITAs need practice teaching opportunity.

And, the following is needed from ITA programs:

4. ITA programs should certify that ITAs who engage in practice teaching be sufficiently fluent and able to talk in English. Not perfectly—otherwise, why would they need practice teaching? But good enough to hammer out what they wish to say in English even if at first it sounds clumsy.
5. ITA programs need to include practice teaching in academic departments in their ITA preparation course planning.
6. ITA programs need to be deliberate and consistent with their feedback to ITAs after teaching observations in academic departments, and also need to encourage ITAs to discuss this feedback with academic department mentors or hosting instructors.

It would be easy to simply keep listing what the various parties could do. But the main points here are the two large, curved arrows connecting ITA programs to academic departments, and academic departments to ITA programs. Because I am an ITA educator, I write from the point of view of ITA programs. ITA programs need the support of academic departments: Departments are likely places for ITAs to find opportunities for procedural knowledge development to learn how to talk in classrooms. It is my hope that the contributions of the authors in this book, which were reviewed for relevance and on-the-ground usability, will support a greater focus on procedural knowledge development for ITAs, whether through planned, centralized ITA programs, or through the individual efforts of faculty members, mentors, supervisors, and other support personnel in academic departments.

In a Nutshell

1. *Talking Theories* is intended for multiple audiences, including faculty members and staff in academic departments.
2. ITA educators, traditionally ESL teachers and/or applied linguists, cannot alone support ITAs as instructors of undergraduate content.
3. This introduction proposes new relationships between ITA educators and the academic departments ITAs study and work in.
4. Together, ITA educators and academic departments need to create opportunities for qualified ITA candidates to team-teach or guest-teach in classes where they will eventually be the primary instructors.
5. Such practice-teaching experience can only be provided by academic departments.
6. Specific feedback on practice teaching performances, and directly relevant language instruction, is most profitably provided by ITA educators.
7. Practice teaching in academic departments and support from ITA educators can together improve ITAs' procedural ability to talk in classrooms through the development of self-efficacy, and the cognitive language learning processes engendered by practice.

References

Bachman, L. & Palmer, A. (1996). *Language testing in practice*. Oxford: Oxford University Press.

Chiang, S. (2009). Dealing with communication problems in the instructional interactions between international teaching assistants and American college students. *Language and Education, 23*(5), 461-478.

Civikly, J. & Muchisky, D. (1991). A collaborative approach to ITA training: The ITAs, faculty, TAs, undergraduate interns, and undergraduate students. In J.

Nyquist, R. Abbott, D. Wulff, & J. Sprague (Eds.), *Preparing the professoriate of tomorrow to teach* (pp. 356-360). Dubuque, IA: Kendall Hunt.

Cook, C. (2013). Texas Tech eclipses 33,000 enrollment for first time. *Texas Tech Today*. Available: http://today.ttu.edu/2013/09/texas-tech-eclipses-33000-enrollment-for-first-time/

DeKeyser, R. (2007a). *Practice in a second language: Perspectives from applied linguistics and cognitive psychology*. Cambridge: Cambridge University Press.

DeKeyser, R. (2007b). Study abroad as foreign language practice. In R. DeKeyser (Ed.), *Practice in a second language: Perspectives from applied linguistics and cognitive psychology* (pp. 208-226). Cambridge: Cambridge University Press.

Ferzli, M., Morant, T., Honeycutt, B., Warren, S., Fenn, M., & B. Burns (2012). Conceptualizing graduate teaching assistant development through stages of concern. In G. Gorsuch (Ed.), *Working theories for teaching assistant development* (pp. 231-274). Stillwater, OK: New Forums Press.

Gorsuch, G. (2006). Discipline-specific practica for international teaching assistants. *English for Specific Purposes, 25*, 90-108.

Gorsuch, G.J. (2011). Exporting English pronunciation from China: The communication needs of young Chinese scientists as teachers in higher education abroad. *Forum on Public Policy, 2011*(3). Available: http://forumonpublicpolicy.com/vol2011no3/archive/gorsuch.pdf

Gorsuch, G. (2012). The roles of teacher theory and domain theory in materials and research in international teaching assistant education. In G. Gorsuch (Ed.). *Working theories for teaching assistant development.* (pp. 421-474). Stillwater, OK: New Forums Press.

Gorsuch, G. (2014). Improving discourse intonation for international teaching assistants: How slow thou art. *ITAIS Newsletter*. Available: http://newsmanager.commpartners.com/tesolslwis/textonly/2014-03-06/6.html

Gorsuch, G. (forthcoming). International teaching assistants at universities: A research agenda. *Language Teaching.*

Gorsuch, G., Meyers, C., Pickering, L, & Griffee, D. (2013). *English communication for international teaching assistants* (2nd ed.). Long Grove, IL: Waveland Press, Inc.

Gorsuch, G. & Sokolowski, J. (2007). International teaching assistants and summative and formative student evaluation. *The Journal of Faculty Development, 21*(2), 117-136.

Graham, S. & Weiner, B. (1995). Theories of principles of motivation. In D. Berliner & R. Calfee (Eds.), *Handbook of educational psychology* (pp. 63-84). New York: MacMillan Library Reference USA.

Gumperz, J. & Cook-Gumperz, J. (2007). Discourse, cultural diversity and communciation. A linguistic anthropological perspective. In H. Kotthoff & H. Spencer-Oatey (eds.), *Handbook of intercultural communication*. Berlin: Mouton de Gruyter, 127-151.

Gunthner, S. (2007). Intercultural communication and the relevance of cultural specific repertoires of communicative genres. In H. Kotthoff & H. Spencer-Oatey (Eds.), *Handbook of intercultural communication* (pp. 127-151). Mouton de Gruyter, Berlin.

Hahn, L. (2004). Primary stress and intelligibility: Research to motivate the teaching of suprasegmentals. *TESOL Quarterly,* 38.2, 201-223.

Halleck, G. & Moder, C. (1995). Testing language and teaching skills of international teaching assistants: The limits of compensatory strategies. *TESOL Quarterly,* 29(4), 733-758.

Hoekje, B., & Linnell, K. (1994). "Authenticity" in language testing: Evaluating spoken language tests for international teaching assistants. *TESOL Quarterly,* 28.1, 103-126.

Hoekje, B. & Williams, J. (1994). Communicative competence as a theoretical framework for ITA education. In C. Madden & C. Myers (Eds.), *Discourse and performance of international teaching assistants* (pp. 11-26). Alexandria, VA: Teachers of English to Speakers of Others Languages. The Institute of International Education (2013). *Open doors 2011/2012 fast facts.* Available: http://www.iie.org/Research-and-Publications/Open-Doors

ITA Interest Section (2013). *ITA programs.* Retrieved from: http://www.ita-is.org/links.html

Kang, O. & Rubin, D. (2012). Intergroup contact exercises as a tool for mitigating undergraduates' attitudes toward nonnative English-speaking teaching assistants. *Journal on Excellence in College Teaching,* 23(3), 159-166.

Kaufman, D. & Brownworth, B. (Eds.)(2006). *Professional development of international teaching assistants.* Alexandia, VA: Teachers of English to Speakers of Other Languages.

Kim, S. & Kubota, R. (2012). Supporting nonnative English-speaking instructors to maximize student learning in their courses: A message from the guest editors. *Journal on Excellence in College Teaching,* 23.3, 1-6.

Kim, Y.Y. (2001). *Becoming intercultural: An integrative theory of communication and cross-cultural adaptation.* Thousand Oaks, CA: Sage Publications, Inc.

LaRocco, M. J. (2012). Chinese International Teaching Assistants and the essence of Intercultural Competence in university contexts. In G. Gorsuch (Ed.), *Working*

theories for teaching assistant development (pp. 609-653). Stillwater, OK: New Forums Press.

Lennon, P. (2000). The lexical element in spoken second language fluency. In H. Riggenbach (Ed.). *Perspectives on fluency* (pp. 25-42). Ann Arbor, MI: The University of Michigan Press.

Levis, J., Muller Levis, G., & Slater, T. (2012). Written English into spoken: A functional discourse analysis of American, Indian, and Chinese TA presentations. In G. Gorsuch (Ed.), *Working theories for teaching assistand-evelopment* (pp. 529-573). Stillwater, OK: New Forums Press.

LoCastro, V. & Tapper, G. (2006). International teaching assistants and teacher identity. *Journal of Applied Linguistics,* 3(2), 185-218.

Magnan, K. (September 27, 2013). Florida colleges make plans for students to opt out of remedial work. *The Chronicle of Higher Education.* A4–A7.

Mestenhauser, J.A. (1988). Adding the disciplines: From theory to relevant practice. In J. Mestenhauser, G. Marty, & I. Steglitz (Eds.), *Culture, learning and the disciplines* (p. 168-182). Washington, D.C.: National Association for Foreign Student Affairs.

Munby, J. (1978). *Communicative syllabus design*. Cambridge: Cambridge University Press.

Smock, R. & Menges, R. (1985). Programs for TAs in the context of campus policies and priorities. In J. Andrews (Ed.), *Strengthening the teaching assistant faculty* (pp. 21-33). San Francisco: Jossey-Bass, Inc.

Snow, R., Corno, L., & Jackson, D. (1995). Individual differences in affective and conative functions. In D. Berliner & R. Calfee (Eds.), *Handbook of educational psychology* (pp. 243-310). New York: MacMillan Library Reference USA.

Tapper, G. & Kidder, K. (2006). A research-informed approach to international teaching assistant preparation. In D. Kaufman & B. Brownworth (Eds.). *Professional development of international teaching assistants* (pp. 17-33). Alexandria, VA: Teaching English to Speakers of Other Languages, Inc.

Texas Tech University (2013). *History and mandated purpose of ITA program*. Available: http://www.depts.ttu.edu/classic%5Fmodern/ita/itabackground.php

Thomas, C., & Monoson, P. (1991). Issues related to state-mandates English language proficiency requirements. In J. Nyquist, R.D. Abbott, D.H. Wulff, & J. Sprague (eds.). *Preparing the professoriate of tomorrow to teach*. Dubuque, IA: Kendall/Hunt Publishing Company, 382-392.

Tyler, A. & Davies, C. (1990). Cross linguistic communication missteps. *Text, 10*(4), 385-411.

Weimer, M., Svinicki, M. & Bauer, G. (1989). Designing programs to prepare ITAs to teach. In J. Nyqist, R. Abbott, & D. Wulff (Eds.), *Teaching assistant training in the 1990s* (pp. 57-70). San Francisco: Jossey-Bass, Inc.

Wulff, D., Nyquist, J. & Abbott, R. (1991). Developing a TA program that reflects the culture of the institution: TA training at the University of Washington. In J. Nyquist, R. Abbott, D. Wulff, & J. Sprague (Eds.), *Preparing the professoriate of tomorrow to teach* (pp. 113-122). Dubuque, IA: Kendall/Hunt Publishing Company.

Appendix

Sample Thank You Letter for Hosting TAs or Instructors

Amazing State University
Even More Amazing Department

December 21, 2014

Dear Mr. XXX (host teacher's name),

    I wanted to thank you for hosting Ms. XXX (ITA's name) for guided teaching in your Physics 1404 class this past semester. It is difficult for new teachers and graduate students at a university to find practice teaching opportunities in their departments. Having such experiences is indispensible to improving teaching at the university. The guided teaching in your class helped give Ms. XXX a realistic view of what is required for her future academic and professional career.

    Many thanks for the time and effort it took for you to host this teacher new to our university.

    Sincerely,

(important person's name here with title)

Contributors, Reviewers, and Acknowledgements

There are two main groups who made *Talking Matters* possible. First were the contributors, and second were the reviewers.

Contributors

Contributors were located by having an open call for contributions in teaching and learning center listservs, ITA education listservs, applied linguistics listservs, and by word of mouth. Contributors sent me lengthy abstracts of their proposed work for the volume. After a period of time, contributors sent me their first full drafts, which I then sent to a panel of reviewers. Reviewers sent me comments and suggestions, and these suggestions, along with my suggestions, were relayed to the contributors. Second drafts were then sent to me, and the manuscripts went through a period of development through intensive reading and editing on my part, and intensive rewriting by the contributors. I wish to thank each and every contributor for their patience, and for their trust in me.

The contributors are a diverse group on just about every measure. I wish to point out in particular the graduate students and other emerging scholars who contributed to this book:

- Hasan Almekdash, Texas Tech University
- Karen Brinkley, University of Tennessee
- Jeremy Gevara, Pennsylvania State University
- Jiyon Im, Suwon High Tech High School
- Wei Jiang, Texas A & M University

- Stephen Looney, Pennsylvania State University
- Meghan Moran, Northern Arizona University

Reviewers

The reviewers are just as diverse. I searched for reviewers in much the same way I found contributors, through teaching and learning center listservs, ITA education listservs, applied linguistics listservs, and by word of mouth. I admit it was difficult to find reviewers, and that this aspect of *Talking Matters* took much more effort than I imagined. It was worth it. The reviewers are:

- Stefanie Borst, Associate Professor of German and Associate Dean of the College of Arts and Sciences and long-time TA and ITA mentor, Texas Tech University
- Beth Grayson, Math Department Co-Chair and materials designer and long-time teacher trainer, Texas Public Schools
- Scott Holaday, Professor of Biological Sciences and long-time ITA mentor, Texas Tech University
- Mara Neusel, Professor of Mathematics and Graduate Director and diversity worker, Texas Tech University
- Victor Peppard, Chair, Department of World Languages, University of Southern Florida
- Niina Ronkainen, Associate Professor of Chemistry, Benedictine University
- James Valentine, Director, American Language Institute, University of Southern California
- Pamela Webster, Director of the Math Skills Center, Texas A & M University at Commerce
- Aubrey White, Senior Business Assistant in University Student Housing and mentor to graduate students in Mechanical Engineering, Texas Tech University

I was privileged to work with these individuals. I wish particularly to commend Mara Neusel who generously offered her time and support on the project before her untimely death. She is much missed.

Behind-the-Scenes Players

There is a final group of behind-the-scenes players who rarely get mentioned. They are proof that no matter how discouraged I may get, there are those who stand behind the scenes who sometimes give the most valuable and timely help. They make my work possible. Thanks to Dale Griffee, beloved spouse, and ITA educator in his own right. Thanks also to Kathy Austin Belz, Douglas Dollar, and Lucy Pickering. Thanks to Stefanie Borst and Erin Collopy for the inspiration to create "In a Nutshell" sections for each chapter.

Part One

ITAs' Talk in and out of Classrooms

Spoken Parentheticals in Instructional Discourse in STEM and Non-STEM Disciplines: The Interaction of the Prosodic, Ideational, and Interpersonal Resources in Signaling Information Structure

By Tammy Slater,[1] John Levis, and Greta Muller Levis, Iowa State University

Parentheticals, information that is not directly relevant to the topic being addressed, appear in all academic lectures and help listeners distinguish important from less important information. Their use is a critical skill for all teachers. Despite their importance, research on parentheticals in teaching is scarce. This chapter explores the instructional discourse of native English-speaking teaching assistants and international teaching assistants regarding the use of parentheticals, primarily in terms of the intonational and informational patterns they exhibit. Our analysis involved discourse data collected from sixteen classes, eight from chemistry (four taught by native English-speaking TAs and four taught by

1. Author contact: tslater@iastate.edu

ITAs) and eight from English (also four taught by TAs and four by ITAs). While our study suggested that parentheticals can be used to connect the teacher and students interpersonally, and to break up the density of the lecture, we uncovered interesting differences between TAs and ITAs. Our findings suggest that ITAs may need to learn how to use parentheticals and prosody to break up the density of their lectures. Moreover, by not incorporating parentheticals well, ITAs may come across as unmoving, overly knowledgeable, and even unapproachable. Educators can use these findings to help ITAs better construct a logical hierarchy of information in extended discourse.

Distinguishing important from less important information in a lecture is a critical skill for all teachers. It is frequently achieved through the use of prosody to signal the relative importance of the information being presented. Focused syllables (e.g., *Now THIS is a critical point*) are one key resource to signal importance, but other prosodic strategies are also employed. One of these strategies involves the use of spoken parenthetical utterances. Parentheticals are "expressions that are linearly represented in a given string of utterance (a host sentence), but seem structurally independent" (Dehé & Kavalova, 2007, p. 1). They are said to be marked by special prosody (Bing, 1980). They also provide information that is not directly relevant to the main topic. Intonationally and informationally, parenthetical information is often overlooked. Our chapter is an exploration of parentheticals in teaching in STEM (Science, Technology, Engineering, Mathematics) and non-STEM fields. These two general areas commonly employ a large number of graduate instructors at North American universities.

Literature Review

Why study parentheticals in instructional discourse? This chapter came about because of our previous study (Levis, Levis, & Slater, 2012) on how Chinese, Indian, and American teaching assistants (TAs) turned content from a beginning physics textbook into the spoken language needed to teach the content. We used a simulated micro-teaching environment in which ITAs were given a short text and 20 minutes to prepare. They then were filmed teaching the topic in a room with a blackboard, a camera, and one researcher. We discovered that in addition to their use of sentence focus to highlight new information and de-stressing to mark old (given) information, TAs (especially the American TAs) also used parenthetical intonation, with a relatively flat, low pitch, often over extended stretches of text. American TAs frequently used this strategy to give information about future classes, in asides that raised topics outside the content of the presentation, in interpersonal connections to their imagined audience, and in a kind of spoken internal commentary on what they were teaching. Given that there was no class present, this surprised us.

Most of the literature on parentheticals in speech that was available at that time (e.g., Bing, 1980; Bolinger, 1989; Ladd, 1980) suggested that typical parentheticals were only a few words long and limited in scope. Early discussion of parentheticals characterized them as quite short, expressing commentary on others (e.g., *He's gone, the jerk*), reflecting differences in politeness strategies (e.g., *I'd like that, please*.) or describing the speech of a narrator in the discourse (e.g., *I'm coming, she said*.). Parenthethicals information in the examples here, and throughout the paper, are underlined. However, we heard something different. Parentheticals were often long and varied in form and function. For example, one of the ways in which American TAs used parenthetical intonation was to give information on what future lectures would include, even though they knew they would not be giving such lectures, as in (1).

(1) and well electric energy /the main way that this is produced then is from Farriday's law / and we'll look at this a little later in the class cause this is a little more complicated / but there's other ways to produce / electric energy too /

The American TAs also used parentheticals to make connections to the lives that the imagined students were presumed to be leading, as in (2), where the TA talks about driving with cell-phones and playing video games.

(2) Now electric energy / umm this is what lights our homes / and it's used for like our everyday appliances and conveniences / and sometimes when I see people driving on the road with their cell phones I kind of wonder why we're even using electric energy /cause not all the forms I guess are that great / but umm / it's also used in like video games and stuff /and I think that's why half of you don't show up some of the time /

Indian and Chinese TAs also used parentheticals, but not in the same ways and not with the same prosodic clues. This raised a question for us: How would parentheticals occur in actual teaching? The differing use of parentheticals in our previous study also raised the question of whether there are differences between Native Teaching Assistants (NTAs) and International Teaching Assistants (ITAs). In this study, NTAs were all American native speakers of English and ITAs were all speakers of other languages learned before English.

Our goal, then, is to determine whether NTAs and ITAs used parentheticals differently. In examining this, we are placing our study within a tradition in ITA research that has demonstrated differences in many areas, not only with pronunciation, but also with grammar and its role in making information accessible (e.g., Tyler, 1992). Research comparing the oral proficiency of NTAs and ITAs has analyzed grammatical and discourse competence, intonation (e.g., Kang, 2010; Levis, et al., 2012; Pickering, 2004), differences in cultural views on teaching, classroom roles, and life outside the classroom (Gorsuch, 2003; Myles & Cheng, 2003), and differences in expectations by the listener (Damron, 2000; Rubin, Ainsworth, Cho, Turk & Winn, 1999). While these studies have demonstrated the differences between NTAs and ITAs, and thus the potential issues involved in students learning from teaching assistants, no studies have examined the use of parentheticals.

What are parentheticals? Parentheticals are clausal or sub-clausal units that are "wedged in" a host sentence or "tagged on at the end" (Bolinger, 1989, p. 185), perhaps carrying some interpretation to the host sentence, as in (3) from Bolinger (1989, p. 186). Parentheticals are underlined.

(3) When the opportunity comes, and it will, **I'll bet**, sooner than you expect, you've got to be ready to grab it.

The host sentence here is *When the opportunity comes, you've got to be ready to grab it* and two parentheticals interrupt the host: a longer one, *and it will sooner than you expect* and ***I'll bet*** which interrupts the longer parenthetical. In this parenthetical, the interruption within the host would be marked prosodically by features such as lower pitch, lack of sentence focus, and greater tempo. However, none of these features are essential in every parenthetical

(Dehé & Kavalova, 2007). In fact, very little about parentheticals is always true. Parentheticals can be defined syntactically (Kaltenböck, 2006) or prosodically (Bolinger, 1989; Dehé, 2007) but attempts to come up with watertight definitions have been unsuccessful.

Semantically and pragmatically, parentheticals are just as varied. They seem to create a parallel level of information and thus evoke a parallel level of informational processing. They do not always contribute to the meaning of their hosts, especially when they are discourse-oriented. They are, in the words of Dehé and Kavalova (2007, p. 1), "a motley crew" of structures that do not all share the same syntactic, prosodic, or semantic features.

This chapter is motivated by our belief that parentheticals are far more common in spoken language, even in the relatively formal language found in the classroom, than the amount of research done on them would suggest. Syntactically, they vary widely. Prosodically, they are of interest in the way that they structure information parallel to the main discourse. Semantically and pragmatically, they function in ways that are barely explored, but which are likely to be critical in determining how information is interpreted as being central or peripheral to the topics being discussed. The use of parentheticals also suggests that the discourse structure of teaching may be more complex than previously thought. This chapter thus uses two analytical frameworks to examine the prosodic and informational characteristics of parentheticals uttered by NTAs and ITAs, as explained in the following section.

Research Questions and Frameworks for Analysis

Our study explores two research questions, one having to do with a prosodic analysis and one having to do with an informational analysis.

1. What are the differences in how prosodic parentheticals are employed by NTAs and ITAs in our study?
2. What are the differences in how informational parentheticals are employed by NTAs and ITAs in our study?

To look at how prosodic parentheticals were used in STEM and non-STEM teaching (RQ #1), we listened to recordings from one day of eight TAs' classes (four NTAs and four ITAs) and identified the elements of their oral discourse that fit the prosodic characteristics associated with parentheticals. Two of the researchers listened to these together, and after every two to four minutes, compared their identifications of parentheticals. To identify prosodic parentheticals, we listened for the most commonly cited features in the research literature: low level pitch, lack of pitch accents within the tone units, level or rising pitch at the end, increased tempo, and decreased volume. Prosodic parentheticals rarely had all of these features, although NTA productions usually had more of these features than ITA productions. Where there were disagreements, we listened or watched again, then discussed until agreement was reached. Later, we went back and classified each parenthetical in terms of its general purpose. Because parentheticals are so varied in prosody (Dehé, 2007, p. 262), and because no other work that we have seen has explored how prosodic parentheticals function in discourse, our analysis of prosodic parentheticals is exploratory.

To respond to the question of how parentheticals connect to the utterances around them (RQ #2), we drew from systemic functional linguistics, a theory of language in context, which views language as a system of meaning-making potential where language enacts the various functions that humans carry out (Halliday, 2004). The TAs in our study used their linguistic systems (their meaning-making potential) to produce specific instances of spoken texts to help their students learn the content being taught. Each text can be examined through three metafunctions: the ideational, the interpersonal, and the textual. See Table 1.

Table 1. Metafunctions in Systemic Functional Linguistics

Ideational	Resources for construing experience
Interpersonal	Resources for construing relationships
Textual	Resources for presenting ideational and interpersonal meanings as a flow of information in texts

Identifying the ideational, interpersonal, and textual resources that the TAs use parenthetically and non-parenthetically may thus provide information about connections to and differences from hosts at the clausal level. Clauses are typically joined together to form clause complexes (sentences), which in turn are integrated into logical stretches of meanings. We used two fundamental types of logico-semantic relationships for our investigation: projection and expansion. See Table 2.

Table 2. Projection and Expansion

Logico-semantic relationship	Specific functions	Linguistic features
Projection	Ideas	Events projected mentally ("I think that")
	Locutions	Events projected verbally ("He said that")
Expansion of prior text	Elaboration	Clarification, restatement, exemplification
	Extension	Addition or contrast
	Enhancement	Qualification or modification with temporal, spatial, causal, or conditional detail

Eggins and Slade (1997) extended these ideas to look at relationships between moves and their sequels in casual conversation. We have adopted Eggins and Slade's ideas to examine the function of parentheticals at the discourse level, looking at what they refer to as "sustaining moves" (p. 195), or moves that allow the speaker to continue speaking. Within the category of sustaining moves are "monitoring" moves, "in which the speaker focuses on the state of the interactive situation, for example by checking that the audience is following" (p. 195), and "prolonging" moves, which involve the three logico-semantic categories of expansion identified by Halliday and described in Table 2.

Method

Participants

Sixteen classes were videotaped and audiotaped, eight from chemistry and eight from English. These disciplines were chosen because they commonly employ NTA and ITA graduate instructors who teach their own classes, and because they are disciplines that are distinct in the way they represent STEM and non-STEM based knowledge. Within each discipline, we recorded two classes taught by two experienced NTAs and two taught by experienced ITAs. The classes taught were on similar topics at about the same time within the disciplines. See Table 3.

Table 3. Native Teaching Assistant (NTA) and International Teaching Assistant (ITA) Participants

	Chemistry		English	
	Name	Number of classes	Name	Number of classes
NTA	Amy[2]	2	Ellen	2
	Peter	2	Tim	2
ITA	Ajith (Hindi)[3]	2	Lihua (Chinese)	2
	Hamed (Arabic)	2	Feng (Vietnamese)	2

Analyses

To answer RQ #1, we looked at differences in how prosodic parentheticals were employed by NTAs and ITAs in our study. To answer RQ #2, we examined differences in how informational parentheticals were employed by NTAs and ITAs in our study. After the recordings of the NTAs and ITAs were transcribed, one researcher read through the transcripts to identify utterances that appeared to be parenthetical only by their placement in the transcripts. This researcher did not listen to the NTAs' and ITAs' recordings while identifying informational parentheticals.

Our separate identification of prosodic and informational parentheticals was intended to address two potential drawbacks of transcribed talk (Halliday, 2004). The first is the omission of intonation and rhythm. To address the first drawback, two researchers followed the transcripts while watching and/or listening to the recordings, and they marked utterances that had the prosody associated with parenthetical utterances. The second is that of "commission," where talk is normalized to make it appear "as though it had been composed in writing" (p. 33). In our study, we transcribed the data in tone groups, without punctuation, thereby addressing the second drawback.

Informational and prosodic parentheticals were then classified into linguistic functions (as per Eggins & Slade, 1997; Halliday,

---
2. All names in this study are pseudonyms.
3. Indicates the first language of ITA participants, if not English.

2004) and into themes of purpose that emerged from the data. A consideration of both types of classification allowed us to better inform ITA pedagogy because parentheticals may be both informational and prosodic, but they do not have to be both.

The transcripts were also run through *AntConc* (http://www.laurenceanthony.net/antconc_index.html), a concordancing and word counting (types and tokens) application, to identify the lexical resources the various speakers used, and through *Compleat Lexical Tutor* (http://www.lextutor.ca/), a corpus analysis tool, to establish the academic level of the words used. These quantitative results, both of the full discourse data and of the parentheticals alone, were compared between speakers to establish patterns of usage. Our analyses aimed to reveal differences in parenthetical prosody and parenthetical information between NTAs and ITAs.

Results

Prosodic Analysis (RQ #1). All TAs (NTAs and ITAs) used prosodic parentheticals as one strategy to teach their classes. All of the TAs taught interactively, that is, they knew what content they intended to cover, but did not necessarily plan in detail what they would say. This suggests that their frequent use of parentheticals served important purposes in achieving their main goals, the communication of course content through an interactive exchange with the students. This gives a clue to a primary function of parentheticals. They are a way that the teacher negotiates a developing classroom understanding.

We looked at three main uses of prosodically marked parentheticals: Regulatory uses, interpersonal connections, and making connections to content. These categories grew out of our listening to and classifying the prosodically marked parentheticals. We have chosen to unify our analysis by using functionally oriented titles to help us understand why parentheticals are used in the classroom context. We have not addressed all uses of parentheticals that we discovered, but only those that were most frequent across a number of TAs, both NTAs and ITAs. In addition, we do not provide pitch tracings as evidence, primarily because the length of many parentheticals and the noisy recording quality of the classroom setting made this difficult.

Regulatory parentheticals. The first use of parentheticals was regulatory, including comments about the classroom context, self-correction, and the use of tags. All TAs used parentheticals to comment on the classroom context, often about something that they noticed in the process of teaching, e.g., Ellen's (NTA) use of *we'll begin again with <u>oh I didn't change the slide um</u>*, when she noticed her presentation was at the wrong place, when writing on the board (e.g., Ajith's (ITA) *point two five plus x, <u>let's do that, point two five plus x</u>*, or in giving the reasons for an action, as in (3) from Amy:

(3) so I'll ... give these back to you, when you are taking the other quiz, <u>so we're not wasting time in class.</u>

A very common regulatory use of parentheticals was question tags. Kaltenböck (2006) included question tags in his syntactic taxonomy of parentheticals. Question tags in our data set were usually *(al)right?* and *(o)kay?* TAs used tags primarily to move the discourse along while maintaining their connection to the students, and at the same time making the exposition of content less dense.

Chemistry TAs frequently used tags, whereas tags were less frequent overall for English TAs. This may be because the chemistry recitations were content-heavy, working through problems and graphs of specific chemical processes while preparing for a quiz over these concepts. The English classes, in contrast, were less content-heavy. In addition, student participation in the chemistry classes was restricted to fairly quick responses to TA questions, while the students in the English classes engaged in more extensive discussion. Tags seemed to be most frequently employed when the TA was explaining a concept without expecting discussion. The tags had a different intonation pattern (high-rise) than other parentheticals, but unlike other rising tags in English, a response was neither expected nor appropriate. Tags were used to continue the discourse, and to engage and encourage. In the next example, a chemistry ITA uses *right* repeatedly, a characteristic of rapid-fire questioning. The intonation of *right* is always a quick, quiet, high-rise. The final use of *Right** is, in contrast, said with long, falling intonation.

Example:

ITA:	...what kind of an acid formic acid is? Is it a strong acid or a weak acid?
Student:	It's a weak acid.
ITA:	It's a weak acid, <u>right</u>? How does it split up? If I have formic acid, HCOH. How does it split up? What are the ions formed?
Student:	HCO negative.
ITA:	HCO negative. And?
Student:	H plus.
ITA:	H plus, <u>right</u>? Good. So this makes it an acid, <u>right</u>? H plus makes it an acid. But what happens when I split up HCOONa? Sodium formate. Is sodium formate an acid or a base or a salt?
Students:	Salt/It's a salt.
ITA:	It's a salt, <u>right</u>? So you, this is a weak acid and you have the salt of a weak acid, <u>right</u>? Right*.

Prosodically, parentheticals are normally described as low pitch and either flat or slightly rising in pitch (Bolinger, 1989). In our data set, the question tags did indeed "feel" parenthetical, but they were often high, quiet and slightly rising. The only consistently different thing in terms of prosody was that for most ITAs, the tag was not always quieter, and therefore did not provide as much of a contrast with the rest of the discourse as they did for NTAs.

Interpersonal parentheticals. Parentheticals were also used to promote interpersonal connections between teachers and students. These took a wide variety of forms, from Amy's (NTA) *I gave you that point <u>just because I know that's what you guys like</u>* to Pete's (NTA) playful recognition of an answer (*and that's right correct <u>thank you some audience participation</u>*) to Feng's (ITA) mild warning about using inappropriate sources (*a lot of you used articles um from the websites and with unknown <u>um author that's not really nice</u>*).

These interpersonal connections sometimes led to unpredictable tangents that introduced topics that connected to popular culture, as in Amy's (NTA) spontaneous use of humor in connecting her first statement to a line from the movie *Mulan*, followed by noticing the wrist recorder in the midst of explaining a concept in (4).

(4) so let's get down to business, <u>not to defeat the Huns</u>, but to talk about some buffers, <u>I got a I got a couple laughs - I think I'm funny okay</u>. So let's start with this, so you have a buffer it has propionic acid [notices recorder] <u>I'm a power ranger today this is kind of cool, right</u>

Amy's contrasts in prosody are striking in this example. She starts with a strongly projected voice including extra high pitch, then drops to a quieter, lower-pitched parenthetical with a slight following pause, then back to strongly projected speech with emphatically stressed syllables, then a lower pitched, modulated voice quality that continues even when she says the *right* of the host sentence. Thus the low-pitched prosody of the parenthetical continues when she says *right*, but informationally *right* acts as a transition back to the topic of buffers, and so we considered it part of the host sentence.

Another interpersonal way in which parentheticals were used was to encourage student responses, as in Ellen's (NTA) solicitation of non-verbal responses in the midst of non-parenthetical content.

(5) your intake of food and what you believe about food affects lot of different areas of your life, <u>right</u>, is that true? <u>Some nods, Brenda a nod</u>. How is it true for you, or how do you see that? <u>you're just nodding cause it felt good um</u>

Lihua (ITA) repeated questions regularly with parenthetical prosody to elicit responses when they were not immediately forthcoming, as in this sequence during observation and discussion of a complex graphic.

(6) the width of two streams, so size contrasts, <u>anything else, anything else besides the size contrasts, what else, what kind of element help you to pick out the story</u>

In a particularly striking use of a whispered parenthetical (in **bold**), Amy (NTA) encouraged a response from a particular student who was looking in the wrong place for the answer. The parenthetical was so quiet that one of the researchers did not hear it at first, yet its effect was an almost immediate answer from the student.

(7) what this equation tells you is there are two distinct factors that contribute to your PH, right, <u>so what are the two</u>, according to this equation, what two things will change the PH. [three second pause] **Just look at the equation**

In all these cases, TAs used prosody to encourage a response. The parenthetical marking seemed less insistent to us, and its effect in the speech of a content-engaged TA was almost always a student response.

Finally, TAs used vocatives to create interpersonal connections in calling on students. Vocatives are included as a subcategory of noun phrases as parentheticals within Kaltenböck's (2006) taxonomy. In teaching, the use of names is an important interpersonal tool. Vocatives in teaching tend not to be tied to a host sentence much of the time. Rather, they are their own phrase, and they often carry the function of calling on, or acknowledging students. Because names are generally optional within this context, they were said quietly, with a low, flat pitch, and possibly with a slight rise at the end. Vocatives were often used to call on a volunteer, so the student first had to indicate a willingness to be called on. The invitation was given with the student's name or with a simple nod with the word *yes* in some form.

In our data, while the actual use of noun phrases was limited to students' names and *you guys* by NTAs and, once, *guys* by an ITA, there were, additionally, numerous times that students were simply called on with *yeah?, yeah you?, again?,* and *yes?* These all were said with the characteristic parenthetical prosody and were invariably accompanied by inviting body language such as a head nod. It is interesting to note that, like the use of actual nouns, these were almost entirely used by NTAs and seldom by ITAs. The use of vocatives by NTAs but not ITAs is another example of the greater ease with which NTAs interact with students. "Calling on/acknowledging" seemed to be tied to the way the information was delivered and the types of questions asked. ITA interaction was almost entirely characterized by explanation mixed in with clear sequences of questions that generally had right or wrong answers. These questions were given to the whole class and responded to by anyone. NTAs were more likely to ask less exacting questions, and to wait longer for responses, looking around for willing volunteers and then calling on them.

Almost all the TAs (NTAs and ITAs) used prosodic parentheticals to achieve interpersonal ends. This was consistent with what we noticed in our earlier study (Levis, et al., 2012). Parentheticals are a way in which teachers negotiate classroom relationships with their students.

Content-connecting parentheticals. Another common use for prosodic parentheticals was to call attention to connections to course content. Thus TAs called attention to what had been covered already, what was going to be covered, and real-world content. All TAs did this, although NTAs did more extensively than ITAs always using low flat pitch in their speech to signal the parenthetical nature of the information. For example, Tim referred to previous course content, e.g., *we have a lot of information that could be written in a paragraph but <u>we've talked about before in the last couple weeks that we also want to account for different types of readers</u>*; future course content, e.g., *it's making it clear to our readers that we're not trying to lie to them uh were in a coup- <u>in an example in a little bit we might see why that might be a problem</u>*; and he mentioned outside connections, e.g., *and it was actually really difficult to find unethical data data displays so I think <u>um I think people are doing doing a much better job than we used to</u>*.

Other TAs used parenthetical references to course content more restrictively, to refer only to topics of immediate interest (but not outside applications of the topic). Ajith, in reviewing chemical titrations said *and the KA value is given how will you find the PH A-<u>minus by HA right that's Henderson Hasselbach equation</u>*, while Feng discussed feedback on writing (*so before I return your papers to you I'd just like to give some comments um on our last paper um let's see <u>some of my feedback is here</u>*).

Some TAs went beyond the course content to make spontaneous connections to outside examples or the larger culture. Ellen, in discussing organic food choices said *there's a whole sort of lifestyle <u>right</u> that seems to go along with it <u>I don't know if any of you all have been paying attention to the whole Gwyneth Paltrow Chris Martin break up but</u> a lot of what is getting talked about is her diet in terms of the reasons for their breaking up.*

The use of prosodic parentheticals to connect course content with past, present, and future information relevant to the content was common to all NTAs. There was no indication that these connections were planned beforehand, so the parentheticals were a way in which the speakers created cohesion between the immediate context, the larger context of the course, and popular culture. All TAs used parentheticals, but there was individual variation in how they made these connections. This makes parentheticals another interesting feature of instructional discourse (see also Smith, 2012 for other features).

Summary of results for RQ #1. To summarize (Table 4), NTAs and ITAs both used prosody for parentheticals, but not identically.

Table 4. Purpose and Pronunciation of Prosodic Parentheticals

		NTAs	ITAs
Parenthetical purpose	Regulatory	Yes	Yes
		Regulatory uses common from NTAs and ITAs. Tags heavily used by both groups, more commonly in STEM classes.	
	Interpersonal	Yes	No
		Widely used by NTAs. Rare for ITAs, even for vocatives.	
	Content-connected	Yes	Sometimes
		NTAs connected widely to course content and outside content. ITAs' connections were restricted to the direct content under discussion.	
Parenthetical prosody	Lower pitch	Yes	No
		Pitch was typically lowered by NTAs. ITAs had more limited pitch range differentiation. Tags for both groups usually had higher pitch with lower volume.	
	Lower volume	Yes	Sometimes
		NTAs consistently used lower volume on parentheticals. Some ITAs used lower volume as a primary cue, but others had little difference in volume from non-parenthetical language.	
	Increased tempo	Sometimes	No
		This was variable for NTAs, who sometimes spoke faster but not always; tempo changes were rare for ITAs when comparing host sentence tempo with parenthetical tempo.	

In general, NTAs used a wider variety of parentheticals and used multiple prosodic markers (lower pitch, lower volume, and sometime faster tempo). ITAs were more limited in their use of parentheticals, using them primarily for regulatory functions, but they did not use them for interpersonal uses such as vocatives that connected them to their students. The only prosodic feature marking ITAs' parentheticals was decreased volume. They did not use pitch to differentiate parentheticals from host sentences, nor did they manipulate tempo. In addition, their use of parentheticals was simply not as frequent, except in the use of question tags.

Results of the Information Analysis (RQ #2). Parentheticals do not need to be marked prosodically to be parentheticals. An examination of the written transcripts alone showed that NTAs uttered parenthetical information more often than the ITAs did, using strong and subtle resources within parentheticals. This section describes these resources, and how they differ in use between NTAs and ITAs. We work first from a quantitative angle in which lexico-grammatical resources from the interpersonal and ideational metafunctions are addressed, and then from a thematic approach, in which functional categories are identified and classified.

Quantitative results: Interpersonal metafunctions. The interpersonal metafunction considers the meaning-making resources we use to enact roles and relationships between speakers and audiences. To compare interpersonal differences between the NTAs and the ITAs, we examined resources that are typical of this metafunction, first by identifying them and using the concordancing software *AntConc* to count tokens and types. We then divided these resources into two categories: 1. ones that involved the audience; and 2. ones that created a stance. Involving the audience typically used resources such as vocatives (names), appeals to others (*as X said*), pronoun use (*we* versus *you*), grammatical structure choice (imperatives or questions), and confirmation seeking (*right?*). Creating a stance involves the use of certain processes involved with knowing and thinking, modal verbs (*can, will*), modal adjuncts (*probably, maybe, really, very*), and appraisal lexis (*wrong, fine, crazy, reasonable*).

For confirmation seeks, imperatives, and questions, the patterns of use were not different between the two groups, whereas the other categories suggested that even parenthetically, the NTAs appeared to involve their audience more than the ITAs did. See Table 5. First, NTAs used vocatives more, as we noted in the earlier section on prosody. Although at times they called individuals by name at these times, such as Ellen saying *Bella, a nod?* most of the time the NTAs used *you guys* to address their audience. There was only one occasion of vocatives being used by ITAs, and this was *guys*. Related to this, and within the English content area only (no examples were found in the chemistry parenthetical data), the NTAs occasionally made appeals to others (*as X claimed* or *as Y said*), both outside of class (i.e., *a scholar in the field*) and inside class (i.e., *a student*), but the ITAs' parentheticals offered nothing similar.

Pronoun use within parentheticals was very different between the NTAs and the ITAs. The NTAs used *we* more, including themselves with their audience, rather than focusing on either the students (*you*) or themselves (*I*). This was also a finding in earlier work comparing NTAs and ITAs (Levis et al, 2012). The ITAs used *I* most frequently, followed by *you*, and finally least often, *we*. This finding supports earlier work on the patterns of pronoun use for Indian-subcontinent TAs found in Levis et al (2012).

In the present study, with regards to creating a stance, the ITAs, specifically the English-content ITAs, used *think* more than twice as often as the NTAs in parenthetical speech, and uttered *know* less than half as often. Non-parenthetically, both NTAs and ITAs used *think* and *know* about the same number of times. Moreover, when adjusted to tokens per 100, the ITAs used more examples of appraisal lexis, modal verbs, and modal adjuncts than did the NTAs, but the types were much more limited in number. The negatively tagged word *wrong* was the most common appraisal word in the chemistry-content ITA's parentheticals, and the positively tagged *fine* was the most used in the English ITA's parentheticals. A similar pattern held for modal verbs, with ITAs in general preferring *will*, as Levis et al (2012) found. The modal adjunct *just* was the most commonly used by chemistry ITAs and *probably* was the most common in English. When taken all together, the use of these stance features can make the ITAs come across as sounding more unmoving and judgmental than the NTAs. Combine this with the lack of inclusion of the audience, and the result can lead to an interpretation of a TA who is "all business."

Quantitative results: Ideational metafunctions. Examining the ideational resources that each group used in general would not reveal much, as the TAs were teaching two vastly different subject areas (chemistry and English). We instead set about looking at the use of vocabulary that is related specifically to an academic content area in contrast to everyday language. To examine this across disciplines, we ran the transcripts through the *Compleat Lexical Tutor* (http://www.lextutor.ca) to explore the kinds of words that the TAs were using in their parentheticals (Table 5). The *Compleat Lexical Tutor* classifies words according to frequency in corpus analyses of written texts (see Laufer & Nation, 1995): the first 1,000 most frequent words in English, or K1; the second 1,000 most frequent, or K2; the *Academic Word List* (*AWL*)(those words which are frequent only in academic contexts); and *Off-list Words*, which are not on the other three lists. In other words, *Off-list Words* are less frequent than the top 2,000 words, and are not commonly used in general academic contexts). The K1 and K2 lists represent almost 85% of the vocabulary used in normal written English. The lists are used as a measure of lexical density.

Table 5. Vocabulary Analysis by L1 and Utterance Type

	ITA		NTA	
	Non-Parenthetical	Parenthetical	Non-Parenthetical	Parenthetical
Tokens	29,683	484	29,881	2,862
Types	2,003	205	2,195	610
Type-token	0.07	0.42	0.07	0.21
Tokens per type	14.82	2.36	13.61	4.69
Lexical density	0.47	0.45	0.46	0.45
K1 words: Function Content Ratio F:C	24,407 82.23% 15,672 52.80% 8,735 29.43% 1.79:1	429 88.64% 265 54.75% 164 33.88% 1.62:1	24,323 81.40% 16,284 54.50% 8,039 26.90% 2.03:1	2,484 86.79% 1,587 55.45% 897 31.34% 1.77:1
K2 words	976 3.29%	21 4.34%	1,044 3.49%	98 3.42%
K1 + K2	85.52%	92.98%	84.89%	90.21%
AWL words	1,445 4.87%	7 1.45%	1,109 3.71%	71 2.48%
Off-list Words	2,855 9.62%	27 5.58%	3,405 11.40%	209 7.30%
AWL + Off-list	4,300 14.48%	34 7.02%	4,514 15.11%	280 9.79%

Note. Compleat Lexical Tutor analysis gave information both about the total number of words (the total number of tokens) and about how often each word occurred (the total number of types). Thus, if one particular word occurred 15 times in the transcript, the analysis would say there was one type with 15 tokens.

Research question 2 asked about differences in uses of informational parentheticals by NTAs and ITAs. The vocabulary that the TAs used gives us information about how technical the language is in the parentheticals and in the non-parentheticals. NTAs used marginally more words in their parentheticals from the *Academic Word List (AWL)* and the *Off-list Words* than the ITAs did, although in the full dataset, ITAs used more words from the *AWL* than did the NTAs.

As expected, the chemistry-content ITAs used more *Off-list Words* than did the English-content ITAs (because the chemistry content has more specialized vocabulary than does the English vocabulary), and the English-content ITAs used more *AWL* words than the chemistry-content ITAs (Table 6). What was interesting was that the English-content NTAs used more words from the *AWL* and *Off-list Words* than the chemistry-content NTAs, suggesting that the NTAs in the chemistry classes may have been attempting to make their recitations more listener-friendly by making the course content less dense and connecting specialized terms to everyday vocabulary. See Table 6.

Table 6. Vocabulary Analysis by Discipline and NTA/ITA Status

	ITA		NTA	
	ENGL	CHEM	ENGL	CHEM
Tokens	259	225	1,231	1,630
Types	133	115	403	374
Type-token	0.51	0.51	0.33	0.23
Tokens per type	1.95	1.96	3.05	4.36
Lex density	0.44	0.46	0.47	0.43
K1 words: Function Content Ratio F:C	231 89.19% 144 55.60% 87 33.59% 1.79:1	198 88.00% 121 53.78% 77 34.22% 1.62:1	1,043 84.73% 649 52.72% 394 32.01% 2.03:1	1,439 88.28% 936 57.42% 503 30.86% 1.77:1
K2 words	14 5.41%	7 3.11%	46 3.74%	52 3.19%
K1 + K2	94.60%	91.11%	88.47%	91.47%
AWL words	5 1.93%	2 .89%	41 3.33%	30 1.84%
Off-list Words	9 3.47%	18 8.00%	101 8.20%	109 6.69%
AWL + Off-list	14 5.4%	20 8.89%	142 11.53%	139 8.53%

Finally, the ratio of function to content words was marginally greater for NTAs than for ITAs. This suggests that the discourse for ITAs was slightly denser, with relatively more content words than function words packed in. Even though the content words the ITAs used were more common (i.e., from the list of the most frequent 1000 words), there were more of them, and thus when combined with the interpersonal features noted above, the ITAs' language may come across as being more dense, even if the words were parenthetical, that is, not specific to the content being taught (Table 6).

Thematic analyses and results. Turning to the thematic approach in which functional categories were examined, we found that NTAs generally used more function categories than their ITA peers and in longer stretches of discourse. The use of these functional categories, defined earlier (see Table 2) as projection (e.g., *I think that... he said that...*), elaboration (clarification, restatement), extension (addition, contrast), enhancement (qualification, modification), and monitoring (checking that the audience is following) will be examined in turn using illustrations from the discourse data, focusing on the parenthetical utterances identified by reading the transcriptions.

Projection. By looking at the quantitative measures as above, we can see that both ITAs and NTAs used projection parenthetically, with ITAs using "think" to project information more often than NTAs (based on tokens per 100), and NTAs using "know" more often. The following examples illustrate this usage:

Feng (ITA):   You could choose your PowerPoint slides. Um brochure—I don't **think** that we designed any brochure in this section—so PowerPoint slides is obviously the only option that you could have.

Amy (NTA):   If you were given the KSP for this particular salt—which I don't actually **know** what it is. We'll just pretend that it's—oh that's probably really wrong but pretend this is the KSP for this salt—How would you find the molar solubility of either one of these ions?

Notice also how the NTAs appear generally to use these sensing verbs in somewhat longer parenthetical utterances, which in fact contain more than one proposition. For example, Amy (NTA) has multiple parenthetical propositions, admitting that she doesn't know what the KSP was, suggesting that the class as a whole (including her) pretend that the number she has offered is a possible KSP, then confirms that the number is probably not the best choice as an example. ITA Feng, on the other hand, used sensing verbs to offer single propositions, making the parenthetical information appear shorter.

Elaboration. All speakers used elaboration in their parenthetical speech to clarify, restate, or exemplify the main line of content in some way, and both used this elaboration in very similar ways, as the following examples illustrate:

Tim (NTA): Since most of these are RFPs for local communities, we're assuming that—<u>uh this might be in like a city hall uh setting or something like that</u>—they've also asked citizens of the community to come along.

Ajith (ITA): How do you find the PH?—<u>Yeah. What is wrong here? I have done something wrong? Is the equation balanced? No what is wrong? Is the water here? It is water. Yeah, then alright. Sorry. Yeah</u>—How do you find the PH?

When functioning as an elaboration, ITAs' parentheticals such as Ajith's example, were at times quite long with multiple propositions. Not using a sensing verb such as "think" to alert the listener to the parenthetical status could make it difficult for the audience to interpret the status of the utterances unless they are marked as parenthetical in some other way, such as prosodically (in which ITAs were inconsistent), or by a shift to the first person (*I* or *we*), as Ajith did. Tim's strategy was to identify the information as an elaboration by using the modal *might* and highlighting that it is an example through his use of *or something like that*.

Of all the teaching assistants, NTA Amy appeared to have the largest range of resources to show she was elaborating parenthetically. Not only did she indicate examples by introducing them with projections such as *we'll just say* or *for example*, she also used subject nominal clauses, as in the following:

Amy (NTA):   What is the PH of the solution—is what we want to find out. All right so—There are two ways to do this.

She also brought students' attention to examples on the board, as in *those are from here* and restated a long stretch of lecture with what appeared to be a parenthetical *there you go* or *that is how a buffer works*, and she clarified a problem-solving effort with *now that makes sense*. Most examples of NTA parentheticals clearly stated that they were elaborating or clarifying through examples or explicit restatements, whereas the ITA elaborations were not always clearly articulated.

Extension. The ITAs used the functional category of extension, which adds to or contrasts with information in the main line of content, much less frequently than did the NTAs. When the ITAs' parentheticals involved single propositions, the identification of the utterance as parenthetical did not come across as problematic, such as in Hamed's example:

Hamed (ITA):   Please uh try to be there early—like ten minutes earlier—for the exam.

Yet when more than one proposition was included in an effort to extend the information, as in Lihua's utterance below, the resulting parenthetical could leave the audience struggling with whether the information is important or not. The parenthetical content offers related information that may require prosodic marking to clarify its informational importance, as with this example:

Lihua (ITA):   But the officials look at report—which is really complicated and technical and most of the NASA officials they may not know about the technical details and probably most of the them are not engineers at all and probably politician so—when they look the report and read the graph...

The NTAs frequently signaled their extensions with *and* and their contrasts with lexical markers such as *although* or *but*. Sometimes these were interjected as single parenthetical words and sometimes as longer stretches, as in the following:

Tim (NTA):   We have uh some of the East Asian countries—<u>Japan Korean China—that that don't have as high of an obesity rate—though I would uh based on recent data in the last year I think there there's a lot of data showing that China would actually be uh be higher at this point</u>—but yeah based on based on this data we can see that...

Note that Tim's first parenthetical is elaboration but the second is enhancement, combining different types of functions in the same chunk of information. Lihua attempts similar extension above, but she repeats the same syntactic structure, coordination, whereas Tim's use of subordination and projection helps organize the information in the parenthetical in a clearer manner, potentially helping the audience see the hierarchy better. A detailed discussion of this phenomenon is beyond the scope of this chapter. For a fuller discussion, see Tyler, (1992).

Enhancement. Both ITAs and NTAs uttered parentheticals that showed enhancement, qualifying their utterances using detail that showed condition or cause in some way. The NTAs frequently had longer parenthetical examples or combined functions of parentheticals within the same host utterance, as in:

Ellen (NTA):   You can still use that—<u>I just stole it as an example cuz it was the first thing that popped into my head</u>—All right so once you have your confusing thing idea your confusing ad...

Lihua (ITA):   But if you look at North Dakota nobody got shot—<u>it's probably because nobody lives there</u>—but anyway it concentrates on the east part of the country.

Monitoring. The most striking difference between NTAs and ITAs with regards to these thematic categories within parentheticals was in the use of the monitoring function. Whereas examples of monitoring were rare in the speech of the ITAs, there were many examples of NTAs using parentheticals explicitly and implicitly to comment about whether their audiences were following along:

Amy (NTA): ...to four point eight one—<u>okay I got nods. Okay. Cool</u>—So again just as we have expected. Increase.

Peter (NTA): So for those of you who do have your book, let's see, it is number seventeen forty-four that I think happens to be on page seven forty-four—<u>I hear approximately three books turning pages so it makes me very happy I guess</u>—So let's see. So this problem says...

The NTAs' parenthetical speech which monitored also included questions (e.g., *Can everybody read the country names?*), tag questions (*I think that was last semester, wasn't it?*), and confirmation checks (*Okay? Right?*). The closest similar monitoring parentheticals from the ITAs were shorter and more directly related to the content being presented, distinguishing them from the NTA examples:

Lihua (ITA): I mean we looked at one of the example—<u>if you remember</u>—sitting is killing you.

Ajith (ITA): I'm going to take point one five moles of propionate sodium propionic so C2H5C—<u>ignore the names if you're uncomfortable</u>—so I have propionic acid point oh one five moles.

Moreover, the ITAs at times used monitoring parentheticals to make assumptions about what their students brought to their understandings in the class:

Lihua (ITA): Is that correlated with regulations of guns in the States? Probably. Do you know about the regulations of states?—<u>Probably you're not familiar with</u>—but if you look closely, do a little

	research, then you probably know that that there is might be a correlation.
Ajith (ITA):	If this is the result—<u>I know you have trouble in calculating them but</u>—if this is the result…

Such assumptions were also noted in Levis, et al., (2012) by the ITAs, who used this strategy to attempt to make connections with their audience; and they often do this as parenthetical interruptions to the main content being taught.

Implications for ITA Teaching

Learning is a complex phenomenon that involves taking in new information and connecting it with what you already know, that is, information that is given. In order to facilitate this, teachers need to present information in learnable chunks and help students make connections. This involves breaking up important content so that learners are not overwhelmed, and we argue that one way teaching assistants (TAs), and other instructors can do this is by using parentheticals. We have identified a number of both simple and complex uses of parentheticals in a two disciplinary teaching contexts. Not all are crucial. However, there are some suggestions that arise from this study that can benefit TAs.

Suggestion #1: Using lower pitch and quieter utterances to more clearly mark parentheticals. Both NTAs and ITAs will help their students learn if they employ parenthetical information and prosody to break up the density of information. They can use standard parentheticals such as *for example* and *okay*? But such short parentheticals may be harder for their students to separate from the main line of information than longer utterances that have multiple propositions. ITAs in particular could benefit from using lower pitch in quieter utterances that either point back to information students have already learned, or point forward to something they are going to discuss in the near future.

Suggestion #2: Using more inclusive language (we, us, I) in parentheticals. ITAs should also understand the importance of connecting to their audience. While connecting the students to content is arguably the most obvious element in a class, interpersonal connection is also extremely important. One advantage TAs have over professors is that they are in a position to be less remote because of age and context. Usually their discussion, recitation, or lab sections consist of 20 to 30 students, and yet are expected to be interactive. All TAs in our study did an admirable job of being interactive in their classes. However, NTAs more successfully established interpersonal connections with the simple parenthetical use of vocatives (especially calling on students using their names) and the personal pronouns *we, us,* and *I.* Using the inclusive *we* rather than an exclusive *you* invited the listeners into the lesson. ITAs would be wise to make use of these simple strategies so that they do not come across as unmoving and overly knowledgeable in stance.

Suggestion #3: Using parentheticals to comment on self and classroom events to connect to students. In addition, ITAs can use parentheticals to ask questions, to comment on and encourage student responses to questions, or to make short personal but harmless comments about themselves or a student (such as the NTA's parenthetical comment to a student in an awkward spot in the room, *sorry, you're stuck in the screen*). Such use of parenthetical language helps make the lesson come across as less dense and more understandable, and can make the TA appear more approachable. The power of interpersonal connectedness in large universities goes beyond the classroom atmosphere. It also makes it easier for students to visit their TAs in office hours, a proven activity to increase student success.

Conclusion

TAs (both NTAs and ITAs) in this study used parentheticals frequently. Their parentheticals served varied purposes, had varied syntactic structures, and were sometimes (but not invariably) marked prosodically. In short, they represent a "disparate and problematic range of phenomena" (Burton-Roberts, 2005, p. 179). But why use parentheticals at all? What communicative resources do parentheticals provide that the far better described "given and new information" in analyses of discourse do not? Part of the answer may come from Bing's (1980) classification of some parentheticals as being intonationally marked by what she called the "O-contour" (for "outside contour"). This type of intonation was to be interpreted outside the dominant intonational system, as part of a separate, parallel system of meaning-making. The "inside" system is one in which syntax and prosody combine to mark information as "new" and "given." But as "outside" phenomena, parentheticals allow speakers to achieve other communicative goals such as providing online commentary on and adjustments to the discourse being created, connections between the current discourse and related content, and interpersonal involvement with the listeners.

Parentheticals as a significant parallel channel of classroom communication. Parentheticals appeared to provide a parallel channel serving as a commentary on the content and a way for the teacher to adjust, in real time, by providing background knowledge or connections that were not thought of before the time of speaking. In teaching situations where lectures are not fully written out, teachers constantly adjust to the classroom environment, to connections they had not intended to exploit, and to student responses. Parentheticals are one way in which teachers create coherence between the information they are presenting and the larger context in which the information is presented. The TAs referred back to previously discussed information from earlier classes, to content that was still to be covered, and to real-world connections that were not planned. Parentheticals then helped serve as a way to anchor the class in a wider context.

Parentheticals were also a way in which the TAs promoted interpersonal involvement with their students. The first job of any teacher is to effectively teach, whatever content or skill is in focus. But teachers also try to connect to their students' lives through humor, small talk, or a variety of other strategies. The value of face-to-face teaching must include the feeling that a teacher knows you personally, is engaged with you, and is not just delivering content. Parentheticals were a way to promote this kind of interpersonal involvement while keeping it separate from the primary content.

Parentheticals, both prosodic and non-prosodic, offered teachers ways to monitor the class, elaborate and enhance content, and promote interpersonal involvement across the teacher-student divide. Parentheticals point out that teachers are not simply "information transfer vehicles" but are guides to the content, helping students see connections that may even be surprising to the teachers themselves. There is little systematic research on parentheticals, especially concerning their use in relationship to their use in classroom teaching and learning. Further research is needed, particularly using approaches such as stimulated recalls that can explore and make explicit why instructors use parentheticals in their teaching, or even how much instructors are aware of their use of parentheticals.

In a Nutshell

1. Teachers need to help students understand which information is more important and which is less important. This happens through vocabulary and grammatical choices, but it also happens through prosody, or suprasegmentals.
2. Teachers call attention to important information, but they also use parentheticals to mark levels of importance of information and interpersonal connections. This is signaled by information changes and special prosody.
3. We examined NTA and ITA use of parentheticals in STEM and non-STEM teaching.
4. NTAs made greater use of parentheticals than did ITAs, with differences in grammar, vocabulary and prosody.
5. The TAs seemed to use parentheticals to create a parallel information track in which they commented on content, made connections, regulated their own and student interaction, and promoted interpersonal involvement.
6. Not all uses of parentheticals are appropriate for ITA training. But some, especially the use of tags, vocatives, and inclusive language (e.g., *we* versus *you*), should be employed by all TAs.
7. Parentheticals are an important way for teachers to be more than information-transfer machines, and to develop interpersonal connections with students.

References

Bing, J. (1980). *Aspects of English prosody*. Bloomington: Indiana University Linguistics Club.

Bolinger, D. (1989). *Intonation and its uses*. Palo Alto, CA: Stanford University Press.

Burton-Roberts, N. (2005). Parentheticals. In K. Brown (Ed.), *Encyclopaedia of language and linguistics* (2nd ed., Vol. 9)(pp. 179-182). London: Elsevier Science.

Damron, J. A. (2000). *Chinese 101, a prerequisite to Math 100? A look at undergraduate students' beliefs about their role in communication with international teaching assistants*. Unpublished dissertation: Purdue University, West Lafayette, Indiana.

Dehé, N. (2007). The relation between syntactic and prosodic parenthesis. In N. Dehé & Y. Kavalova (Eds.), *Parentheticals* (pp. 261-284). Amsterdam: John Benjamins.

Dehé, N., & Kavalova, Y. (2007). Parentheticals: An introduction. In N. Dehé & Y. Kavalova (Eds.), *Parentheticals* (pp. 1-22). Amsterdam: John Benjamins.

Eggins, S., & Slade, D. (1997). *Analysing casual conversation.* London, UK: Cassell.

Gorsuch, G. (2003). The educational cultures of international teaching assistants and U.S. universities. *TESL-EJ*, *7*(3), 1-17.

Halliday, M.A.K. (2004). *An introduction to functional grammar* (3rd ed.). London, UK: Hodder Arnold.

Kaltenböck, G. (2006). Spoken parenthetical clauses in English: A taxonomy. In N. Dehé & Y. Kavalova (Eds.), *Parentheticals* (pp. 25-52). Amsterdam: John Benjamins.

Kang, O. (2010). Relative salience of suprasegmental features on judgments of L2 comprehensibility and accentedness. *System*, *38*(2), 301-315.

Ladd, D. R. (1980). *The structure of intonational meaning.* Bloomington, Indiana: Indiana University Linguistics Club.

Laufer, B., & Nation, P. (1995). Vocabulary size and use: Lexical richness in L2 written productions. *Applied Linguistics 16* (3), 307-322.

Levis, J., Levis, G.M., & Slater, T. (2012). Written English into spoken: A functional discourse analysis of American, Indian, and Chinese TA presentations. In G. Gorsuch (Ed.), *Working theories for TA and ITA development* (pp. 529-572). Stillwater, OK: New Forums Press.

Myles, J., & Cheng, L. (2003). The social and cultural life of non-native English speaking international graduate students at a Canadian university. *Journal of English for Academic Purposes*, *2*(3), 247-263.

Pickering, L. (2004). The structure and function of intonational paragraphs in native and nonnative speaker instructional discourse. *English for Specific Purposes*, *23*(1), 19-43.

Rubin, D., Ainsworth, S., Cho, E., Turk, D., & Winn, L. (1999). Are Greek letter social organizations a factor in undergraduates' perceptions of international instructors? *International Journal of Intercultural Relations*, *23*(1), 1-12.

Smith, K. (2012) The instructional discourse of domestic and international teaching assistants. In G. Gorsuch (Ed.), *Working theories for TA and ITA development* (pp. 483-528). Stillwater, OK: New Forums Press.

Tyler, A. (1992). Discourse structure and the perception of incoherence in international teaching assistants' spoken discourse. *TESOL Quarterly*, *26*(4), 713-729.

Achieving Successful Instructional Interaction in a Chemistry Laboratory: Participant Perspectives

by Barbara Gourlay,[1] Brown University

Research on communication between international teaching assistants (ITAs) and undergraduates in college science courses has focused on the language of the ITAs, excluding the language of the students. This study investigated communication and interaction in an introductory chemistry lab, and differed from previous research in two ways: First, it examined both sides of interactions; and second, it relied on the perspectives of both ITA and student participants to assess the success of interactions. Participants reported successful interactions when the ITAs grasped undergraduates' questions and understood their needs. This key finding guided further analysis of ITA/undergraduate communication, revealing that the questions undergraduates initiated were frequently expressed ambiguously and depended on reference to physical objects and gestures to complete meaning, requiring skillful disambiguation on the part of ITAs. Thus, this finding highlights ITAs' receptive skills. Findings also underscore the role of visual channels of communication (gesture and physical setting), and how they coordinate with verbal communication. Specific suggestions are offered for providing improved institutional support for ITAs in order to enhance the educational experience and learning outcomes for both ITAs and their undergraduate students.

Early and more recent controversies surrounding international teaching assistants (ITAs) in American classrooms (Bailey, 1984; Bailey, Pialorsi, & Zukowski Faust, 1984; Brown, Fishman, & Jones, 1991; Finder, 2005; Gravois, 2005; Yankelovich, 2005) have focused

---
1. Author contact: barbara_gourlay@brown.edu

on the language and communication skills of ITAs, framing and setting the agenda for much ITA research and ITA program curricular design (Kaufman & Brownworth, 2006; Nyquist, Abbot, Wulff, & Sprague, 1991; Smith, Byrd, Nelson, Barrett & Constantinides, 1992). The resulting research on ITA talk and communication has identified how features of spoken English contribute to well-articulated, fluent, intelligible, and comprehensible speech, and how those features (linguistic, paralinguistic, cultural, non-verbal) contribute to communication success and breakdown between ITAs and their undergraduate students (Benrabah, 1997; Bradlow & Brent, 2008; Davies & Tyler, 1994; Derwing & Munro, 1997, 2001, 2005; Derwing, Rossiter, Munro & Thompson, 2004; Derwing, Thomson, & Munro, 2006; Fayer & Krasinski, 1995; Field, 2005; Fortanet, 2004; Gonzalez, 2004; Hahn, 2004; Jenkins & Parra, 2003; Levis, 2004; Lippi-Green, 1997; Llurda, 2000; Major, Fitzmauric, Bunta, & Balasubramanian, 2002; McGregor, 2007; Munro & Derwing, 1995, 1998, 1999; Munro, Derwing, & Morton, 2006; Pickering, 2001, 2004; Plakans, 1997; Riggenbach, 2000; Tyler, 1992, 1995; Wennerstrom, 1998, 2000; Williams, 1992).

In-classroom ITA Research

Going beyond studies of decontextualized language or language in simulated contexts, in-context ITA research has examined language and communication in actual teaching settings and found that the characteristics of a teaching environment (office hours, laboratory teaching, or lecture-style classes) place different communicative demands on teaching assistants (Axelson & Madden, 1994; Byrd & Constantinides, 1992; Hoekje & Williams, 1992; McChesney, 1994; Rounds, 1994). However, ITA research from actual classrooms (Myers, 1994; Rounds, 1987; Tanner, 1991; Williams, Inscoe, & Tasker, 1997) has focused on the discourse of the instructor and how that language guides undergraduate learning. ITA communication research has not yet explored the interactive nature of ITA-undergraduate communicative exchanges to the extent that educational research in other educational environments has looked at communication between teachers and students (Cazden, 2001; Roth, McGinn, Woszcyna, & Boutonné, 1999; Yerrick & Roth, 2005).

What Guides Research on ITA Talk

Three main assumptions have apparently guided research on ITA communication. First, it has been assumed that ITAs will be successful classroom communicators in American universities when their speech approaches that of native-English speakers. Conversely, the more ITA speech deviates from native-speaker norms the less successful they will be as communicators (Pickering, 2004; Tyler, 1992; Williams, 1992). Second, it has been assumed that the significant language in the classroom is the language that originates with the instructor (McChesney, 1994; Myers, 1994; Tanner, 1991; Tyler, 1992; Wennerstrom, 1998). And finally, when evaluating the speech and communication of non-native speaking teaching assistants, the opinions of people external to the communicative exchange provide sufficient understanding of when communication is and is not successful (Bresnahan, Ohasi, Nebashi, Liu, & Shearman, 2002; Derwing, Rossiter, Munro, & Thomson, 2004; Hahn, 2004).

A Contrasting Orientation for Research on ITA Talk

The research presented here has approached the study of international teaching assistant-undergraduate communication with significantly different assumptions. First, this study assumes, as Williams (1997) suggests, that ITAs achieve successful communication with their undergraduate students in ways that differ from their native speaking counterparts. Second, this research explores the real-world communication patterns in science labs, learning environments where undergraduate engagement in the learning process requires them to communicate actively with their instructors. Finally, this research project gained the perspectives of those involved in the communicative exchanges to understand what constitutes successful communication and interaction for them in this educational environment.

Research Purpose and Research Questions

The purpose of this research was to learn more about the communication and interaction patterns between ITAs and their undergraduate students, and thus to better understand how successful communication in academic environments can be encouraged and supported. This study investigates the talk and communication strategies between non-native speaking teaching assistants and native speaking undergraduates, and their approaches to negotiating information in the interactive setting of an introductory-level university chemistry laboratory. This is a learning environment where a high number of international students are placed in teaching positions (see contribution of Griffee & Gorsuch, this volume). The research questions guiding this study were:

1. In university-level chemistry laboratories, what constitutes successful communication and/or successful negotiation of information between native-English speaking students and their teaching assistants who are advanced non-native speakers of English?
2. What communication skills (i.e., linguistic, paralinguistic, non-verbal, cultural, pedagogical) contribute to successful classroom interactions between non-native English speaking teaching assistants and their native-speaking undergraduate students?

Method

Setting

This study took place in the first-semester chemistry labs of an introductory-level chemistry course at an elite, mid-sized university in the Northeast. Over the course of the semester, data were gathered from 36 hours of chemistry lab instruction. This included 9 hours of the weekly one-hour pre-lab lecture conducted by a professor, and 27 hours of the first hour of nine weekly lab sessions, headed by ITAs, for three sections. Observation data included field notes, audio recordings (six hours) and video recordings (nine hours). Additional data were collected in the form of participant questionnaires and approximately 25 hours of one-on-one semi-structured interviews.

Participants

In order to understand the characteristics of successful communication and interactions from the participants' perspectives, three different constituencies are represented: undergraduates, international teaching assistants (ITAs), and the professor responsible for the course. The perspectives of all three constituencies, obtained through semi-structured interviews, provided triangulation of data sources (Patton, 2002), and thus were needed to accurately determine the success of an interaction, strengthening the consistency and reliability of the findings.

The undergraduates. Of the 51 undergraduates who enrolled in the three lab sections studied, 45 undergraduates participated in the study. The six undergraduates who did not participate included one international undergraduate, one undergraduate who was below the age of consent to participate, and four undergraduates who did not attend with sufficient regularity to complete the course. In essence, all eligible, regularly attending undergraduates participated in the study. The 45 undergraduate participants were essentially randomly selected, as they were the undergraduates who were randomly assigned to a lab section on their preferred day by the faculty member teaching the course. The participating undergraduates seemed interested in and receptive to contributing to a study that was intended to improve communication and facilitate learning in the labs. The undergraduates demonstrated themselves to be intelligent, engaged in, and dedicated to learning in the course.

Background characteristics of the undergraduates in this study, obtained through participant questionnaires, identified that they were almost equal proportions of male (47%) and female (53%) students. The majority (87%) were 18 to 19 years old, and mostly freshman (51%) and sophomores (42%). While nearly all (89%) were science majors, only one self-specified as a chemistry major. The undergraduates reported being raised in the United States (91%), mostly in suburban areas (69%). While English was the predominate language spoken at home for almost all (98%), English was the exclusive language for the majority (68%). Nearly everyone (93%) had studied a foreign language, and more than half (65%) had traveled abroad. Academically, nearly all (93%) had studied chemistry in high school, with some (38%) having studied AP chemistry. Undergraduates identified that their high school chemistry class may or may not have had a lab component. More than half (64%) had taken some college math, but all had extensive high school math backgrounds, taking calculus (91%) and taking four years of high school math (73%). For the questionnaire used to generate this information, see the Appendix.

The international teaching assistants. The five ITAs in this study were chosen by purposeful sampling. In order to minimize potential communication difficulties related to cultural adjustments to a new educational environment, only ITAs who had been in the United States for at least one year were chosen. These ITAs had experienced one full academic year of graduate work at an American university, and had teaching experience in their field at the university level in the United States. In total, five international graduate students participated, with three being the primary teaching assistants. All were native speakers of Mandarin Chinese, and four were male and one was female. All spoke with some degree of accented English, but all had demonstrated sufficient English language proficiency in the university's local performance test to assume teaching duties in the lab environment. For information on locally set language standards see: http://www.brown.edu/academics/gradschool/international-students-language-proficiency-toefl-or-ielts

Rather than focusing on communication in one lab section between a single teaching assistant and the undergraduates in that section, multiple lab sections for the course were selected to reduce the chance that the communication patterns observed were idiosyncratic. This also increased the possibility of obtaining a greater variety of communicative interactions, to provide a broader understanding of successful communication in this context.

The professor. The professor for the laboratory component of the course was a female native-speaker of English, with 19 years of university-level teaching experience in chemistry and 14 years experience of administration. During the semester of data collection, she was the sole faculty member for this laboratory course, overseeing the instruction of approximately 500 students. She had taught or co-taught the course in previous years and contributed to the lab manual for the course. The professor was responsible for all curricular and logistical aspects of the laboratory component of the course, including designing and determining the lab experiments, presenting the weekly pre-lab lectures, and overseeing all teaching assistants.

Procedure

Three procedures were established to answer the study's two research questions of what constitutes successful communication and/or negotiation of information in chemistry labs and what communicative skills contribute to successful communication. First, through lab observations the interaction and communication patterns that occurred in the chemistry labs were documented and analyzed to provide a profile of communication in this setting. Second, semi-structured interviews established what successful communication was, according to those engaged in the actual communicative exchanges. The interview process also obtained participant group perspectives and opinions on what communicative strategies and practices contributed to successful interaction. Finally, interaction analysis reviewed a subset of all lab interactions, obtained in the interview process, to examine interactions for characteristics of successful communication.

Interactions as units of analysis. The methodology of this study was driven by the research goals of having the participants define successful communication and by examining the communication of both the teaching assistant and the undergraduates. Therefore, this investigation took the unit of analysis as an "interaction," defined as two or more alternating, uninterrupted turns (Fairclough, 2003). One consequence of using an "interaction" as the unit of analysis is that real-world interactive classroom communication and the interactions that occur are seen as a process of collaborative communication, where both the teaching assistant and undergraduate contribute to communication and must work together to create the interactions and negotiate understanding. In other words, interactive lab communication between ITAs and their undergraduate students is seen as a spontaneous, meaningful, two-way negotiation and exchange of ideas and information.

Lab observations. The purpose of the lab observations was to understand the communicative demands of this educational environment. In addition, the audio and video materials collected in this phase of the investigation served as the source material for the later, interview phase of this project. From fifteen hours of recorded lab sessions, all interactions were identified, coded, and checked for accuracy. Primary coding categories included: *lab session, lab section, start time, stop time, location, participants, participant gender, initiator of the interaction, activity or task topic.*

The coding categories for the activity or task topic of the interactions were initially established in consultation with the chemistry course faculty member, and later refined and finally checked for reliability with two independent coders. The resulting categories for activity or task topic included the following: *equipment, lab preparation, materials, procedures, safety, social.* Table 1 provides the definitions used in coding lab communication for activity types.

Table 1. Coding categories and definitions for activities discussed in lab communication

Category	Topics discussed
Equipment	Tools, devices, and equipment of the laboratory. Examples: standard equipment such as test tubes, beakers, funnels, and stir bars were included in this category, as were specialized equipment such as pH meters.
Lab Preparation	Advance preparation for the lab. Examples: questions related to the pre-lab quiz, the pre-lab questions, returned assignments, sample assignment, or undergraduates being organized into working groups.
Materials	Solutions or samples used in an experiment, i.e., experimental materials. Examples: NaOH (sodium hydroxide), reagents, types of water used, and samples to be analyzed.
Procedures	How to carry out the procedures of the experiment as directed by the lab manual. Examples: setting up vacuum filtration or titration.
Safety	Actions related to the health and well being of those present in the lab. Examples: wearing goggles, cleaning up broken glassware, or working appropriately under the hood with proper ventilation.
Social	Conversational exchanges that were carried out in the lab but were not directly related to the experiment. Their function was maintaining a sense of social cohesiveness in the lab.
Unassigned	Communicative exchanges where classification was not possible, the result of part of the exchange being inaudible.

Interview purpose and timing. The purpose of the interview phase of this project was to identify successful communication or interactions, as determined by participants involved in the communicative exchanges. The interviews also served to develop an understanding of what contributed to the success of the interactions, once again from the participants' perspectives. As soon as the audio and video recordings and the accompanying files documenting information in the recordings had been prepared, interviews were conducted. The participants provided their feedback on interactions in which they were involved through one-on-one semi-structured interviews. The interview process was initiated as soon as possible after the interactions occurred to increase the likelihood that when reviewing the interactions the participants would remember clearly the details of the communicative exchange.

The first participants interviewed were the undergraduates, followed by teaching assistants, and finally the faculty member. For the convenience of the faculty member, her interviews were conducted in the month after the course had finished. In the interviews, interactions were played back for the participant as many times as necessary for the participant to be comfortable with their grasp of the exchange. Participants were always free to ask questions or provide other information at any time during the interview process. All participants responded to a 10-item, 7-point Likert scale interview instrument where 1 indicated strong disagreement and 7 strong agreement with a given statement (one item). See Table 2.

The semi-structured interviews elicited information on ten different dimensions (Table 3) of the communicative interaction. This was done to address the study's research questions by identifying successful communication in the chemistry labs from the participants' perspectives, and gaining insight into what the participants believed contributed to the success of the interactions. The dimensions examined both sides of the instructional interaction: The question an undergraduate posed (Table 2, interview items 1 - 5) and the response the teaching assistant provided (Table 2, interview items 6 - 9). Participants also had to identify explicitly whether they believed the interaction was or was not successful (Table 2, interview item 10).

The dimensions were establish to obtain feedback on the participants' understanding of the question and response (Table 2, interview items 1 and 6), as well as obtaining perspectives on participant comfort and satisfaction with the information exchanged (Table 2, interview items 2, 3, 7, 8, and 9). Also of interest was participants' understanding of the intended question function (Kearsley, 1976) of the undergraduate questions (Table 2, interview items 4 and 5). Specifically, the dimensions focused on whether the teaching assistant understood the question, how easy it was for the undergraduate to ask the question, what motivated the undergraduate to ask the question, whether the undergraduate understood and was satisfied with the response, whether the response provided sufficient information, and the overall impression of whether this was a successful communicative interaction.

Table 2. Interview Prompts

Interview item	Undergraduate	Teaching assistant	Faculty
1	The teaching assistant understood my question.	I understood the undergraduate's question.	I think the teaching assistant understood the question.
2	I was comfortable approaching the TA with my question.	The undergraduate's question was easy to answer.	The undergraduate's question was clearly expressed.
3	I wasn't sure how to explain (or phrase) my question.	The undergraduate had difficulty asking the question.	The undergraduate had difficulty expressing the question.
4	I needed to have instructions or information clarified.	The undergraduate wanted information clarified.	The undergraduate was seeking clarification of information.
5	I was checking to make sure that I understood what to do; i.e., I was seeking confirmation.	The undergraduate was checking to make sure that he/she understood what to do.	The undergraduate was seeking confirmation that what he/she was doing was correct.
6	I understood the TA's response.	The undergraduate understood my response.	The undergraduate understood the response.
7	I was satisfied with the TA's response.	The undergraduate was satisfied with my response.	The TA responded accurately.
8	The TA provided sufficient information for me to understand the response.	I was satisfied with my response.	The TA provided sufficient information in the response for the undergraduate to understand the response.
9	I wish the TA had responded differently.	I now realize that another response would have been better.	The TA should have responded differently.
10	Overall this was a successful question/answer exchange.	Overall, this was a successful question/answer exchange.	Overall I think this was a successful question/answer exchange.

Note. All participants could provide additional explanations for each item. For example, in Interview Item 9, participants could describe what a different response should include.

Table 3. Interview Item Dimensions

Interview item	Dimension captured
1	Teaching assistant comprehension of the question
2	Undergraduate comfort asking the question
3	Undergraduate difficulty expressing the question
4	Undergraduate requesting clarification of content information
5	Undergraduate requesting confirmation or reassurance
6	Undergraduate comprehension of the response
7	Undergraduate satisfaction with the response
8	Sufficient information included in the response
9	Wish for another response
10	Overall success of the interaction

The interview prompts (Table 2) for all three groups of participants were similar, though each prompt was written to reflect the perspective of the constituency being interviewed. The actual interview prompts allowed participants to offer opinions on their contributions to the communicative exchange and on the contributions of their communicative collaborator. All participants were invited to add comments whenever they felt that additional information was important to be included or had not been addressed. An interaction was classified as successful or unsuccessful based on the Likert scale response to interview item 10, with the additional requirement that there be unanimous agreement among the participants.

Interaction analysis. The final phase of this project examined the interactions identified in the interview process to better understand what features or communication skills contributed to successful classroom interactions between the ITAs and the undergraduate students. The interview process yielded a subset of 50 recorded interactions that participants classified by their degree of success. These interactions were then analyzed for their content and characteristics. Information obtained in the interview process from the Likert scale responses and participant comments guided the analysis of the interview interactions. Broad transcription of the interview data provided sufficient detail for interaction analysis. Turn-taking behaviors were examined, and using a framework from Flowerdew and Miller (2005) of conversational listening, the interaction analysis examined how the communicative exchanges were opened, were closed, and how topics were established.

Results

This study investigated two research questions. What constitutes successful communication and/or negotiation of information between non-native English speaking teaching assistants and their undergraduate students in introductory-level chemistry labs (RQ #1), and what are the communicative skills that contribute to successful communication between these two populations (RQ #2). Results of this study are organized into three areas, based on the type of data collected (observation, interview, and interaction analysis). First, analysis of data collected through direct observations, audio-recordings, and video-recordings provided a profile of the types of negotiation of information that occurred in the first hour of the chemistry laboratory sessions, addressing RQ #1. Second, semi-structured interviews addressed the first research question by identifying successful communication through the quantitative measure of Likert scale responses to interview items (RQ #1), and also addressed the second research question by obtaining qualitative data of participant opinions about the communication skills contributing to the success of lab interactions, which provided a more complete understanding of the responses to the Likert scale data (RQ #2). Participants also provided their views on ways that communication could be improved. Third, analysis of lab interactions addressed both research questions by providing an expanded understanding of those features of the instructional exchanges that contribute successful negotiation of information and a more in-depth understanding of how participants negotiate information (RQ #1 and RQ #2).

Observation of lab communication, RQ #1: Analysis of lab communication provided insight into patterns of communication, including how frequently interactions occurred, how long the interactions were, who initiated the interactions, the gender of the participants involved, and what activities were discussed. It quickly became apparent that the chemistry labs are a learning environment where undergraduates initiate a high proportion of the classroom discourse and teaching assistants are responsible for responding to undergraduate requests quickly and efficiently. Successful communication and negotiation of meaning here requires that the teaching assistants demonstrate the linguistic and pedagogical skills of handling short, frequent questions arising on regularly occurring topics.

Interaction frequency and length. Communication between the ITAs and the undergraduates was frequent and brief. In total, there were 877 identifiable interactions in the 15 hours (900 minutes) of recorded labs involving the ITAs. While the average number of interactions for the labs was approximately one per minute, a preliminary survey of the data revealed that in general interactions were brief. Interaction length, calculated from start and stop times in the digital recordings, was organized in categories of ten-second intervals for interactions of less than one minute to ensure reliable and accurate measures from the recordings. A category was established for interactions of one to two minutes, and another for interactions over two minutes. Table 4 illustrates this finding.

Interactions that took less than 30 seconds (f = 641 where f = frequency) accounted for 73% of the lab interactions and occurred more frequently than interactions that took longer than 30 seconds (f = 236). In addition, 92% of all interactions in the labs were a minute or less in length. Only 8% of all interactions were over one minute in length, and of these, two-thirds (14 out of 21) occurred in initial part of the lab, when the teaching assistants and undergraduates were located in the classroom area and were engaged in interactions related to the lab overview and preparing for the labs.

Table 4. Frequency and Percentage of Interactions by Length of Interaction

Interaction length in seconds	Frequency	Percentage	Cumulative percentage
1-10	285	33%	33%
11-20	223	25%	58%
21-30	133	15%	73%
31-40	81	9%	82%
41-50	47	5%	88%
51-60	38	4%	92%
61-120	49	6%	98%
> 120	21	2%	100%
Total	877	100%	

Note. Frequency counts and percentages illustrate the communicative demand placed on international teaching assistants in the lab environment during the first hour of the labs. All data from non-participants have been excluded from student analysis.

Interaction initiation. The 877 interactions the ITAs participated in during the recorded labs demonstrate the high communicative demand place on them during the first hour of the labs. However, only 799 interactions were analyzed for interaction initiation. About 9% of the interactions were excluded from the analysis of interaction initiation: 70 interactions involving non-participating undergraduates and 8 interactions occurring with others in the setting (the lab manager, other teaching assistants, or the faculty member). While these interactions are an important part of the duties of these teaching assistants and the activities of the labs in general, they were not central to, nor available for, use in this study and were therefore removed from analysis of interaction initiation. As a result, 799 interactions were examined for who initiated the interaction—the undergraduate or the teaching assistant. In this study, undergraduates initiated a higher proportion of the interactions. Of the 799 undergraduate-ITA interactions, the ITAs initiated 39% (f = 308, again where f = frequency) and the undergraduates initiated 61% (f = 491). Table 5 provides an overview of the frequency and percentages of interaction initiation.

Table 5. Frequency and Percentage of Interactions by Interaction Initiation

	Participant Interactions	
Interaction Initiation	Frequency	Percentage
ITA	308	39%
Undergraduate	491	61%
Total	799	

Topic of interaction. Topics of lab communication were categorized into six main areas: equipment, lab preparation, materials, procedures, safety, and social. There were 803 interactions available for this analysis and assignment to one of the six coding categories. Removed from this analysis were the 70 interactions from non-participants and 4 additional interactions that could not be assigned a category. Due the complexities of recording in a lab environment, at times crucial audio and video data were not captured adequately enough to assign some interactions to an activity category. When the interactions were analyzed, the categories that emerged as having the highest frequency of occurrence were lab preparation (f = 283 where f = frequency), procedures (f = 303), equipment (f = 127), and materials (f = 48). Interactions discussing safety (f = 24) and social (f = 18) aspects of the labs occurred less often. Table 6 shows the frequencies and percentages for the activity types of the interactions.

Table 6. Frequency and Percentage of Lab Interactions by Topic of Activity

Activity	Interaction with assignable activity topics	
	Frequency	Percentage
Equipment	127	16%
Lab Preparation	283	35%
Materials	48	6%
Procedures	303	38%
Safety	24	3%
Social	18	2%
Total	803	

The lab preparation interactions were a substantial number of the interactions, second only in frequency to interactions related to procedures. However, the lab preparation interactions differed from the other types of interactions in this study in that many originated in conversations and activities occurring prior to the hands-on portion of the lab experiment. Here, undergraduates were frequently asking questions about prior pre-lab preparation: the pre-lab questions, the pre-lab lecture, or the information provided in the lab manual. The ITAs were frequently repeating instructions from the faculty member or carrying out routine activities related to classroom maintenance. These interactions were more often ones that were based in texts (written or spoken) of other speakers. When the teaching assistants were involved in interactions related to lab preparation, they were frequently engaged in planned discourse (e.g., giving a recap of the lab at the start), communicating information from the faculty member (e.g., making announcements), or discussing the logistics of the lab.

The interactions related to the other activity types (equipment, materials, procedures, and safety) were those that occurred primarily while the undergraduates were engaged in the experiment for that week. These interactions were based on questions, conflicts, and dilemmas the undergraduates faced when carrying out the experiment. The interactions required ITAs and undergraduates to communicate spontaneously and to negotiate and respond to issues, concerns, and topics that arose while they worked through the lab experiment.

Interaction initiation and topic of activity. Analysis of interaction initiation by topics revealed that interactions for certain activities were more likely to be initiated by the ITAs and other types of interactions by the undergraduates (Table 7). ITAs initiated four-fifths (83%) of all safety-related interactions, slightly more than half (55%) of lab preparation interactions, and more than half (53%) of social interactions. Undergraduates initiated four-fifths of all interactions related to equipment (80%) and materials (81%), and almost three-fourths (71%) related to procedures.

Table 7. Interaction Topic by Initiation

Activity of interaction	Interaction initiation		Percentage of all interactions
	ITA	Undergraduate	
Equipment	20%	80%	16%
Lab Preparation	55%	45%	35%
Materials	19%	81%	6%
Procedures	29%	71%	38%
Safety	83%	17%	3%
Social	53%	47%	2%

Summary of results for Observation of lab communication, RQ #1: The findings show the teaching assistants and undergraduates engaged in frequent, brief interactions, making the chemistry labs vigorous, fast-paced learning environments, where undergraduates guided much of the classroom discourse by initiating the majority of interactions. Additionally, patterns of communication emerged as to the types of interactions the participants initiated. Teaching assistants more often initiated interactions that discussed topics related to lab preparation and safety, and undergraduates predominately initiated interactions discussing experimental equipment, materials and procedures. An expanded discussion of lab communication and interactions can be found in Gourlay (2008).

Interviews: RQ #1 and RQ #2. Data collected through semi-structured interviews (Likert scale responses and participant comments) established which interactions were successful for the participants, provided data to compare patterns of agreement among the participants, and elicited comments about lab communication. Analysis of interview data addressed both research questions by clearly identifying successful communicative exchanges and by discovering the communication skills and strategies participants saw as contributing to successful communication, or in some cases improving it. Further, the benefits of using a research methodology that gained participant perspectives became apparent with the variety and depth of opinions obtained, providing a level of an understanding not available to an external observer. Participant groups prioritized different aspects of the interactions, even though they engaged in and experienced the same interaction.

Of the 45 undergraduate study participants, 16 (36%) participated in the interviews. The faculty member and the teaching assistants participated in all interviews requested. In total, data collected through the interview process included 50 undergraduate-initiated interactions. The 50 interactions were representative of all lab interactions in many important ways, such as length, gender of participants, and activity discussed (Table 6). These undergraduate-initiated communicative exchanges were the ones used later for interaction analysis (Table 7).

Likert scale responses. Interaction success classification (*successful, partially successful, and unsuccessful*) was determined from a Likert scale item (RQ #1). As previously discussed, the purpose of Interview Item 10 (*overall, this was a successful exchange,* see Table 2) was for the participants to identify successful interactions. To be classified as successful, an interaction had to be rated as successful by all three participants, with a three-way consensus. No undergraduate and no ITA rated an interaction as unsuccessful. The faculty member rated one interaction as unsuccessful. While the faculty member acknowledged that the exchange in question had been successful linguistically, i.e., the participants "seemed to have succeeded in communicating something," the information exchanged was insufficiently accurate. Therefore, from her perspective, it was an unsuccessful exchange. The undergraduate and the ITA, however, agreed on the success of this interaction.

Because no interaction could be unanimously classified as an unsuccessful exchange, interactions were classified as successful ($f = 28$) and partially successful ($f = 22$), meaning that at least one of the participants viewed a given interaction with a sufficient degree of certainty as being a successful exchange, and that at least one of the participants rated the success of the interaction with an insufficient degree of certainty (3, 4, or 5 on the Likert scale). As a result, all 50 of the interactions examined during the interview were classified as either successful (56%) or partially successful (44%).

Consensus of success categorizations by participant group. Satisfaction was high for many of the 50 interactions within each participant group. Each participant group identified 78% of the interactions as categorically successful (Item 10: Overall, this was a successful question/answer exchange). However, finding complete consensus of opinion among the participants on overall interaction success (Item 10) was more challenging. Though all participants were generally satisfied with the interactions and saw them as being successful to some extent, they could not agree with sufficient degrees of certainty which interactions were entirely successful.

Consensus of opinion was higher for Interview Item 10 when looking at agreement between two participant groups, in a two-way comparison. Agreement between the ITAs and the faculty member (both content-area specialists) was 68%. Agreement between the undergraduate and faculty member (both native speaker groups) was similar, at 66%. Slightly lower agreement occurred between the ITAs and undergraduates (both participants in the instruction) at 62%.

Of the 28 successful interactions with three-way consensus, only one interaction had complete three-way consensus for all 10 interview items. In other words, all three participant groups rated all interview items (Items 1 - 10, see Table 3) identically. Here, agreement in two-way comparisons (i.e., identical responses on each of the 10 interview dimensions) was highest for the faculty member and the ITAs, at 20%. The rate of agreement in the other two-way comparisons was lower. Both the ITA and undergraduate agreement rate, and undergraduate and faculty member agreement rate on all 10 interview dimensions was 6%. Table 8 shows the frequency and percentage rates for agreement of opinion.

Table 8. Overview of Agreement of Successful Interactions as Identified by Interview Item 10 and Complete Consensus on all Interview Items 1 - 10

	Successful interaction interview item #10		Agreement on all 10 interview prompts	
	Frequency	Percentage	Frequency	Percentage
Participant group				
Undergraduates	39	78%	--	--
ITAs	39	78%	--	--
Faculty member	39	78%	--	--
Two-way consensus				
Undergraduate and ITA	31	62%	3	6%
Undergraduate and faculty member	33	66%	3	6%
ITA and faculty member	34	68%	10	20%
Three-way consensus				
Undergraduate, ITA, and faculty member	28	56%	1	2%

Interview comments: *RQ #2.* During the interview process, the participants often provided comments directly related to each of the ten interview items (see Table 2). At the end of the interviews, they also offered various comments about communication and learning in the labs, providing background information and helping to explain the Likert scale ratings, and setting the stage to address RQ #2 on what communication skills contribute to successful classroom interactions. For example, opinions diverged in two interview items: Interview Items 4 and 5, the two dimensions asking about the function of an undergraduate question (Table 3).

For Interview Item 4 (*Undergraduate requesting clarification of content information*), teaching assistant and undergraduate comments clarified the source of their divergent opinions regarding the type of content information the undergraduates were requesting. The teaching assistants interpreted questions as asking for specific answers, but the undergraduates were trying to locate information they knew they needed, but couldn't find. Similarly, in Interview Item 5 (*Undergraduate requesting confirmation or reassurance*), participants' comments revealed that the differing opinions occurred because the undergraduates intended their questions to be heard as asking for confirmation or reassurance from their teaching assistants. However, the ITAs heard the questions as requests for content information only, not recognizing that the undergraduates intended their questions be interpreted as simultaneously requesting content information and confirmation or reassurance. This finding underscores the importance for ITAs (and all teaching assistants, for that matter) to interpret undergraduate questions as multifunctional, in that they sought content information and reassurance at the same time, even if not explicitly expressed as such.

Faculty member's comments. The faculty member's comments covered a wide range of topics, including undergraduate performance, teaching assistant performance, and issues related to teaching in the chemistry lab in general. Her comments were positive about the work of everyone in the labs. She felt that the ITAs supported and guided student learning, and that the undergraduates were committed to developing their skills in the chemistry lab necessary to understanding chemistry. Her comments are summarized below in Table 9.

Table 9. Summary of Faculty Member's Comments on Undergraduate and ITA Communication

Summarized comments on positive features of undergraduate and ITA communication patterns

- ITAs coordinated demonstration with description and explanation, "essential for teaching in the chemistry labs."
- Undergraduates and ITAs took steps to ensure that they were talking about the same place in an experiment, which often requires negotiation and more than one attempt to be talking about the same point.
- By working through and solving problems with the undergraduates, the ITAs modeled for the undergraduates how to think and act like chemists.

Summarized comments on challenges to successful communication

- Undergraduates sometimes had difficulties expressing their questions and using the appropriate terminology, e.g, calling a flask a burette or heavy dependence on "this."
- Undergraduates were sometimes too precise when it was not necessary, but were not precise enough in other situations.
- At times, undergraduates collapsed multiple questions into one, making the ITA's job of teasing apart the questions more complicated.
- Pedagogically, in some cases the ITAs should have spent a little more time explaining why something happened or why something should be done in a particular way to the undergraduates.

ITAs' comments. The ITAs commented mostly on the skills and abilities of their undergraduates as a class. All enjoyed teaching the undergraduates and were very positive about them, reporting that the undergraduates were capable, well prepared, and dedicated to learning the material. In general, the ITAs were the most critical of all study participants of their *own* language skills. They felt that quicker responses with less hesitancy were better, and that hesitating to think about a response before saying it was potentially distracting or confusing for the undergraduates. The ITAs were also concerned about giving the right amount of information in a response, not too much and not too little, especially when the response required was complicated or "complex."

Undergraduates' comments. The 16 undergraduates who participated in the interviews eagerly offered many comments about learning and communicating in the labs. Three themes emerged from their discussions of successful interactions, and one theme from their discussion of partially successful interactions.

Successful communication: Comprehension and understanding. In the interactive lab, undergraduates prioritized ITAs' understanding and comprehension skills. The undergraduates clearly identified that they had different expectations for communication skills of teaching assistants based on the type of teaching. In a lecture format, typical of the pre-lab overview, clear pronunciation was a priority. However, in the question-answer format of the labs, while still important, pronunciation was not seen as problematic and was not seen as a barrier to communication. For the undergraduates, comprehension skills were the most important communication skill in the lab environment.

In the interview process, undergraduates shifted the meaning of the ITAs' understanding from the purely linguistic level to a broader interpretation. "Understanding" included the context and situation in which the verbal interaction was embedded. The undergraduates reframed the interview phrase "understand the question," and they repeatedly identified that it was crucial in the labs that their teaching assistants "understand me and my situation." Undergraduates needed their teaching assistants to understand what they were saying and doing. At the same time, the undergraduates reported that the teaching assistants needed to have a clear understanding of where in the experiment the undergraduates were.

The undergraduates also recognized that they themselves often had difficulties articulating what they wanted, primarily because they did not have or were not sure of the vocabulary to express themselves. Comments that illustrate this sentiment included *I know what I wanted. I didn't know what it was* or *I ended up phrasing it okay, but I didn't specify things clearly, but he [the teaching assistant] understood.* Or *Using the word 'electrode' would have helped make this clearer, rather than just 'this.'*

Successful communication: Instructional trust and comfort. The undergraduates felt comfortable, respected and supported. They were comfortable communicating with their teaching assistants and trusted that the teaching assistants were committed to helping them learn the material. Undergraduate comfort and trust with their ITAs made it easy for them to ask questions. Further, they were comfortable pursuing questions because in the lab environment they did not expect communication to be successful immediately.

Early on, the ITAs had established rapport with their students and provided a learning environment that supported student questions. The undergraduates viewed their ITAs as friendly and enjoyed interacting with them, though they did not want to be seen as asking "stupid" questions. They appreciated that the ITAs made themselves available for questions by walking around the lab, but many undergraduates preferred that the teaching assistants not interrupt them with questions because they found such interruptions distracting from their work.

Undergraduates also recognized that successful communication required negotiation to achieve mutual understanding of the question or problem to be resolved. They frequently mentioned *On the second try we got it right* or *On the second time around the ITA understood. At first, the teaching assistant didn't understand what I was misunderstanding, but we eventually worked it out.* One undergraduate commented on the length of time it took for an interaction to be successful, but that eventually the exchange was successful because both the teaching assistant and the undergraduate worked together to resolve the undergraduate's question or problem.

Successful communication: Verbal and visual information. Undergraduates strongly believed that the coordination of verbal information and visual information was crucial to their learning in the chemistry labs and an important constituent of successful communication. The undergraduates emphasized how they wanted and needed their teaching assistants to respond to their questions by demonstrating what to do, in addition to expressing the information verbally. In cases where the ITA used only verbal explanations, the undergraduates expressed an interest in seeing what to do in addition to hearing about what they should do. As one undergraduate stated: *I've never been in a chem lab and I haven't used the equipment before. They [faculty member and teaching assistants] assume that we are familiar with it [the equipment], but we aren't. Reading the chapter [in the lab manual] doesn't show you how to use the equipment.*

Improving Communication: Assume student questions have multiple functions. From the interactions that were categorized as partially successful, the undergraduates were consistent in wanting their teaching assistants to understand and respond to two unspoken needs embedded in their questions: First, assume questions were always asking *why*, and second, assume questions are simultaneously asking for content information and reassurance. The undergraduates wanted the teaching assistants to tell them *why* what they were doing correctly was correct and *why* what they were doing incorrectly was incorrect. They wanted their teaching assistants to interpret their questions as multifunctional, even if not explicitly expressed as such. Undergraduates consistently reported that when they approached their teaching assistants, they were asking the ITAs for discrete (content) information and simultaneously asking them to confirm (reassure) that what they were doing was right or not.

Summary of results for interviews, RQ #1 and RQ #2: Adopting a research methodology that sought the perspectives of the actual participants in the interactions lead to rich and varied data, providing a more complete and accurate account of communication in the labs by revealing information unavailable through direct observation. Data from the interview phase of the project included quantitative and qualitative data. In semi-structured interviews, participants identified, through Likert scale responses, instances of successful communication, addressing the first research question of what constitutes successful communication. The semi-structured interview process also allowed participants to provide qualitative data, comments that provided support and explanation about why interactions were successful, which addressed RQ #2 about what communication skills and features contribute to successful communication. Participants were also comfortable suggesting ways communication could be improved.

Participants were, in general, positive about the interactions in which they took part. In the majority of cases, participants had similar overall views of interactions, but often with different degrees of certainty of success. From multiple participant perspectives, the predominant communication skills that contributed to successful communication included fully comprehending undergraduate questions (e.g., contextualizing the question, addressing unspoken needs), having sufficient trust and comfort among the participants to encourage negotiation of information and persistence through miscommunication, and communicating information verbally and visually through coordinated description and demonstration. Further, the one theme that emerged for improving communication was for ITAs to assume questions have multiple functions: a question that on the surface is asking for content information is often also asking for confirmation or reassurance, as well as requesting justification.

Interaction analysis: RQ #2. Interaction analysis of the 50 undergraduate-initiated interactions from the interview phase of this study provided an opportunity to understand in greater detail lab communication to address the second research question of what communication skills contribute to successful communication. Interaction analysis examined turn-taking behaviors and, using a framework of conversational listening (Flowerdew and Miller, 2005), structural and functional features of the interactions. This section includes subsections on turn-taking, opening an interaction, closing an interaction, and establishing an interaction topic, and also a focus on syntactic patterns, lexical choices, and types of information requested in the high-frequency undergraduate-initiated interactions. Together, these subsections address RQ #2 by highlighting the importance of linguistic, non-linguistic, and pedagogical aspects of lab communication, such as monitoring and responding to the actions, as well as verbal communication; deciphering ambiguity in interactions; and having familiarity and understanding of regularly occurring types of information needed by the undergraduates.

Turn-taking. Turn-taking behavior within the interactions consisted of a pattern of alternating turns between the undergraduates and the ITAs, with successful interactions having slightly fewer turns than the partially successful interactions. However, some communicative exchanges challenged the definition of what constituted a communicative turn. In this setting, both actions and language could be conversational turns. In some instances, a turn was only verbal expression (Example 1). However, in some interactions, a participant's turn was the action or activity alone (Example 2). These "action" turns could not be monitored by the other participant through listening. Rather, these turns had to be monitored visually. In the examples "ITA" means international teaching assistant, and "UG" or "UG2" means undergraduate. Some interactions were accomplished by an ITA and two undergraduates.

Example 1: Verbal turn taking

UG	And do we need to elevate them?
ITA	Elevate?
UG	Yeah like
ITA	Oh, uh. No it's better clamp it
UG	This one?
ITA	Clamp, yeah.
UG	Just so it doesn't move.
UG2	Yeah, cuz it was falling.
ITA	Yeah, and this one too.
UG	We'll probably need another one.

Example 2: Action turn taking

UG	Well, I don't know I'm having trouble.
ITA	Hold this down. The tips to the… ahh… This is… Yeah, You adjust the height of the burette and then put the tips into the uhh…uhhh.
UG	[Student carries out instruction]
ITA	A little lower.
UG	[Student carries out instruction]
ITA	Yeah. Now press the bottle and let it go. The solution will go up.
UG	[Student carries out instruction]
ITA	Yeah. Now you can close this.
UG	Close this?
ITA	Yeah, this one is closed when it is vertical.
UG	So, it's closed.
ITA	Yeah, Yeah.

Opening an interaction. Undergraduate-initiated interactions were opened by gaining an ITA's attention using his or her name (Examples 3 and 4) or some other vocalization, e.g. "Uhm." However, undergraduates also signaled their questions, with no introduction, by just asking the question. As one undergraduate stated: *I'm really comfortable with the TA. You can tell because I don't have to use his name. I just ask the question.* Rarely did an undergraduate explicitly indicate an intention to ask a question with overt discourse marking, such as *I have a question.*

Example 3: Opening an Interaction

UG [Says ITA's name]
ITA Uhm.
UG Where do we get the two grams of borax? Is it in the back?

Example 4: Opening an Interaction

UG [Says ITA's name]
ITA Yep.
UG Ah, what do we do if all the thermometers are giving us different readings?

Closing an interaction. Closing interactions also had identifiable patterns (Examples 5 and 6). One of the participants, either the undergraduate or the ITA, would close an interaction with some sort of confirmation, word or vocalization, that the interaction was over: *okay, thank you, alright, good idea, yeah,* or *uh hum.* ITAs closed the interactions more frequently, two-thirds of the time.

Example 5: Closing an Interaction

UG Should we dump it out or it can stay there?
ITA It can stay there. Yeah, yeah.

Example 6: Closing an Interaction

UG How much is enough?
ITA Maybe five, five grams. Five grams, yeah.

Interaction topic. Undergraduates established the topics of their interactions usually in either their first or second speaking turns. They used five common syntactic patterns, which are given below. They also depended heavily on lexically ambiguous choices. Finally within the high-frequency undergraduate-initiated topics (equipment, materials, procedures), they requested consistent types of information.

Interaction topic: Syntactic patterns. The five common syntactic patterns undergraduates initiated interactions with included: Wh-questions, Yes/No questions, questions with alternative choices signaled by *or*, statement of a problem, and statement of a situation followed by a question. Here are some examples:

Wh-Questions
- How much NaOH and HCl should we pick up?
- Uh...How do we do this?

Yes/No Questions
- Is that the right way to set it up?
- Is this a Hirsch funnel?

Questions with Alternatives Signaled by or
- Do we actually have to clamp this in or can I just put it in so it rests on the bottom?
- Is that good enough or do we have to put iodine in?

Statement of a Problem
- It still isn't working.
- It won't go out.

Statement of a Situation Followed by a Question
- Um... On the actual bottle it says .019 molarity. Is that okay for the NaOH?
- When I measure the pH of the seawater and it's not 8.2, do I adjust it to 8.2 or do I leave it like that?

Interaction topic: Lexical choices. Analysis of question forms confirmed what participants reported: When asking their question, undergraduates expressed their questions using a range of lexical choices and degrees of lexical precision. In some instances, undergraduate questions were clearly stated, syntactically well-formed, expressed using precise terminology, and easily understood from the information available in the question itself. Unfortunately, questions of this type were in the minority. In most instances, questions were expressed with heavy dependence on deictic reference (referring to an assumed shared knowledge), and were thus ambiguous.

When examining the ambiguously expressed questions, it was demonstrably impossible to adequately or appropriately respond to the question as it was stated, if a listener were to depend only on the linguistic code of the question. See the examples below:

Information-dense and unambiguous question
> [ITA's name] do you know how much solid sodium borate we're supposed to put in this thing to heat over the Bunsen flame?

Context-dependent and ambiguous question
> [ITA's name] should I pour this in there?

In an examination of the ambiguously expressed questions, ambiguity was tied to the use of deictic reference (*this* and *there*). Reference was most often situational (exophoric) reference rather than textual (endophoric) reference (Halliday & Hassan, 1976). In order for the ITAs to disambiguate the question, they needed additional information provided by the context. The act of hearing and responding to a question required that an ITA understood the visual information that accompanied the verbal expression of the question. The teaching assistant needed to understand the situation to make the question meaningful.

Interaction topic: Information requested on equipment and materials. Undergraduates most frequently initiated interactions on topics related to equipment, materials and procedures. In this section, the interactions discussing equipment and materials are discussed together because they shared similarities in the type of information undergraduates wanted. Procedure-related interactions are discussed separately. Undergraduate-initiated questions about equipment and materials centered on the undergraduates developing familiarity and dexterity with the resources of a chemistry lab by using, understanding, and talking about them. The undergraduate-initiated questions concerning materials and equipment encompassed three primary types of information:

1. Locating and acquiring equipment or materials (*Where is it?*)
2. Identifying the appropriate item (*What is needed?*)
3. Understanding how a piece of equipment works (*Is it functioning properly?*) or measuring materials (*How much is needed?*)

First, the undergraduates needed to develop familiarity with the physical environment of the labs and understand how to acquire the equipment and materials that they needed for the experiments (see Example 7). For these types of questions, the undergraduates knew what they needed, but were not sufficiently familiar with the labs and resources for obtaining what they needed. A large proportion of these questions had very simple responses: for equipment, *get it from the stock room*, and for materials, *it's on the back bench*.

Example 7: Locating and acquiring equipment or materials

UG   [Says ITA's name]
ITA Yep.
UG   We don't have a pH meter in our thing.
ITA You, you can I I think that one one. Use that one. You can just take it.
UG   Can we just take it over?
ITA Yeah.

The second type of questions for equipment and materials were ones in which the undergraduates needed help determining the appropriate piece of equipment or materials they needed (Examples 8, 9, and 10). The undergraduates were developing judgments for their work as chemists, which required that the teaching assistants provide supporting explanations to the undergraduates. In some cases, the undergraduates had a clear sense of what they needed, but in other instances, the undergraduates needed more support and information from the teaching assistant.

Example 8: Identifying the appropriate type

UG   Can we use a beaker of this size to…?
ITA Yeah, sure.

Example 9: Identifying the appropriate type

UG   Uhm.
ITA Yep.
UG   For part four do we use natural seawater?
ITA Natural seawater, yeah.

Example 10: Identifying the appropriate type
UG   When we do the sample B, we we use that with deionized water, right?
ITA   Yeah, Yeah.
UG   Ok.
ITA   Uhum.

The last type of question related to equipment and materials illustrates how the undergraduates were developing a sense of proportion and precision (Examples 11 and 12). In these cases, undergraduates were developing their sense of how a piece of equipment functioned or whether it was functioning properly. They learned what type of precision was needed in measuring and using the materials.

Example 11: Equipment function
UG   [Says ITA's name]
ITA   Yep.
UG   Ah, what do we do if all the thermometers are giving us different readings?
ITA   I think ah these two are really close. And maybe this is not so good.
UG   Okay.
ITA   Uh yeah, I think you can use either either of these two.

Example 12: Material quantity
UG   How much NaOH and HCl should we pick up?
ITA   I [prolonged pause]
UG2   For part 4.
UG   For aeration. Like how much should I take so we don't waste any?
ITA   Uhm.
UG   About how much.
ITA   I think 10 milliliters should be enough.
UG   10 milliliters.
ITA   Yeah.

Procedures. Procedure-related interactions, the most frequently occurring type of all interview interactions, were in many respects the more complex questions because these interactions included not only issues and concerns related to equipment and materials, but also to how things worked together. For the procedure-related questions, undergraduates were asking for assistance on three areas:

1. What needs to be done?
2. How is a procedure carried out?
3. How is a problem solved?

Procedures: What needs to be done? The most common question about procedures that undergraduates asked their teaching assistants was what they should do (Examples 13 and 14). Often, these questions were situations in which the undergraduates were reading the instructions in the lab manual and were double-checking with the teaching assistants about what they should be doing. One undergraduate described how these types of questions were crucial, especially at the beginning of the experiment, since it was often the case that what seemed like a minor step to the undergraduates early in an experiment, had significant consequences later on.

Example 13: What needs to be done?
UG So, after the first like five minutes we have to like cover it?
ITA Um, yeah.

Example 14: What needs to be done?
UG Uhm. It says adjust volume to 100. If ours is like at 97
ITA Ok.
UG Does that mean, do we add water or do we just
ITA Add water.
UG Add water.
ITA Add 3 milliliters.
UG Ok

Procedures: How is a procedure carried out? The undergraduates needed help from the teaching assistants to explain and demonstrate how to complete a step in an experiment (Examples 15, 16, and 17). For example, in setting up a vacuum properly, the information that was provided in the lab manual described the procedure, but when the undergraduates where confronted with the hands-on experience of setting up a vacuum, they needed additional support and information from the teaching assistants.

Example 15: How is a procedure carried out?

UG Uhm, Are we going about setting up the vacuum right?
ITA Umm
UG How do we set up the vacuum?
ITA You need another flask and yeah put the funnel in.
UG Another flask just like that?
ITA Yeah….And you have a an adapter for the funnel to seal to the flask….

Example 16: How is a procedure carried out?

UG Uhm, Are we going about setting
UG2 Uhm, We don't keep that in there while we titrate it do we?
ITA The what?
UG The…uhm…pH meter.
ITA The electrode uhh
UG Do we keep it in there while we add
ITA I would say you don't have to, but uh, I don't think there are any problems if
    you
UG Oh, we can just keep it in there?
ITA Yeah,
UG2 So then we just leave it. It's easier then we don't have to go clean it out.

Example 17: How is a procedure carried out?

UG [Says ITA's name]
ITA Yep.
UG Could you show me how to uhm…sorry…How to like.
ITA Oh, You need a adapter.
UG Where do I get … I was just looking for one of those.
ITA Ah
UG Those in there?
ITA [ITA looks for an adapter] Adapter…Adapter…Oh, it's a Oh, it's a stopper….It looks almost the same except the the adapter is hollow

Procedures: How is a problem solved? The most complicated and longest interactions were those procedure-related questions involving problem-solving. These were situations in which the undergraduates had completed the steps in an experiment as detailed in the lab manual, but for some reason the outcome was not successful or not as anticipated (Examples 18 and 19). The undergraduates needed the teaching assistants to help troubleshoot, requiring the teaching assistant to verbally "walk through" the steps of the experimental procedure using the apparatus that the undergraduates had constructed. The ITA had to help locate the problem and then offer a solution.

Example 18: How is a problem solved?
UG   Uhm, [Says ITA's name]
ITA Yep.
UG   I plugged this in, but I don't think it's on.
ITA Okay….Is this on? …. Maybe this?...Yeah, it's on now.
UG   Hum.
ITA I mean I mean the the power is on. The power supply is on.
UG   Okay. Shouldn't that be at seven though?
ITA I…yeah. It should be seven because you are using the pH seven buffer. Yeah.
UG   But it's not.

Example 19: How is a problem solved?
UG   Uhm… Wha Ours. Something won't go out. It can't
ITA Okay. So…
UG   It won't go out.
ITA Let me see. The container is not good enough.
UG   No. I mean…I can't get the. It's not the container. It's that I can't get the liquid out of here. I can't get the liquid up or out.
ITA That's not enough
UG   No, No. It won't come out.
ITA Right. Because of this part. Because of this part...

In the procedure-related questions, undergraduates were seeking the advice, support, and help from their ITAs as the undergraduates worked through the chemistry experiments. The procedure-related questions demonstrated that the undergraduates were developing their understanding of and judgments about how to approach the work in the chemistry laboratory, as well as their abilities to discuss the activities of the experiment and lab.

The ITAs in this study all had different teaching and communication styles of working through the procedure-related questions, especially when they were troubleshooting. One ITA tended to be more expressive verbally, modeling for the undergraduates how chemists talked. Another ITA tended to use less language modeling, requiring the undergraduates to express the information for themselves. Both styles were seen as successful by the participants, though the interactions in the labs in which the ITAs allowed the undergraduates to express the information tended to take slightly longer.

Summary of results for interaction analysis: RQ #2. Interaction analysis explored in greater depth aspects of undergraduate-initiated interactions with their ITAs. Findings in this section revealed that undergraduate-initiated interactions often present requests for information ambiguously, requiring their teaching assistants to skillfully disambiguate undergraduate questions using the contextual resources of the educational setting. The findings also revealed that the high-frequency undergraduate-initiated interaction topics related to experimental equipment, materials and procedures, demonstrating recurring patterns of undergraduate requests for and negotiation of information. Undergraduates' questions also reflected their development as chemists, in understanding how to approach and judge their own work in the chemistry labs.

The successful communication that occurred in these chemistry labs was not about what one participant group (ITAs and undergraduates) did. Rather, it was what individuals of both groups did together in their efforts to understand each other. Only when the ITAs understood the needs of the undergraduates, and the source of their questions, could they supply responses that addressed the concerns of the undergraduates. Undergraduates had to do the same, and when they thought that communication was not working, they had to persist by monitoring their understanding of the teaching assistant's information and redirecting the exchange. This was, in essence, the discourse of the classroom.

Conclusion

The findings of this study make important contributions to our understanding of communication between non-native speakers placed in instructional positions (ITAs) and their native speaking students in three significant ways. First, in interactive chemistry labs communication frequently originates with and is directed by undergraduates, a rich area for future research, and which also has implications for policy decisions (see the contribution of Kang and Moran, this volume). Second, research investigating communication between the ITAs and undergraduates benefits from methodologies that obtain the perspectives of *both sets of participants* involved in lab communication. As demonstrated by this study, success in communication could only be identified by the participants engaged in the interaction, and not by an observer external to the communicative exchange, which is arguably a much more common pattern in ITA education. And third, understanding communication between ITAs and undergraduates using strictly linguistic frameworks which exclude gesture, physical resources, artifacts of the setting, and context, will not be able to capture and account for the rich and needed ways that members of this educational setting communicate. Promoting and supporting successful communication between these two groups needs to be understood as a collaborative experience in which both teachers and learners contribute to the process.

In a Nutshell

1. ITA preparation programs (curricula and evaluation) can benefit from departmental collaborations to develop familiarity with and understanding of the real-world discourse demands of a discipline, allowing programs to more effectively tailor their support for ITAs and the demands of their departmental duties.
2. This study is an example of one such collaboration. It could not have been realized without interest, support and willingness to participate from the faculty member, the teaching assistants, and the undergraduates.
3. For the interactive educational environment of a university-level chemistry lab, ITAs should be prepared to handle brief, rapidly asked questions, which are often stated with ambiguity and imprecision, as undergraduate students are developing control of the discourse of the discipline. Further, ITAs should be familiar with the high-frequency questions of the discipline.
4. In the lab, successful undergraduate-ITA interactions should include both explanation and demonstration, with shared meaning and understanding coming from the coordination of language, resources, and gesture.
5. In order to meet undergraduate learning needs, ITAs' responses to undergraduate questions should include additional support

and information, including the reason *why* something is as it is. They need to supply frequent reassurances about undergraduate thinking and approaches to the coursework.
6. Undergraduates should be encouraged to express their tacit concerns and questions.
7. ITA and undergraduate rapport should be established early and be maintained throughout for undergraduate engagement, participation, and learning in a course.
8. Universities should ensure that ITAs have the requisite teaching skills and preparation for their duties in the classroom.
9. Research methodologies that elicit the perspectives of those engaged in and invested in classroom communication should be used to clearly understand the intentions and motives of the participants in these educational environments.

References

Axelson, E. R., & Madden, C. G. (1994). Discourse strategies for ITAs across instructional contexts. In C. Madden and C. Myers (Eds.), *Discourse performance of international teaching assistants* (pp. 153-185). Alexandria, VA: TESOL Publications.

Bailey, K. M. (1984). The "foreign TA problem." In K. M. Bailey, F. Pialorsi, & J. Zukowski/Faust (Eds.), *Foreign teaching assistants in U. S. universities* (pp. 3-15). Washington, DC: National Association for Foreign Student Affairs.

Bailey, K. M., Pialorsi, F., & Zukowski Faust, J. (Eds.)(1984). *Foreign teaching assistants in U. S. universities*. Washington, DC: National Association for Foreign Student Affairs.

Benrabah, M. (1997). Word-stress: A source of unintelligibility in English. *International Review of Applied Linguistics in Language Teaching, 35*, 157-166.

Bradlow, A. R., & Bent, T. (2008). Perceptual adaptation to non-native speech. *Cognition, 106*, 707-729.

Bresnahan, M. J., Ohasi, R., Nebashi, R., Liu, W.Y., & Shearman, S.M. (2002). Attitudinal and affective response toward accented English. *Language & Communication, 22*, 171-185.

Brown, K. A., Fishman, P. F., & Jones, N. L. (1991). Language proficiency legislation and the ITA. In J. Nyquist,, R. Abbot, D. Wulff, & J. Sprague (Eds.), *Preparing the professoriate of tomorrow to teach: Selected readings in TA training* (pp. 393-403). Dubuque, Iowa: Kendall/Hunt Publishing Company.

Byrd, P., & Constantinides, J. (1992). The language of teaching mathematics: Implications for training ITAs. *TESOL Quarterly, 26*, 163-167.

Cazden, C. B. (2001). *Classroom discourse: The language of teaching and learning* (2nd ed.). Portsmouth, NH: Heinemann.

Davies, C. E., & Tyler, A. E. (1994). Demystifying cross-cultural (mis)communication: Improving performance through balanced feedback in a situated context. In C. Madden & C. Myers (Eds.), *Discourse performance of international teaching assistants* (pp. 201-220). Alexandria, VA: TESOL Publications.

Derwing, T. M., & Munro, M. J. (1997). Accent, intelligibility, and comprehensibility: Evidence from 4 L1s. *Studies in Second Language Acquisition, 19,* 1-16.

Derwing, T. M., & Munro, M. J. (2001). What speaking rates do non-native listeners prefer? *Applied Linguistics, 22,* 324-337.

Derwing, T. M., & Munro, M. J. (2005). Second language accent and pronunciation teaching: A research-based approach. *TESOL Quarterly, 39,* 379-398.

Derwing, T. M., Rossiter, M. J., Munro, M. J., & Thomson, R. I. (2004). Second language fluency: Judgments on different tasks. *Language Learning, 54,* 655-679.

Derwing, T. M., Thomson, R. I., & Munro, M. J. (2006). English pronunciation and fluency development in Mandarin and Slavic speakers. *System, 30,* 183-193.

Fairclough, N. (2003). *Analyzing discourse: Textual analysis of social research.* New York: Routledge.

Fayer, J., & Krasinski. (1995). Perception of hesitation in nonnative speech. *Bilingual Review, 20,* 114-121.

Field, J. (2005). Intelligibility and the listener: The role of lexical stress. *TESOL Quarterly, 39,* 399-424.

Finder, A. (2005, June 24). Unclear on American campus: What the foreign teacher said. *New York Times,* pp. A1, A18.

Flowerdew, J. & Miller, L. (2005). *Second language listening: Theory and practice.* New York: Cambridge University Press.

Fortanet, I. (2004). The use of 'we' in university lectures: Reference and function. *English for Specific Purposes, 23,* 45-66.

Gonzalez, V. (2004). *Second language learning: Cultural adaptation processes in international graduate students in U.S. universities.* Lanham, MD: University Press of America, Inc.

Gourlay, B. (2008). *An investigation of communication patterns and strategies between international teaching assistants and undergraduate students in university-level science labs.* (Doctoral dissertation, University of Rhode Island/Rhode Island College). Retrieved from http://digitalcommons.ric.edu/etd/12/

Gravois, J. (2005). Teach impediment. *The Chronicle of Higher Education.* Retrieved from: https://chronicle.com/article/Teach-Impediment/33613

Hahn, L. (2004). Primary stress and intelligibility: Research to motivate the teaching of suprasegmentals. *TESOL Quarterly, 38,* 201-224.

Halliday, M. A. K., & Hasan, R. (1976). *Cohesion in English.* Essex, England: Pearson Education Limited.

Hoekje, B., & Williams, J. (1992). Communicative competence and the dilemma of international teaching assistant education. *TESOL Quarterly, 26,* 243-270.

Jenkins, S., & Parra, I. (2003). Multiple layers of meaning in an oral proficiency test: The complementary roles of nonverbal, paralinguistic, and verbal behaviors in assessment decisions. *The Modern Language Journal, 87,* 90-107.

Kaufman, D., & Brownworth, B. (2006). Collaborative paradigms and future directions in international teaching assistant professional development. In D. Kaufman & B. Brownworth (Eds.), *Case studies in TESOL practice series: Professional development of international teaching assistants* (pp. 1-13). Alexandria, VA: TESOL Publications.

Kearsley, G. P. (1976). Questions and question asking in verbal discourse: A cross-disciplinary view. *Journal of Psycholinguistic Research, 5,* 355-375.

Levis, J. (2004). Intonation and discourse: Three approaches. *TESOL Quarterly, 38,* 353-356.

Lippi-Green, R. (1997). *English with an accent: Language, ideology, and discrimination in the United States.* New York: Routledge Press.

Llurda, E. (2000). Effects of intelligibility and speaking rate on judgments of non-native speakers' personalities. *International Review of Applied Linguistics in Language Teaching, 38,* 289-300.

Major, R., Fitzmaurice, S., Bunta, F., & Balasubramanian, C. (2002). The effects of non-native accent on listening comprehension: Implications for ESL assessment. *TESOL Quarterly, 36,* 173-190.

McChesney, B. J. (1994). The functional language of the US TA during office hours. In C. Madden & C. Myers (Eds.), *Discourse performance of international teaching assistants* (pp. 134-152). Alexandria, VA: TESOL Publications.

McGregor, A. (2007, March). Comprehensibility of international teaching assistants. Paper presented at the annual meeting of the Teachers of English to Speakers of Other Languages, Seattle, WA.

Munro, M. J., & Derwing, T. M. (1995). Processing time, accent, and comprehensibility in the perception of native and foreign-accented speech. *Language Learning, 45,* 289-306.

Munro, M. J., & Derwing, T. M. (1998). The effects of speaking rate on listener evaluations of native and foreign-accented speech. *Language Learning, 48,* 159-182.

Munro, M. J., & Derwing, T. M. (1999). Foreign accent, comprehensibility, and intelligibility in the speech of second language learners. *Language Learning, 49,* 285-310.

Munro, M. J., Derwing, T. M., & Morton, S. L. (2006). The mutual intelligibility of L2 speech. *Studies in Second Language Acquisition, 28,* 111-131.

Myers, C. L. (1994). Question-based discourse in science labs: Issues for ITAs. In C. Madden & C. Myers (Eds.), *Discourse performance of international teaching assistants* (pp. 83-102). Alexandria, VA: TESOL Publications.

Nyquist, J., Abbot, R., Wulff, D., & J. Sprague (Eds.). (1991). *Preparing the professoriate of tomorrow to teach: Selected readings in TA training.* Dubuque, IA: Kendall/Hunt Publishing Company.

Patton, M. Q. (2002). *Qualitative research & evaluation methods* (3rd ed.). Thousand Oaks, CA: Sage Publications, Inc.

Pickering, L. (2001). The role of tone choice in improving ITA communication in the classroom. *TESOL Quarterly, 35,* 233-255.

Pickering, L. (2004). The structure and function of intonational paragraphs in native and nonnative speaker instructional discourse. *English for Specific Purposes, 23,* 19-43.

Plakans, B. (1997). Undergraduate experiences with and attitudes towards international teaching assistants. *TESOL Quarterly, 31,* 95-119.

Riggenbach, H. (Ed.). (2000). *Perspectives on fluency.* Ann Arbor: The University of Michigan Press.

Roth, W.M., McGinn, M. K., Woszcyna, C., & Boutonné, S. (1999). Differential participation during science conversations: The interaction of focal artifacts, social configurations, and physical arrangements. *The Journal of the Learning Sciences, 8,* 293-347.

Rounds, P. (1987). Characterizing successful classroom discourse for NNS teaching assistants. *TESOL Quarterly 21,* 643-671.

Rounds, P. (1994). Student questions: When, where, why, and how many. In C. Madden & C. Myers (Eds.), *Discourse performance of international teaching assistants* (pp. 103-115). Alexandria, VA: TESOL Publications.

Smith, R. M., Byrd, P., Nelson, G. L., Barrett, R. P., & Constantinides, J. (1992). *Crossing Pedagogical Oceans: International Teaching Assistants in U.S. Undergraduate Education*: (ASHE-ERIC Higher Education Report No. 8). Washington, DC: The George Washington University School of Education and Human Development.

Tanner, M. W. (1991). *NNSTA-student interactions: An analysis of TAs questions and students' responses in a laboratory setting.* Unpublished doctoral dissertation, University of Pennsylvania, Philadelphia.

Tyler, A. (1992). Discourse structure and the perception of incoherence in international teaching assistants' spoken discourse. *TESOL Quarterly, 26,* 671-688.

Tyler, A. (1995). Cross-cultural miscommunication: Conflicts in perception, negotiation, and enactment of participant role and status. *Studies in Second Language Acquisition, 17,* 129-152.

Wennerstrom, A. (1998). Intonation as cohesion in academic discourse: A study of Chinese speakers of English. *Studies in Second Language Acquisition, 20,* 1-25.

Wennerstrom, A. (2000). The role of intonation in fluency. In H. Riggenbach (Ed.), *Perspectives on fluency* (pp. 102-127). Ann Arbor: University of Michigan Press.

Williams, J. (1992). Planning, discourse marng, and the comprehensibility of international teaching assistants. *TESOL Quarterly, 26,* 693-711.

Williams, J., Inscoe, R., & Tasker, T. (1997). Communication strategies in an interactional context: The mutual achievement of comprehension. In G. Kasper & E. Kellerman (Eds.), *Communication strategies: Psycholinguistic and sociolinguistic perspectives* (pp. 304-322). New York: Addison Wesley Longman.

Yankelovich, D. (2005, November 25). Ferment and change: Higher education in 2015. *The Chronicle of Higher Education,* B6.

Yerrick, R. K., & Roth, W.R. (2005). *Establishing scientific classroom discourse communities: Multiple voices of teaching and learning research.* Mahwah, NJ: Lawrence Erlbaum Associates.

Appendix

Questionnaire used for background information on undergraduate participants

1. Name:
2. Age:
3. Sex: _____ Male _____ Female
4. Home town and state:
5. Did you grow up primarily in an urban, suburban, or rural environment?

6. Entry Year:	7. Concentration: If you have not selected your concentration, what is a likely concentration?

8. Contact information for follow interview questions. Telephone: E-mail:
9. What language(s) do you speak at home with your family?
10. Indicate other languages you have studied and your proficiency level.

11. Please describe any experience of travel or living abroad.			
Location	Length of time	Dates	Purpose

12. Have you taken chemistry in high school?　　　　　　YES　　　NO

    If YES, please answer the following:
    How many semesters have you studied chemistry?
    In what year did you study Chemistry:　　　　9th　　10th　11th　12th
    Did you take an AP Chemistry course?　　　　　　　YES　　　NO
    Have you studied Calculus?　　　　　　　　　　　　YES　　　NO
    How many years of Math did you study in high school?

Area of Math	Semesters Studied

How many semesters of Math have you studied in college?

Area of Math	Semesters Studied

Interaction and Discourse Markers in the ITA-led Physics Laboratory

by Stephen Daniel Looney,[1] Pennsylvania State University

Research has pointed out that international teaching assistants (ITAs) use fewer discourse markers (DMs) in a more restricted fashion than American teaching assistants and that these differences impede listeners' comprehension of lectures. Strikingly, studies have ignored a common environment in which ITAs and undergraduates interact: science, technology, engineering, and mathematics (STEM) laboratories. This study investigates the use of DMs by a first-year physics ITA and two native English-speaking undergraduates during an experiment, "The Diffraction Grating Spectrometer." The question guiding the analysis is: How do ITAs and undergraduates use the DMs so and okay in physics lab interaction to display and demonstrate? Okay and so are of interest because of their salient sequential position in turns-at-talk, and because they function independently (okay, and so) and as a single construction (okay so) in both undergraduate and ITA speech. Okay, so, and okay so function to display understanding of prior utterances and to project space to verbalize an understanding, thus allowing the lab procedure to move forward. A lengthy interactional sequence is analyzed, in which multiple procedural errors are located and corrected in two undergraduates' lab reports. By demonstrating how okay and so function in both ITA and undergraduate speech, this paper provides insight on specific features of a shared interactive practice, locating and correcting misunderstanding, in which ITAs and undergraduates engage in multiple contexts at many North American universities. ITA educators and mentors can use recorded and transcribed interactional data from university classrooms to draw ITAs' attention to these important linguistic features.

---

1. Author contact: sdl16@psu.edu

For over two decades, social scientists and pedagogues have been interested in understanding and improving international teaching assistant (ITA) performance in the classroom, as well as finding ways for ITAs to improve rapport with undergraduates. The "ITA problem" with English communication has been recurrently oversimplified to ITAs' variation from idealized native English speaker (NES) communication norms both in academic and popular media reports (Clayton, 2000; Finder, 2005) with little discussion of literal language from university contexts. While academic articles have provided insight into ITAs' and undergraduates' experiences and effectiveness, only a handful of studies have taken a detailed look at ITA and/or undergraduate speech. This report begins with the assumption that the lack of focus on actual ITA and undergraduate speech is still a significant blind spot in our understanding of ITAs' tasks as teachers, as well as ITA and undergraduate interaction. See Table 1 for areas and authors of previous studies.

Table 1. Published Research on ITA-undergraduate Talk

Topics	Authors and dates of publication
The use of modals and directives in office hour and lab interactions	Reinhardt (2010); Tapper (1994)
Types of questions used by ITAs and undergraduates	Myers (1994); Rounds (1994)
The prosodic patterns of ITA lectures	Hahn (2004); Pickering (2001, 2004)
Intercultural effects on classroom pragmatics	Davies & Tyler (2005)
The development of interactional competence in ITA office hour role-plays	Rine & Hall (2011)
Undergraduates' discursive strategies for negotiating misunderstanding in office hour meetings	Chiang (2009); Chiang & Mi (2008)
Discourse markers in ITA lectures	Liao (2009); Tyler (1992); Williams (1992)

In large part, the research shown in Table 1 has illuminated differences between ITA speech and native speaker English (NES) speech, or models of NES speech, and proposed how divergence from native speaker norms may negatively impact classroom interaction and undergraduates' learning. This body of literature's contribution to our understanding of ITA talk is indisputable, but there are still gaps, in this case caused by reliance on traditional linguistically oriented frameworks, and perhaps also by studying language use in contexts where student-teacher interaction cannot be adequately modeled, for example role-plays or studies where speech raters listen to pre-recorded lectures.

This report contributes to the understanding of ITA and undergraduate interaction in an Introduction to Physics lab at a large U.S. university. A micro-analytic perspective is used here, which is informed by Interactional Competence (Hall, Hellermann, & Pekarek Doehler, 2011; Young, 2011), which itself emerges from a confluence of Conversation Analysis, Sociocultural Theory, and Language Socialization (Kasper, 2001). This perspective views language not as a fixed set of prescribed rules for usage, but as a collection of largely generic interactive resources co-constructed and socio-historically situated within interactive practices. In other words, "relying on the informational, semantic, and propositional content of words and utterances will fail to get at what utterances (and silences) might be doing as actions in a sequence of detailed interactional events" (Jacoby & Ochs, 1995, p. 176). Thus, minute details of interaction, such as discourse markers (DMs) that are often overlooked in structuralist linguistic analyses, may be critical to the co-construction of knowledge and understanding between speakers. By looking at these oft-ignored features, this chapter will give readers a deeper appreciation of how interlocutors align their understandings of lab procedures through the use of DMs.

The stance of the current research is that ITA program personnel and individual faculty mentors working with ITAs can raise ITAs' awareness of interactive resources in Science, Technology, Engineering and Math (STEM) laboratories by using recorded and transcribed interactional data from university classrooms. Such transcriptions can be used to draw attention to important interactional features that have been perhaps under-recognized in traditional English as a second language (ESL) instruction. This study's findings have implications that extend to ITAs' academic mentors, whether they are ESL educators, or faculty members and support staff in academic departments. By tending to ubiquitous yet overlooked details of interaction during course observations and teaching practicums, academic and professional mentors can provide targeted feedback to ITAs on how to use English in a fashion that guides student thinking and promotes critical engagement as suggested by the National Science Foundation (NSF) and the National Science Board (NSB)(Beering, 2009). *Okay* and *so* may seem too simple and unimportant for analysis, but this report demonstrates their crucial organizational and interactive functions in academic discourse.

Literature Review

Discourse markers in ITA lectures. Early comparative studies (Tyler, 1992; Williams, 1992) between ITA and NES discourse provided insights into ITA discourse; namely, how it differs from NS speech, and how it affects listener comprehension and processing. Tyler (1992) and Williams (1992) tested undergraduates' perceptions of ITA lectures as well as the efficacy of pre-lecture planning to improve ITAs' abilities to mark information structure in their lectures. A primary concern of both studies was the use of discourse markers (DMs) by ITAs. Williams' (1992, p. 697) findings supported the hypothesis that ITAs' advance planning improves comprehensibility of ITAs' lectures. Findings further revealed that ITAs used DMs in a more systematic manner if provided an opportunity to plan their explanations. This suggested that ITAs were aware of the need for discourse marking and were able to employ DMs, but also that their state of L2 development at that time may have inhibited their ability to explicitly mark their discourse in real time.

Tyler (1992, p. 716) investigated one ITA's use of sequential DMs such as *first*, *next*, and *finally* in academic presentations given in an ITA preparation course. Tyler (1992, p. 719) showed that while the ITA's explanation opened with NES-like sequential DMs, the DMs became less explicit and more ambiguous (e.g., *and then* and *also*) as the lecture progressed. This had the effect of making the ITA's presentation seem "confusing [and] incoherent" (Tyler, 1992, p. 723). Following her analysis of the ITA's speech, the author provided an analysis of corresponding aspects of a NES teaching assistant's (TA's) lecture, which was more coherently organized in regards to the rhetorical expectations of Standard American English. In other words, the NES TA maintained the use of numerical DMs (e.g. *first*, *second*, etc.) as opposed to the ITA who started with numerical DMs and abandoned them early in the presentation. The findings pointed out clear differences between the ITA's and NES TA's use of DMs, and demonstrated that inconsistent and unclear use of DMs can negatively impact listeners' perception and comprehension of pre-recorded lectures. Listeners to lectures and explanations lacking clear and consistent DMs struggle to identify key points and logical relationships between pieces of information.

In a later study, Liao (2009) looked at how the use of DMs differs from speaker to speaker, as well as how context affects DM usage among a group of Chinese ITAs at an American university. Like past research, Liao (2009, p. 1318) showed that while ITAs and TAs used similar DMs, such as *oh, like, okay*, and *well*, the functions of the DMs differed or were limited in the case of the ITAs. For example, NES TAs regularly use the DM *well* as a delay marker in responses to questions while only one of Liao's (2009) ITA participants used *well* in this manner. Following her comparison of ITAs to TAs, Liao (2009) looked at how the use of DMs was influenced by discourse style, gender, and individual identity. Liao (2009, p. 1316) pointed out, "when discussing the use of DMs by NNSs [non-native speakers], we should not only aim to find a general pattern, but also seek to realize the voice behind each individual's choice of using DMs." This view shifted the paradigm, going beyond previous research by showing ITAs as active language users who consciously adapt to different interactional situations. Liao (2009) contributed to the ITA discussion by providing a dynamic picture of language users, whether they are native English speakers or non-native English speakers.

Summary. Thus three major themes emerge from the ITA literature on DMs:

1. ITA and TA discourse marking of information in lectures differs.
2. Planning explanations ahead of time helps ITAs structure their discourse in a more effective manner.
3. The use of discourse markers (DMs) is influenced by numerous factors including context, individual variation, and language proficiency.

These studies have helped ITA preparation programs better address the linguistic challenges ITAs face by looking at language use in lectures. At the same time, lecturing is only a small part of most ITAs' and TAs' responsibilities. Strikingly, studies have ignored the use of DMs in STEM laboratories. To give a more well-rounded and accurate view of ITA responsibilities and ITA and undergraduate interaction, this report looks at the use of DMs in face-to-face interaction during an actual physics lab session.

Discourse markers in interaction. Discourse markers (DMs) are an integral and often overlooked aspect of face-to-face interaction. According to Heritage (1984, p. 335), DMs have been treated "as an undifferentiated collection of 'back channels' or 'signals of continued attention' [which] seriously underestimate[s] the diversity and complexity of the tasks that these objects are used to accomplish." In contrast to traditional views of DMs, talk-in-interaction research has shown that DMs function as change-of-state tokens, modifiers of agreement or disagreement, information managers, and observable displays of cognitive processes (Bangerter & Clark, 2003; Buysse, 2012; Condon & Čech, 2007; Fraser, 1990, 1999; Gaines, 2011; Heritage, 1984, 2002, 2005; Müller, 2005; Redeker, 1990; Schiffrin, 1987). It is clear how important these functions would be to giving explanations, giving lengthy answers to questions, and trouble-shooting events in a lab. By tending to the interactional qualities of DMs, talk-in-interaction analyses go beyond traditional linguistic perspectives by investigating how interlocutors make sense of the world through the turn-by-turn unfolding of talk instead of focusing on *post hoc* analyses of "grammatically correct" utterances that exclude the "messy details" of talk.

Why focus on okay and so? The functions of DMs *okay* and *so* are crucial to both mundane and institutional interaction including that in the Physics lab. *Okay* seems to have two functions, as a marker of common ground and a transition within joint projects. *Okay* is focused on as these two functions are commonly found in Physics lab interactions, and are sequentially salient, meaning they appear at the beginning of or individually in turns. The functions marked by *okay* are involved in the practice of displaying understanding. *So* seems to have three functions, those of drawing a conclusion, marking a question, and turn management. These functions are also often seen in Physic lab interactions, are also sequentially salient, and are involved in the practice of demonstrating understanding.

Okay. As Condon and Čech (2007, p. 19) point out, much research has identified *okay* simply as a backchannel device. This perspective views *okay* as a backward looking resource, an acknowledgement that the prior turn at talk was received, and that repair is not required. But *okay* is not so simple. Other studies from a talk-in-interaction perspective have looked at the multiple discourse functions of *okay* in various contexts such as phone conversations (Bangerter & Clark, 2003; Schegloff, 1968, 1979; Schegloff & Sacks, 1973), police interviews (Gaines, 2011), and computer-mediated interactions (Condon & Čech, 2007). This report particularly focused on two functions of *okay:* A transition in interactional sequences, or joint activities (Bangerter & Clark, 2003); and a marker of common ground (Condon & Čech, 2007). It is not always easy to disentangle these two functions as the literature has pointed out and this chapter's analysis will demonstrate.

According to Condon and Čech (2007), interlocutors use *okay* to display to one another that at that point in the currently unfolding interaction they believe that they share a common understanding of the immediate context of interaction. Drawing on the discussion of DMs that display and show understanding by Schegloff (1982), Condon and Čech (2007, p. 20) point out that *okay* is "maximally informative about the speaker's construal of the previous talk, while consuming minimal resources and avoiding an explicit representation of what is understood." In terms of the Physics lab, this means that the ITA understands what the students have done in the lab prior to an interaction, and that the students understand what the ITA expects them to do in the lab moving forward. Uses of *okay* may also mark transitions in interactional sequences, as will be seen in this report's analysis. Beach (1993, p. 338) emphasizes the "dual character" of *okay* that is both backward and forward-looking. This dual character is perhaps most clearly articulated in a discussion about transitions in joint activities.

According to Bangerter and Clark (2003), people engage in joint activities, such as planning a vacation, a date, or a business meeting, that require two or more parties to align their understanding and coordinate future action. A joint activity like planning a vacation can be subdivided into sub-projects like making a budget, purchasing airfare, reserving lodging, and planning an itinerary. Other joint projects, like completing a Physics lab, can be similarly subdivided and interlocutors transition within and between these subdivisions when engaging in joint projects. Bangerter and Clark (2003) call these transitions between sub-projects *vertical transitions,* and these transitions are often marked by *okay.* Bangerter and Clark (2003, p. 217) also note that "*okay* is clearly used more often in dialogues that reflect well-defined tasks." Condon and Čech (2007) have pointed out that the frequency of *okay* as a DM token falls when interaction is computer-mediated, but that *okay* in computer-mediated interaction still functions as it does in face-to-face interaction. Therefore, the use of *okay* as a DM is influenced both by the goal of interaction, and by the context of interaction. Both of these observations have implications for current study in that Physics labs are well-defined tasks that take place in a face-to-face context.

So. The second DM of interest to this study is *so*, which has been widely investigated. In both L1 and L2 speech, *so* has been noted to have multiple functions and also to occur in different contexts (Bolden, 2009; Buysse, 2012; Lam, 2009, 2010; Local & Walker, 2005; Müller, 2005; Raymond, 2004; Schiffrin, 1987). *So* serves as a linguistic road sign to cue interactants as to what is coming up in a turn at talk. They contribute to a context in which student and teacher collaborate to complete a lab. These three functions of *so* are:

1. Drawing conclusions
2. Marking questions
3. Turn management

Like the functions of *okay* presented in the previous section, it is not always easy to distinguish these functions. For instance, an utterance following *so* could be a conclusion posed in the form of a question. This is seen in Table 9 when a student says, *so change this to blue?*

Drawing a conclusion so. The first function of *so* focused on in this report is drawing conclusions. Buysse (2012, p. 1768) writes, "a possible paraphrase for a conclusive structure is: "from state of affairs X I conclude the following: Y"." Due to the imprecise nature of student questions in science labs (*Did we do this correctly?*)(See also Gourlay's contribution in this volume.), it is often left up to instructors to assess the state of affairs by looking at students' lab setup and/or lab manual, asking questions about the procedure the students have gone through, and then drawing a conclusion about where mistakes may have been made. Following the assessment of the state of affairs and before the explicit statement of the conclusion the instructor has reached, the DM *so* may be found. This is the case in the analysis and results presented below.

Interestingly, as shown in the analysis and results section, this drawing-a-conclusion at times appears in the form of a question, and/or demonstrates genuine misunderstanding. For this reason, this report will refer to drawing-a-conclusion *so* as demonstrating-(mis)understanding *so*. Demonstrating (mis)understanding is a way in which a speaker shares her understanding (correct or incorrect) of the world for a confirmation, denial, or amendment by a listener in hopes of aligning with the listener. Demonstrating (mis) understanding is often done in the form of a question which may be genuinely seeking affirmation or amendment, or may be serving the pedagogical purpose of engaging students and directing their attention to missing information (missing units of measurement, for example) or procedural mistakes. These utterances by the ITA implicitly demonstrate understanding of how the lab should be completed.

***Marking questions* so.** The second function of *so* of relevance to this report is marking the speech act of questioning. Only two studies have explicitly categorized instances of *so* marking questions (Müller, 2005; Schiffrin, 1987) while others have demonstrated how *so* is integral to the interactional functions of some question utterances (Bolden, 2009; Lam, 2009). Both Müller (2005, p. 82) and Schiffrin (1987) have pointed out that marking-questions *so* denotes that the question is "motivated" either by immediately prior discourse or by prior shared knowledge between speakers that may not be explicitly present in the interactional sequence. Myers (1994) has shown that university science lab discourse is question-based. The data presented in this report will demonstrate that questions marked by *so* are motivated by prior utterances or observations about the context of interaction.

***Turn management* so.** The final function of *so* relevant to this report is turn management, in other words, holding the floor and/or prompting a turn. Buysse (2012) and Lam (2009) have characterized holding-the-floor *so* as having a rising tone and elongated vowel, and being a device for signaling in-the-moment speech processing. This type of *so* thus often appears in conversation sequences near pauses, fillers, and repairs. Buysse (2012) and Lam (2009, p. 364) have also pointed out that prompting-a-turn *so* can appear as its own intonation unit with a level or falling tone with a short vowel. This type of *so* more broadly occurs "in text types which have a more flexible allocation of speaker roles." Raymond (2004) has also noted what is best termed the stand-alone *so*. Bolden (2009) looked at *so* as a resource to prompt incipient action that both speakers are aware of based on prior knowledge of the context.

All of these findings about turn management functions of *so* are relevant to this report because of the interactionally messy nature of the science laboratory. That is, turn taking is not rigidly defined in the Physics lab, and overlapping and connected speech is prevalent. It is in these "messy" sequences of interaction that ITA and undergraduate co-construct talk, and the contextual nature of interaction and language use become observable.

Summary of Okay and So. In summary, the DMs *okay* and *so* have been noted to have numerous functions. *Okay* has been identified as a marker of common ground and as a transitional marker between parts of a larger task. Tables 2 and 3 show how *okay* functions in both ways and at times in both ways at the same time as a minimal display of understanding. Later excerpts (Tables 9 and 10) reveal *okay* as a display of understanding that requires an accompanying demonstration of understanding to ensure that intersubjectivity is established.

Three functions of *so* that are relevant to this chapter are conclusive *so*, questioning *so*, and turn management *so*. In this chapter, all of the excerpts containing *so* (Tables 4-11) are examples of conclusive *so* but will be referred to as demonstrating (mis) understanding. Demonstrations of (mis)understanding are often in the form of questions (Tables 4, 5, 6, 9, and 10) and marked by overlapping and latched speech (Table 4, 9, and 10). The questions may serve pedagogical functions, seek information, or both but are all demonstrate an understanding of the lab procedure that needs affirmation, denial, or amendment. Instances of turn management *so*, also demonstrate understanding of the unfolding interaction and lab procedure as well as reveal that interlocutors are closely monitoring co-participants' speech and accordingly adjusting their own (or their interlocutor's) understanding of the immediate context.

How this study fits in. This report investigates the use of *okay* and *so* by a novice Physics international teaching assistant (ITA) and two NES (native English speaker) undergraduates in a consequential and authentic institutional setting. The ITA in the study is a Mandarin Chinese and English bilingual. This study draws on past taxonomies and conversation analytic approaches to discourse markers (DMs) to describe how *okay* and *so* function in interaction in a Physics lab. This article adds to past ITA research by looking at DMs in interaction from a view of co-construction (Jacoby & Ochs, 1995) and conversation analysis (Sacks, Schegloff, & Jefferson, 1974). This is a break from traditional ITA research in which the full communicative burden has been placed upon the ITA, with little attention paid to the role that undergraduate students play in ITA - student interaction (see also contributions by Gourlay, Kang and Moran, and Trebing in this volume). By demonstrating how *okay* and *so* function in both ITA and undergraduate speech, this paper provides insight on specific features of interactions in which an ITA and undergraduates locate and correct misunderstanding about lab procedures.

Research Purpose

This study investigates the use of discourse markers (DMs) by an ITA and two American undergraduates during an experiment in an Introduction to Physics lab titled "The Diffraction Grating Spectrometer" (see lab worksheet in Appendix A). The question guiding the analysis is: How do discourse markers (DMs) *okay* and *so* function in a lab interaction to help interactants co-construct understanding in the Physics lab? Readers will come away from this chapter with a deeper appreciation for the minutiae of speech and the critical role that underappreciated little words like *okay* and *so* play in accomplishing work in the university.

Method

The Data and the Setting

The data presented in this article comes from an extended sequence of recorded interaction between an ITA and two undergraduates in which multiple procedural errors were located in the students' lab worksheet. After errors were located and accounted for in the interaction, it became clear to the ITA that the students did not understand the instructions given by the ITA's teaching partner, nor did they understand the directions on the lab worksheet. This sequence was chosen for analysis because it exemplified an interactive practice (Hall, 1995) typical of ITA-undergraduate interaction in the Introduction to Physics lab, namely, locating and correcting misunderstanding. The lab worksheet, photographs of lab equipment, and observation field notes were used to supplement the analysis. The lab worksheet is included as an appendix (Appendix A).

This report comprises part of a larger study investigating the co-construction and development of interactional competence in a university Introduction to Physics lab at a large, public research university in the United States. Multiple lab sessions, from which this study drew on, were led by a first-year ITA working in tandem with a more experienced ITA or NES TA. Each lab session had approximately 40 American undergraduates. The undergraduates worked in pairs to complete an experiment that demonstrated a physical phenomenon covered in a lecture outside the lab sessions. In every lab session, the first-year ITA wore a wireless lapel microphone to capture the audio from interactions with students. The recordings were transcribed according to CA conventions (Woofitt, 2005) and submitted to a line-by-line analysis.

The Focus Participants

At the time of data collection, the ITA participant (Yao, not his real name) was in his second semester of teaching Introduction to Physics lab sessions. Yao was a first-year Ph.D. student in the Physics Department, came from China, and had no previous teaching experience before arriving in the U.S. The two undergraduate focal participants (Jan and Ann, not their real names) were both female, and were NES students enrolled in the second part of a two-part Introduction to Physics course sequence. In addition to the two-hour-per-week lab session, the undergraduates also took part in a three-hour-per-week lecture led by a tenure-track faculty member who had no direct contact with Yao or his teaching partner.

Analysis and Results for *Okay*[2]

As mentioned earlier, *okay* generally functions as a marker of common ground that also marks transitions between sub-projects within larger joint projects. The following analysis reinforces these findings. In Table 2, we see Yao explain to two undergraduates (Jan

---

2. The excerpts in this article are all drawn from the same interactional sequence. They are not presented in chronological order because they illuminate different features. See Appendix B for the complete sequence in chronological order.

and Ann) that the line that they have measured as a red line, is actually the "central line." Following Yao's correction, Jan displays her understanding with an *okay*.

Table 2. Displaying Understanding

56.		Jan:	huh↑
57.		Yao:	this is not the: the right line the
58.			central line the central line is (.) is
59.			uh: it looks like red ↓ but actually it's
60.			not it's uh it's kind of a mixture of all
61.			kinds of >light it< looks like red. but
62.			it's not the so called red. lines.=
63.	→	Ann:	=okay=

Table 2 opens with Jan's second pair part expressing confusion regarding Yao's incomplete statement in line 54: *this is not the*. Following Jan's utterance indicating confusion (huh↑), Yao launches into an explanation that what the students have perceived and recorded as being red light is actually a mixture of all kinds of light that looks red (lines 57-62). Ann displays her understanding of Yao's explanation in line 63 with the DM *okay*. To paraphrase Condon and Čech (2007), Ann's turn in line 63 is maximally informative about her state while having the minimal form. That is, *okay* functions here to make it clear that she understands the previous turn. She immediately yields the floor, allowing Yao to complete his explanation in succeeding turns.

Table 3 reveals another function of *okay*: Closing a sequence, and moving between sub-projects (transitioning). It is difficult to completely distinguish this function and the previous function of confirming understanding (finding common ground). Sequentially speaking, these occurrences of *okay* are located clearly at the end of a sub-project while the *okay* in Table 2 occurs within a sub-project. It also bears noting that in lines 32 and 33 both undergraduates say *okay* while in Table 2 only one student does so. Both students are displaying understanding after Jan has demonstrated understanding. See Table 3:

Table 3. Transitioning Between Sub-projects

28.		Jan:	okay so change this to [blue.
29.		Yao:	[yes.=
30.		Jan:	=and say we couldn't find violet.
31.		Yao:	yes:
32.	→	Jan:	okay=
33.	→	Ann:	=°okay°=

Table 3 begins with Jan demonstrating understanding of what she and her partner should change in their lab report to correct it (line 28). In line 29, Yao provides a minimal affirmative response, *yes*. Jan then continues stating her understanding of what she should do, *say we couldn't find violet*, in line 30. Her utterance is once again followed by a minimal affirmative response by Yao in line 31. In lines 32 and 33, Jan and Ann close the sub-project with *okay* tokens.

Summary of okay. The uses of *okay* to display understanding in Tables 2 and 3 reflect what prior literature suggested about the DM *okay*, specifically that it is a marker of common ground and a transitional marker (Bangerter & Clark, 2003; Condon & Čech, 2007; Schegloff & Sacks, 1973). As both examples here show, *okay* is often found alone in a latching or overlapping turn at the end of a sub-project (i.e., resolving a question). The analysis shows how *okay*, while generally ignored in ITA research, is crucial to co-construction of shared understanding in the Physics lab. Yao, Jan, and Ann use the DM to display understanding of the prior turn (Tables 2 and 3) and, at times, that they are ready to close a sub-project and move to the next one (Table 3). At the same time, *okay* does not demonstrate understanding but only displays it. The next DM this analysis will focus upon, *so*, precedes the demonstration of understanding.

Analysis and Results of *So*

In Table 4, Jan opens the sequence with a question about her lab work (lines 1-2). Yao initially responds affirmatively with *wow, it's really good* in line 3. Following a brief pause, Yao deploys *oh* as a change-of-state token (Heritage, 1984). Yao's utterance is followed by a pause in line 4 before he resumes the turn, uttering *so* which is followed by a justification for *missing the blue* on Jan's lab report. See Table 4:

Table 4. Drawing a Conclusion and Turn Management

1.		Jan:	did we do all of this right? does it
2.			look right?=
3.		Yao:	=wow its really good (.) O::H
4.			(0.9)
5.	→	Yao:	s:o=
6.		Jan:	=>and< we couldn't see [anything
7.		Yao:	[>you missed< the
8.			blu:e↑

Table 4 is an example of the DM *so* prefacing a demonstration of understanding (drawing conclusions) by both Yao (teacher) and Jan (student). In lines 1 and 2, Jan asks Yao if her work has been done correctly. After looking at her lab report, Yao utters *so*. Immediately following Yao saying *so* in line 5, Jan latches on (begins speaking immediately as Yao stops speaking) and explains that she and her partner *couldn't see anything* (line 6). Line 6 shows Jan orienting to Yao's *so* as a prompt for an explanation of why she has not recorded measurements for *blue*. Jan is demonstrating that she had already located the absence of measurements for the blue light as a problem and was waiting for Yao to point to this problem. Therefore, Yao's turn (*so*) prompts incipient action (Bolden, 2009). Jan's preemptive response to Yao's forthcoming question reveals that she is actively participating in the lab, not merely waiting for Yao's correction.

Mis(understanding). Following Jan's latched-on turn in line 6, Yao retakes the floor in an overlapping turn (talk from two or more people occurring at the same time) and asks if the students *missed the blue*. Yao's turn in lines 7 and 8 demonstrates his understanding of the students' lab procedure. He does this in the form of a question, *you missed the blue,* marked with rising final intonation. Yao demonstrates his understanding as "misunderstanding." In this case, the "misunderstanding" serves a pedagogical function. To clarify, Yao knows that the students *missed the blue*. He can see that on the lab worksheet (Appendix A) but he engages his students through questioning instead of directly pointing out a mistake. Thus, when we look at this excerpt from an *emic* perspective of co-construction (looking to see how those "inside" the conversation treat utterances), it demonstrates that DMs can have multiple and multi-layered functions that are contingent on the perceptions and actions of each interlocutor as their talk unfolds.

Table 5 also shows the DM *so* preceding a demonstration of understanding (drawing conclusions) in the form of a question. In line 34, Jan asks Yao if she and her partner have calculated *D correctly*. After a pause of 2.3 seconds in line 35, Yao opens his response with *so* followed by a micro-pause (line 36). Yao then produces the interrogative *what is the unit* (line 36). Once again, marking the speech act of questioning. See Table 5:

Table 5. Turn Management and Marking Questions

34.		Jan:	=and did we calculate D correctly?
35.			(2.3) ((looking at WB))
36.	→	Yao:	**so.** (.) uh wh- what is the unit
37.		Jan:	we di::d
38.		Yao:	millimeter?
39.		Jan:	the:: the first
40.			(3.8)
41.		Jan:	>this is in< nano meters bu?t we put theta
42.			(in it) on that.=

It bears pointing out that the fact that Yao's second pair part (an obligatory response of any kind to a first pair part) to Jan's first pair part (line 34) indicates a non-preferred response (Raymond, 2003). Non-preferred simply means Yao's answer in line 36 is not quite what Jan expected, and that Jan is going to need to adjust to a new trajectory in the talk. Therefore when Yao utters *so*, the undergraduate may be aware that Yao is most likely identifying trouble with her work. The question that demonstrates understanding in this case is quite different from the example in Table 4 above. This *so* precedes a question that seems to demonstrate genuine misunderstanding as well as serving a pedagogical purpose. In contrast to the question in Table 4, the question in Table 5 is a *wh-* question (*wh- what is the unit*). Students commonly omit units of measure on their lab worksheets and by directing the students' attention to this omission, Yao is implicitly reminding students of the importance of units of measure in Physics. Through questioning, Yao is engaging his students in the lab procedure instead of only pointing out and correcting mistakes. This shows a degree pedagogical sophistication.

In Table 6 below, Yao once again uses *so* as a DM marking the speech act of questioning. He is orienting himself to the non-verbal context of the lab, the lab worksheet in this case. He asks his undergraduate interlocutors if they had recorded the *initial position* (line 45).

Table 6. Marking Questions

41.		Jan:	>this is in< nano meters bu?t we put theta
42			(in it) on that.=
43.		Yao:	=oh wai- wai- wait wait a minute (.)
44.			this angle (4.0) oh °le- >let me borrow<
45.	→		this° **so** did you record the initial
46.			position?

The excerpt in Table 6 opens (lines 41-42) with Jan's response (following a repair and a restart) to Yao's question *What is the unit?* that he posed in line 36 (Table 7). In lines 43-45, we see Yao deploy a change-of-state token *oh* (Heritage, 1984). The change-of-state in this case is that Yao is no longer concerned with the unit of measure but is instead focused on the procedure that the undergrads have undertaken. This change-of-state is further realized in lines 45 and 46 (Table 6) when Yao asks *did you record the initial position?* This question is a *do*-support question and once again demonstrates a genuine misunderstanding.

In Table 7, line 48 is the undergraduate's second pair part response to Yao's interrogative turn constructional unit in Table 2, line 45-46: *Did you record the initial position?*

Table 7. Drawing a Conclusion

48.		Jan:	the yeah cause this was th-=
49.		Yao:	=th- the <u>cen.tral max.</u> >i mean<=
50.		Ann:	=yeah=
51.		Jan:	=yeah the red it was this one fifty two point
52.			eight that was our cen.tral. (0.7) line.=
53.		Ann:	=°then we went°=
54.	→	Yao:	<u>oh so</u> sorry this is not the
55.			(0.5)

The undergraduate, Jan, replies that she and her partner did record the initial position and begins to account for having done so. Yao interrupts the undergraduate to self-repair his use of *initial position* (Table 6) with the construction *central max* (Table 7, line 49), which more closely aligns with the lab manual and past lab sessions investigating the properties of light waves. In line 50, the other undergraduate Ann again confirms that she and Jan have recorded the central maximum and in lines 51 and 52 Jan recommences her accounting for their actions by reading out their measurement of the *central line*. In line 53, Ann attempts to continue accounting for the students' procedural moves *(then we went)* but is interrupted by Yao in line 54 (*oh so sorry this is not the*). Again, Yao displays cognition as well as softening disagreement using *oh* (Heritage, 1984). He then utters *so* (line 54), marking his verbalized understanding that the angle that the students have measured and recorded is not actually the central maximum.

In Table 8, Ann displays her understanding of what Yao just explained (*this is our central*, line 71) and her understanding that *everything else* (the answers), with the exception of the *second red* (line 73) is correct. At this point, it becomes obvious that the students are unclear about the relationship between the procedure they are conducting, the measurements they are recording, and the calculations they are making. If they have been measuring a spectrum of light from a central point and that central point was incorrect, one should be able to deduce that all of the corresponding measurements and thus the resulting calculations would be incorrect. Following a quite long pause of 3.2 seconds in line 74, Yao first verbalizes confusion (*sorry what*) about Ann's prior turn. He then expresses understanding (*so oh, I see the problem*) in line 75 that the students do not understand the procedure. He concludes his turn by accounting for the students' misunderstanding with a reference to his teaching partner's (*xxxxxx*, line 76) apparently lacking pre-lab activity lecture.

Table 8. Drawing a Conclusion

71.		Ann:	=okay. >so this is our central.< so.
72.			>everything else is right.< we just need to
73.			go find our second red.
74.			(3.2)
75.	→	Yao:	°sorry° what (.) so oh↑ i see the pro.blem.
76.			xxxxxx didn't explain the procedure very
77.			[clearly
78.		Jan:	[yeah::

The *so* in line 75, like the other examples precedes a demonstration of understanding. The understanding is explicitly demonstrated in Yao's utterance following his saying *so oh* with *I see the problem* (line 75). This conclusion is not only based upon Ann's prior turn (lines 71-73) but also upon the previous problems Yao has located in the undergraduate's lab report and procedure. It is the amalgamation of these issues that leads Yao to draw the conclusion that the undergraduates did not clearly understand his teaching partner's explanation of the lab procedure, or as Yao puts it the other TA (*xxxxxx*) *didn't explain the procedure very clearly* lines 76-77. Yao is finally left to re-explain the lab procedure to the same pair of undergraduates.

Summary of *so*. This section has unpacked how *so* precedes utterances demonstrating understanding in five excerpts from a Physics lab interaction. These demonstrations of understanding are done using both declarative and interrogative syntax and often involve latched (very closely spaced) or overlapping turns at talk. Tables 4, 5, and 6 are all examples of Yao demonstrating (mis) understanding through the use of questions following the DM *so*. Using *so* and the questions not only help Yao understand how his students have reached the point they have in their lab procedure, but also to orient students' attention to key information (units of measurement) and misunderstandings. Overlapping and latched talk following *so* also seems to be significant to the co-construction of shared understanding. The latched and overlapping turns in Table 4 show that the interlocutors are keenly attuned to the other interlocutors' understanding based on prior knowledge and non-verbal resources such as lab manuals.

Tables 7 and 8 are different. They are examples of *so* preceding a demonstration of understanding of how the lab should be done or why the students have conducted the lab procedure incorrectly. They are posed in declarative syntax and are accompanied by nearby *oh* and *sorry*, DMs which mark changes in state, and the non-preference for other-correction, respectively. Again, as stated earlier, non-preference simply means something unexpected in a conversation. Yao assumes that being corrected by others is non-preferred by his interactants. Thus he softens his overt correction.

Okay so as a Collocation

A final discourse marker (DM) highlighted in this report is the collocation *okay so*. It has been mentioned in previous literature but has not been deeply investigated. Three excerpts from the data collecting for this report illustrate how *okay so* functions as a phrasal DM that looks both backward (*okay*) to display understanding and forward (*so*) to demonstrate understanding. In first example, shown in Table 9, students are seeking clarification regarding Yao telling them that what they have recorded as violet light in their lab report is actually blue light.

Table 9. Displaying and Demonstrating Understanding

20.		Jan:	=really? because it looked=
21.		Ann:	=yeah [really. purple
22.		Jan:	[really. purple=
23.		Yao:	=yeah↑ (.) i- i know it's looks like purple
24.			but we call that blue be- because there is
25.			another li:ne (1.2) uh darker than this so we
26.			call that that one is the violet one
27.			(1.5)
28.	→	Jan:	**okay so** change this to [blue.
29.		Yao:	[yes.=

The excerpt in Table 9 begins with the two undergraduates requesting clarification (*really*) and justifying their work (*because it looked really purple*) in lines 20-22. Following the students' justification of their answer, Yao demonstrates that he understands why the students are confused, and that even though the blue light looks violet, it is blue and the violet light is too dark for the students to see (lines 23-26). Yao's explanation is followed by a substantial 1.5-second pause in line 27. Student Jan then says, *okay so change this to blue* (line 28) and Yao responds, *yes* (line 29). In Jan's turn, she displays understanding (*okay*) and then demonstrates her understanding (*so change this to blue*) in the form of a question that Yao can affirm or reject.

Table 10 contains two instances of the phrasal DM *okay so*. During this segment of interaction, Yao is showing the students the difference between the red lines and the central line. After his explanation, one of the students posits her understanding of the prior interaction and what she should do to appropriately complete the lab.

Table 10. Displaying and Demonstrating Understanding

64.		Yao:	=the red lines should be right here.
65.		Jan:	the what?
66.		Yao:	the sh- the the <u>true</u>↓ red lines should be
67.			right her:e.=
68.	→	Ann:	=okay [so
69.		Yao:	[you turn >at an< angle so so this is
70.			the central line i think an-=
71.	→	Ann:	=okay. >so this is our central.< <u>so.</u>
72.			>everything else is right.< we just need to
73.			go find our second red.

The excerpt above opens with Yao pointing out where the *red lines should be* (line 64). In line 65, Jan poses a request for clarification. Yao then repairs his previous utterance by restating that the *red lines should be right here* (lines 66 and 67). In his self-repair, Yao also contrasts the red lines that he is pointing out with the red lines that the students have incorrectly recorded with the word *true* being stressed. After Yao's self-repair, Ann takes the next turn with an *okay so* (line 68). Unlike the use of *okay so* in Table 9, this one is followed by an overlapping turn in which Yao continues his explanation, talking through Ann's *(okay) so*, showing the students the *central line* (lines 69 and 70) which is what they had originally thought was the red line. Ann latches (speaks immediately) onto Yao's previous turn in line 71 with another *okay so* followed by a statement of her understanding, moving forward, to be confirmed or rejected by Yao in the next turn.

Finally, Table 11 shows an instance of Yao using *okay so*. This excerpt is taken from early in the interactional sequence after Yao says *you missed the blue* (Table 11, lines 7-8).

Table 11. Displaying and Demonstrating Understanding

9.		Ann:	we couldnt find <u>any</u>. blue
10.	→	Yao:	**okay so** <u>ac</u>tually↓ usually↓ (0.7) >what you
11.			find< is the uh is the blue.
12.			(0.8)
13.		Jan:	huh?
14.		Yao:	yeah.
15.			(0.6)

The *okay so* presented in Table 11 bears a surface similarity to the previous instances examined in Tables 9 and 10. The *okay* component is a display of Yao's understanding of the prior utterance in which the student has reported not seeing *any blue* (line 9). However, the *so* here is different. Instead of Yao's proposing understanding for confirmation or correction, it is correcting misunderstanding and demonstrating understanding of how the lab *should* be done and not how it has been done.

Table 11 opens with the statement *we couldn't find any blue* (line 9). Yao's second pair part response begins with an *okay so* (line 10). As mentioned above, the *so* DM in this case is not serving to mark the speech act of questioning, as it did in the two student tokens of *okay so* analyzed above. It is marking Yao's correction of his student's misunderstanding. Yao's sensitivity with this interactive practice becomes clear as his turn unfolds. Following his utterance of *okay so* Yao twice modifies his correction with the hedges *actu-*

ally usually (line 10). He then tells the students that what they have found is the blue light (lines 10-11). The almost second-long pause in line 12 indicates trouble. This trouble is made verbally apparent in line 13 when the student utters, *huh?* Yao responds with *yeah* (line 14) before a brief pause (line 15) and an explanation, some of which can be seen in Table 8, that what the students have recorded as violet light is actually blue light.

Summary of collocation okay so. Thus, the final three excerpts (Tables 9, 10, and 11) presented here show how *okay so* functions in Physics lab interaction to display and then precede demonstrating understanding. Like the individual examples of *okay* (Tables 2 and 3) and *so* (Tables 4-8), the examples of *okay so* are located at the beginning of turns and, in the case of *so*, are followed by *yes-no* questions or statements correcting misunderstanding. In Tables 9 and 10, undergraduates use *okay* to display that they have understood prior correction from the ITA (Yao) and *so* to mark a demonstration of understanding in the form of a *yes-no* question in declarative syntax to be affirmed or denied by Yao. Table 11 shows Yao using *okay* to display that he understands his students' (Jan and Ann) misunderstanding. He then uses *so* to mark the beginning of a demonstration of understanding his students' misunderstanding, as well as a demonstration of his own understanding of how the lab ought to be conducted. So perhaps more clearly than the individual examples of *okay* and *so,* these examples of *okay so* as a collocation reveal shared construction of meaning in the Physics lab through the display and demonstration of understanding.

Discussion

This report has shown that discourse markers (DM), though often overlooked from an interactional perspective in ITA research and pedagogy, are an essential component of face-to-face interaction in science labs. In general, we have seen that *okay* displays understanding and often occurs in turns that mark transitions from one sub-project to another. We have seen that *so* precedes utterances that demonstrate understanding and that this demonstration of understanding can be spoken in the form of a question or a statement. The DM *so* is also located near overlapping talk (two or more individuals speaking at one time) and other DMs such as *oh* and *sorry*. Finally, we have seen that *okay* and *so* can function as a collocation *okay so* that displays understanding and precedes an utterance demonstrating understanding.

These findings are significant to ITA mentors, and ITA and English for Specific Purposes educators and researchers, for two reasons: 1. They shed light on the use of DMs in interaction within authentic instructional situations from the perspective of interactional competence, and 2. They reveal the significance of DMs in the sequential co-construction of understanding in the university Physics lab. The use of real-life, real-time classroom data to analyze the talk of the university is a key contribution of this report. As past research has shown, ITA-undergraduate interaction is largely based around aligning the novice understanding of the undergraduate with the expert understanding of the ITA. This seems to be done through question and answer sequences using various interactive resources (Chiang, 2009, 2011; Chiang & Mi, 2008; Myers, 1994; Rounds, 1994; Tapper, 1994). In the excerpts analyzed above, we have seen that two of the resources undergraduates and an ITA use in this alignment are the DMs *okay* and *so* which can signal the display and demonstration of understanding. By displaying understanding using *okay*, students and the ITA are propelling interaction forward using a deceptively small word to signal their receipt of information from the prior turn, their understanding of that information, and to their attention transitioning to a next task.

Oftentimes, a display of information is inadequate for successfully co-constructing understanding, and a demonstration of understanding is needed. As we have seen, *so* can precede utterances that demonstrate understanding. Demonstrating understanding can be done in the form of a question or a statement and can serve interactional, informational, or pedagogical functions. Interactionally, *so* prompts ITAs and students that a question may be coming in the turn. It also occurs around overlapping and latched talk in which students and the ITA might both be demonstrating understanding. Informationally, *so* alerts interactants that there could be a problem in the interaction that requires questioning for resolution. In the case of this report, the ITA needed some information (the unit of measurement) from the students to properly understand the context. At the same time, *so* can precede a student utterance demonstrating understanding of the lab procedure, for confirmation or amendment by the ITA. Both of these cases are has been termed demonstrating (mis)understanding. Pedagogically, the demonstrations of (mis)understanding through questions that *so* marks, allow the ITA to engage the students in active learning and solving their own problems.

DMs and ITA preparation or mentoring. These findings on DMs in Physics lab interactions add up to some significant implications for ITA and English for Specific Purposes programs, and for informal mentoring. In ITA research, the study of DMs has been somewhat restricted to the context of lectures. While the use of DMs in lectures is undoubtedly important and deserving of attention, lecturing is only part of what ITAs have to do. ITAs must also be able to use and interpret DMs in lab and office hour interactions. Because this feature of spoken language has been overlooked in language instruction, ITAs have been left to develop their use of these interactional resources (or not) on their own. With the advent of affordable technology and the availability of databases of language in use like MICASE (http://quod.lib.umich.edu/m/micase/) and TalkBank (talkbank.org), those involved in ITA preparation or mentoring can use such resources to raise ITAs' awareness about these features, and how or when to use them.

There are multiple ways that the analysis and data presented in this chapter can be used as lessons for those involved in ITA preparation as well as for developing at-hand strategies for lab coordinators and academic advisors. First, those involved in ITA preparation could use video clips and transcripts to raise ITAs' awareness about DMs and how they are used in teaching contexts. In addition to awareness-raising, ITA trainers can use video and transcript data to develop cloze and discourse completion task activities in which ITAs "fill in the blanks" with DMs that they would use in specific contexts. An example of such an activity with transcripts is included in Appendix B.

What ITA mentors can do. One need not be an applied linguist or ESL specialist to take away some important ideas for mentoring ITAs. First, discipline-specific mentors can encourage ITAs not to settle for displays of understanding, and to seek demonstrations of understanding from students. Simultaneously, they can instruct ITAs to demonstrate their own understanding in the form of questions that direct student attention, instead of always providing direct instruction. Mentors can also share common questions in specific labs. This way, ITAs can strategize how to answer questions, and to use questions to demonstrate understanding and guide student thinking. Finally, discipline-specific mentors can team up with ESL and pedagogy specialists to maximize the effectiveness and relevance of research on interaction in STEM settings.

Conclusion

In conclusion, this chapter has looked at the uses of the DMs *okay* and *so* by two undergraduates and an ITA in an Introduction to Physics lab at a U.S. university. The analysis reveals that discourse markers (DMs) are used in similar ways by the undergraduates and the ITA. In addition, the DM functions are tied to both the social context of interaction and the interlocutors' institutional identities as teacher and student. These findings add to our understanding of classroom talk by demonstrating that DMs function to help teachers and students locate and correct misunderstanding, as well as to display and demonstrate understanding in the context of the science lab. These findings suggest that continued close analysis of ITA-undergraduate classroom interaction could further inform ITA training and in turn improve teaching in the American university.

In a Nutshell

1. The ITA literature has suggested that ITA and native English speaker speech are markedly different and that such differences have negative consequences for listener comprehension and classroom interaction, but little ITA research has focused on how ITAs and American undergraduates together accomplish the work of the university classroom.
2. The ITA and English for Specific Purposes (ESP) literatures, and some pedagogical materials, ignore aspects of language that do not fit neatly into traditional grammars. Interactional discourse markers are one example of a relatively unexplored area.
3. In the data presented here, an ITA and two undergraduates use the discourse markers *okay* and *so* in similar sequential positions for similar classroom communicative functions.
4. *Okay* and *so* are used separately and in tandem (as *okay so*) to mark displays and demonstrations of understanding.

5. Inexpensive recording equipment makes possible the preparation of simple teaching materials to provide ITAs with explicit instruction about discourse markers *okay* and *so,* drawing on real classroom language use.
6. These findings also provide a starting point for faculty and staff in mentoring positions to identify critical linguistic aspects of classroom interaction that have positive impact on the pedagogy of ITAs.
7. Future research should continue to look at the minutiae of classroom interaction with the aim of understanding how language functions in the classroom and how pedagogical materials may be developed to address ITAs' classroom language.

References

Bangerter, A., & Clark, H. (2003). Navigating joint projects with dialogue. *Cognitive Science, 27*, 195-225.

Beach, W. (1993). Transitional regularities for 'casual' "Okay" usages. *Journal of Pragmatics, 19*, 325-352.

Beering, S. C. (2009). *National Science Board STEM education recommendations for the President-Elect Obama administration.* Washington DC.

Bolden, G. (2009). Implementing incipient actions: The discourse marker 'so' in English conversation. *Journal of Pragmatics, 41*, 974-998.

Buysse, L. (2012). *So* as a multifunctional discourse marker in native and learner speech. *Journal of Pragmatics, 44*, 1764-1782.

Chiang, S. (2009). Dealing with communication problems in the instructional interactions between international teaching assistants and American college students. *Language and Education, 23*(5), 461-478.

Chiang, S. (2011). Pursuing a response in office hour interactions between international teaching assistants and US college students. *Journal of Pragmatics, 43*(14), 3316-3330.

Chiang, S., & Mi, H.F. (2008). Reformulation as a strategy for managing 'understanding uncertainty' in office hour interactions between international teaching assistants and American college students. *Intercutural Education, 19*(3), 269-281.

Clayton, M. (2000, September 5). Foreign teaching assistants' first test: the accent. *The Christian Science Monitor.* Available: http://www.csmonitor.com/2000/0905/p14s1.html

Condon, S., & Čech, C. (2007). OK, next one: Discourse markers of common ground. In A. Fetzer & K. Fischer (Eds.), *Lexical markers of common ground* (pp. 17-45). New York: Elsevier.

Davies, C.E., & Tyler, A. (2005). Discourse strategies in the context of crosscultural institutional talk: Unconvering interlanguage pragmatics in the university classroom.

In K. Bardovi-Harlig & B.S. Hartford (Eds.), *Interlanguage pragmatics*. Mahwah, NJ: Lawrence Erlbaum Associates.

Finder, A. (2005, June 24). Unclear on American campus: What the foreign teacher said. *The New York Times*. Available: http://www.nytimes.com/2005/06/24/education/24assistant.html?pagewanted=all&_r=0

Fraser, B. (1990). An approach to discourse markers. *Journal of Pragmatics, 14*, 383-395.

Fraser, B. (1999). What are discourse markers? *Journal of Pragmatics, 31*, 931-952.

Gaines, P. (2011). The multifunctionality of discourse operator *okay*: Evidence from a police interview. *Journal of Pragmatics, 43*, 3291-3315.

Hahn, L. (2004). Primary stress and intelligibility: Research to motivate the teaching of suprasegmentals. *TESOL Quarterly, 38*(2), 201-223.

Hall, J.K. (1995). (Re)creating our worlds with words: A sociohistorical perspective of face-to-face interaction. *Applied Linguistics, 16*(2), 206-232.

Hall, J.K., Hellermann, J., & Pekarek Doehler, S. (2011). *L2 interactional competence and development*. Buffalo, NY: Multilingual Matters.

Heritage, J. (1984). A change-of-state token and aspectes of its sequential placement. In M. Atkinson & J. Heritage (Eds.), *Structures of social action: Studies in conversation analysis* (pp. 299-345). New York: Cambridge University Press.

Heritage, J. (2002). Oh-prefaced responses to assessments: A method of modifying agreement/disagreement. In C.E. Ford, B.A. Fox & S.A. Thompson (Eds.), *The Language of turn and sequence* (pp. 196-224). New York: Oxford University Press.

Heritage, J. (2005). Cognition in discourse. In H.T. Molder & J. Potter (Eds.), *Conversation and cognition* (pp. 184-202). New York: Cambridge University Press.

Jacoby, S., & Ochs, E. (1995). Co-construction: An introduction. *Research on Language and Social Interaction, 28*, 171-183.

Kasper, G. (2001). Four perspectives on L2 pragmatic development. *Applied Linguistics, 22*(4), 502-530.

Lam, P. (2009). The effect of text type on the use of *so* as a discourse particle. *Discourse Studies, 11*(3), 353-372.

Lam, P. (2010). Toward a functional framework for discourse particles: a comparison of *well* and *so*. *Text & Talk, 30*(6), 657-677.

Liao, S. (2009). Variation in the use of discourse markers by Chinese teaching assistants in the US. *Journal of Pragmatics, 41*, 1313-1328.

Local, J., & Walker, G. (2005). Methodological imperatives for investigating the phonetic organization and phonological structures of spontaneous speech. *Phonetica, 62*, 120-130.

Müller, S. (2005). *Discourse markers in native and non-native English discourse*. Philadelphia, PA: John Benjamins Publishing Company.

Myers, C. (1994). Question-based discourse in science labs: Issues for ITAs. In C. G. Madden & C. L. Myers (Eds.), *Discourse and performance of international teaching assistants* (pp. 83-102). Alexandria, VA: Teachers of English to Speakers of Other Languages, Inc.

Pickering, L. (2001). The role of tone choice in improving ITA communication in the classroom. *TESOL Quarterly, 35*(2), 233-255.

Pickering, L. (2004). The structure and function of intonational paragraphs in native and nonnative speaker instructional discourse. *English for Specific Purposes, 23*, 19-43.

Raymond, G. (2003). Grammar and social organization: Yes/No interrogatives and the structure of responding. *American Sociological Review, 68*(6), 939-967.

Raymond, G. (2004). Prompting action: The stand-alone "so" in ordinary conversation. *Research on Language and Social Interaction, 37*(2), 185-218.

Redeker, G. (1990). Ideational and pragmatice markers of discourse structure. *Journal of Pragmatics, 14*, 367-381.

Reinhardt, J. (2010). Directives in office hour consultations: A corpus-informed investigation of learner and expert usage. *English for Specific Purposes, 29*, 94-107.

Rine, E.F., & Hall, J.K. (2011). Becoming the teacher: Changing participant frameworks in international teaching assistant discourse. In J. K. Hall, J. Hellermann & S. P. Doehler (Eds.), *L2 interactional competence and development* (pp. 244-274). Buffalo, NY: Multilingual Matters.

Rounds, P. (1994). Student questions: When, where, why, and how many. In C.G. Madden & C. Myers (Eds.), *Discourse and performance of international teaching assistants* (pp. 103-115). Alexandria, VA: Teachers of English to Speakers of Other Languages, Inc.

Schegloff, E. (1968). Sequencing in conversational openings. *American Anthropologist, 70*, 1075-1095.

Schegloff, E. (1979). Indentification and recognition in telephone conversational openings. In G. Psathas (Ed.), *Everyday language: Studies in ethnomethodology* (Vol. 23-78). New York: Irvington.

Schegloff, E., & Sacks, H. (1973). Opening up closings. *Semiotica, 7*, 289-327.

Sacks, H., Schegloff, E., & Jefferson, G. (1974). A simplest systematics for the organization of turn-taking for conversation. *Language, 50*, 696-735.

Schiffrin, D. (1987). *Discourse Markers*. New York: Cambridge University Press.

Tapper, J. (1994). Directives used in college laboratory oral discourse. *English for Specific Purposes, 13*(3), 205-222.

Tyler, A. (1992). Discourse structure and the perception of incoherence in international teaching assistants' spoken discourse. *TESOL Quarterly, 26*(4), 713-729.

Williams, J. (1992). Planning, discourse marking, and the comprehensibility of international teaching assistants. *TESOL Quarterly, 26*(4), 693-711.

Woofitt, R. (2005). *Conversation analysis and discourse analysis: A comparative and critical introduction*. London: Sage.

Young, R. F. (2011). Interactional competence in language learning, teaching, and testing. In E. Hinkel (Ed.), *Handbook in research in second langague teaching and learning* (Vol. 2). New York: Routledge.

Appendix A

Name: _____ Date/Time: _____
Instructor: _____
Lab Partner: _____

18 Work Sheet

The Diffraction Grating Spectrometer

DATA TABLE

1. **MERCURY SPECTRUM**

Color	λ (nm)	θ_L	θ_R	θ_{avg}	$\sin\theta_{avg}$	d.
yellow	579.0					
green	546.1					
blue	435.8					
violet	404.7					

Average value of d = _____ m

2. **HYDROGEN SPECTRUM**

Color	N	θ_L	θ_R	θ_{avg}	$\sin\theta_{avg}$	λ_{exp} (nm)	λ_{Th} (nm)	Error (%)
Red	1						656.3	
Red	2						656.3	
Blue-green	1						486.1	
Blue-green	2						486.1	
Blue	1						434.0	
Blue	2						434.0	
Violet	1						410.2	
Violet	2						410.2	

18–5

Appendix B

Classroom Learning Material: The Location and Function of Okay *and* So *Worksheet*

Directions: After introducing the functions of the discourse markers (DMs) *so* and *okay*, as outlined in this paper, have students locate and classify the *okay* and *so* DMs in the following excerpt. Share answers as a class and discuss any alternative DMs that might be used in the same location for similar functions.

1.	F1.1:		did we do all of this right? does it
2.			look right=
3.	ITA:		=wow it's really good (.) O:::H (.) so:=
4.	F1.1:		=we couldn't see [anything
5.	ITA:		[>(you missed)< the blu:e
6.	F1.2:		we couldn't find any blue
7.	ITA:		okay so actually usually what you find is
8.			the uh is >°the°< blue
9.	F1.1:		huh↑
10.	ITA:		yeah
11.			( )
12.	ITA:		this i mean this slit is for blue (.)what
13.			you can see is usually blue the vi-
14.			violet one is (1.0) really really dark
15.			and it's difficult to see=
16.	F1.1:		=<u>real</u>ly because it looked=
17.	F1.2:		=yeah=
18.	F1.1:		=really (purple)=
19.	ITA:		=yeah i- i know it's looks like purple
20.			but we call that that one is the violet
21.			one
22.			(.)

23.	F1.1:	ok so change this to [blue
24.	ITA:	[yes=
25.	F1.1:	=and say we couldn't find violet
26.	ITA:	yes:
27.	F1.2:	[°okay°
28.	F1.1:	[okay and did we calculate d correctly
29.		(.)
30.	ITA:	so uh wh- what is the unit
31.	F1.1:	uni::t=
32.	ITA:	millimeter↑s
33.	F1.1:	the:: the first
34.		(.)
35.	F1.1:	this is in nano meters but we put theta
36.		(in it) on that=
37.	ITA:	=oh wai- wai- wait wait a minute (.)
38.		this angle (4.0) oh °le- >let me borrow<
39.		this° so did you record the initial
40.		position
41.		(1.0)
42.	F1.1:	the yeah 'cause this was th-=
43.	ITA:	=th- the central max i mean=
44.	F1.2:	=yeah=
45.	F1.1:	=yeah the red it was this one 52.8 that
46.		was our central line=
47.	F1.2:	=°then we went°=
48.	ITA:	oh so sorry this is not the (0.5)=
49.	F1.1:	=huh
50.	ITA:	this is not the: the right line the
51.		central line the central line is (.) is
52.		uh: it looks like red but actually it's
53.		not it's uh it's kind of a mixture of all
54.		kinds of >light it< looks like red but

55.			it's not the so called red lines=
56.	F1.2:		=okay=
57.	ITA:		=the red lines should be right here
58.	F1.1:		the what
59.	ITA:		the sh- the the true red lines should be
60.			right here=
61.	F1.2:		=okay [so (i just)
62.	ITA:		[you turn >at an< angle so so this is
63.			the central line i think an-=
64.	F1.2:		=okay so this is our central so
65.			everything else is right we just need to
66.			go find our second red
67.			(2.0)
68.	ITA:		°sorry° what (.) so oh i see the problem
69.			xxxxxx didn't explain the procedure very
70.			[clearly
71.	F1.1:		[yeah::
72.	ITA:		okay so central is first you record the
73.			central max=
74.	F1.2:		=right=
75.	ITA:		=record that position=
76.	F1.2:		=okay=
77.	ITA:		=okay [and for
78.	F1.2:		[so that would be this=
79.	ITA:		=yes and for each lines define the angle
80.			and we what we record here is difference
81.			between the lines and the [initi-
82.	F1.1:		[the central max=
83.	ITA:		=and the central max=
84.	F1.1:		=okay=
85.	ITA:		=and then we do the average we do the s-
86.			sin theta tha- that's the procedure=

87.	F1.2:	=okay=
88.	ITA:	=okay
89.		(.)
90.	F1.1:	what=
91.	ITA:	=have you have you done the difference
92.	F1.1:	we will but we'll okay we'll redo all
93.		those 'cause we didn't >get it right< we
94.		didn't do it correctly okay=
95.	ITA:	=yeah so=
96.	F1.1:	=but i understand what you're saying
97.	ITA:	yeah
98.	F1.1:	okay
99.		(.)
100.	F1.1:	thank you
101.	ITA:	you're welcome

Judgments of Non-standard Segmental Sounds and International Teaching Assistants' Spoken Proficiency Levels

by Jiyon Im,[1] Suwon Hightech High School and John Levis, Iowa State University

Mispronunciations of vowel and consonant (segmental) sounds are among the most frequent and identifiable types of difficulties in second language speech. This study examined the extent to which the pronunciation of non-standard segmental sounds contributed to how often listeners noticed difficulties in understanding, and how the assessed spoken proficiency levels of nonnative English speakers were related to the native English speaking listeners' understanding. Five linguistically-trained native American English listeners watched video-recorded teaching demonstrations of three Korean speakers of English whose oral proficiency in English had been rated at three different levels (low, intermediate, and advanced). The speakers were international teaching assistants (ITAs), or in preparation to be one. The listeners, using think-aloud techniques, paused whenever they had difficulty understanding. They then verbally described the nature of the difficulty they experienced, similar to the procedure used by Zielinski (2008). The findings showed that listeners stopped more frequently for the ITAs who had been rated as low and intermediate in oral ability than they did for the advanced speaker. In addition, the reasons for stopping varied according to the speakers' levels. The findings of this study indicate that final consonants should be treated as an important carrier of grammatical, topical, and

---
1. Author contact: augeynyc@gmail.com

discoursal cues in academic talk. The findings also indicate that accuracy in some stressed vowel sounds is particularly important, and should be highlighted in teaching and mentoring ITAs.

A commonly accepted goal of teaching pronunciation to nonnative speakers is the development of intelligible pronunciation. Intelligibility involves the ability to be understood despite an accent or the production of non-standard segments (often called "errors"), both normal features of second-language speech learned in adulthood. For example, a native listener might be able to recognize *grids* as intelligible even though she would agree that it actually sounded like *grease* as observed in our data. We use the term non-standard segment(s) to refer to these mispronunciations in this paper, following Zielinski (2008).

While intuitively appealing as a goal, intelligibility is complex in practice. According to Smith and Nelson (1985), understandable speech involves at least three considerations. First, listeners must be able to decode the individual words spoken. Second, listeners must be able to understand the meaning of what is said. And finally, listeners must be able to interpret the utterance successfully. Smith and Nelson (1985) named these three kinds of understanding 1. intelligibility, 2. comprehensibility, and 3. interpretability. The import of this is that listeners may notice the pronunciation of a non-standard segment even when understanding is not affected. The distinction between intelligibility and comprehensibility has been regarded as somewhat blurry in the field of pronunciation, yet the two levels of understanding turn out to be distinct in practice. For example, a native listener elaborated how both types of understanding were operative, saying "I can catch the words [intelligibility] but I don't understand what he is talking about [comprehensibility]" in the course of our think-aloud session. Such noticing of the ways that understanding may be differently impacted by speaker's speech and listeners' potential responses to their speech, is central to this study.

Intelligibility, segmentals and suprasegmentals. While interpretability, Smith and Nelson's third category above, is rarely examined in relation to pronunciation (see, however, Low, 2006), measurements of intelligibility and comprehensibility and their impact are central to current research on second language (L2) pronunciation (Derwing & Munro, 1997; Isaacs & Trofimovich, 2012; Levis, 2005; Munro & Derwing, 1995). The first goal of intelligibility research is to examine the central role of the listener in understanding accented speech, using listener responses to sentence level or discourse level stimuli. And while the listener may be "a silent partner" (Zielinski, 2008) in examining intelligible speech, it is important to look at listener responses in greater detail because intelligibility involves a mutual construction of understanding between speakers and listeners (Fiksdal, 1990; Jenkins, 2002; Zielinski, 2006a). In this study, intelligibility is defined by how features of pronunciation cause listeners to stop and comment on the clarity of ITAs' speech.

Another goal of intelligibility research is determining which elements of language are the most important in making speech more intelligible. A number of studies have attempted to determine which general phonological categories seem to most affect listeners' ability to understand. For example, Derwing, Munro and Wiebe (1998) examined the effect of pronunciation instruction for two groups of learners, one taught with an emphasis on segmentals and one taught with an emphasis on suprasegmental/global features. Although both groups improved their comprehensibility in more controlled contexts, such as reading sentences aloud, only the group to whom suprasegmental/global instruction had been given was perceived as being more comprehensible in spontaneous speech. See Table 1 (p. 116) for additional studies which examined which elements of language seem important in making speech more intelligible.

Other writers have also asserted the superiority of suprasegmentals. McNerney and Mendelsohn (1992) argued that short-term pronunciation courses should emphasize suprasegmentals as most likely to lead to improvement that will be noticed. Firth (1992) likewise noted that oral improvement is most likely starting with the widest possible scope (i.e., speaking), then narrowing down to suprasegmentals, and finally to segmentals. Implicitly, then, segmentals should <u>not</u> be taught if we take these arguments to a logical conclusion.

Arguments for focusing on segmentals in pronunciation programs. We argue in this report, however, there is little evidence for such a strong anti-segmentals stance when designing pronunciation training programs. Although improvement in segmentals does not invariably lead to improvement in how easily listeners understand an L2 speaker in the short run, they may be important nonetheless.

Munro and Derwing (2006) demonstrated that not all segmentals are equal, and that those with a high functional load (those that are are involved in many minimal pairs, such as /n/ and /l/, as in *need* pronounced as *lead* or *library* said as *nibrary*) impact comprehensibility to a much greater extent than those with a low functional load. In a strong assertion of the importance of segmentals, Jenkins (2000) studied nonnative speakers and nonnative listeners in in-

Table 1. The Phonological Aspects of Pronunciation in Key Studies

	Segmentals	Suprasegmentals
Key Studies	Jenkins (2002) Intelligibility is compromised by errors in core segmental items: certain consonants in word initial positions (e.g., phonemic variations, voiceless stops, consonant clusters); accurate vowel quantity (e.g., shortening and lengthening vowels); and consistent vowel quality in a regional variation. Also, nuclear stress errors compromise intelligibility.	Gallego (1990) More communicative breakdowns were reported when the speaker wrongly placed word stress in teaching assistant (TA) presentations.
	Munro and Derwing (2006) High functional load (FL) errors (e.g., the /l/-/n/ contrast, as in *need-lead* or *library* said as *nibrary*) affected listeners' perceptions of accentedness and comprehensibility more than low FL errors (e.g., the /ð/-/d/ contrast, as in *the-duh* or *then-den*).	Hahn (2004) Correctly placed primary phrase stress (for new-given information) led to better comprehension than incorrect or missing primary phrase stress.
	Bent, Bradlow, and Smith (2007) Vowel production accuracy and word-initial consonant accuracy correlated with the intelligibility of the read-aloud sentences produced by Mandarin speakers of English.	Kang (2010) Comparatively faster native speaker (NS) speech seemed to positively affect listeners' rating of comprehensibility more than slower NS speech.
	Zielinski (2008) The effect of non-standard segmentals on intelligibility varied according to different syllabic positions and the L1 background of the speaker. Neither segmental nor suprasegmental features should be more advocated.	

Jenkins (2000)

teraction and found that segmental pronunciation errors were the most important category influencing unintelligibility, with suprasegmental errors playing a relatively unimportant role. Based on her research, Jenkins' (2002) proposals for features which should be taught included certain consonants in word initial positions (e.g., phonemic variations as in *vowels* being heard as *bowels*, voiceless stops as in [pʰɪn] (*pin*) as compared with /spɪn/ (*spin*), consonant clusters as in *promise, string*, etc.), and accurate vowel quantity (e.g., shortening and lengthening vowels as in between *live* and *leave*.

Zielinski (2008) claimed that both segmental and suprasegmental features are important in pronunciation classrooms, and that attempting to talk about one without the other makes no sense. In her study, Zielinski had three native English speakers transcribe utterances chosen from three non-native speakers' conversational speech (Mandarin, Vietnamese, and Korean L1). She used the places where listeners had difficulty in the transcriptions and follow-up questioning of the listeners to identify "sites of reduced intelligibility" (p. 71). The sites of reduced intelligibility were compared with a detailed phonetic transcription created by a trained phonetician, to determine what features in the speech caused the listeners to not understand. Zielinski concluded that English-speaking listeners depended heavily on the pattern of strong and weak syllables in the syllable stress pattern produced by L2 speakers (a suprasegmental feature) in order to identify the words spoken. In addition, the presence of non-standard segments in strong (stressed) syllables had a greater impact on loss of intelligibility.

Zielinski's results, along with the findings of Munro and Derwing (2006) and Jenkins (2000), indicate that segmentals impact intelligibility. There is clearly reason to investigate how listeners respond to non-standard segments in L2 speech. Non-standard segments are extremely common in L2 speech, whether from L1 (first language) interference or because of developmental issues. For example, Zielinski (2008) argued that the segmental deviations in different syllable positions seemed to be significantly affected by L1 backgrounds. Likewise, Bent, Bradlow, and Smith (2007) found that Mandarin speakers of English tended to produce the syllable-final clusters the least accurately, which may be a result of transfer from Mandarin Chinese. These syllable-final clusters are also salient to native English listeners, who are often able to accurately identify vowels and consonants that do not match what is expected. The frequency of these non-standard segments has also been argued to be critical in judgments of intelligibility (Prator & Robinett, 1985).

What the current study does. Even though the contribution of non-standard segments to reduced intelligibility is clear, we know little about <u>which</u> non-standard segments most seriously affect a listener's ability to understand. Zielinski (2008) led the way in beginning to identify what listeners respond to in sites of reduced intelligibility. This study modifies her methodology by asking listeners to notice the features of L2 speech in general, not only where pronunciation reduces intelligibility but also where pronunciation or other language features cause listeners to respond in some way to what they noticed.

Literature Review

Extended discourse. We now discuss three issues which motivate the research methodology used in this study, including using speech samples of extended discourse, the influence of overall second language proficiency on intelligibility, and concurrent verbal reports of listeners. The type of speech sample appears to influence judgments of intelligibility. Previous research, such as that cited above, has used both very short and much longer speech segments. While all types of speech samples have led to the conclusion that pronunciation is a major contributor to loss of intelligibility, it is our belief that intelligibility, while reliably measurable at the sentence level, is more realistically measured when listeners have access to full linguistic and visual context in understanding, elements that are common in most speech events. In a study where the speech sample did not include the full discourse context, Munro and Derwing (1995), subjects listened to about ten seconds of a description of a series of pictures. The listeners in Zielinski (2006a, 2008) also listened to excerpts selected from a stretch of conversation, each of which was a clause or sentence consisting of an average of ten words. The sentences were from natural speech in extended discourse, but they were excised from the larger discourse context for the intelligibility transcription task. This deprived listeners of access to the discourse context.

Some other studies have used discourse contexts to examine intelligibility or comprehensibility. Listeners in Hahn (2004) responded to a mini-lecture in which sentence stress was manipulated. Results demonstrated that misplaced sentence stress led to loss of comprehension. In another study, Gallego (1990) had subjects listen to short lectures given by three international teaching assistants (ITAs) and identify the features that caused loss of intelligibility. Word stress was the main factor identified, followed by vocabulary and flow of speech (i.e., fluency).

L2 speakers' proficiency level. L2 oral proficiency levels also seem to influence listeners' judgments of intelligibility. Most studies have examined intelligibility using intermediate to advanced proficiency speakers. This is justifiable since the pronunciation difficulties of lower-level speakers may be strongly affected by their weaknesses in being able to produce fluent, automatic speech. The impact of proficiency may be the cause of paradoxical findings in two studies. Munro and Derwing (1995) found that segmental errors, intonation, grammar, and the length of utterance were related to listeners' perceptions of accentedness (a measure of how much a speaker's pronunciation differs from a local norm). They also found that non-standard intonation and ungrammatical phrases affected perceived comprehensibility (the amount of work needed to understand). However, Derwing and Munro (1997) noted that segmental errors, intonation, grammar, and the length of utterance were not significantly correlated with accentedness ratings. The two studies used different speaker subjects at different proficiency levels.

Proficiency in speaking is not clearly related to proficiency in other aspects of language. In many studies of ITAs, the students being examined are arguably high proficiency in their grammar and reading (and sometimes in listening), while they are less able to speak fluently and clearly. Often, this is the result of educational systems that emphasize standardized testing of grammar, vocabulary, and receptive language skills (reading and listening). Speaking and pronunciation, in contrast, are often neglected. Thus, spoken performance may be quite different from other aspects of language knowledge and performance. In this study, intelligibility was examined for three otherwise advanced learners whose oral proficiency varied according to a test of ITA teaching performance. No other oral testing was used to determine the relative proficiency levels of the three ITAs.

Concurrent verbal reports. This study used a concurrent verbal report, sometimes called a think-aloud report, to collect judgments of listener understanding. The concurrent report is a form of introspective thinking in which participants describe their successive thinking processes during a task. Although introspection has been used in psychology as a way of observing a subject's mind since the early 20th century, the establishment of think-aloud reports as a valid research method is indebted to Ericsson and Simon (1983). In second language learning, think-aloud reports began to be used in the 1980s and have been used to examine learner strategies in reading, vocabulary acquisition, and testing (Cohen, 1996; Douglas & Hegelheimer, 2007; Ellis, 1991; Faerch & Kasper, 1987; Green, 1998). However, think-aloud reports have not been used frequently in pronunciation research, with the exception of Zielinski (2008), who used verbal reports to pinpoint which phonological features most commonly were implicated in sites of reduced intelligibility.

Research Questions

This study examined three questions:
1. When asked to stop for difficulties in understanding, how much more do listeners stop during the presentations of lower oral proficiency speakers than for more advanced oral proficiency speakers?
2. How often are non-standard segments the reason for listeners to stop listening?
3. Which non-standard segments appear to be most likely to make listeners stop listening and comment?

Methodology

Participants

Five American English speakers and three Korean speakers of English participated in this experiment. The native American English speakers (two male, three female) had all taken at least a few basic linguistics courses and were comfortable describing pronunciation using an accepted, standard descriptive system. All were graduate students in the MA or PhD program in TESL/Applied Linguistics at the institution where this study took place. One listener had been trained as a TEACH (ITA speaking test) rater previously, while other listeners had no experience of having worked as a rater for any speaking tests.

The Korean speakers were all graduate students in various academic departments at the university. The advanced-level student had been in the U.S. for six months, the intermediate-level student for a year, and the low-level student less than one month. The low-level ITA (a male) was from Busan, a regional city in Korea, while the other two participants (both female) were from Seoul, the capital city of Korea. The low-level speaker was a graduate student in Industrial and Manufacturing Systems Engineering (ISME), the intermediate speaker was in Human Health and Performance (HHP), and the advanced speaker was in Art and Design.

All the speakers had TOEFL scores above 550 (Paper) or 213 (CBT). Their level of English speaking ability, however, varied as measured by the results of the locally administered TEACH tests. The TEACH test is an institutional test of oral performance given to prospective international teaching assistants at the university. It is scored on a scale of 0-300. The test is based on a face-to-face microteaching exercise from the students' fields of study. Students received a topic in advance and had two hours to prepare. The teaching was conducted before a panel of raters including ESL experts and undergraduate students and video-recorded. The advanced-level student scored 240 (fully certified to teach), the intermediate-level student scored 200 (limited teaching responsibilities), and the low-level student 140 (not certified to teach).

Materials

Three types of materials were used in this study: A think-aloud training video clip for the listeners, the Korean speakers' TEACH demonstration video clips (see description above), and the screen capture recorder *Camtasia* (see http://www.techsmith.com/camtasia.html). In order to provide training for the think-aloud procedures for the listeners, a five-minute training film was developed. A native English speaker was filmed demonstrating the think-aloud procedures, while pushing pause buttons and saying what occurred to him. The sample verbalization included talking about what was confusing, how the speech was understandable, replicating what was heard, commenting on both global and specific aspects of the speech, and making free comments. Each ITA's video-recorded TEACH demonstration included a five-minute microteaching session by the Korean TAs on a topic from their field of study. To record the think-aloud reports by listeners, *Camtasia Studio*, a laptop-based screen recorder and video editor that comes with *Camtasia* studio software, was used. Verbalizations as well as actions related to the video recording, including the actions of pressing pause buttons and playback buttons were recorded. The listeners spoke into a microphone attached to the laptop.

Procedure

The first author met each of the five native English-speaking listeners to record their verbal reports. Each session took about one hour including the following interview. First, listeners took part in a ten-minute training session. The listeners were asked to watch the think-aloud training video and were given verbal instructions by the researcher. Next, the listeners were asked to watch each video clip and pause whenever they found it hard to understand the Korean speakers' presentations. The listeners were asked to verbalize their thoughts about the communicative breakdowns they were experiencing and to focus on pronunciation issues in the speech materials. A five-minute break was given between each rating session. Finally, the author asked each listener to clarify any think-aloud comments that were unclear.

Analysis

Preliminary data analysis included a number of steps. First, all TEACH presentations were transcribed. Second, all listeners' verbal reports were transcribed. Third, each stop location was identified according to its location in the TEACH transcripts. Finally, the reasons for stopping were classified according to the reasons given by the listeners.

To answer RQ #1, *t-tests* were used to determine if proficiency level (advanced versus intermediate, intermediate versus low, etc.) was connected to the number of stops made by the listeners. The utterances made by listeners that did not specify a communicative breakdown were not considered in counting the number of stops the listeners made. The examples of such excluded utterances included comments to praise a speaker's performance, personal remarks related to the text, listeners' suggestions for the particular speaker, and listener self-evaluations.

To answer RQ #2, *t-tests* were used to determine if the speakers' proficiency level was connected to the number of non-standard segments implicated in the stop locations indicated by the listeners. The stop locations where non-standard segments were identified and classified according to the linguistic features at those stop locations. Next, phonological reasons were divided into suprasegmental versus segmental features. Non-phonological reasons for stopping were classified as related to grammar, inappropriate use of language, and awkward expression.

To answer RQ #3, the segmental features where the listeners stopped were classified to examine which non-standard segments caused listeners to stop most often. A sequence of steps was used to identify the locations where linguistic features contributed to reduced intelligibility. The classification of the linguistic features was grounded in Zielinski's (2008) classification of the phonological features in terms of the segments according to syllable position, syllable strength, and syllable stress patterns. Non-standard vowels and consonants in syllable initial and final position, and in strong and weak syllables were counted, as these were the most common in the results. For example, if a listener identified *leading* as sounding like *reading*, we would classify this as an initial consonant in a strong syllable.

Results

RQ #1. The results showed that listeners stopped more often for speakers who had been rated with lower oral proficiency (Table 2). The number of stops was strongly related to level for the advanced- and intermediate-level students ($p = 0.0238, p < 0.05$) and between the advanced and low-level students ($p = 0.0069, p < 0.05$). The mean number of stops made was $M = 13.8$ for the advanced ($SD = 4.08$) and $M = 24.2$ for the intermediate speaker ($SD = 9.06$). There was no significant difference between the low- and intermediate-level ($p = 0.2481, p < 0.05$). The mean number of stops made was $M = 28.4$ for the low speaker ($SD = 9.5$).

Table 2. The Number of Times the Five Listeners Stopped While Listening to Each Recording

	Advanced speaker (TEACH score 240)	Intermediate speaker (TEACH score 200)	Low speaker (TEACH score 140)
	Total pauses	Total pauses	Total pauses
NS 1	20	34	41
NS 2	15	34	34
NS 3	13	17	27
NS 4	12	16	16
NS 5	9	20	24
Total	69	121	142
Mean	13.8	24.2	28.4
SD	4.08	9.06	9.5

RQ #2. RQ #2 examined the number of stops where non-standard segments were identified by the listeners (Table 3). There was a significant difference observed in between the intermediate- and advanced-level speakers ($p = 0.01177$, $p < 0.05$). There was also a significant difference between the low-level and advanced speakers ($p = 0.0074$, $p < 0.05$). The mean number of stops where non-standard segments were recognized was $M = 7$ for the advanced speaker ($SD = 6.55$) and $M = 20$ for the intermediate speaker ($SD = 8.09$). In addition, the mean number of stops where non-standard segments were recognized was $M = 23.4$ for the low-level speaker ($SD = 9.86$). The difference between the low-level and intermediate speakers, however, was not statistically significant ($p = 0.2838$, $p < 0.05$). Like the previous results, listeners made a clear distinction between the advanced and the non-advanced proficiency speakers, but they did not make the same distinction between the two lower proficiency speakers.

Table 3. The Number of Times Where Segmentals were Identified as the Reason for Stopping the Recording

	Advanced speaker		Intermediate speaker		Low speaker	
	Total stops	Number of stops where segmentals were identified	Total stops	Number of stops where segmentals were identified	Total stops	Number of stops where segmentals were identified
NS 1	20	18	34	34	41	40
NS 2	15	2	34	20	34	23
NS 3	13	6	17	16	27	21
NS 4	12	7	16	15	16	14
NS 5	9	2	20	15	24	19
Total	69	35	121	100	142	117
Mean	13.8	7	24.2	20	28.4	23.4
SD	4.08	6.55	9.06	8.09	9.55	9.86

RQ #3. RQ #3 examined in detail the non-standard segments that were identified by listeners. The order of the reasons for listeners stopping the recording differed according to the proficiency level of the speakers (Table 4).

Non-standard segments in strong syllables versus those in weak syllables. It is clear that non-standard segments in strong syllables (both vowels and consonants) were noticed more frequently than those in weak syllables (unstressed syllables). Two-thirds (66.8%) of identified segmental errors were found in strong syllables, consistent with previous research (Bond & Small 1983; Cutler & Butterfield 1992; Cutler & Carter 1987; Zielinski 2008). Specifically, 28.3% of non-standard consonants were identified in strong syllable final positions and 21.5% in strong syllable initial positions out of the all non-standard segments. Vowels were identified for 17% of the all non-standard segments. Vowels in weak syllables only were noticed in large numbers for the low-level speaker. This speaker was perceived as having made 9.6% of the total non-standard segments with 4.6% in the strong syllables and 5.0% in the weak syllables. Meanwhile, both the advanced speaker and the intermediate speaker were perceived as having produced the fewest number of non-standard vowels (respectively, 3.1% and 6.8% of the total non-standard segments).

Table 4. Rank of Non-standard Segments Identified as Reasons for Stopping

Rank	Advanced speaker		Intermediate speaker		Low speaker	
1	Syllable Final consonants (Strong) e.g., pa*ge*	8.7 %	Syllable Final Consonants (Strong) e.g., ba*ll*	12.8 %	Syllable Final Consonants (Weak) e.g., inve*n*tory	10.9 %
2	Vowels (Strong) e.g., gr*i*d	3.8 %	Syllable Initial Consonants (Strong) e.g., *p*ins	10.9 %	Syllable Initial Consonants (Strong) e.g., *f*unction	9.8 %
3	Syllable Initial Consonants (Weak) e.g., mar*g*in	3.4 %	Vowels (Strong) e.g., b*ow*ling	7.5 %	Syllable Initial Consonants (Weak) e.g., or*d*er	7.2 %
4	Syllable Initial Consonants (Strong) e.g., s*p*are	0.8 %	Syllable Initial Consonants (Weak) e.g., to*t*al	3.8 %	Syllable Final Consonants (Strong) e.g., ca*l*culate	6.8 %
5	Syllable Final Consonants (Weak) e.g., archite*ct*	0.8 %	Vowels (Weak) e.g., *a*	0.8 %	Vowels (Weak) e.g., inv*e*ntory	6.0 %
6	Vowels (W*e*ak)	–	Syllable Final Consonants (Weak) e.g., happe*n*	0.4 %	Vowels (Strong) e.g., c*a*rrying	5.7 %
Total		17.4 %		36.2 %		46.4 %

Note. Percentages are rounded to the nearest tenth.

Breakdown of non-standard vowels in both weak and strong syllables. Table 5 below shows the breakdown of non-standard vowels in both weak and strong syllables. The intended (standard) vowels are listed in the first row of symbols, while the non-standard production by level is listed below the intended vowels. Some of these non-standard vowels productions were identified by more

Table 5. Non-standard Vowels Identified Classified by Weak and Strong Syllables

Intended	Non-Standard Vowels In Strong Syllables											Total Type (Tokens)
	Reduced Vowels (weak)	Lax Vowels				Tense Vowels				Diphthongs		
	ə	ɪ	ʊ	ɛ	æ	ow	ey	ɔ		ay	aw	
Advanced speaker		iy(6)	ɪ(3)					ø(1)				3 (10)
Inter-mediate speaker	ɪ(2)	iy(1)		ey(1) ay(2)	ay(1) ey(3)		e(1) a(1)	ow(2) ɔy(1) e(1)		a(1)	ɔ(5)	13 (22)
Low speaker	ʌ(13) ɔ(1) ɪ(3)	iy(1)			ɪ(1) a(2) ɔ(1) e(1)	ɔ(1) e(2)	iy(1)	ʌ(3) e(1)				10 (31)
Totals	19	8	3	3	9	3	3	8		1	5	26 (63)

Note. ( ) denotes the number of occurrences (tokens) for the various pronunciation features.

than one listener. The total vowel types and tokens identified for each level are in the final column while the total number of times each intended vowel caused listeners to stop are listed in the bottom row.

It is evident that certain non-standard vowel productions were noticed more frequently than others. Specifically, /ɪ/, /æ/, /ɔ/, and /aw/ (e.g.,/ɪ/- *this* , /æ/- *add*, /ɔ/- *ball*) accounted for nearly half of the times that listeners stopped and commented. It is also noticeable that vowels that should have been pronounced with a reduced quality (that is, with a schwa-like sound as in the final vowel in *sofa*), but were instead produced as though in a strong syllable, also caused difficulty for listeners. That is, while vowels in weak syllables caused listeners to stop less frequently overall than vowels in strong syllables, they remained an important problem area.

It is also of interest that the greatest difficulty was in identifying /ə/ as /ʌ/ as in *procure**e**nt* and *opp**o**site* in the low-level speaker's speech. Often there is little difference in quality between these vowel symbols, one symbol being used for the unstressed vowel and one for the stressed vowel. Clearly, it appears that stressing the vowel, thus increasing its quantity (that is, lengthening the vowel) while keeping the same general vowel quality, caused listeners to stop more frequently. Jenkins (2000) argued for vowel quantity (length) to be emphasized over vowel quality (exact target sounds) in her *Lingua Franca Core* (LFC), which sought to specify what features of pronunciation were actually necessary for intelligible speech. She argued that the reduced vowel /ə/ (the most frequent vowel in English) is not important for intelligibility. Our results suggest that when two vowels have a similar quality, as do the stressed vowel /ʌ/ and the reduced vowel /ə/ (as in the two vowels in the word *FUNgus*), length may be critical to differentiate between strong and weak syllables. In other words, saying the word *funGUS* may be difficult to understand because of the stress even though the vowel sounds are very similar.

Non-standard final consonants. For all three speakers, non-standard segments in syllable final positions had a strong impact on listeners (see Table 6 below). There were 112 total times that the listeners noticed these types of segments (25, 35, and 47 for the advanced, intermediate, and low-level speakers, respectively). For the advanced and intermediate-level speakers, final consonants were

Table 6. Non-standard Final Consonants in Strong and Weak Syllable by Level

	Syllable	Non-Standard Syllable Final Consonants																Type (Token)
		m	f	v	θ	t	d	z	s	n	l	dʒ	r	k	ŋ			
Advanced speaker	Strong	ø(3)				ø(2)	n(1) ø(3) t(2)		z(1)	r(1)	r(2)	z(2) s(2) ʒ(3)		g(1)			8 (23)
	Weak					ø(1)								ø(1)				1 (2)
Intermediate speaker	Strong	n(1)			s(4) st(3)	ø(2) f(1)				ŋ(3) ø(5)	r(9) ø(3) f(1)		ø(1) l(1)					8 (34)
	Weak									r(1)								1 (1)
Low speaker	Strong	ø(2)	k(1)	ø(1)		ø(1)					r(4) n(1) ø(4)		ø(3) l(1)					5 (18)
	Weak			və(1) vɑ(1) vi(1)		ø(2) θ(5)		s(2)		l(1) ø(1)	p(1) r(3) ø(5)		ø(3)		n(2) ø(2) l(2)			11 (29)
Totals		6	1	4	7	18	6	3	1	12	33	7	9	2	6			19 (112)

Note. ( ) denotes the number of occurrences (tokens) for the various pronunciation features.

noticed most in strong syllables but for the low-level speaker, final consonants in strong and weak syllables were both noticed, with those in weak syllables noticed more frequently. The importance of final consonants in strong syllables is consistent with the previous research of the pronunciation of English learners with Vietnamese and Mandarin first language backgrounds (Bent, Bradlow, & Smith, 2007; Zielinski, 2006a). In the current study, one striking result was that in 43 of the 110 times that final consonants were noticed, they were noticed because they were omitted or switched. Reading down the columns in Table 6, a small number of final consonants (i.e., /m, v, t, d, s, z, l, r/) dominated the ones noticed (69 out of 112), with final /l/ alone being nearly 30% of the overall total. This may be a source of difficulty for listeners since those consonants can also signal contractions or grammatical endings. In this study, about 23% (18 out of 80) fell into this category. A final observation is the striking difference between the low-level speaker and the others. It was only for the low-level speaker that final consonants in weak syllables were noticed to any great extent, suggesting that his accuracy in segmentals was a significant weakness across all syllables.

Non-standard initial consonants. Non-standard consonants in syllable initial position, for example, *bowling, pins, carrying, for,* and *cost,* caused listeners to stop frequently for the intermediate and low-level speakers but rarely for the advanced speaker. Other studies have also found that strong syllables are particularly important in how listeners access a speaker's intended words (Cutler & Butterfield, 1992; Cutler & Carter, 1987), although the difference according to speaker proficiency level had not been documented before (Table 7). The advanced speaker had few non-standard segments (4.2% out of the all non-standard segments) noticed at the beginning of her words, which may be a contributing reason for her higher rating. In contrast, the initial consonants of the two other speakers frequently caused listeners to stop (14.7% for the intermediate speaker and 17% for the low-level speaker). For the intermediate speaker, segments starting strong syllables were most important, while for the low-level speaker, initial consonants in both strong and weak syllables were noticed at similar rates. It is not surprising that common difficulties for Korean learners of English (/l-r/as in *like, class*; /p-f/ as in *pin, happen, opposite*; /b-v/ as in *bonus, bowling* and sibilants as in *margin, change, stage*)

Table 7. Non-standard Initial Consonants Noticed by Listeners by Proficiency Level

Syllable		Non-Standard Syllable Initial Consonants																Type (Tokens)
		p	b	m	w	f	v	ð	t	d	s	n	l	tʃ	dʒ	r	k	
Advanced speaker	Strong																	2 (2)
Advanced speaker	Weak								d(1)		ø(1)					ø(1)		3 (9)
Intermediate speaker	Strong	θ(2) f(1) ø(1)	v(12) ø(1)			v(1)		d(4)					n(1) r(1)	t(2)	3(1) ʃ(7)		t(2)	8 (29)
Intermediate speaker	Weak	b(1) f(1)	v(1)			ø(1)			ø(2)		ø(1)		t(1) r(1)			ø(2)		6 (10)
Low speaker	Strong	d(1)					m(1)				p(1) d(1) dʒ(2) ʃ(5)		r(6)					8 (26)
Low speaker	Weak	f(1)		ø(1)	v(1) ø(2)	ø(1) p(5)	ø(1) m(5)			ð(1)		ø(1)	ø(1) r(1)			ø(2) n(2) l(2)	g(1)	8 (19)
Total		8	14	1	3	8	7	4	3	1	11	1	12	2	8	9	3	16 (95)

Note. ( ) denotes the number of occurrences (tokens) for the various pronunciation features.

dominated the initial consonants noticed (Avery & Ehrlich, 1992; Swan & Smith, 2001).

Discussion

The frequency of communication breakdowns and levels of speaking ability. RQ #1 examined the number of times listeners stopped during the presentations of the three Korean speakers of English. The advanced speaker's words were perceived as the easiest to identify, as shown in the lower number of total stops for the five listeners (advanced = 69; intermediate = 121; low-level = 142). Most listeners commented that the pronunciation of the advanced speaker was very clear. None of the listeners made such a comment about the other two speakers.

The number of stops for the intermediate and low-level speakers was not significantly different. This was somewhat surprising, since the intermediate speaker scored considerably higher on the original TEACH test (200, compared to the low-level speaker's score of 140). On the one hand, this difference in results may have occurred from the demands of the original test on the speakers, versus the demands of the think-aloud listening task on the listeners. In the TEACH test, the intermediate speaker was noticeably more interactive and engaged with the audience. Although she had many difficulties with pronunciation and other aspects of language, her interactivity seemed to help compensate. This was not true of the low-level speaker, whose manner was noticeably less interactive. On the other hand, the listeners may have had a hard time in deciding exactly what part of the sounds or words they should click on when they struggled to decode the low-level speakers' teaching demonstrations. As one of the listeners reviewed his state of understanding, he stated that "it is hard to grasp exactly what he is saying. I know what he is generically talking about, it's pretty hard to follow... I don't know part of it seems like there is not enough variance of consonants, they sound so similar." In addition, the intermediate speaker's topic, bowling, was one that raters of the TEACH test would have had previous knowledge of. The low-level speaker, however, spoke on a topic that was more technically demanding of listeners. Topic familiarity, then, may also have allowed the original raters to compensate for the intermediate speaker's language.

Although listeners stopped primarily for pronunciation, they also paid attention to non-pronunciation features of language, especially in the advanced speaker's speech. The pronunciation of the advanced speaker was deemed clear overall. However, listeners also commented that her choice of expressions and discourse organization was not up to the standard of her pronunciation. One listener remarked that:

> Again all of the words are very very clear I don't know why she's struggling to put it into complete sentences, it's almost like the way I speak Spanish. There are hesitations because I translate it as I go from my English thoughts to Spanish. It's amazing she is not being very fluent, she's got the words but she hasn't got the syntax.

The discrepancy between the number of times listeners stopped and the TEACH scores of the intermediate and low-level speakers, coupled with listeners' attention to non-phonological aspects in the advanced speaker's speech, led to further analysis of the features which caused listeners to stop. As presented in Table 8 below, the advanced speaker's speech was particularly perceived as having grammatical deviations and inappropriate use of language. The number of the listener comments about these two non-phonological areas decreases as oral proficiency judgments go down, approaching zero for both the intermediate and low-level speakers. Since the intermediate and low-level speakers had many more grammatical difficulties and struggled more with vocabulary choices than the advanced speaker, this was surprising. It is likely that the greater frequency of non-standard segments for the lower-proficiency speakers made it less possible for listeners to pay attention to grammar, expression, and pragmatics. The low-level speaker in particular may not have reached the "threshold level of pronunciation" (Hinofotis & Bailey, 1981, p. 120) necessary for intelligible speech. One reason for missing such a threshold may have been the wide range and large number of non-standard segments in his speech.

Table 8. Features Noted by Listeners in the Speech of the Three Speakers

	Total stops	Pronunciation		Other language features		
		Seg-mentals	Supraseg-mentals	Grammar	Prag-matics	Awkward expression
Advanced speaker	69	35	1	24	7	2
Intermediate speaker	121	100	1	3	2	12
Low speaker	142	117	24	2	0	0

Note. The total stops may not match individual numbers because listeners sometimes stopped for more than one reason.

Perceived segmental accuracy and levels of speaking ability. Research question number 2 and part of research question number 3 addressed how the listeners perceived non-standard segmental features. Figure 1 below suggests that segmental accuracy may be critical for a non-native speaker to be rated as being advanced. No matter how effective a speaker is with other communicative skills, frequent non-standard pronunciation of vowels and consonants may keep the speaker from being rated as advanced in oral proficiency. Paradoxically, fewer non-standard segments seemed to allow listeners to notice other language features, such as the morphosyntactic features noticed for the advanced speaker. This suggests that most of the non-standard segments of the advanced speaker did not lead to breakdowns, likely because of the generally intelligible language she exhibited. Although the intermediate and low-level speakers both had similar numbers of non-standard segments, the difference in their TEACH scores (240 versus 200 versus 140) suggests a potential flaw in the testing procedure at lower levels. The speaker's topic may have a strong effect on ratings, or the interactive, compensatory skills of the intermediate speaker led to fewer breakdowns than might otherwise have been the case.

In contrast, the frequent non-standard segments of the intermediate and low-level speakers appear to have made it difficult for listeners to notice other features of their language during the listening task.

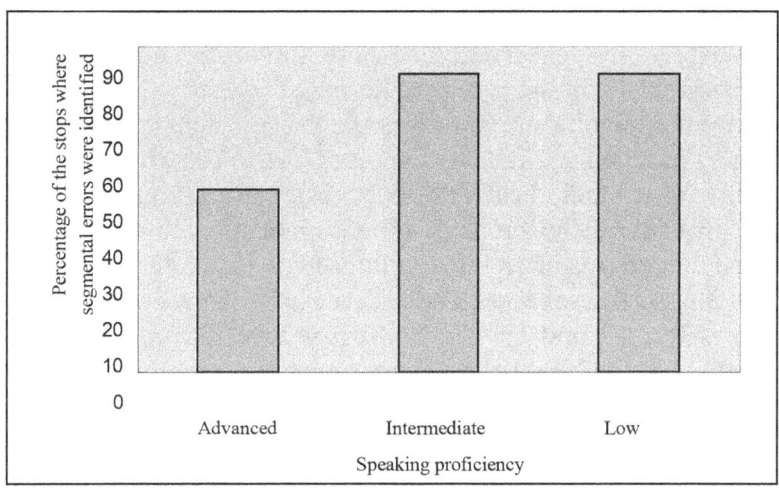

Figure 1. How often non-standard segments were identified as reasons for stopping.

Segments which contributed to reduced intelligibility. RQ #3 addressed the non-standard segmental features which were noticed by listeners. Not all non-standard segments were noticed by all listeners, and indeed, some non-standard segments were not noticed at all. This is not surprising. It is extremely difficult to do a fine-grained analysis of non-standard segments in a five-minute sample of teaching talk. Even trained listeners will identify some segments as problematic while ignoring others. The value of the process by which we identified non-standard segments was that we used trained listeners who could bring their own English as a second language (ESL) teaching expertise to the task of listening. A full phonetic analysis would not have told us which segments were salient to non-phoneticians.

The results suggest that the Korean dialects used by speakers may be a variable that can affect a Korean speaker's English. Busan Korean (the dialect of the low-level speaker) consistently places word stress on the second from the last syllable of the word. In this study, the low-level speaker consistently stressed the penultimate syllable of the word, perhaps leading to listeners noticing a greater number of suprasegmental features for the low-level speaker. Consequently, the listeners noticed both non-standard stress and non-standard vowels. This may also have caused the particularly high number of vowels in weak syllables noticed for the low-level speaker. All the speakers studied were Korean, but not all Korean speakers speak the same type of Korean.

Another significant point was the specific non-standard consonants in syllable initial position used by the Korean speakers of English. Avery and Ehrlich's (1992) observation about /dʒ/ typically pronounced by Koreans was not supported by this study. They stated that /dʒ/ is often mispronounced as /g/ or /d/, but in this study, the Korean speakers tended to replace /dʒ/ by other sibilants such as /ʃ/, /z/, and /ʒ/. The findings in this study indicated two things about /dʒ/. First, this particular consonant was identified as important in final position only for the advanced speaker. In syllable initial position, /ʃ/ and /ʒ/ were pronounced instead of /dʒ/. See some of the examples below, which illustrate this at the word level. In our examples, an examination of the locations where listeners stopped suggests some reasons the non-standard segments in syllable final position were salient to the listeners. First, often they were in words that carried crucial information about grammar, such as number (singular/plural), possession, and tense (Gilbert, 1995) as in (1).

> (1) NS 3. Beg: Utterance 26.: Plural
> *quantities* /kwantətiz/ → *quantitiest* /kwantətɪst/
>
> NS 1. Int: Utterance 34. Possessive
> *man's total* /mænztotəl/ → *math total* /mæθtotəl/
>
> NS 3. Int: Utterance 1. Tense
> *will* /wɪl/ → *were* /wər/

Second, key terms provided an important semantic "axis," or central point of reference, in processing the content of a lecture. The terms such as *titles* and *calculate* were important for understanding the low-level speaker's presentation about techniques for inventory planning and control. Similarly, *ball* was the most important word for the intermediate speaker who talked about bowling and scoring. See (2) below:

(2) NS 1. Beg: Utterance 13.
titles /taytɪlz/ → *type* /tayp/

NS 1. Beg: Utterance 25.
calculate /kælkyuleyt/ → *kyoongreet* /kyuwngreyt/

NS 2. Int: Utterance 16.
Ball /bɔl/ → *vur* /vər/

Conclusions and Implications for ITA Educators and Mentors

Methodological contributions of the study. An important methodological contribution of this study is the use of think-aloud verbal reports to learn how listeners processed speech. Like Zielinski (2006b), the study shows that this methodology can be very helpful in identifying causes of reduced intelligibility in ITAs' extended speech. According to Ericsson and Simon (1983), a listener first recognizes the audio-acoustic [phonological] features in speech first, and proceeds to further levels by relying on a complex mixture of memory and other cognitive activity. Although segmental features were the most important contributor to intelligibility in this study, most listeners stopped for other reasons also, especially while listening to the advanced speaker. Listeners first recognized difficulties in phonological features. When these features were adequately perceived, other parts of the message, including word choice and morphosyntax, became more noticeable. The large number of non-standard segmentals (and suprasegmentals) in the speech of the intermediate and low-level learners overwhelmed the listeners' ability to identify other types of language difficulties.

Another methodological contribution of this study was the use of screen capture recording, which provided an environment in which the presentations were watched in close to a real-life setting. Listeners watched the teaching simulation sessions on the LCD and had access to visual cues including facial expressions, gestures, and eye contact with the original audience, and ITAs' use of the blackboard. Using video files made it easy to use for the listeners, and to locate the data for the researchers. Finally, the type of speech sample used in this study made it possible to model the complex nature of intelligibility in understanding spoken discourse.

Implications for TA training, mentoring, and testing. ITA educators specializing in English as a Second Language (ESL) should try form-focused instruction which helps ITAs with prioritized segmental sounds, which we have suggested in this study. Given our finding that articulating the segments located in syllable-final positions plays a role in successfully communicating with the listeners, this deserves teachers' attention as the segments in syllable final positions often are a means to access lexical and grammatical information in academic discourse. It may be especially important for ITAs from some L1 backgrounds (for example, Chinese, Vietnamese, and Korean) that lack some consonants or consonant clusters in syllable/word final positions, to practice speaking with this in mind (Bent, Bradlow, & Smith, 2007; Zielinski, 2006a, 2008).

Implications for ITA mentors who are not ESL teachers. This chapter is written from the perspective of experienced ESL teachers. For those who are not trained language teachers, a clear implication is that pronouncing wrong sounds matters. Sounds, however, are only important as they are pronounced within words. Our results suggest that calling attention to the key vocabulary that is mispronounced by ITAs is very important, even if the ITA's mentor is not a trained language teacher. Research on what makes words intelligible usually uses native speakers who are not trained teachers, because native speakers have good intuitions about what is confusing and what is not. We suggest that mentors trust their intuitions about the words that need to be prioritized. Key words, especially those that are in the field or are general technical terms (e.g., *calculate*), are likely to make a difference in intelligibility. General words, especially words like *the, then, think*, etc., do not sufficiently impact understanding to justify working on them, no matter how much they may irritate a mentor to hear them pronounced wrongly.

Testing implications. This study indicates that, despite the predictive value of non-standard segments, a single linguistic factor cannot completely explain a speaker's oral proficiency, as shown in the differential ratings on the TEACH test with the similar number of non-standard segments noticed by listeners for both the intermediate and low-level speakers. ITA trainers are routinely encouraged to focus on not only phonological aspects of language but other aspects as well (Smith, Meyers, & Burkhalter, 1991). In fact, effective performance in other communication areas is thought to help compensate for deficiencies in pronunciation. Clear organization may be especially important for advanced speakers because the listeners pay more attention to non-phonological aspects of a speech when pronunciation is good. With good organization on the part of the speaker, listeners likely will find it easier to follow a speech despite non-standard segments in pronunciation.

Other compensatory strategies are also important, of course, such as interactivity. Although the intermediate speaker was similar to the low-level speaker in terms of the types and number of non-standard segments she spoke, she was rated as performing better than the low-level speaker, perhaps because of her effective presentation skills. Such a mastery of effective presentation skills will benefit all speakers, but it may especially help lower-level speakers. These compensatory strategies, however, can only take a speaker so far.

Speech in other professional domains. Although this study looked at ITA speech, the findings may extend beyond academic domains into other professional domains where high-stakes decisions are made, such as workplace presentations, in-depth interviews, and conference talks. Particularly, ITA educators or mentors who have limited time and energy, but who find themselves needing to effectively communicate with non-active English speaking partners, may benefit from our findings about which segments to prioritize. Instead of including all vowels and consonants as prescribed in pronunciation reference books, ITA candidates as language learners are recommended to focus on practicing the most "noticeable" segments in the most "noticeable" rhythmic and syllable positions.

In a Nutshell
1. Non-standard segmentals (vowel and consonant sounds) are frequently identified as difficulties in the speech of nonnative speakers. This is especially true for professional contexts such as education.
2. The TEACH tests (an ITA test of oral performance) of three Korean TAs (previously rated as advanced, intermediate, and low-level) were listened to by five linguistically sophisticated native English-speaking listeners. The listeners stopped the

recording each time they noticed a difficulty in understanding the TAs' talk.
3. Each difficulty was explained by listeners using a think-aloud technique. The reasons were then identified according to phonological and non-phonological causes.
4. Non-standard segments were the overwhelming reason for stopping the recording by the listeners. Segments in strong (stressed) syllables were much more likely to be noticed than those in weak (unstressed) syllables.
5. ITA educators may emphasize the importance of consonants in stressed syllable initial as well as syllable final positions, because syllable final syllables often signal listeners to access to grammatical and lexical information whereas syllable initial segmentals influence lexical search strategies in accessing what word was intended.
6. Mispronunciations matter, but they should always be corrected in key vocabulary that may cause confusion for ITAs. Native speakers of English, even those who are not trained ESL teachers, have good intuitions about which words make the biggest difference. They should develop and trust these intuitions.
7. Non-standard segments were noticed at a significantly higher rate for the intermediate and low-level TAs than for the advanced-level TA. Non-phonological factors (grammar and lexis) were noticed only for the advanced TA, although grammatical and lexical difficulties were more frequent for the other TAs. This may be because these factors are more noticeable when a TA's pronunciation is more standard.
8. The higher TEACH test rating for the intermediate level speaker was not borne out by a lower number of non-standard segmentals. It is possible that the TA's better teaching style led to a higher rating.
9. The high number of non-standard segments noticed by listeners suggests that segments play a particularly important role in how TAs are rated in ITA performance tests, and that segmentals, especially at lower levels of performance, should play a central role in instructional objectives.

References

Avery, P. & Ehrlich, S. (1992). *Teaching American English pronunciation.* Oxford: Oxford University Press.

Bent, T., Bradlow, A.R., & Smith, B. (2007). Segmental errors in different word positions and their effects on intelligibility of non-native speech: All's well that begins well. In M.J. Munro & O.S. Bohn (Eds.), *Second language speech learning: The role of experience in speech perception and production* (pp. 331-347). Amsterdam: John Benjamins Publishing Company.

Bond, Z.S. & Small, L.H. (1983). Voicing, vowel, and stress mispronunciations in continuous speech. *Perception & Psychophysics, 34*(5), 470-474.

Cohen, A. D. (1996). Verbal reports as a source of insights into second language learner strategies. *Applied Language Learning, 7*(1&2), 5-24.

Cutler, A. & Butterfield, S. (1992). Rhythmic cues to speech segmentation: Evidence from juncture misperception. *Journal of Memory and Language, 31*(2), 218-236.

Cutler, A. & Carter, D.M. (1987). The predominance of strong initial syllables in the English vocabulary. *Computer Speech & Language, 2*(3), 133-142.

Derwing, T.M. & Munro, M.J. (1997). Accent, comprehensibility, and intelligibility: Evidence from four L1s. *Studies In Second Language Acquisition, 19*, 1-16.

Derwing, T.M., Munro, M.J., & Wiebe, G. (1998). Evidence in favor of a broad framework for pronunciation instruction. *Language Learning, 48*(3), 393-410.

Douglas, D. & Hegelheimer, V. (2007). *Strategies and use of knowledge in performing new TOEFL listening tasks.* Unpublished research report.

Ellis, R. (1991). Grammaticality judgments and second language acquisition. *Studies in Second Language Acquisition, 13*, 161-186.

Ericsson, K.A. & Simon, H.A. (1983). *Protocol analysis: Verbal reports as data.* (Rev. ed.), Cambridge, MA: MIT Press.

Faerch, C. & Kasper, G. (Eds.). (1987). *Introspection in second language research.* Clevedon: Multilingual Matters.

Fiksdal, S. (1990). *The right time and pace: A microanalysis of cross-cultural gatekeeping interviews.* Norwood, NJ: Ablex.

Firth, S. (1992). Pronunciation syllabus design: A question of focus. In P. Avery & S. Ehrlich, *Teaching American English pronunciation* (pp. 173-183). Oxford: Oxford University Press.

Gallego, J.C. (1990). The intelligibility of three nonnative English speaking teaching assistants: an analysis of student-reported communication breakdowns. *Issues in Applied Linguistics, 1*, 219-237.

Gilbert, J. (1995). Pronunciation practice as an aid to listening comprehension. In D. J. Mendelsohn & J. Rubin (Eds.), *A guide for the teaching of second language learning* (pp. 97-112). San Diego: Dominie Press.

Green, A. (1998). *Using verbal protocols in language testing research: A handbook.* Cambridge: Cambridge University Press.

Hahn, L.D. (2004). Primary stress and intelligibility: Research to motivate the teaching of suprasegmentals. *TESOL Quarterly, 38*(2), 201-223.

Hinofotis, F. & Bailey, K. (1981). American undergraduates' reactions to the communication skills of foreign teaching assistants. In J. Fisher, M. Clarke & J. Schachter (Eds). *On TESOL '80 - Building bridges: Research and practice in teaching English as a second language* (pp. 120-133). Washington, DC: TESOL.

Isaacs, T. & Trofimovich, P. (2012). Deconstructing comprehensibility. *Studies in Second Language Acquisition, 34*(3), 475-505.

Jenkins, J. (2000). *The phonology of English as an international language.* Oxford: Oxford University Press.

Jenkins, J. (2002). A sociolinguistically based, empirically researched pronunciation syllabus for English as an international language. *Applied Linguistics, 23*(1), 83-103.

Kang, O. (2010). Relative salience of suprasegmental features on judgments of L2 comprehensibility and accentedness. *System, 38*, 301-315.

Levis, J.M. (2005). Changing contexts and shifting paradigms in pronunciation teaching. *TESOL Quarterly, 39*(3), 369-377.

Low, E.L. (2006). A cross-varietal comparison of deaccenting and given information: Implications for international intelligibility and pronunciation teaching. *TESOL Quarterly, 40*(4), 739-761.

McNerney, M. & Mendelsohn, D. (1992). Suprasegmentals in the pronunciation class: Setting priorities. In P. Avery & S. Ehrlich, *Teaching American English pronunciation* (pp. 185-196). Oxford University Press.

Munro, M.J. & Derwing, T. M. (1995). Foreign accent, comprehensibility, and intelligibility in the speech of second language learners. *Language Learning, 45,* 73-97.

Munro, M.J. & Derwing, T.M. (2006). The functional load principle in ESL pronunciation instruction: An exploratory study. *System, 34*(4), 520-531.

Prator, C.H. & Robinett, B.W. (1985). *Manual of American English pronunciation.* New York: Holt, Rinehart, and Winston.

Smith, J.A., Meyers, C.M., & Burkhalter, A.J. (1991). *Communicate: Strategies for international teaching assistants.* Englewood Cliffs, NJ: Regents Prentice Hall.

Smith, L.E. & Nelson, C. (1985). International intelligibility of English: Directions and resources. *World Englishes, 4*(3), 333-42.

Swan, M. & Smith, B. (2001). *Learner English: A teacher's guide to interference and other problems.* Cambridge: Cambridge University Press.

Zielinski, B. (2006a). *Reduced intelligibility in L2 speakers of English.* Unpublished PhD dissertation, La Trobe University, Bundoora.

Zielinski, B. (2006b). The intelligibility cocktail: an interaction between speaker and listener ingredients. *Prospect, 21*(1), 2-25.

Zielinski, B. (2008) The listener: No longer the silent partner in reduced intelligibility. *System, 36,* 69-84.

Cohesion and Perceived Proficiency in ITA Oral Communication across Engineering and the Sciences

By Jennifer Haan,[1] University of Dayton

International Teaching Assistants (ITAs) often require additional instruction because their speech is not easily understandable. This lack of perceived proficiency may be attributable to mistakes in sentence level grammar or pronunciation, but may also be affected by discourse level structures including overall organization and coherence of talk. This chapter examines spoken data from an ITA proficiency test to better understand the relationship between cohesion – the linguistic property used to build coherence – and perceived comprehensibility of ITAs. The study analyzes the use of cohesive ties (such as pronouns and conjunctions), across different proficiency levels in order to characterize and describe how ITAs at varying levels of language proficiency use different patterns of discourse in their talk. Results indicate that although ITAs at lower proficiency levels do use cohesive ties, they display difficulty using certain types correctly, and are more likely to have unproductive pauses when attempting extended discourse. These results have significant implications for ITAs teachers and mentors interested in developing strategies to help ITAs use extended discourse for the pofessional purpose of teaching. The strategies include consciousness-raising activities for ITAs as well as sample outlines of organizational

---

1. Author contact: jhaan1@udayton.edu

schemas from science and engineering with particular importance placed on framing words and cohesive ties.

Successful teaching requires the use of extended discourse. Classroom instructors use lectures, tutors develop extended explanations and definitions, and laboratory instructors provide instructions and descriptions. Across different contexts and classrooms, it is vitally important for international teaching assistants (ITAs) to be able to talk in a way that is comprehensible to their undergraduate students. And, while it is sometimes easy to recognize *when* an ITA *is* comprehensible in the classroom, it is much more difficult to define the specific characteristics that lead to, or detract from, that comprehensibility. Undergraduates, when complaining about ITAs, often attribute their lack of understanding to the ITA's "accent" or "pronunciation," or may even focus on the instructor's "grammar." Certainly, violations of expected pronunciation patterns or syntactic structures do play an important role in impeding intelligibility (Tyler, Jefferies & Davies, 1988), but it is easy to fall into the misconception that comprehensibility *only* relates to sentence-level grammatical accuracy and pronunciation. It is easy to forget the role that discourse level features play in the overall spoken ability of ITAs. The types of classroom talk, however, that ITAs must be able to use involve discourse units that are longer than phrases or sentences. Therefore, when trying to describe the specific language features that comprise communicative ability in the classroom, it is important to move beyond the sentence to understand how the structure of the discourse can facilitate or detract from successful communication. If we can better understand how features of longer discourse affect the perceived comprehensibility of ITAs, then we can teach ITAs how to use those features effectively to better communicate with their students.

This chapter looks at ITA oral communication beyond the sentence level to examine which features in longer units of discourse affect the perceived communicative ability of non-native English speaking international graduate students who are participating in an ITA testing and training program. In particular, the study uses 40 spoken responses from an ITA English proficiency test to examine discourse features related to cohesion, including the use of cohesive ties and pausing, across longer units of spoken text. The study asks: 1. What types of cohesive ties are used across different proficiency levels of speech that either facilitate or detract from overall comprehensibility? 2. How are these cohesive ties used differently across different proficiency levels? and 3. What additional linguistic features play a role in facilitating or detracting from the overall coherence and comprehensibility of ITAs' extended discourse? Throughout the chapter I describe the relationship between the use of cohesive ties and perceived communicative ability, and also describe how ITA educators, whether from the field of ESL or not, can address cohesion to help ITAs develop more comprehensible and coherent speech, and thus more effectively communicate ideas to U.S. undergraduates.

Literature Review

Key Terms in Second Language Learning: Communicative Competence and Discourse Competence

Communicative competence. Throughout the 1970s and 1980s the second language learning/applied linguistics community shifted the focus of language teaching and learning from grammatical accuracy to communicative competence. Communicative competence is "the ability to function in a truly communicative setting – that is, in a dynamic exchange in which linguistic competence must adopt itself to the total informational input, both linguistic and paralinguistic, of one or more interlocutors" (Savignon, 1972, p. 8). This definition broadens the view of language proficiency to include aspects other than the correct usage of grammatical rules. ITA educators coming from the English as a second language (ESL) field have used this concept of communicative competence as a starting point for ITA instruction and training, focusing specifically on the ways that ITAs communicate in an authentic academic classroom setting. More recent definitions of communicative competence have included a number of more narrowly construed competencies which ITAs must be able to perform in order to be successful. See Table 1.

Table 1. Components of Communicative Competence

Competence	Definition	Examples
Grammatical competence	The ability to correctly employ the sentence-level linguistic code of the language.	Correct use of tenses, articles, pronunciation, intonation.
Sociolinguistic competence	The way in which the linguistic code can be manipulated appropriately in different settings and contexts.	Appropriate choice of words in the given context and audience.
Strategic competence	The ability to use compensation strategies when linguistic resources are inadequate.	Talking around a word that is unfamiliar, using specific language learning and communication strategies.
Discourse competence	The way that speakers use specific linguistic features in order to appropriately structure written and oral texts beyond the sentence level.	Connecting phrases and sentences in ways that are coherent and understandable.

Note. Drawn from Canale & Swain, 1980; Crossley, Salisbury, & McNamara, 2010; Halliday & Matthiessen, 2004; Riggenbach, 1999.

Although ESL specialists and ITA educators have long been interested in the role of grammatical competence in successful classroom communication, less has been written about the role of specific discourse features and their relationship to perceived communicative ability. Because ITAs are required to produce long, discourse level speech in their pursuit of teaching content to undergraduate students, the current study focuses on the feature of cohesion in developing discourse competence.

Discourse competence and ITAs. Discourse competence is the ability to produce texts beyond the clause and sentence level to "form structures, convey meanings, and accomplish actions" (Shiffron, 1994, p. 6). In the context of ITAs' talk in classrooms, this means being able connect examples to definitions, transition from one topic to another, or explain logical connections between points in such a manner so as to help undergraduates understand the course content. This type of communicative ability is important for ITAs, and for all teachers in higher education, for a number of reasons. In their role as ITAs, non-native English speaking graduate students are expected to be able to participate in extended types of discourse in their second languages, both oral and written. As tutors, lab instructors, and recitation leaders in engineering and the sciences, ITAs are expected to give U.S. undergraduates definitions of complex, discipline-specific terms and ideas; provide instructions for laboratory procedures, tests, and homework assignments; and respond to student questions in one-on-one tutoring sessions. They have to give extended explanations, descriptions, and examples. A deeper understanding of the features of successful extended discourse can help ITAs develop these types of talk in ways that are clear and understandable for undergraduates.

Key Terms for this Study: Coherence and Cohesion

Coherence. In order to be comprehensible, extended stretches of talk (discourse) must be coherent. Here I define coherence as a general sense of connectedness in a text. A number of features go into the creation of a coherent text: topic, theme, rationality, and development, but at its core, coherence has to do with whether or not the entirety of the discourse can be interpreted as a unit by the listener or reader (Anderson, 1995). From a psycholinguistic perspective, coherence has to do with how relationships are perceived and represented in the minds of both the speaker and the listener (Crossley et al, 2010). Because coherence has to do with relationships within the discourse, a number of features can lead to a perception of incoherence in a spoken text, in turn causing communication breakdown. For example, if an instructor begins a lecture discussing one topic and abruptly changes to a different topic, the lecture might be deemed incoherent because the relationship between the two topics is not logically defined. Similarly, if a tutor is providing instruction and her response to a question does not show a clear relationship to the question asked, her response may be considered incoherent. So, for an ITA to communicate effectively and coherently, his/her talk needs to convey relationships in ways that the listener can understand and interpret.

In order to develop coherence, speakers use both content (theme, logic, topic) and linguistic properties (words and grammatical constructions). The use of linguistic properties to develop coherence is called cohesion, and it involves the use of vocabulary items (often termed cohesive ties or discourse markers) to build relationships (Halliday & Hasan, 1976; Liao, 2009) and strategic pausing to show phrasal structure (Chiang, 2011).

Cohesion. If coherence is the global sense of interconnectedness of the ideas in speech communication, then cohesion comprises the specific *linguistic* tools speakers use to bring this coherence about. According to Halliday and Hasan (1976), cohesion is brought about when speakers use vocabulary and grammatical structures to indicate connected meaning both within and across sentence boundaries. Some examples include the use of conjunctions, the use of clearly connected phrases (through rhythm, intonation, and pausing), and thought groups (Chiang, 2011), and the use of repeated words or synonyms.

Cohesion is integral in creating a unified, coherent meaning in spoken texts, and the vocabulary words and grammatical structures used to bring this about are often referred to as cohesive ties, which "enable readers or listeners to make the relevant connections between what was said, is being said, and will be said" (Castro, 2004, p. 215). The definition of cohesive ties goes back to Halliday and Hasan's 1976 work, but variations on these cohesive features in both speaking and writing have been examined under a wide variety of terminologies, including "discourse markers" (Fung & Carter, 2007), "cohesive devices" (Lui & Braine, 2005), and "small words" (Hasselgreen, 2005). All of these terms are used to describe the specific lexico-grammatical features that speakers use to build relationships between different parts of the discourse. Speakers use these linguistic features in combination with logical content and/or argumentation to build an overall coherent discourse. The current study uses Halliday and Hasan's 1976 theoretical framework to focus specifically on the relationship between the use of cohesive ties and overall comprehensibility. See Table 2.

Table 2. Types of Cohesive Ties

	Definition	Types	Classroom Examples
Referential Cohesion	Lexical items which must be interpreted in accordance with another element in the discourse.	Pronominals	*For homework, do the binomial equations in the book.* **They** *are on page seven.*
		Demonstratives	*You should always show your work.* **That** *is part of being a good student.*
	Two categories are exophoric – referring to concepts outside the text and endophoric – referring to an item within the text.	Definite articles	*We are learning about Newton's 3rd law.* **The** *law states that…*
		Comparatives	*Some students study very little. Those who want good grades study* **more** *often.*
		Collocation	*In the fraction 4/5, 4 is the* **numerator** *and 5 is the* **denominator**.
Substitution	The replacement of one lexical item with another item that is not a personal pronoun	Nominal	*Read problems 1-30 in your textbook. Complete the even* **ones**.
		Verbal	*Take your time to work through the problems.* **Doing** *them quickly will lead to errors.*
Ellipsis	Substitution by zero	N/A	*Are you returning our tests on Friday? I am. (returning your tests)*
Conjunctival Cohesion	The use of conjunctions, connectors, or transitional words to bring together clauses, paragraphs, or discourse.	Simple additive	*To do well in this class, you must attend each class session. You must* **also** *hand in each assignment on time.*
		Simple adversative	*Pick partners for you next project.* **However**, *make sure you have not worked together before.*
		Causal and reverse causal	**Because** *you are having difficulty with the concepts, I am postponing the test until next week.*
		Temporal and sequential	**First**, *develop a hypothesis.* **Then** *test it.*
		Complex	**If** *you do not hand in your homework,* **then** *you will receive a 0 on the assignment.*

Notes. Drawn from Halliday and Hasan (1976). Collocation, under referential cohesion, is defined as two or more words that frequently co-occur and are used to build lexical cohesion because of their systematic, semantic relationships (*numerator/denominator, boys/girls, dollars/cents, stand up/sit down*).

Previous Research on Cohesion and Comprehensibility

A number of studies on spoken language have examined the use of cohesive ties and discourse markers in the perceived comprehensibility of speech. One study by Tyler, Davies, and Jeffries (1988) examined teaching demonstrations of eighteen Chinese and Korean teaching assistants whose students had complained about their ITAs' language ability. They noted: "although pronunciation problems do contribute to their comprehensibility...even if their pronunciation were NOT a source of difficulty, these students would STILL be perceived as being incoherent by American English listeners" (p. 102). They argued that discourse structure is as important as pronunciation when it comes to communicating effectively.

A second study by Tyler (1992) looked at the discourse patterns of a Chinese graduate teaching assistant's spoken English and compared it with that of a native speaker of North American English. The Chinese teaching assistant's English had been perceived as hard to follow by native English speakers, and Tyler contended that the ITAs' use of discourse structuring devices caused breakdowns in communication. The ITA in her study mixed different types of lexical discourse markers, starting the lecture with sequential discourse markers such as *and then* and *after that*. The ITA then shifted to additive markers such as *also* and *and*. According to Tyler, "the additive markers give ambiguous signals. It is not clear if they are signaling the elaboration of an already established topic or the introduction of a new major point" (p. 719). From this analysis, Tyler suggested that discourse-based differences contribute substantially to communication difficulties, and are, therefore, important to address. Additional studies have also found that the correct and explicit use of discourse markers and cohesive ties can lead to *greater* comprehensibility. Publishing in the same year as Tyler, Williams (1992) found that ITAs who used explicit connecting words to build relationships between sentences were rated as more comprehensible than those who did not.

How cohesive ties are used and the issue of "distance." As shown previously, existing research has indicated that using a greater number of cohesive ties increases comprehensibility in extended discourse. But it may be the case that the use of these cohesive ties is only helpful in facilitating communication when they are used correctly and there is not an over-reliance on a particular form. So, it is not only the number of ties that seems to matter, but also the *way* that the ties are used. If the ties are used incorrectly, or only a narrow range of cohesive ties are used or are overused (such as *yeah*, Liao, 2009), then the extended discourse and talk of TAs may sound incomprehensible to listeners.

An additional factor seems to be *distance* between the referent and the word to which it refers. The lower the distance between the tie and the reference, the more discoursally competent the extended speech will be. Compare: *Here is your* assignment. *It begins on page 54*, with *Here is your* assignment. *After you read through the chapter we will be having a quiz and conducting an experiment.* It *begins on page 54.* In the second example, because of the distance between the tie and the referent (*assignment* and *it*), the meaning of the cohesive tie is obscured. A large distance between a cohesive tie and the referent could involve a longer length of time, perhaps due to pausing, or could also involve the insertion of additional phrases or sentences, as can be seen in the second example. Although previous studies have provided important information about how ITAs use cohesive ties and discourse markers to build coherence and increase comprehensibility, more information is still needed to understand how non-native speakers are using these lexico-grammatical features in speech.

How Other Linguistic Features Add to or Detract from Comprehensibility

Although not usually addressed in formal theories of cohesion, some previous research indicates that linguistic features such as rate of speech and pausing patterns are of significance to the overall comprehensibility of second language learner speech. Excessive pausing has been found to be especially problematic when it comes in the middle of phrases and sentences, and breaks up "focus clusters" of information (Chafe, 1985). When considering the comprehensibility of non-native speaker teaching assistants, Rounds (1987) states, "if there is not a smooth flow of talk with silences at phrase boundaries…students may begin to lose what is commonly called the train of thought. Such silences tend to diffuse attention rather than focus it" (p. 654). These silences also lead to a lack of cohesion in the text by increasing the distance between cohesive ties and their referents.

Research Questions

The current study examines the use of cohesive features across different proficiency levels of an Oral English Proficiency test given to ITAs at a large research university. The overall research purpose is to explore ITA candidates' use of cohesive ties such as one of the tasks of an Oral English Proficiency Test. The current study adds to the literature cited above, and in addition makes suggestions easily adapted to program-level, course-level, and mentor-level interventions. In particular the research asks:

1. What types of cohesive ties are used across different proficiency levels of oral communication that either facilitate or detract from overall comprehensibility?
2. How are these cohesive ties used differently across different proficiency levels, in terms of number and distance from referent?
3. What additional discourse level linguistic features such as rate of speech and pausing patterns play a role in adding to or detracting from the overall coherence and comprehensibility of the extended discourse?

Method

Participants

The study participants were 40 international graduate students with a variety of first languages including Korean, Chinese, Arabic, Bengali, Turkish, Ukranian, Kannada, and Greek. The participants were matriculated students who were enrolled in engineering or science graduate programs. These students were typical for international graduate students going through an Oral English Proficiency Program at the institution where this study took place. In this program, students typically take a locally constructed oral proficiency test, which is described in the Materials section below. The test is given to determine if they can be placed as a TA in a classroom with U.S. students, or if they need additional training and instruction in English before taking up their teaching. Typically students take this test at the beginning of the preparation program, after participating in a short online orientation. Students' responses are recorded in this test, some of which formed the data set for this study. After testing, ITA candidates' responses are scored and put into proficiency levels. For this study, ten recordings from each of the four higher levels of proficiency were randomly selected, resulting in 40 samples of responses to a specific item on the test. Because the language samples were rendered anonymous and collected randomly from among a pool of responses, and because the samples comprised existing data routinely captured for program purposes, the study was exempt from review by the Institutional Review Board.

The participants' responses to the items on the test were scored by holistically by two independent raters on a scale from three to six. Participants with scores of three and four were deemed not comprehensible enough to be placed in a classroom, and were asked to complete a one-semester oral English course before becoming TAs, while individuals getting scores of five and six were considered comprehensible and proficient enough to be exempt from the course. They could immediately be certified to begin teaching or serving in an instructional capacity in contact positions with undergraduates. If participants did not take this local oral proficiency test, they could also achieve certification by scoring a 27 or higher on the speaking section of the TOEFL iBT (Educational Testing Service, 2014; see also Griffee & Gorsuch, this volume), a 76 or higher on the Pearson Test of Spoken English, or a 50 or higher on the Test of Spoken English (TSE).

Materials

The main material for this study was an Oral English Proficiency Test designed to test the oral English ability of international graduate students who were offered funding to be TAs at a large U.S. research institution. The test, designed by applied linguists and ESL-based ITA training specialists, has been in use for over ten years, and consists of seven items which were thought to capture the graduate students' ability to communicate in a variety of academic situations. The test item tasks include a read-aloud of an institutional document, a graph interpretation task, an opinion response task, a compare and contrast task, a giving advice task, a pass-on-this-information memo item, and a pass-on-this-information telephone message item.

Table 3. Oral Proficiency Test Items

Read Aloud	Graph Interpretation	Opinion Response	Compare and Contrast	Advice Giving	Pass on Information: Memo	Pass on Information: Telephone
Test takers read aloud a provided university document.	Test takers are given graphs to explain and interpret.	Test takers read and respond to a short opinion piece.	Test takers compare and contrast different texts.	Test takers give advice to a student with a problem.	Test takers read a memo and pass the information on to a colleague.	Test takers hear a voicemail message and pass the information on to a colleague.

The test takers are given two minutes to think about their answers and then respond, out loud, to the prompts given. They are given a maximum of two minutes to respond, but they do not have to talk for the entire two minutes. The test is semi-direct and computer-based, and test takers' responses are monologic; that is, there are no interlocutors.

This study focuses specifically on participants' responses to the advice-giving item, which elicits speech that is spontaneously constructed without the aid of other types of written materials (such as graphs or articles). The prompt states:

Dear instructor,

In one of my other classes, I have a foreign teaching assistant. I believe that you are both from the same country. My problem is that I cannot understand anything she says. If I come to your office hours today, can you please give me some advice about how to handle this?

Respectfully,
Joe Smith

Procedure and Analysis

The 40 speech samples were transcribed and coded according to the number and type of cohesive ties, sample length, and rate of speech. In order to answer RQs #1 and #2, I analyzed the use of cohesive ties according to Halliday and Hasan's (1976) framework, including their classifications of five primary classes of cohesive ties: reference, substitution, ellipsis, conjunction, and lexical cohesion (see Table 2). After these five categories were coded, they were then broken down further into sub-types of reference (pronomial, demonstrative or definite article, or comparative), types of conjunction (additive, adversative, casual, and temporal), and types of lexical cohesion (reiteration or collocation)(see Table 2). To better understand how these features were used across different proficiency levels, after the items were coded, I analyzed the cohesive ties for their number and density across different proficiency levels, the distance between the cohesive tie and the referent across proficiency levels, the type of cohesive ties across proficiency levels, and the manner of use of the cohesive ties across levels. In order to address research question 3, I analyzed additional discourse level linguistic features, namely rate of speech and pausing, across different proficiency levels to determine their effect on the perceived comprehensibility and proficiency of the speakers.

Results and Discussion

Research Questions 1 and 2. The research questions were: 1. What types of cohesive ties are used across different proficiency levels of oral communication that either facilitate or detract from overall comprehensibility? 2. How are these cohesive ties used differently across different proficiency levels? An analysis of the use of cohesive ties across proficiency levels revealed that students in the two highest levels, five and six, used both more and different types of cohesive ties than students at middle levels three and four. Table 4 below summarizes the general findings; these are then explained in more detail in each section thereafter. Please refer to Table 2 for a review and examples of cohesive ties.

Table 4. Average Number and Characteristics of Cohesive Ties Across Proficiency Levels

	Level three	Level four	Level five	Level six
Number of referential ties	6	9	11	12
Characteristics of referential ties	Use of personal pronouns only in reference to the prompt (*she, her*).	Use of personal pronouns in reference to prompt, plus additional pronouns (*it, that*) in reference to other issues or problems.	Use of personal pronouns and additional pronouns, additional inclusion of relative pronouns (*which, that*).	Use of personal pronouns and additional pronouns, additional inclusion of relative pronouns (*which, that*).
Number and characteristics of ellipsis and substitution	None	None	None	None
Number of conjunctions	7	9	14	14
Characteristics of conjunctions	Few conjunctions, 95% simple additive (*and, also, but*); incorrect use of simple connectors.	65% simple (*and, also, but*), generally used correctly; also include internal temporal connectors (*first, second*) inconsistently.	Only 56% simple (*and, also, but*). Consistent use of different types of conjunctions including internal temporal, causal (*because*), and complex conjunctions (*if...then*).	Only 54% simple (*and, also, but*). Consistent use of different types of conjunctions including internal temporal, causal (*because*), and complex conjunctions (*if...then*)
Number of repeated words (lexical cohesion)	8	7	4	4
Characteristics of repeated words (lexical cohesion)	Reliance on non-productive repetition (*This...this... this...problem*).	Reliance on non-productive repetition (*You should talk... talk*).	Less repetition overall, more repetition to strategically connect ideas.	Less repetition overall, more repetition to strategically connect ideas.

Referential cohesive ties. The most common references across all of the levels were given in reference to the advice prompt (Table 3). These, first of all, included pronomial reference items such as *she* and *her* to refer to the teaching assistant described in the prompt. A second common reference to the prompt was in the use of the demonstrative article *this* as well as the definite article *the* when talking of *the problem* or *the situation* that was described in the prompt. Higher-level participants seemed more willing to use pronomial, comparative, and demonstrative articles than participants at the lower levels. In level three, only one respondent made use of referential items to refer to anything in her discourse other than *the problem* and *the TA* in the prompt. In levels four through six, however, additional pronomial and demonstrative reference items were used. Participants at these higher levels seemed more comfortable using these reference items to talk about elements other than within the prompt itself. Many used *it*, *this*, or *these* to refer to the advice they were giving; they also used *that*, or *this* to refer to notes or materials from the imagined class. Some used *them* or *they* to refer to other students. These subtle trends suggested that students at higher levels of proficiency were more comfortable with the ambiguity of reference that can sometimes come with the use of referential ties. Level three participants, on the other hand, seemed to prefer to repeat lexical items directly from the test prompt so as to avoid this ambiguity, rather than build cohesion by way of referential items.

One additional difference between the middle level (three and four) and the higher level (five and six) participants had to do with their use of relative pronouns such as *who* or *which* as referential ties. Eight of the ten participants at levels five and six made use of at least one relative pronoun in their responses. This use was significantly lower at the level four, while at level three, no participants used relative pronouns in a subordinating clause. Participants at the higher levels displayed the ability to use relative pronouns to build cohesion. This seemed to be an indication of their ability to use referential cohesive ties to develop more complex sentences, while building relationships between concrete and abstract people and ideas.

Ellipsis and substitution. No evidence of either ellipsis or substitution was found across any of the recorded responses in the Oral English Proficiency Test Data. This is likely due to the fact that both of these types of cohesive ties are found most often in oral communication between two or more people. Although this test examines oral proficiency, the item chosen here did not elicit interactive speech.

Conjunction. Data indicates that while participants in all proficiency levels used a number of transitional devices within their discourse, these connectors became more prevalent and complex for participants in the higher levels. Participants in level three used the fewest number of conjunctions in their responses, averaging only seven per two-minute response. These participants used simple additive connectors such as *and* and *also* most frequently in their discourse. 54% of the level three responses is the conjunction *and*, and if *also* is added to that, the two ties together comprise 64% of the conjunction use. Virtually all of the conjunctions participants used in level three fall into the categories of simple additive, simple adversative, or simple causal. Some examples of these conjunctive ties from participants in level three were:

(1) *I think you can ask him or her to speak slowly...***and***...uh...you should encourage him to express himself...freely.*

(2) *I* also *had the similar experiences.*

Although the level three participants used these types of simple connectors, including *but* and *so*, they sometimes experience difficulty using them in expected ways. One level three participant said:

(3) *I'm sorry...***but***...I will try to talk with her about this problem.*

The use of the adversative conjunction *but* in relation to the *I'm sorry* leads the listener to expect something negative. By following the conjunction with a positive statement, the listeners' expectations are confounded. Other examples which may confound listeners were the simple causal conjunction *so*:

(4) *She wants to always wants to help you...***so***...uh...the problem between you and her come from always come from communication.*

(5) *The problems are...uh...overcome by written and reading form...***so***...I know you have the difficult procedure.*

The use of *so* prepares the listener for a causal relationship between the two parts of the discourse (i.e. *she wants to help you,* **so** *feel free to talk to her*); but instead, the speakers go back to reiterate the problems and difficulties. The cohesive tie *so*, then, has the effect of leaving the listener waiting for a causal relationship while the speaker goes on to address a different topic altogether.

In the level four speech samples, participants used *and* in 54% of the total number of conjunctions, much like level three respondents. 65% of all the lexical cohesive ties are simple conjunctions. Each respondent at this level included some type of either internal temporal or correlative sequential conjunctive tie. These conjunctions are used to organize the discourse and move it from one point to the next, and include such connectors as *first, second, finally*, and *next*. Although the level four test takers used these connectors to try to give direction to the text, they did not use them consistently and therefore potentially violating the expectations of the listeners. In other words, just because a participant used *second* as a connector, he or she did not necessarily mean there was an explicit *first* or *third* spoken.

Participants in levels five and six did not differ from each other, but together they differed from level three and four participants in their consistent use of internal temporal and correlative sequential conjunctions. This was also true for their use of complex conjunctive constructions such as *not only...but also* as well as reversed causal connectors such as *because*. These participants were engaged in a higher level of discourse in that they were not only giving advice, *per* the test item, but were also giving reasons for that advice. They are able to construct the discourse using appropriate cohesive ties to demonstrate that logical connection.

(6) *My best advice would be to go and talk to him about it* **because** *um you need to get a good grade.*

(7) *I would suggest you to uh go to the professor uh who's in charge of this course and talk to him about the situation* **because** *the situation is completely inappropriate.*

(8) **Not only** *is this situation a problem for you,* **but it is also** *a problem for other students.*

In addition to using reverse causal connectors to offer reasons for their advice, participants at levels five and six were able to hypothesize about a variety of situations by using *if…then* constructions. The ability to use these complex constructions allowed the test candidate to be specific in his/her advice to the student.

(9) **If** *I can't be of any assistance,* **then** *I'll try to find someone who will be able to help you out.*

(10) **If** *you think speaking to her is not going to make any difference and that um she is really not going to be able to help you* then *maybe it would be a good idea to go and speak to the person who has assigned the teaching assistant to your class.*

The participants made use of complex conjunctival relationships which allowed them to be more specific and enhance their perceived proficiency in the role as a teacher using English. They also brought different types of cohesive ties together in close proximity to each other in the utterance in order to show the logical connections between points. Both examples (9) and (10) included simple additive conjunctions, complex "if…then" conjunctival statements as well as relative pronouns for subordination. This potentially allows listeners to attend more easily, thereby increasing the perception that the speaker is proficient in English.

Lexical cohesion. In all four of the levels examined (see Table 4), the participants reiterated terms such as *the problem*, *the situation*, or the *teaching assistant*. This simply means that some participants used words more than once in their discourse to connect ideas. Participants in levels three and four incorporated a higher percentage of reiteration throughout their test responses than did participants in levels five and six. At first glance, this may suggest a higher overall cohesive quality to the spoken responses, but upon closer analysis, this reiteration might actually detract from the coherence of their talk. Participants at levels three and four seemed to be using reiteration not as a cohesive tie, but rather as a type of non-productive lexical item which might be used to compensate for limitations in vocabulary.

(11) *You cannot* **understand…understand** *her talking.*

(12) *I also* **have...have...similar...similar** *problem.*

(13) *It can help you to* **make up for...make up for what you... what you** *left behind.*

Research question 3. The research question was: What additional discourse level linguistic features play a role in facilitating or detracting from the overall coherence and comprehensibility of the extended discourse? From the data, two additional features emerged as significant discourse level factors impacting the overall coherence and comprehensibility of participants' extended discourse. These were the rate of speech, and the number and type of pauses in talk. Even though it is natural for fluent speakers of a language to have a certain amount of pausing within a two-minute talk, an analysis of participants' responses in this study indicated that as one goes up in terms of test levels three, four, five, and six, the number and length of pauses used by participants decrease. The test candidates were give a two-minute time limit to talk, but they were not required to talk the entire two minutes. Eight of the ten level three participants talked for two minutes, but because of their slow rate of speech and excessive pausing, they said fewer words in two minutes than participants in levels five or six said in one minute, on average. Stated in numerical terms, participants in level three averaged .77 words per second. Level four participants averaged 1.48 words per second, and level five participants used 2.23 words per second on average. Level six participants used on average 2.43 words per second.

Certain types of pausing, particularly pausing in the middle of phrases (example 14) and pausing that increases the distance between anaphors and their antecedents (examples 15 and 16), may reduce the comprehensibility of extended talk. Here are examples from participants in levels three and four:

(14) *I understand your* [pause] *situation.*

(15) *The problem is* [pause] *a* [pause] *difficult* [pause] *difficult* [pause] *problem.*

(16) *The teaching assistant has* [pause] *problem* [pause] *the problem* [pause] *she* [pause] *has to improve* [pause] *her* [pause] *English.*

During these pauses, the participants seemed to be searching for a word or a grammatical form. This caused them to pause within information units, and seem less proficient in English.

Discussion and Implications for ITAs

This study presented a qualitative analysis of ITAs' extended talk across different proficiency levels. See Table 5.

Table 5. Characteristics Across Proficiency Levels

Proficiency Level	Rate of Speech	Repetition/Pronoun use	Use of Conjunction
Level 3	Slow speech (.77 words/minute), pausing within phrases and constituents.	Excessive repetition of words, particularly unproductive repetition. Little use of pronomial reference (*it, this, she*), rather continued repetition of nouns.	Incorporation of few conjunctions, primarily simple additive connectors (*and, also*); often misuse conjunctions.
Level 4	Somewhat quicker speech (1.43 words/minute), continued pausing within phrases as well as extended time between anaphor and antecedent.	More use of personal and demonstrative pronouns, some unproductive repetition, but less than at the lower level.	Use of conjunctions, but rely heavily on simple additive, adversative, or causal; include temporal and sequential conjunctions as well (*first, second; next*).
Level 5	Acceptable rate of speech (2.23 words/minute), some pausing, and not within phrases or constituents.	Little unproductive repetition, personal and demonstrative pronouns are used, additionally relative pronouns are used to subordinate clauses and build cohesion.	Use of temporal and correlative sequential conjunctions as well as complex conjuctival constructions (*not only...but also*) and reversed causal connectors (*because*)
Level 6	Faster speech (2.43 words/minute, fewer pauses overall, pauses at appropriate phrase boundaries.	Repetition is used primarily to build cohesion, personal and demonstrative pronouns are used, additionally relative pronouns are correctly used to subordinate clauses and build cohesion.	Use of temporal and correlative sequential conjunctions as well as complex conjuctival constructions (*not only...but also*) and reversed causal connectors (*because*)

For ITA mentors and instructors across different disciplines, an awareness of these differences in discourse patterns at different levels of proficiency can be helpful both to identify ITAs and ITA candidates at particular proficiency levels, and then provide instruction so as to improve their speech comprehensibility. If ITA educators and mentors recognize the importance that cohesion plays in the comprehensibility of extended talk, then they can provide ITAs with important tools for developing the needed skills. ITAs can be taught to notice the ways that referential items and conjunctive ties organize discourse in lectures, explanations, and discussions. This type of explicit noticing instruction can help the students to increase their awareness of these types of discourse markers and the ways they are used in their disciplines.

Noticing activities. Mentors and ITA instructors can use a variety of noticing activities to help ITAs see the way that discourse is structured. Here is one: The following excerpt is from *A Handbook for Mathematics Teaching Assistants* published by the Mathematical Association of America (2014).

> Calculus is usually split into two types: differential and integral. Differential calculus deals with instantaneous rates of change: how things change right now, not over six years or ten miles (those are average rates of change), not over six seconds or six one-hundredth of a second, but right now, this instant. We will be learning about this instantaneous change this so-called derivative, how to find it, how to manipulate it, and how to use it in problems from physics and chemistry to business and economics. For instance, if the instantaneous change takes place over time, then this derivative is the velocity of the object that is moving, and this concept is of special interest to physicists and engineers; it is one of their tools for explaining the physical world. When Isaac Newton wrote F = ma, for instance, he was saying that forces are related to acceleration, and acceleration is a derivative, a rate of change.

To help students better understand how repetition, conjunction, and discourse markers are used in this type of lecture, mentors can have ITA candidates read this type of text doing different tasks. As a first step, ITAs can read through the text looking for repetition of terms and ideas for cohesion (*differential, derivative, instantaneous,* etc.) and discuss how this repetition shapes the discourse and helps to move it along. We can see, for example, that already in the first line the repetition of the term *differential* helps to organize the talk because it becomes clear that the overall lecture will be about two types of calculus, but at this moment the instructor is discussing the first type (*differential*).

As a second step, ITAs can also find pronouns throughout the excerpt and discuss how those pronouns make connections between different parts of the text. ITAs can discuss the use of the pronoun *it* when referring back to *derivative*. Mentors and ITA instructors might point out that the pronoun is used in close proximity to the antecedent to which it refers, but when the lecturer begins a new sentence about the same topic, the noun can be repeated rather than the pronoun, to avoid potential ambiguity. ITAs can be led through a discussion of the use of the demonstrative *this* to build connections, particularly when talking about the derivative. Instructors and mentors can draw ITAs' attention to different types of conjunctions and discourse markers throughout the text that help to organize it. Some of these are simple (*and, or*), but there are also more complex ties including *not...but* as well as *if...then*, and *for instance*. Finally, once ITA candidates are able to notice these cohesive ties, instructors and mentors can guide ITAs to develop lecture excerpts of their own using appropriate cohesive ties. For example, mathematic ITAs could be asked to think through and compose a paragraph addressing integral calculus along the lines of the structure presented in the excerpt above.

Providing models, outlines, and handouts. In addition to these types of noticing activities, ITA educators and mentors in engineering and the sciences can also provide models, outlines, or handouts to help ITAs incorporate cohesive ties appropriately according to the discourse conventions of their fields. Wankat and Oreovicz (1992) note that when teaching beginning level engineering students, "organiz[ing] the lecture in a linear, logical fashion" (p. 94) can be helpful. The same authors encourage engineering teachers to "include stage directions in their lecture notes" (p. 95). ITA educators and mentors could provide outlines of different discourse organizational schemes in lectures, brief explanations, recitations, and lab instructions using the types of conjunctive ties typical to the lecture context, so that ITAs can more appropriately organize their discourse. Here is one example: One of the tasks of many newly-arrived ITAs in the sciences is to lead laboratory sections. Because lab experiments are procedural by nature, the use of internal temporal conjunctions, such as *first, second, third*, are of importance in instructing undergraduate students on the relationships between steps in the experiment. ITA mentors can offer a sample outline that includes these types of cohesive ties. When ITAs are developing their own procedural instructions, they can follow the example. See Table 6.

Table 6. Sample Lab Procedure

Sample Lab Procedure	Sample Outline
First, add 5 drops of ionic liquid to the test tube. Then, record your observations.	First…
	Then…
Second, add 5 drops of a second ionic liquid to the same test tube.	Second…
Third, mix the liquids using a clean stirring rod.	Third…
After you have mixed the liquids, record your observations.	After…
	Then…
Then, repeat the experiment in a different tube with different solutions.	

Felder (2000), suggests that much instruction in engineering and the sciences takes place using an explanation plus practical application or example discourse structure. This is a communication context where the relationships between different segments of the discourse must be clearly delineated in order for students to follow the flow of the activity. ITAs can be provided with sample organizational schemas, to show the relationships between explanation and application. See Table 7.

Table 7. Schema for Explanation Plus Example

Sample Schema for Explanation plus Example	Sample Organization
In this section we are going to talk about function and function notation.	In this section…
First, what is a function? An equation is a function if for any x in the domain of the equation the equation will yield exactly one value of y.	First… Now…
Now, let's look at an example. **Example 1** Determine if each of the following are functions. (a) $y = x^2 + 1$ (b) $y^2 = x + 1$	Example 1… This first one… This second one… Now…
Solution (a) This first one is a function. Given an x, there is only one way to square it and then add 1 to the result. So, no matter what value of x you put into the equation, there is only one possible value of y. (b) This second one is not a function. The only difference between this equation and the first is that we moved the exponent off the x and onto the y. This small change is all that is required, in this case, to change the equation from a function to something that isn't a function.	
Now we need to take a quick look at function notation…	

Note. Adapted from tutorial.math.lamar.edu

    This explicit instruction and modeling of cohesion in discourse can make ITAs feel more comfortable in the overall structuring of their explanations, while at the same time providing their students with tools to understand the material being discussed. ITAs need to develop the ability to present coherent extended discourse in English. As shown in this report, this involves more than a focus on sentence level grammar and pronunciation. Attention to cohesion as a feature of coherent and comprehensible speech is indispensible to build ITAs' repertoire for successful professional communication.

In a Nutshell

1. In longer oral and written discourse (language use beyond the sentence level), cohesive ties play an important but complex role in organizing texts and aiding listener comprehensibility.

2. 40 two-minute recordings of ITAs at four different levels of proficiency were analyzed for cohesive ties. ITAs were assigned to middle proficiency levels 3 and 4, and higher proficiency levels 5 and 6 according to a locally administered speaking performance test designed to determine ITAs' readiness to teach.
3. There were marked differences in how ITAs at different levels of proficiency used cohesive ties, resulting in less, and more, comprehensibility.
4. Participants at levels 5 and 6 seemed more able to incorporate relative pronouns (*which, that*) to correctly develop subordinate clauses (*This small change is all that is required, in this case, to change the equation from a function to something* **that** *isn't a function.*)
5. At lower-level 3 participants used fewer conjunctions to relate ideas together, and often used conjunctions incorrectly (overuse of *so*). At higher-level 4, participants were able to use more conjunctions and more correctly, but continued to rely on simple conjunctions. Participants at levels 5 and 6 were able to use complex conjunctions (*because* and *if... then*).
6. Repetition of ideas may, in some cases, increase cohesion in talk. However, ITAs at lower proficiency levels upon arrival used excessive, unproductive repetition, where ideas were being repeated in very close proximity without regard for cohesion. ITAs tested at higher levels, however, were able to use repetition to build connections between different parts of their talk (*This small* change *is all that is required, in this case, to* **change** *the equation from a* **function** *to something* **that** *isn't a* **function**.)
7. As participants' proficiency level increased, so did their rate of speech. At lower levels, pauses within units of information and phrase boundaries, and excessive listening time between antecedent and anaphor seemed to lead to a lack of comprehensibility (*The problem is* [pause] *a* [pause] *difficult* [pause] *difficult* [pause] *problem.*)
8. ITAs can benefit from noticing activities which help them to pay attention to the kinds of cohesive ties used to organize speech in academic settings. ITA instructors and mentors

can build these types of activities into their instruction or mentoring by having ITAs listen to in-discipline lectures while focusing on cohesive ties such as productive repetition, and conjunctions.

9. Mentors and instructors can provide sample outlines of discourse to show how to use connecting words and cohesive ties to organize their speech. References

References

Anderson A.H. (1995).Negotiating coherence in dialogue. In M.A. Gernsbacher & T. Givon (Eds.), *The negotiation of coherence* (pp. 41-58). New York: John Benjamins.

Canale, M. & Swain, M. (1980). Theoretical bases of communicative approaches to second language teaching and testing. *Applied Linguistics*, 1, 1-47.

Castro, C. (2004). Cohesion in the social structure of meaning in the essays of Filipino college students writing in L2 English. *Asia Pacific Education Review,* 5, 215-225.

Chafe, W. (1985). Some reasons for silence. In D. Tannen & M. Saville-Troike (Eds.), *Perspectives on silence* (p. 77-89). Norwood, New Jersey: Ablex.

Chiang, S. Y. (2010). Pursuing a response in office hour interaction between U.S. college students and international teaching assistants. *Journal of Pragmatics,* 43, 3316-3330.

Crossley, S., Salisbury, T. L., & McNamara, D. S. (2010). The role of lexical cohesive devices in triggering negotiations for meaning. *Issues in Applied Linguistics*, 18(1), 55-80.

Educational Testing Service (2014). *TOEFL iBT: About the test.* Available: https://www.ets.org/toefl/ibt/about

Felder, R.M. (2000). The future of engineering education II. Teaching methods at work. *Chemical Engineering Education, 34,* 26-39.

Fung, L., & Carter, R. (2007). Discourse markers and spoken English: Native and learner use in pedagogic settings. *Applied Linguistics*, 28(3), 410-439.

Halliday, M.A.K., & Hasan, R. (1976). *Cohesion in English.* London: Longman.

Halliday, M.A.K., & Matthiessen, C. M. I. M. (2004). *An introduction to functional grammar.* London: Arnold.

Hasselgreen, A. (2005). *Testing the spoken English of young Norwegians: A study of test validity and the role of "smallwords" in contributing to pupils' fluency: Studies in language testing.* Cambridge: Cambridge University Press.

Liao, S. (2009). Variation in the use of discourse markers by Chinese teaching assistants in the U.S. *Journal of Pragmatics, 41,* 1313-1328.

Liu, M., & Braine, G. (2005). Cohesive features in argumentative writing produced by Chinese undergraduates. *System, 33*(4), 623-636.

Mathematical Association of America (2014). *A handbook for mathematics teaching assistants*. Available: http://www.maa.org/programs/students/student-resources/a-handbook-for-mathematics-teaching-assistants

Riggenbach, H. (1999). *Discourse analysis in the language classroom.* Ann Arbor: University of Michigan Press.

Rounds, P. (1987). Characterizing successful classroom discourse for NNS teaching assistant training. *TESOL Quarterly, 21*, 643-671.

Savignon, S. J. (1972). *Communicative competence: An experiment in foreign-language teaching.* Philadelphia: Center for Curriculum Development.

Schiffrin, D. (1994). *Approaches to discourse.* Oxford: Blackwell Publishers.

Tyler, A. (1992). Discourse structure and the perception of incoherence in international teaching assistants" spoken discourse. *TESOL Quarterly, 26*, 713-729.

Tyler, A., Jeffries, A., and Davies, C. (1988).The effect of discourse structuring devise on listener perceptions of coherence in non-native university teacher's spoken discourse.*World Englishes, 7*, 101-110.

Wankat, P.C., & Oreovicz, F. (1992).*Teaching engineering.* Purdue University: McGraw-Hill.

Williams, J. (1992). Planning, discourse marking, and the comprehensibility of international teaching assistants. *TESOL Quarterly, 26*, 693-711.

Part Two

University Community Entry and Creating Contexts for ITAs' Talk and

Communication Enhancement Through Positive Contact Activities Between International Students and U.S. Undergraduate Students

By Okim Kang[1] and Meghan Moran, Northern Arizona University

The current study introduced structured intergroup contact activities as a way of enhancing communication between U.S. undergraduates and international students, and, by extension, international teaching assistants (ITAs). It examined the effects of contact interventions on undergraduates' perceptions of ITAs' and international students' oral performance. It also investigated the impact of such interventions on international students' attitudes toward U.S. students and U.S. culture. 285 students participated: 1.) 100 U.S. undergraduates in a contact group, 2.) 100 U.S. undergraduates in a non-contact group, and 3.) 85 non-matriculated international students attending an intensive English program on campus. The contact-group students participated in structured contact activities (e.g., solving puzzles or joining fun activities). The undergraduates from both contact and non-contact groups evaluated recordings of 9 non-native English speakers' speech (6 ITAs and 3 intensive English program students) at the beginning

---

1. Author contact: okim.kang@nau.edu

and at the end of the semester. The constructs of the listening task were U.S. undergraduates' perceptions of speaker comprehensibility, accentedness, stereotyping, and oral proficiency. Results showed that after the contact exercises, undergraduates in the contact group evaluated the accented speech in ITAs' recordings more positively compared to what they had previously and to those in the non-contact group. The contact intervention also brought about international students' positive attitude changes. The findings suggest a possible classroom model to improve U.S. students' communication in linguistically diverse contexts.

Problematic Pedagogy and a Culture of Negativity

A simple search in an academic database for international teaching assistants (ITAs) will return thousands of hits. These include articles on evaluation of ITA training courses, ITAs' cultural beliefs and the teaching practices they engender, and improving ITAs' speaking fluency, among many others. An implicit trend quickly emerges from the literature: ITAs are different from American TAs, these differences are problematic for undergraduate students and as such, the differences should be identified, explored, and if possible, corrected. From this viewpoint, learning is seen as a uni-directional imparting of information rather than a co-construction of knowledge between students and their instructors. Far less research focuses on students of ITAs and their role in the creation of problematic pedagogy. In other words, the communicative burden is being placed largely on ITAs; because they are the non-native speakers of English, it is often considered their responsibility to do what is necessary to make themselves understood in the academic realm. This is in contrast to a co-construction of language that assigns equal responsibility to both the ITA and the U.S. undergraduate student in interaction (see also Trebing's contribution in this volume).

Students' complaints regarding their international teaching assistants have been documented for decades. This culture of negativity towards ITAs has been dubbed "The ITA Problem" (Fitch & Morgan, 2003). A student learning that she or he has been assigned a lab or class taught by an ITA can lead to what has been referred to as "The Oh-No Syndrome" (Rao, 1995). In students' global perceptions of ITAs' identities, details of ethnicity, nationality, status, and academic positions are secondary. What is of primary importance is their foreignness (Fitch & Morgan, 2003). The act of meaning-making in an ITA-fronted classroom is complex and involves various perceptual factors such as linguistic stereotyping and reverse linguistic stereotyping, as well as actual linguistic factors (such as segmental and suprasegmental features) that could serve to lower intelligibility. At best, students may complain about their ITAs, and at worst, they may completely avoid enrolling in classes taught by ITAs. This animosity is inherently problematic to a learning and teaching environment; furthermore, it is compounded by recent findings that students' negative attitudes towards non-native accents can actually lead to a decrease in their comprehending ITAs' talk (Ahn & Moore, 2011).

Negative Effects on International Students as Well as on ITAs

In fact, ITAs are not the only ones affected by these attitudes. International undergraduate students also experience discrimination and isolation, finding it difficult to form friendships with American undergraduates (Mak, Brown, & Wadey, 2014), and to face American undergraduates' negative attitudes in culturally mixed group work in which they must talk (Summers & Volet, 2008). American undergraduates ascribe unfavorable attitudes toward international students and reported feeling uncomfortable, impatient, and frustrated when encountering communication difficulties. These emotions have been attributed to factors such as "accented speech, cultural differences in non-verbal communication styles, and cultural variations in values, norms, and customs" (Spencer-Rodgers & McGovern, 2002, pp. 623-624). Moreover, this broad range of adverse emotions surrounding interactions between members of different ethnolinguistic groups can be a contributing factor to intergroup hostility (Spencer-Rodgers & McGovern, 2002).

Given these findings, how can we, as teachers and teacher trainers of both native and non-native English speaking university students and teaching assistants, promote successful, open-minded communication in the classroom? Due to its nature as a dynamic co-construction between speaker and listener, issues in intelligibility must be addressed through both dimensions. First, teacher trainers of ITAs should make sure their students are well-equipped with linguistic strategies that can give them agency over their interactions with undergraduate students (Zhang, 2012). ITAs who have low speaking proficiency skills also should undergo pronunciation training that will focus on specific, research-informed segmental and suprasegmental features that have been found to increase intelligibility of speech. However, there are many instances of ITAs who are accented yet still highly intelligible. In these cases, we must work to overcome undergraduate listeners' biases and stereotyping, which are contributors to breakdowns in understanding. This study will address the latter of these by using specific and replicable programs of contact activity.

Although little is known as yet about the necessary dimensions for improving U.S. undergraduates' comprehension of accented English speech, it is commonly believed that language attitudes are malleable. The current study provides evidence for the mitigation of undergraduates' attitudes by applying the Contact Hypothesis (Allport, 1954). Together with contemporary work such as Kang and Rubin (2012); Staples, Kang, and Wittner (2014); and Kang, Rubin, and Lindemann (2014), it adds to our understanding of doing practical and principled interventions to improve ITA-led classrooms' learning environments. While the previous studies have commonly employed an intervention that is independent of existing classroom curricula, the current study investigates the feasibility of embedding intercultural contact activities directly into existing classrooms and existing course syllabi.

Literature Review

U.S. undergraduates and ITAs, and linguistic stereotyping.
It can be convincingly argued that ITAs are devalued in U.S. higher education because of their actual talk or perceived talk. Reading the literature, some of which is cited in the introduction, suggests that learning from an ITA involves expenditures of increased cultural, linguistic, and cognitive resources by U.S. undergraduates. Students may impose self-fulfilling negative expectations regarding this burden of mental effort. These expectations can likewise affect the success of American students' interactions with non-native speakers and deter U.S. undergraduate students from talking effectively with ITAs (Lindemann, 2002). While successful comprehension of ITAs' talk is in part a function of undergraduates' familiarity with accented speech (Gass & Varonis, 1984), their lack of familiarity

with varieties of accents creates anxiety that detracts from their listening comprehension (Derwing, Rossiter, & Munro, 2002). From the ITAs' points of view, ITAs may feel self-conscious of their own linguistic proficiency and their ability to establish rapport and maintain social relationships with their American students (Zhang, 2012), and thus increase communicative tensions.

We wish to argue that students' complaints are more a function of their stereotyped judgments than of ITAs' actual talk (Rubin, 2002). Students' biases have been studied through a linguistic stereotyping paradigm from the field of social psychology. Stated briefly, listeners ascribe stereotyped features to speakers on the basis of their speech (Lambert, Hogdson, Gardner, & Fillenbaum, 1960). In other words, brief samples of speech varieties lead language users to build associations with low-prestige groups, such as working-class people, or uneducated people. This in turn cues negative attributions regarding individual speakers.

Reverse linguistic stereotyping and linguistic expectancy. What is even more salient to this study is the phenomenon of reverse linguistic stereotyping (RLS), illustrated by Kang & Rubin (2009). In RLS, listeners hear a non-standard accent in talk where none may be present. The social identity ascribed to the speaker by the listener evokes linguistic expectancy, which then leads to a stereotyped evaluation of language performance. Like any other social group, undergraduate students' expectations and stereotypes of talk are based on attributions of group membership, and therefore on distorted perceptions of a speaker's language style and proficiency. It can be argued students judge the style of a speaker not on the actual linguistic characteristics of the speech, but on the linguistic characteristics *they believe they hear* in the talk (see Kang & Rubin, 2009, for empirical evidence).

Ameliorating problems using an alternative point of view. Researchers turned their attention toward finding ways to facilitate the success of ITAs' and undergraduates' interactions. Yook and Albert (1999) split 422 undergraduate students into groups depending on treatments the researchers devised: These included participation in an intercultural training method (*Intercultural Sensitizer*, see Albert, 1983), role plays, role plays plus Intercultural Sensitizer, and a control group with no treatment. Participants were randomly assigned to disclosure or no-disclosure conditions, meaning that for some participants in any of the treatment groups, the ITA presentation that they watched came with a statement that the speaker was speaking in his or her second language. The complex measures and results in this study indicated that training with the Intercultural Sensitizer, alone or in combination with role plays and/or the disclosure condition resulted in a situation where empirically, students blamed ITAs less for their non-native speech patterns. When students placed less blame on the ITAs, their emotions of anger, disgust, and surprise decreased, while their feelings of sympathy increased. This in turn seemed to lead to higher evaluations of the ITAs' talk. These results led Yook and Albert to conclude that, "intercultural sensitivity training can help U.S. undergraduates have a more positive attitude toward learning from an ITA" (1999, p. 16).

Each of the interventions employed in Yook and Albert (1999) attempted to increase sympathy on the part of the listener, although none of them involved actual in-person interactions between American undergraduates and international students or teachers. Smith, Strom, and Muthuswamy (2005) took a different tack and employed a version of the *jigsaw classroom* (Aronson, Stephan, Sikes, Blaney, & Snapp, 1978) to bring about in-person interaction between undergraduates and international students. Their hypothesis was that as undergraduate students report more interactions with international students while solving problems, the higher they will rate ITAs as English speakers, and as teachers. Each week, approximately half of the 90 undergraduates participating in the study met with an international student and completed exercises that complemented the class material in the intercultural communication course that all participants were enrolled in. The undergraduates then took surveys over time that elicited information about domestic TAs, ITAs, and "non-specified" TAs. Smith et al (2005) found that undergraduates who interacted with an international student were not statistically significantly different in their perceptions than undergraduates in the no-interaction condition. However, the experimental (interaction) group was less likely to rate ITAs progressively worse throughout the semester than was the control group. This leads us to consider a significant theoretical framework, the Contact Hypothesis.

The Contact Hypothesis. Kang and Rubin (2012), Kang et al (2014), and Staples et al (2014), assessed undergraduate students' perceptions on the speech of non-native English speakers both prior to, and after, interactions in which undergraduates met with international students in a planned intervention situation. They have relied upon the Contact Hypothesis developed by Allport (1954,) and extensively refined and revised by social psychologists over the past sixty years. The Contact Hypothesis claims that prejudice would be reduced between two groups with different characteristics if members of the groups got to know each other better. Later versions of the original tenet specified that certain conditions must be present in order for the hypothesis to work. These conditions are as follows: 1.) contact must be voluntary; 2.) groups must be of equal status and composition; 3.) contact should extend beyond an immediate task; 4.) contact must be non-superficial (i.e., have acquaintance potential); 5.) contact should have mutually beneficial outcomes; 6.) the intervention task cannot be accomplished without mutual input; and 7.) there must be clear institutional support.

Studies on interactive treatments based on the Contact Hypothesis. Kang and Rubin (2012) conducted two trials in which approximately half of the American students, the experimental group in the study, participated in a structured contact activity with ITAs. The activity involved groups of four or five American students talking with two ITAs in order to solve mystery puzzles. Prior to the activity, all students had rated eleven ITAs' presentations of a five-minute mini-lecture on ITAs' comprehensibility, overall oral proficiency, degree of accentedness, and teaching competence. Results showed that students who had participated in the contact activity rated ITAs higher on comprehensibility and teaching competence in a post-test, whereas the control group, who had no interactive activity with ITAs, did not change their ratings on ITAs from the beginning to the end of the study. Interestingly, the experimental group students in the interaction group who, at the outset of the study, claimed that their grades had been negatively affected in the past by poor teaching on the part of ITAs, displayed the most dramatic improvement in ratings.

In a similar set of studies, Kang et al (2014) confirmed that despite low levels of contact, the intervention (i.e., structured contact between international teaching assistants and American students) had a consistent and replicable effect on the undergraduates. Confirming Kang and Rubin (2012), American students who had had interpersonal, structured contact with ITAs listened to speech samples from non-native English speakers, and attributed more comprehensibility and instructional competence to the speakers. The contact was comprised of one hour informally conversing and then collaborating to solve mystery puzzles. This indicates that even brief interactions between undergraduates and ITAs can mitigate undergraduate students' negative perceptions of ITAs' speech and instructional competence. However, Kang and Rubin (2014) concluded with the suggestion that qualitative data collection, such as direct interviews with ITAs and undergraduate students, needs to be done to gain insight into participants' impressions of the intergroup collaboration and its effects. This then motivates the current study, which uses a qualitative component to address the need for more detailed information.

Staples et al (2014) differed from Kang et al (2014) and Kang and Rubin (2012). First, the structured contact between undergraduates and international students extended over half of a semester. Contact group participants interacted with their international partners during hour-long sessions at least once per week for eight weeks. Second, the interactions focused on important issues surrounding tensions between undergraduates and international students, with both groups giving advice and suggestions, and even role-playing in the position of the other. Third, Staples et al (2014) overtly addressed one of the tenets necessary for the Contact Hypothesis to be most successful: Institutional support. Staples et al's (2014) contact activities were part of a long-standing undergraduate program whose aims were to help international students improve their language, intercultural communication skills, and instructional skills. Quantitative findings from this study showed that the undergraduate contact group rated their international counterparts' speech samples as less accented, more comprehensible, and more instructionally competent. Undergraduates' control group ratings worsened for each construct. We note that data were not collected from the international partners because the study primarily focused on perceptual changes of U.S. undergraduate students. We address international students' perceptions in the current study in upcoming sections.

Proposing contact activities in undergraduate core courses. The current study is unique in that it integrated intercultural contact activities between undergraduate and international students into a pre-existing curriculum of an anthropology course focused on culture and communication. In other words, the activities had the aim of improving undergraduate students' attitudes towards international students and their accented speech, while simultaneously meeting course objectives. The goals of the course include introducing cultural and linguistic diversity based in linguistic anthropological perspectives. The contact activities offered such diversity opportunities. This is important because extracurricular contact interventions rely on student volunteers who may be more open-minded than the general student population. More importantly, the current study provides a model that could be replicated in required courses at any university, such as core courses in the Humanities. Embedding intercultural contact activities within the curriculum exemplifies institutional support, a Contact Hypothesis condition that continues to be under-discussed in the literature. We now turn our attention to the literature on international students' and ITAs' perspectives.

International students' and ITAs' attitudes toward U.S. undergraduate students. International teaching assistants (ITAs) often have to speak a second language when they teach abroad, and they also sometimes have trouble adapting to the culture and academic features in a new country. Oftentimes, the more "distance" there is between two cultures, the more difficulty the student has in adjusting in the new setting (Bennett, 1995). Furnham and Alibhai (1985) showed that international students themselves prefer friends from the same or similar countries. However, Kovtun (2011) showed that courses especially designed to help international students adapt to their new university and their new culture can help international students academically, and in their interactions with students from the host culture.

Research conducted more exclusively on ITAs has examined ITAs' behavior rather than their attitudes and perceptions (Gorsuch, 2003). However, there have been a handful of studies that have investigated ITAs' feelings towards American courses and American students. In one such case, Ates and Eslami (2012) analyzed the teaching blogs of three ITAs, and data from semi-structured interviews with them. One of the themes that emerged was the awareness on the part of the ITAs with regard to their non-native speaker status. ITAs commented that U.S. students concentrated on her or his English language skills more so than the content of her or his talk (Ates & Eslami, 2012). Also, ITAs believed that some students used their perceptions of ITAs' linguistic competence as an excuse for their own shortcomings in class. In a similar case study, Liu (2005) elicited information on the perceptions of four Chinese ITAs who taught freshman composition to American undergraduate students. Liu's interviews focused on the ITAs' teaching experiences and their beliefs about students' attitudes towards them. That data revealed that the ITAs found their language-related challenges to be the largest obstacle to effective communication between them and their students. They felt that because they were unable to demonstrate linguistic advantages over native speakers in the areas of vocabulary, idioms, accuracy, and fluency in speaking, they were less confident when talking to their students.

It can be argued that ITAs feel they must make accommodations in order to be successful in their pedagogical responsibilities. Previous studies have shown that these accommodations are met with various levels of success. For example, by analyzing interviews with seven Chinese ITAs, LaRocco (2012) has suggested that ITAs have meta-knowledge regarding norms of their own culture as well as American culture, which helps them to develop intercultural competency and skills in navigating intercultural interactions. Zhang (2012) points out that before ITAs are culturally competent in a new educational culture, they use the interactional framework of their home countries as guidelines for communication with undergraduate students. That is, until they are confronted with socio-pragmatic problems. As ITAs improve in their intercultural interactions, they must "constantly negotiate their perceptions and behaviors in order to find appropriate ways of dealing with different situations happening in the target culture" (Zhang, 2012, p. 387).

Study Purpose

The current study involves a number of features that have not been present in previous contact intervention studies. First, the activities administered in the current study involved a more elaborate contact design than previous studies, occurring three times throughout the semester. Second, the design was embedded within a Liberal Arts core course. Because the contact activities were designed to align with the course goals, this study offers insight into how contact intervention can be integrated into a course curriculum. Finally, pre- and post-intervention surveys are collected from both U.S. undergraduate participants, and international student participants. While many of the international student participants were not yet matriculated to a university, they were in the U.S. and studying at an intensive English program to pursue this possibility.

The purpose of this study was to investigate the outcomes of a program of structured contact between international students and U.S. undergraduates that adhered to the principles of the Contact Hypothesis. The research questions investigated were:

Research question #1. What are the effects of contact interventions between U.S. undergraduate students and international students on the undergraduates' attitudes toward ITAs? Specifically, how do undergraduate students' evaluations of international students' accentedness, comprehensibility, and oral proficiency change after strategic interactions with international students? Will their measures of stereotyping change? How will undergraduates in a control group compare?

Research question #2. How do international students' (or ITAs') attitudes regarding U.S. undergraduate students differ after contact activities with U.S. undergraduates?

Method

Participants

"Listeners." There were two groups of "listeners" who participated in the contact activities and also provided ratings on ten speech samples. One group was U.S. undergraduates, and one group was international students attending a nearby intensive English program (IEP). The first group was comprised of two hundred U.S. undergraduate students, split evenly between a control "no-contact" group (100 students) and an experimental "contact" group (100 students). These students were enrolled in two sections of "Anthropology 103: Culture in Communication" at a state university in the Southwest. The two sections of the course were taught by the same instructor with an identical curriculum. According to the university, this course "offers a comparative global perspective on communicative forms, especially languages, as systems of social signs. Primary emphasis on case studies are from non-western societies" (Northern Arizona University, 2014). Due to natural attrition, the number of students from each group who completed both the pre- and the post-survey were 73 in the control group and 81 in the experimental group. Eighty-two of the U.S. undergraduates were female and 72 were male. Their ages ranged from 18 to 24. Their ethnic backgrounds included Caucasian White (87%), Hispanic (5%), Black (5%), Asian (1%), and multi-ethnic or others (2%). Participants' first languages were largely English (96%). The majority of the participants (89%) responded *yes* to the question, *Do you often interact with non-native speakers of English?*

A second group of "listeners" and contact activity participants was 85 unmatriculated international students. The international students joined their U.S. undergraduate colleagues in contact activities as described below. The actual number of participants varied for each of the three consecutive activities, ranging from 72 to 101 due to this group's attendance status. Terms of study in IEPs are somewhat shorter than quarters or semesters of study at American universities. Thus, this group was somewhat of a moving target. One thing in common between them was that they were composed mainly of Arabic- and Chinese-speaking students. Of the international students, 32 completed a language and culture survey (Appendix A) before and after each of the three contact activities. The optional nature of the survey might have led to the low response rate with the IEP students.

"Speakers." Nine non-native speakers (NNSs) of English provided speech samples for the U.S. undergraduate listeners to rate. Six were ITAs from various departments, and three were international students who were enrolled in an intensive English program (IEP). The three IEP students were assumed to have lower speaking abilities than the ITAs and were thus included to assure variance in the speech samples representing a range of oral proficiencies. The nationalities of the non-native English speakers providing speech samples included three Arabic speakers, three Chinese speakers, one Spanish speaker, one Russian speaker, and one South African (Zulu) speaker. Finally, a tenth and final speech sample was provided by a native speaker of English who was an M.A. student in a Teaching English as a Second Language program. This last sample provided a needed benchmark of high proficiency.

Activity Facilitators. A total of 17 graduate students and teachers from the Intensive English Program volunteered to assist in the structured contact activities. Although most of them participated in all three contact sessions, some of them facilitated only one or two sessions out of the total three. The activity facilitators' roles included guiding both U.S. undergraduates and international students to their designated groupings, facilitating the activities, mediating interactions among participants, and/or participating in the actual activities. After the contact activities, ITAs provided their reflection on their experience as activity facilitators.

Materials

Speech samples for the listeners to rate. The ten speech samples provided by the "speakers" were recorded. The speakers were shown a cartoon with a series of pictures about construction sites and asked to describe what they saw. This speech elicitation method is similar to the one used in Derwing and Munro (1997). The actual recordings lasted for about one minute, and 30-second segments within the total recording times were selected for rating. The selected segments started and ended with full phrases.

Pre- and post-contact activity speech sample ratings*.* In a pre- and a post-intervention survey that was administered electronically, both groups of U.S. students in the anthropology course (i.e., control and experimental) were asked to listen to ten speech samples and then rate the speech performance of the ten speakers on the constructs of comprehensibility, accentedness, and oral proficiency. The U.S. students were also asked to complete survey items which captured the extent to which they may have been stereotyping, based on the speech samples. Note that the IEP students did not participate in this speech rating. The pre- and post-contact activity surveys were identical to each other except that the ten speech files appeared in a different order to control for order effect. The pre-survey was administered 12 weeks prior to the post-survey, with the intervention activities spaced approximately equally in the intervening weeks. Likewise, for both the pre- and post-intervention surveys, there existed different versions of the survey achieved through item randomization in order to eliminate the possibility of order effect. Each survey consisted of the 10 speech files with a corresponding set of 11 items used to evaluate comprehensibility (3 items), accentedness (4 items), and oral proficiency (4 items). For each of the constructs, 7-point analytic rating scales were employed.

Comprehensibility. The dependent variable of comprehensibility is consistent with Derwing and Munro's (1997) view of the construct, that is, native speakers' perceptions of intelligibility. In other words, these three items captured how much effort the listeners felt they had to put forth in order to understand the language itself (although not necessarily the content). The three questions used to assess this construct were that the speaker (1) *was easy/hard to understand*; (2) *required little/lots of effort to understand*; and (3) was *incomprehensible/was highly comprehensible*.

Accentedness. The second dependent variable, accentedness, was defined here as the degree to which a speaker's speech pattern differs from that of the listener (Derwing & Munro, 2005) and is seen as a separate, though related, construct from comprehensibility. The listener was prompted, *The speaker to whom I just listened* and then given the choices: (1) *speaks with a foreign/an American accent*; (2) *has no accent/has a strong accent*; and (3) *speaks like a non/native speaker of English*.

Oral proficiency. Next, the oral proficiency scale consisted of constructs commonly found on the performance tests, such as pronunciation/accent, English grammar, English vocabulary, and overall ability to communicate in English. It was adopted from Kang's (2012) study. Students chose how much each of these constructs interfered with understanding by marking a point on a 7-point scale. A sample item was *The speaker's English vocabulary: Did not interfere with understanding/Interfered completely with understanding.*

Stereotyping. For the fourth construct, stereotyping, a reduced version of Zahn and Hopper's (1985) *Speech Evaluation Instrument* (SEI) was adapted with a seven-point Likert scale. The adaptations consisted of eliminating questions that were unclear, overlapped with other items or other parts of the survey, or were not relevant to the study. Previous studies have utilized the SEI as stereotyping and attitude measures (e.g., Kang & Rubin, 2009; Rubin & Smith, 1990). The original SEI was composed of three dimensions with 33 items: (a) *superiority*, (b) *social attractiveness*, and (c) *dynamism*. The adapted stereotyping measure used here included ten items: four from superiority (e.g., *How would you rate the speaker you just heard? poor/rich*), three from social attractiveness (e.g., *kind/unkind*), and three from dynamism (e.g., *lazy/energetic*). Internal consistency on each of the four constructs met or exceeded .91 (see Table 1). The pre- and post-contact activity surveys are available upon request from the corresponding author.

Table 1. Constructs and Internal Consistency of Survey Questions

Construct	Number of Items	Measured	Alpha Level
Comprehensibility	3	Low – High	>.94
Accentedness	4	No Accent – Heavy Accent	>.91
Oral Proficiency	4	Grammar, Vocabulary, Pronunciation, Overall Ability to Communicate	>.95
Stereotyping	10	Unlikeable – Likeable	>.94

Language and culture survey. In order to examine international students' attitudes toward American students and culture, and perhaps any effect of the contact activities, a language and culture survey was developed. See the Appendix. An initial bank of 20 questions for this survey were selected from Neulip and McCroskey's (1997) ethnocentrism scale and the Bogardus (1925) social distance scale. Additional questions were written that were target- and context-specific. This initial selection was then refined through discussion to a final subset of 10 questions in order to reduce the chance of participant fatigue and resulting non-responses on the questionnaire.

Items 3, 4, and 9 were reverse-coded for analysis, so that all high numbers represented a positive aspect of attitudes, whereas all low numbers characterized negative attitudes. For example (see also the Appendix):

It is ok for us as international students to study here and then remain in the United States.
1 = Strongly Agree   7 = Strongly Disagree
1   2   3   4   5   6   7

For the interest of the paper, which is international students' willingness to communicate with American students and to adopt American culture, the survey items were categorized into three themes: Interaction Inclination, Collaboration Comfort, and Culture Model. For Interactional Inclination, items 1, 6, 7, and 9 were combined as a composite value. Here is an example item:

I try to avoid talking with American students because I'm afraid I won't be able to understand them.
1 = Strongly Agree   7 = Strongly Disagree
1   2   3   4   5   6   7

The internal consistency Cronbach's alpha for the four-item measure was .71 at pre-test and .73 at post-test, respectively.

Collaboration Comfort included items 4 and 10. The internal consistency reliability of these two items was .69 and .72 for the pre-test and post-test administrations, respectively. For example:

I feel uncomfortable when American people speak English around me.
1 = Strongly Agree   7 = Strongly Disagree
1   2   3   4   5   6   7

Culture Model included a single item, 8:

My culture should be the role model for other cultures.
1 = Strongly Agree   7 = Strongly Disagree
1   2   3   4   5   6   7

Lastly, students completed an additional thirteen items that elicited basic demographic information as well as self-reports on foreign language skills, amount of time spent interacting with non-native speakers, frequency of travel outside of the United States, and proficiency at understanding non-native accents. These items can be provided upon request from the corresponding author.

Procedures

Structured contact activities. Three times throughout the semester, the experimental group of students met with the international students and were placed in groups of 3 - 4, with 1 - 2 international students and 1 - 2 anthropology undergraduate students per group. The groups were randomly assigned for each contract activity, increasing the likelihood that the undergraduates would have contact with international students from various regions and of both genders. Once groups were formed with the assistance of the activity facilitators, directions for the activity were given by the corresponding author.

First session. During the first 50-minute session, each group was given pictures with non-verbal gestures (e.g., a thumbs-up sign). They were asked to discuss as a group what the gestures meant in American culture, whether they had a similar or different meaning in the culture of the international students. The groups were asked to discuss and demonstrate other gestures used by members of their cultures. The activity provided a basis to initiate communication so that students did not merely sit in an uncomfortable silence. The universal reliability of the topic was also conducive to conversation. Once they had established a comfortable communicative environment, conversations often digressed to other topics.

Second session. In the second session, the mixed groups of students shared opinions about cultural values and proverbs. They each received a "culture puzzle" as a prompt developed by the corresponding author and the intensive English program teachers. A simpler example can be found in the following link: http://www.everythingesl.net/inservices/culture_puzzles.php. As with the previous activity, this provided a foundation for students to share customs from their own cultures and relate them to others in the group. However, the topics were not so detailed or strictly guided that students felt bound to them for the entirety of the session.

Third session. The third session took place in a gymnasium with light refreshments to encourage participation and establish a fun and informal atmosphere. Mixed groups of four to five students were first given a long dowel (a skinny, lightweight, wooden rod). They were instructed to place one finger each upon the dowel and attempt to lower it to the ground. This game, called "helium stick," is an ice-breaker that encourages communication and teamwork in order for the team to achieve its goal.[2] The aim of the second activity in this session was for each group to build the tallest structure

---

2. For more on the helium stick activity, please see http://www.wilderdom.com/games/descriptions/HeliumStick.html.

possible out of marshmallows and uncooked spaghetti.[3] Both of these activities combined a kinesthetic component to the interactions between the undergraduates and the international students. Due to the open layout of the gymnasium, participants were able to see other groups' progress in each of the activities, thus establishing a somewhat competitive but fun atmosphere. Activity facilitators circulated the gymnasium, monitoring and encouraging student progress.

Speech sample rating survey administration. All speech sample rating surveys were created and distributed online through the institution's survey website and in consultation with an IT specialist. In accordance with the institution's Internal Review Board, students' responses were anonymous. The timeline for this project spanned one 16-week academic semester. In the second week, all anthropology undergraduates (both control and experimental) signed a consent form and completed the online pre-test speech sample rating surveys. The experimental group then participated in the intercultural contact activities in weeks 5, 9, and 12, while the control group had no contact activities. Lastly, in week 14, both groups completed the post-test speech sample rating surveys. At the end of the semester, the undergraduates in the experimental group were additionally asked to reflect on their experience with the following prompt: *If you participated in the in-class activities this semester, write a paragraph about your experience in the activities. Has this experience changed your perspective on people from other cultures?*

Language and culture survey administration. International students took the language and culture survey (Appendix) at the beginning and at the end of the semester. The survey was distributed in class optionally and the instructor collected the completed responses a day after the distribution.

Data Analyses

In order to examine the first research question, i.e., the effects of contact interventions on undergraduates' attitudes toward their international student colleagues, we entered the experimental group undergraduates' ratings on all ten items comprising each

---

[3]. For more on the spaghetti towers activity, please see http://youthworkinit.com/spaghetti-and-marshmallow-tower/.

of the four constructs into a statistical program. The same procedure was done for the control group's ratings. We conducted four 2 (contact group versus noncontact group) x 2 (pretest versus posttest) mixed factorial ANOVAs with the second of these factors constituting a repeated measure. A single ANOVA was run for each of the four dependent variables captured in the speech sample rating survey (comprehensibility, accentedness, oral proficiency, and stereotyping). Post-hoc analyses were performed to compare means in each cell. To examine international students' attitudes toward U.S. undergraduates, survey responses were estimated using descriptive statistics, and paired pre- and post- semester t-tests were computed. For the multiple comparisons, a Bonferroni adjustment was made; i.e., by starting with an overall *alpha* of .10, the significance threshold in the current study was set at $p < .025$.

The qualitative data (the undergraduates' written comments) collected from the contact group were carefully reviewed multiple times. When themes emerged in this content analysis, the correctness of the interpretation was checked with the participants who provided the information. This procedure allowed us to gather additional insights about students' perceptual changes as a result of the contact activities. Overall, they were used as supportive evidence to elaborate and help explain the quantitative data results (Creswell & Clark, 2007).

Results

Undergraduates' responses towards ITAs' and graduate students' speech samples. Table 2 shows cell means for the four dependent variables in the study, divided by group (contact versus no contact) and by time (pretest versus posttest). It illustrates the changes of participants' speech rating scores before and after the contact interventions.

Table 2. Contact Condition (2) x Time (2) Means for Four Dependent Variables

Dependent Variables	Contact (n = 90)				Noncontact (n = 90)			
	Time 1 (pre-test)		Time 2 (post-test)		Time 1 (pre-test)		Time 2 (post-test)	
	Mean	SD	Mean	SD	Mean	SD	Mean	SD
Comprehensibility	3.65	1.98	4.05	1.77	4.09	1.77	4.00	1.33
Accentedness	2.88	1.77	3.39	1.68	3.16	1.62	3.44	1.64
Oral proficiency	3.79	1.41	4.20	1.81	4.30	1.93	4.26	1.71
Stereotyping	3.98	1.20	4.21	.93	4.26	1.17	4.31	1.10

Note. All ratings are on a scale of 1 = negative attribute to 7 = positive attribute.

Effects of contact activities on comprehensibility ratings. The *Time* (2) x *Contact* (2) mixed factorial ANOVA for comprehensibility ratings showed a statistically significant main effect for *Time* ($F_{1,152} = 6.23$, $p = 0.013$). That is, all participants' posttest ratings ($M_{post} = 4.06$, $SD = 1.70$) were higher than their pretest ratings ($M_{pre} = 3.75$, $SD = 1.95$) when they rated the speech files for comprehensibility (a difference of .31 on a 7-point scale). A non-significant interaction for the contact variable by time of testing emerged ($F_{1,152} = 3.17$, $p = 0.042$, eta² = .02). Even though the interaction effect was not significant according to our Bonferroni-adjusted significance threshold of .025, our additional analysis showed that the contact group rated the speech samples more comprehensible on the posttest ($M = 4.05$) than they did on the pretest ($M = 3.65$, or a .40 increase on a 7-point scale), while the no-contact group did not show such change ($M = 4.09$ for the pretest and $M = 4.00$ for the posttest, or a .09 decrease). In other words, although the no-contact group (pretest $M = 4.09$) happened to perceive the ITAs' speech as more comprehensible than the contact group (pretest $M = 3.65$) to begin with (a difference of .44), only the contact group showed an improvement in their ratings over the period of the study. We note that the contact group, using intact classes, showed relatively lower rating scores at pre-test compared to the no-contact group. In other words, members of the experimental group started off a little more stringent than those of the no-contact group. Therefore, the result of this finding should be carefully interpreted, given that the increase in the contact group can be due to regression to the mean in this one group.

Effects of contact activities on accentedness ratings. The mixed factorial ANOVA (*Time* x *Contact*) for perceived accentedness ratings showed that there was a statistically significant main effect for *Time* ($F_{1, 152} = 16.39$, $p = 0.000$, $eta^2 = .12$). This means that all participants found speakers less accented on the posttest ($M_{post} = 3.41$, $SD = 1.64$) than they did on the pretest ($M_{pre} = 2.98$, $SD = 1.32$, a difference of .43 on a 7-point scale). However, no significant interaction effect was found between time and contact groups. One explanation is that the control group, while not participating in intergroup collaborative activities, were nonetheless enrolled in an anthropology class which utilized a curriculum that might have enhanced the improvement in this construct.

Effects of contact activities on oral proficiency ratings. For oral proficiency ratings, no main effect achieved statistical significance ($F_{1, 152} = 2.02$, $p = 0.16$). However, the *Time* x *Contact* group interaction effect was statistically significant ($F_{1,152} = 7.27$, $p = 0.007$, $eta^2 = .025$). Tukey's HSD procedure was conducted to analyze the interaction between time and contact group. The contrasts revealed that the contact group rated the ITAs' and graduates students' speech samples higher on the posttest ($M = 4.20$) than they had on the pretest ($M = 3.79$, or a difference of .41), while the no-contact group's scores did not really differ between pretest ($M = 4.30$) and posttest ($M = 4.26$). However, as seen in the comprehensibility ratings above, the two groups were different from the outset with their pre-tests. Some additional variables that have not been identified in this study could cause the lack of change in the no-contact group. At the same time, some idiosyncratic interpersonal dynamics of the contact meetings might have influenced the change of the contact group's ratings. Future research can replicate the collaborative activities with other classes of undergraduate students to confirm the effects of the contact intervention.

Effects of contact activities on stereotyping ratings. A statistically significant main effect for *Time* ($F_{1,152} = 5.44$, $p = 0.010$, $eta^2 = .016$) was found for stereotyping ratings such that both participant groups' posttest scores ($M_{post} = 4.25$, $SD = 1.42$) exceeded pretest scores ($M_{pre} = 4.08$, $SD = 1.30$, or a .17 increase on a 7-point scale). An interaction effect (*Time* x *Contact*) was not significant ($p = 0.088$, $eta^2 = .014$). Nonetheless, the increase in the contact group from pretest ($M = 3.98$) to posttest ($M = 4.21$, or a .23 increase) was higher than that in the non-contact group (pretest M = 4.26, posttest M = 4.31, or a .05 increase).

Undergraduates' answers to the reflection questions at the end of the speech sample rating survey. The reflection question responses provided insight into the impact of the interventions throughout the semester. The qualitative responses from the contact group supported the quantitative findings in that the contact activities indeed affected undergraduate' attitudes toward ITAs or international students in general.

> ..... Growing up in the U.S., it was always very clear to me how different we were to everyone else in the world, through the media. But now that I've interacted with the students from other cultures, I realize that yes we are different in some ways, like our cultures, history, but we are more alike than the American media tends to portray.

> ... now I feel like I have become a little more open-minded towards individuals from other nationalities. .... Prior to those experiences, ... I would not go out of my way to make conversation with those particular individuals...After interactions, I feel like I would be more willing to interact with those individuals.

> Throughout the activities this semester, I can say that they have helped me see a greater perspective on people from other cultures....I can see that their culture [and] way of speaking serves a purpose and must be respected just like we treat our own [language/culture]. I think that these activities were also beneficial to the rest of the class as well.

International students' attitudes toward undergraduate students. Thirty-two international students who had participated in the contact activities completed the language and culture surveys. First, findings showed that international students' willingness to interact or communicate with American students changed significantly from before to after the intervention (t = 3.76, p = 0.001, Cohen's d = .78). The effect size was moderate to large. Students' responses were in the mid-range, suggesting perhaps a non-committal stance, but at the pretest period when international students did not have a chance to interact with any American students, their responses were lower and thus less positive (M = 3.14). Nonetheless, after the three-time contact activities, they appeared to be more positive, and inclined to interact with American students (Interaction inclination), and look for chances to communicate with them (*M* = 4.07, or a difference of .93 on a 7-point scale). Given that IEP students in the U.S. can find it very difficult to meet and interact with English speakers on campus, this finding is especially noteworthy.

Table 3. Pretest and Posttest Means for Three Attitude Aspects

Variables	Contact (*n* = 32)			
	Pretest		Posttest	
	Mean	SD	Mean	SD
Interaction inclination	3.14	1.21	4.07	1.19
Collaboration comfort	3.45	.61	4.43	.86
Cultural model	3.78	1.21	3.72	.98

Note. All ratings are on a scale of 1=negative attribute to 7=positive attribute.

International students' collaboration willingness with American students was also examined (Collaboration comfort). A paired *t*-test was conducted to compare mean scores between pretest and posttest. After the contact experience, international students felt significantly more confortable in collaborating with American students than they did before such experience, with the effect size being strong ($t = 8.04$, $p = 0.000$, Cohen's $d = 1.31$). Their mean score went from 3.45 for the pre-test to 4.43 for the post-test, or a difference of .98 on a 7-point scale. However, the contact intervention did not influence students' perspectives of their own culture.

Discussion

The current study showed that three sessions of structured contact activities between U.S. undergraduate and international students over the course of one semester could bring a positive change in their attitudes toward each other. Undergraduate students' contact with international students in collaborative activities led them to change some of their perceptions of ITAs' audio-recorded speech performances. The results of four repeated measures 2 (Time) x 2 (Contact) ANOVAs revealed that although all students were enrolled in an anthropology class called *Language and Culture*, students who participated in the contact activities evaluated ITA speech as more comprehensible and orally more proficient than those who took part in the traditional curriculum alone. In terms of comprehensibility, even though the interaction effect missed the significance threshold of $p < .025$, the contact group showed some changes in the improvements of their ratings after the contact intervention. Some qualitative responses made by undergraduates suggested an increased respect for people from other cultures. The contact activity did not necessarily affect their accent perception ratings; that is, both groups of students found the ITAs' speech less accented at post-test compared to their pre-test ratings, which is consistent with previous findings (Kang et al, 2014).

This positive impact of the contact experience on people's perception has been well documented (Pettigrew & Tropp, 2006; Kang & Rubin, 2012; Kang et al, 2014; Staples et al, 2014). This result supports the previous studies of intergroup contact in that structured contact situations which meet the optimal conditions of Contact Theory (Allport, 1954) can lead to listeners' prejudice reduction even in classroom contexts. In this study, the intervention was unique because it was embedded in the classroom activities at three points during the semester. Students in the contact group did not have to look for opportunities to interact with international students. In fact, this is a good case in point. More often than not, students who are opened-minded and willing to adapt to new cultures and diversity may voluntarily participate in various intercultural activities. However, those who are really in need to change their stereotyped attitudes or perceptions may not seek any intervention opportunities themselves. The findings of the current study were especially important because it was targeted at those who were in the latter category and still showed that changes could be made to those groups of people.

Contact activities in the context of an undergraduate course. From the perspective of undergraduate studies' course curriculum, the current study attracts its own attention. As part of Liberal Arts core curriculum requirements, it is common for undergraduate students to take an Anthropology 101 (or equivalent) class, which intends to introduce various cultures and languages, and make a case for diversity. However, the current study demonstrated that simply taking the class itself may not bring pronounced attitude changes to students. In the current study, students in the no-contact group took the class but did not participate in any face-to-face activities with international students. They only changed their ratings of perceived accent, but not of comprehensibility, oral proficiency, or stereotyping. This suggests that it is important to incorporate hands-on contact experience in the curriculum, which can benefit both undergraduate and intentional students. While some universities may have clubs, seminars, and classes that help both international students and American undergraduates interact together, these are not common at most universities in the U.S., but should be supported and promoted (Kovtun, 2011). Overall, the elaborated procedure of the current study, although a bit labor intensive, provides a blue print for individuals in other schools who want to implement interventions in their courses.

The ITAs or three international students who provided the speech samples were not the ones with whom the undergraduate students interacted. That is, there was no actual contact with the speakers who provided the speech samples. Nevertheless, some of the undergraduates' ratings were influenced by the intervention. That means that undergraduate students who engage in structured contact activities with international students can rate ITAs as more comprehensible and orally proficient. In addition, it should be noted that in order to change undergraduate students' attitudes toward ITA speech, they did not have to interact with ITAs themselves. In this study, they simply interacted with other international students.

Attributing issues with ITA speech to other sources. As Kang and her colleagues (2014) argue, the criticism of ITA speech is not directly prompted by the ITAs' language proficiency, but rather is a reflection of inter-group prejudice and stereotyping (Lindemann, 2002). The stereotyping measure itself did not turn out to be significantly different before and after the contact intervention in the current study. Nonetheless, the overall perception of international students' speech (oral proficiency) improved after the contact activities. The participants reported how much they enjoyed the activities and how beneficial they were to them. Although the intervention was between international students and U.S. undergraduate students, this result may have implications for the ITA community. It might be possible that U.S. undergraduate students hold negative stereotypes (Miller, 2002) simply because they consider ITAs as foreigners or outsiders. However, through structured, positive contact, U.S. undergraduates might re-categorize ITAs or all international students as a mutual identity, as can be seen from an undergraduate student's comment, *"but we are more alike than the American media tends to portray."*

Uses of contact interventions on U.S. campuses. Graduate teaching assistants teach undergraduate courses in every major research university in the United States, and many of these are international TAs (Minchew & Couvillion, 2003). Accordingly, improving U.S. students' attitudes or willingness to engage with non-native speakers of English will not only help them better learn from ever-growing numbers of international instructors on campus but also better interact with their future international classmates. Accordingly, these types of activities incorporated in an undergraduate core course can open up a promising future for campus globalization. Examples of possible activities include role-plays between ITAs and students, cultural discussions about differences or similarities, cooperative puzzle solving games, or team building activities. Furthermore, some of the activities implemented in this study can be used as a complement in ITA training programs or workshops. They can be further incorporated in student orientations in science, technology, engineering, and math (STEM) fields or international faculty training programs.

What is also important is the impact of this contact on international students or ITAs. Participating in this positive contact and interacting with U.S. undergraduates in a structured manner has helped them positively change their attitudes toward U.S. students. Although the current study involved as-yet unmatriculated international students in the actual intervention, and not actual ITAs, it can be argued that this activity would be effective in promoting ITAs' interaction with U.S. students. It would be interesting to directly measure how ITAs' self-confidence or the level of interaction with undergraduate students might change after this kind of contact intervention.

Conclusion

Still most colleges and universities do not often make tangible efforts toward improving students' intercultural understanding

(Rubin, 2002; Kang et al, 2014). As a way to remedy this common shortcoming, this study illustrated a concrete model of how we could apply such an idea, and its effectiveness on students' rating behaviors and attitude changes. In line with the arguments of previous studies (Fitch & Morgan, 2003; Kang & Rubin, 2012; Staples et al, 2014), we maintain that universities, colleges, and departments should promote views of international students and ITAs as essential agents who can foster real globalization on our campus.

Areas for further research. The importance of contact interventions in higher education can be further supported with more extended research. First, due to the large number of undergraduate students involved in this study, the current research design could not arrange a matching number of ITAs who could participate in the intervention. Accordingly, largely ESL international students were the primary interlocutors with U.S. students, and the changes of their attitude were examined in this study. Future research can directly investigate the impact of contact interventions on ITAs' performances or their interaction skills with undergraduate students in the classrooms. In addition, it is important to find out how participants' evaluations of ITA speech changes over time. Possibly the effect of the contact on undergraduates' perceptions of accented spoken English may not persist over time; that is, whether or not the effect is only for a short period of time is worth examining. Another area to improve the research design is systematic administration of the intervention. Whoever plans to administer these contact activities should prepare specific guidelines for each party and supervise each participant to ensure that everyone can fully understand the procedures and enjoy the activities.

Finally, contact activities themselves can be evaluated for their effectiveness. If they are implemented in the classroom with a large number of participants, some activities may work better than others. For example, our second day activity, "cultural values and proverbs," was not as well received as others for the interaction among students. It was speculated that certain expressions were somewhat too advanced or vague for some international students to utilize. On the other hand, the third activity, the "helium stick and spaghetti tower" activities in the gym, was excellent in terms of getting participants engaged. In-depth qualitative studies including face-to-face interviews with ITAs or undergraduate students can be conducted after each contact activity so that we can gain insights into participants' reaction to a certain activity.

In a Nutshell

1. It may be that U.S. undergraduate students' complaints are frequently more a function of students' stereotyped expectations than of ITAs' objective language and communication skills.
2. Lower level (freshman) core courses provide an excellent opportunity to integrate intercultural contact activities, which simultaneously achieve course objectives and improve the campus learning environment.
3. Structured activities between U.S. students and international students that meet the ideal conditions of the Contact Hypothesis (Allport, 1954) may lead U.S. students to evaluate ITA speech as more comprehensible and more orally proficient.
4. Both groups of students (i.e., U.S. and international) are more inclined to interact with each other after such activities, generating an inclusive student population and more preparation to successfully navigate a globalized world post-graduation.
5. Students who are more open-minded about L2-accented (ITA) speech may in fact have more positive experiences and more successful learning in ITA classrooms.
6. Results showed that after the contact exercises, undergraduate students in the contact group evaluated the accented speech of recorded ITAs significantly more positively compared to what they had previously and to those in the non-contact group.
7. The contact intervention also brought about international students' positive attitude changes.
8. The findings demonstrate a possible classroom model to improve U.S. students' communication in linguistically diverse contexts.

References

Ahn, J., & Moore, D. (2011). The relationship between students' accent perception and accented voice instructions and its effect on students' achievement in an interactive multimedia environment. *Journal of Educational Multimedia and Hypermedia, 20*(4), 319-335.

Albert, R.D. (1983). The intercultural sensitizer or culture assimilator: A cognitive approach. In D. Landis & R. Brislin (Eds.), *Handbook of intercultural training: Vol. 2. Issues in training methodology* (pp. 186-217). New York: Pergamon.

Allport, G.W. (1954). *The nature of prejudice.* Cambridge, MA: Addison-Wesley.

Aronson, E., Stephan, C., Sikes, J., Blaney, N., & Snapp, M. (1978). *The jigsaw classroom.* Beverly Hills, CA: Sage.

Ates, B., & Eslami, Z.R. (2012). Teaching experiences of native and nonnative English-speaking graduate teaching assistants and their perceptions of preservice teachers. *Journal on Excellence in College Teaching, 23*(3), 99-127.

Bennett, C. I. (1995). Preparing teachers for cultural diversity and National Standards of Academic Excellence. *Journal of Teacher Education, 46*(4), 259-265.

Borgardus, E.S. (1925). Measuring social distances. *Journal of Applied Sociology, 9*, 299-308.

Creswell, J. W., & Plano Clark, V. L. (2007). *Designing and conducting mixed method research.* Thousand Oaks, CA: Sage Publications.

Derwing, T.M., & Munro, M.J. (1997). Accent, intelligibility, and comprehensibility: Evidence from four L1s. *Studies in Second Language Acquisition, 19*(1), 1-16.

Derwing, T.M., & Munro, M.J. (2005). Second language accent and pronunciation teaching: A research-based approach. *TESOL Quarterly, 39*(3), 379-397.

Derwing, T.M., Rossiter, M.J., & Munro, M.J. (2002). Teaching native speakers to listen to foreign-accented speech. *Journal of Multilingual and Multicultural Development, 23*(4), 245-59.

Fitch, F., & Morgan, S.E. (2003). "Not a lick of English:" Constructing the ITA identity through student narratives. *Communication Education, 52*, 297-310.

Furnham, A., & Alibhai, N. (1985). The friendship networks of foreign students: A replication and extension of the functional model. *International Journal of Psychology, 20*(6), 709-722.

Gass, S., & Varonis, E.M. (1984). The effect of familiarity on the comprehensibility of nonnative speech. *Language Learning, 34*(1), 65–87.

Gorsuch, G. (2003). The educational cultures of international teaching assistants and U.S. universities. *TESL-EJ, 7*(3), 1-18.

Kang, O. (2012). Impact of rater characteristics on ratings of international teaching assistants' oral performance. *Language Assessment Quarterly, 9*, 249-269.

Kang, O., & Rubin, D.L. (2009). Reverse linguistic stereotyping: Measuring the effect of listener expectations on speech evaluation. *Journal of Language and Social Psychology, 28*, 441-456.

Kang, O., & Rubin, D. (2012). Inter-group contact exercises as a tool for mitigating undergraduates' attitudes toward ITAs. *Journal of Excellence in College Teaching, 23*(3), 159-166.

Kang, O., Rubin, D., & Lindemann, S. (2014). Mitigating U.S. undergraduates' attitudes toward International Teaching Assistants. *TESOL Quarterly.* DOI: 10.1002/tesq.192

Kovtun, O. (2011). International student adaptation to a U.S college: A mixed methods exploration of the impact of a specialized first-year course at a large Midwestern institution. *Journal of Student Affairs Research and Practice, 48*(3), 349-366.

Lambert, W.E., Hodgson, R.C., Gardner, R.C. & Fillenbaum, S. (1960). Evaluational reactions to spoken language. *Journal of Abnormal and Social Psychology, 60*, 44-51.

LaRocco, M. (2012). Chinese international teaching assistants and the essence of intercultural competence in university contexts. In G. Gorsuch (Ed.), *Working theories for teaching assistant development* (pp. 609-653). Stillwater, OK: New Forums Press.

Lindemann, S. (2002). Listening with an attitude: A model of native-speaker comprehension of non-native speakers in the United States. *Language in Society, 31*(3), 419-441. DOI:10.1017/S0047404502020286

Liu, J. (2005). Chinese graduate teaching assistants teaching freshman composition to native English speaking students. In E. Llurda (Ed.), *Non-native language teachers: Perceptions, challenges and contributions to the profession* (155-177). New York, NY: Springer.

Mak, A.S., Brown, P.M., & Wadey, D. (2014). Contact and attitudes toward international students in Australia: Intergroup anxiety and intercultural communication emotions as mediators. *Journal of Cross-Cultural Psychology, 45*(3), 491-504.DOI:10.1177/0022022113509883

Miller, N. (2002). Personalization and the promise of contact theory. *Journal of Social Issues, 58*, 387–410. DOI: 10.1111/1540-4560.00267

Minchew, S.S. & Couvillion, M.B. (2003). A comparison of American and international students' lifestyles and perceptions of the university experience. *National Forum of Applied Educational Research Journal, 13*(3), 1-8.

Neulip, J.W., & McCroskey, J.C. (1997). The development of a U.S. and generalized ethnocentrism scale. *Communication Research Reports, 14*, 385-398. DOI:10.1080/08824099709388682

Northern Arizona University (2014). 2013-2014 LOUIE Course Catalogue. Retrieved from https://www.peoplesoft.nau.edu/psp/ps90pr_1/EMPLOYEE/HRMS/c/SA_LEARNING_MANAGEMENT.CLASS_SEARCH.GBL?Page=SSR_CLSRCH_ENTRY&Action=U.

Pettigrew, T.F., & Tropp, L.R. (2006). A meta-analytic test of intergroup contact theory. *Journal of Personality and Social Psychology, 90*, 751–783.

Rao, N. (1995). The Oh No! syndrome: A language-expectation model of undergraduates' negative reactions toward foreign teaching assistants. *Paper pre-

sented at the annual meeting of the International Communication Association, Albuquerque, NM.

Rubin, D.L., & Smith, K. (1990). Effects of accent, ethnicity, and lecture topic on undergraduates' perceptions of non-native English speaking teaching assistants. *International Journal of Intercultural Relations, 14,* 337-353.

Rubin, D.L. (2002). Help! My professor (or doctor or boss) doesn't talk English! In J. Martin, T. Nakayama, & L. Flores (Eds.), *Readings in intercultural communication: Experiences and contexts* (pp. 127-137). Boston, MA: McGraw-Hill.

Smith, R.A., Strom, R.E. & Muthuswamy, N. (2005). Undergraduates' rating of domestic and international teaching assistants: Timing of data collection and communication intervention. *Journal of Intercultural Communication and Research, 34*(1), 3-21.

Spencer-Rodgers, J., & McGovern, T. (2002). Attitudes toward the culturally different: The role of intercultural communication barriers, affective responses, consensual stereotypes, and perceived threat. *International Journal of Intercultural Relations, 26*(6), 609-631. DOI:10.1016/S0147-1767(02)00038-X

Staples, S., Kang, O., & Wittner, E. (2014). Considering interlocutors in university discourse communities: Impacting U.S. undergraduates' perceptions of ITAs through a structured contact program. *English for Specific Purposes, 35,* 54-65.

Summers, M., & Volet, S. (2008). Students' attitudes towards culturally mixed groups on international campuses: Impact of participation in diverse and non-diverse groups. *Studies in Higher Education, 33*(4), 357-370. DOI:10.1080/03075070802211430

Yook, E., & Albert, R.D. (1999). Perceptions of international teaching assistants: The interrelatedness of intercultural training, cognition and emotion. *Communication Education, 48*(1), 1-17. DOI:10.1080/03634529909379148

Zahn, C.J., & Hopper, R. (1985). Measuring language attitudes: The speech evaluation instrument. *Journal of Language and Social Psychology, 4*(2), 113-123. DOI:10.1177/0261927X8500400203

Zhang, Y. (2012). Rapport management of international teaching assistants in their teaching. In G. Gorsuch (Ed.), *Working theories for teaching assistant development* (pp. 367-392). Stillwater, OK: New Forums Press.

Appendix

Language and Culture Survey

Your Name:
Your home language:

1. I do not like to interact with American people.*
   1 = Strongly Agree   *7 = Strongly Disagree*
   1   2   3   4   5   6   7

2. I would not want an American roommate.*
   1 = Strongly Agree   *7 = Strongly Disagree*
   1   2   3   4   5   6   7

3. It is ok for us as international students to study here and then remain in the United States.*
   1 = Strongly Agree   *7 = Strongly Disagree*
   1   2   3   4   5   6   7

4. I would feel comfortable working with American students on class projects.*
   1 = Strongly Agree   *7 = Strongly Disagree*
   1   2   3   4   5   6   7

5. I try/will try to sit apart from American students in the class, if I have a chance.*
   1 = Strongly Agree   *7 = Strongly Disagree*
   1   2   3   4   5   6   7

6. I try to avoid talking with American students because I'm afraid I won't be able to understand them.*
   1 = Strongly Agree   *7 = Strongly Disagree*
   1   2   3   4   5   6   7

7. I try to avoid talking with American students because I don't think they'll be able to understand me.*
   1 = Strongly Agree   *7 = Strongly Disagree*
   1   2   3   4   5   6   7

8. My culture should be the role model for other cultures.*
   1 = Strongly Agree   *7 = Strongly Disagree*

1   2   3   4   5   6   7

9. I look for a chance to speak with American people.*
1 = Strongly Agree   *7 = Strongly Disagree*
1   2   3   4   5   6   7

10. I feel uncomfortable when American people speak English around me.*
1 = Strongly Agree   *7 = Strongly Disagree*
1   2   3   4   5   6   7

ITAs' Perceptions of ITA Teaching and Training: The Importance of Ongoing and Contextualized Training and Mentoring Programs

By Diana Trebing,[1] Saginaw Valley State University

This qualitative descriptive study analyzes the ways in which international teaching assistants (ITAs) understand and make sense of their roles as international instructors on a central U.S. university campus. This study also suggests necessary changes and additions to ITA training programs, and support as specified by the research participants themselves. Following a qualitative interviewing approach, this study drew upon 15 in-depth interviews with first time and returning ITAs. Analyses revealed that, despite their differences in cultural, educational, and linguistic backgrounds, the ITAs went through similar experiences when adjusting to their teaching assignments in the U.S. For instance, many research participants were passively aware of cultural and social rules of U.S. classrooms, but were not able to apply this knowledge actively in a classroom context. The data also revealed that ITAs see communication as a two-way street between teachers and students. Finally, the results showed that ITAs should receive contextualized and ongoing ITA training and support while they are teaching for the first time in the U.S. It appeared that many research participants were not able to understand the classroom information they were given prior to their first teaching assignment.

---

1. Author contact: dtrebing@svsu.edu

Due to phenomena such as international tourism, migration, and the Internet, our contemporary world is developing into a global village. No matter where we live, we need to be able to communicate with people from other cultures and countries as millions of people leave their homes to embark on journeys to other places in the world. The reasons for and length of these travels are manifold (Christofi & Thompson, 2007; Spencer-Rodgers, 2000). One group of these international sojourners is international students in the U.S. educational system. According to the Institute of International Education (2014a), 819,644 international students are currently studying in the U.S., the majority of whom are seeking graduate degrees. According to Spencer-Rodgers (2001), these students are often considered a homogeneous group. Instead, they represent over 185 countries and differ markedly with regard to native language, ethnicity, and educational background. Furthermore, Skow and Stephan (2000) emphasize that expectations of international students, U.S. students, and faculty might vary significantly due to "differences in cultural values, learning and teaching styles, and verbal and nonverbal ways of speaking" (p. 357). Therefore, understanding U.S. classroom behavior can be a complicated endeavor for international students. However, it is even more complicated for international teaching assistants (ITAs) who are expected to function "effectively" in the U.S. classroom almost immediately after their arrival in the U.S., both as student *and* as teacher.

The author as an ITA. Being an ITA myself who had sole responsibility for teaching two courses one week after my arrival in the U.S., I know how difficult and challenging it can be to effectively fulfill the simultaneous roles of international student and graduate teaching assistant. After coming to the U.S. from Germany in the Fall Semester of 2000 to pursue a master's degree, I was fortunate to be offered an assistantship teaching courses in English as a Second Language (ESL) to international undergraduate and graduate students who wanted to study at U.S. colleges and universities. Like so many other ITAs, I had to get accustomed to teaching in another culture since my experiences studying and teaching in Germany and the U.S. were very different. Like so many other ITAs, I also had only a one-week time period in between my arrival in the U.S. and stepping into the classroom for the first time. Looking back, this transition period was a rather scary experience since I questioned my English language and teaching skills. I wondered every day whether my students were actually learning in my classes. Fortunately enough, my department and supervisors were very supportive and always listened to my concerns. I found their comments and support very helpful and comforting, and thus I gradually gained confidence as an international teacher in the U.S. However, this slowly-gained confidence was quickly shattered during my first semester teaching in my doctoral program a few years later.

A shift to teaching American undergraduates. Instead of teaching international students, I was now faced by American undergraduate students who told me that my English was incomprehensible. Again, I asked my supervisors and fellow doctoral students for advice and was told that it was not my level of English language ability, but that there might be other issues in the classroom that were leading to student complaints. I have to admit that to this day I am not exactly sure what happened in this specific class that I was teaching my first semester in the doctoral program. It was probably a combination of my unfamiliarity with course content and U.S. undergraduate student expectations, different expectations in teaching styles, and the students' unfamiliarity with international instructors that made my classroom lectures difficult to follow. This experience had two effects on my academic career: First, I had to regain confidence as an international teacher in the U.S., and second, I started exploring research studies on ITAs in order to make sense of my personal experiences. Apart from gaining more knowledge through these research studies on ITAs, I also became active in the training workshops and courses my university offered to ITAs. In this context, I spoke to incoming ITAs about my experiences and co-conducted training workshops with American ITA mentors and teachers. Throughout this time, I was also the only ITA who became part of an ITA mentoring group consisting of American ESL specialists who visited the ITAs' courses to give advice and offer feedback on teaching and to listen to any concerns the ITAs might have had. These personal experiences and my role as a mentor for incoming ITAs brought me to this research study, a study that focuses on the experiences of 15 ITAs from various countries who shared their own ideas on how to enhance their university's ITA training program.

Literature Review

ITAs in U.S. colleges and universities. Graduate students have been employed as teaching assistants (TAs) at U.S. colleges and universities for several decades. According to Smith, Byrd, Nelson, Barrett, and Constantinides (1992), the reason for establishing a TA system at U.S. colleges and universities was the shortage of qualified faculty immediately after World War II. Since then, basic undergraduate courses have often been taught by graduate students pursuing either master's or doctoral degrees. Although some TAs might be assisting professors in grading exams or giving lectures, the title "teaching assistant" is ambiguous. With regard to teaching, they may lead laboratory experiments, discussion groups, recitation sections, or might even be in charge of independent courses and thus have sole responsibility for developing course materials, grading exams, and assigning final grades.

In her dissertation, Bailey (1982) discussed the dual role of TAs, both domestic and international, as they are positioned in between faculty and students. She further pointed out that, although many undergraduate courses are taught by TAs, many TAs are not recruited for their interest or abilities in teaching. Instead, students often take these positions to finance their graduate degrees. As a result, the TA system came under scrutiny when numerous parents and students asked for senior faculty to teach undergraduate courses. As a result, many colleges and universities started implementing TA training workshops in the 1970s and 1980s to improve undergraduate teaching and learning. At the same time as the TA system received a lot of attention, the number of graduate students from the U.S. decreased. Vacancies in graduate programs, therefore, were filled with increasing numbers of international students who were also offered assistantships in order to finance their graduate degrees. According to the Institute of International Education (2014a), of the 819,644 international students who are currently studying in the U.S., 339,993 are registered at the undergraduate level and 311,204 at the graduate level, with the remaining 73,528 pursuing non-degree options. Most of these international students are from China (233,597), India (96,754), South Korea (70,627), and Saudi Arabia (44,566). Looking at the fields of study, 21.8% (or 178,984) international students are enrolled in Business and Management degrees, followed by degrees in the STEM fields: 18.8% (or 154,186) in Engineering and 9.5% (or 77,560) in Math and Computer Science (see also Institute of International Education, 2014b). Additionally, 21% of all international students receive funding from their respective U.S. colleges and universities, mostly in the form of teaching, research, or administrative assistantships. Taking on the role of a TA is complicated for ITAs as "these students face the challenge not only of entering the American way of life, but also of coming to terms with the role of student and teacher and the expectations attached to these roles within the American university system" (Ross & Krider, 1992, p. 279).

As early as 1968, the National Association for Foreign Student Affairs (NAFSA) reported a growing nation-wide concern about the role of ITAs on U.S. campuses (Meesuwan, 1992). These early complaints on the effectiveness of ITAs led to various responses. While the general public usually responded with outrage about the perceived poor performance of many ITAs, several states passed laws that mandated testing for ITAs and sometimes even for international faculty (Hoekje & Linnell, 1994; Smith et al, 1992; Thomas & Monoson, 1991). Apart from legislative responses, professional organizations and the colleges and universities themselves started addressing ITA issues and implemented training and testing programs for ITAs.

A rise in ITA research. All of these events contributed to an increase in research on ITAs. The extant literature shows that many American undergraduate students complain about their ITAs' level of English proficiency, especially as it relates to pronunciation and intonation patterns, and thus object to being taught by ITAs. As a result, numerous research studies on ITAs focused on the perceptions of American undergraduate students toward their international instructors (Plakans, 1995, 1997; Rubin & Smith, 1990, Yook & Albert, 1999) and on challenges in the classroom based on various conceptualizations of communicative competence (Hoekje & Williams, 1992, 1994; Neves & Sanyal, 1991; Rubin, 1992). Additionally, other studies focused on creating effective ITA training programs and workshops (Briggs, 1994; Stevenson & Jenkins, 1994; Tang & Sandell, 2000), and improving teaching and cross-cultural skills in the classroom (Bailey, 1982; Bresnahan & Cai, 2000; Gorsuch, 2003; Smith, 2012). Only a few studies, however, have actually focused on the perceptions of ITAs themselves (LaRocco, 2012; Meesuwan, 1992; Ross & Krider, 1992; Tavana, 2005).

Communicative competence. The literature on ITA scholarship illustrates that the core of the ITA debate from the undergraduates' perspective is the ITAs' perceived lack of English language proficiency. It further shows that researchers have argued that ITAs do not only need to have linguistic proficiency (i.e., grammar and vocabulary), but also effective sociolinguistic and discourse skills (i.e., classroom behavior, levels of formality, classroom management) in order to be successful teachers in U.S. classrooms. All of these factors are part of communicative competence, a key concept in second language learning.

Initially, theorists such as Chomsky (1965) only related this concept to linguistic competence (i.e., the correct use of grammar and syntax). Later on, the knowledge of norms of social interaction, nonverbal communication, and discourse patterns was included (Grimshaw, 1973; Hymes, 1974; Savignon, 1997). Based on reconceptualizations such as these, Canale and Swain (1980) created an integrative model, as modified by Canale (1983), suggesting that communication in classroom contexts involves four aspects: grammatical, sociolinguistic, discourse, and strategic competencies.

Grammatical (linguistic) competence and ITAs. Grammatical competence is defined as the knowledge of the rules of morphology, syntax, lexical items, semantics, and phonology (pronunciation) in order "to determine and express accurately the literal meaning of utterances" (Canale & Swain, 1980, p. 30). With regard to ITA training, grammatical competence has received most attention since numerous research studies focused on the inadequate English language proficiency of ITAs. As a result, many ITA training programs include activities targeting pronunciation and grammar skills. As Hoekje and Williams (1992, 1994) point out though, focusing on grammatical competence is difficult since "the time for [ITA] training is short, whereas the improvement of grammatical accuracy can be a time-consuming, long-term process" (p. 248, 1992). As a result, departmental ITA mentors, ESL specialists or not, should provide language support to ITAs, but not focus their efforts solely on improving the grammatical competence of ITAs, as will be argued below.

Sociolinguistic competence and ITAs. Sociolinguistic competence refers to the knowledge of the sociocultural rules for speaking and rules for discourse. For ITAs, sociocultural knowledge is very important as they need to learn cultural and social rules as they pertain to U.S. classrooms. For instance, rules related to interactive teaching styles, appropriate student-teacher relationships, and knowledge of departmental and college rules and standards are crucial for successful teachers. As the responses of the ITAs in this study show, many ITAs struggled with this particular competency. Although they had a basic understanding, they wanted to learn more about teaching methodologies, the undergraduate students' cultural backgrounds, U.S. culture, and the role of TAs in general.

Suggestions for ITA support personnel. In this context, personnel in universities and departments can provide a lot of support, particularly if they are not ESL specialists, and who may not feel qualified to work directly with ITAs on language learning. For example, engaging in interactions with undergraduate students outside the classroom, or observing experienced TAs, can help ITAs understand the standards of a classroom. Besides, departments can provide sample syllabi or teaching activities so that ITAs can learn how to effectively structure their own lesson plans.

Discourse competence and ITAs. Discourse competence, as defined by Canale (1983), is the ability to produce cohesive and coherent discourse at both the productive and interpretive levels. In other words, ITAs not only need to be aware of grammatical and sociolinguistic rules, they also need to be able to apply them effectively in the classroom to help U.S. undergraduates digest content. Several studies (e.g., Axelson & Madden, 1994; Hoekje & Williams, 1992, 1994) have shown, however, that many ITAs fail to elaborate on key ideas in their lectures, use circular instead of linear communicative approaches, and have difficulty interpreting students' questions. It seems that many ITAs have passive discourse competence, but cannot apply the rules actively. This finding is supported in the current study.

Suggestions for ITA support personnel. As a result, instead of just telling ITAs about the university's rules and regulations or about how to teach a certain course, ITA mentors need to contextualize this information and give ITAs an opportunity to practice it. For instance, ITAs could be recorded during office hour role-plays or mini-teaching lessons so they can be guided to self-identify their strengths and weaknesses in the teaching talk which good discourse competence underpins. Departments could offer weekly meetings for both domestic and international TAs so that new ITAs can learn about the experiences of English native-speaking TAs, and pick up handy phrases and discourse structures to better organize their talks.

Strategic competence and ITAs. Strategic competence is defined as the knowledge of verbal and nonverbal strategies that may be used to compensate for the limitations in the other three areas of competence or to increase communicative effectiveness in general. As Hoekje and Williams (1992, 1994) note, this aspect of communicative competence may be crucial for ITA training as most ITAs have challenges with grammatical, sociolinguistic, and discourse competencies.

Suggestions for ITA support personnel. The authors suggest that instead of making English native-speaker competence the goal of ITA training, ITAs should be taught compensatory strategies. For example, mentors can train ITAs to use more written materials in class, to post lecture notes online and refer to them while in class, or to offer additional office hours to further discuss course content. Gorsuch and Sokolowski (2007) found that one Chinese physics ITA came to class early and put detailed outlines on the board and referred to them while giving his pre-lab talk. U.S. undergraduates who were later surveyed found this an effective compensatory communication tool.

Off the beaten path: Relational competence. Spitzberg and Cupach (1984, p. 109) created yet another, lesser-known component of communicative competence, which they named "relational competence." They argued that:

> [T]he perception of competence is a graduated phenomenon in which behaviors, affective responses, and cognition are enmeshed within an unfolding dynamic process of conversation. This dynamic process leads to impressions of a person or conversation as more or less appropriate and effective.

An important contribution of this concept is its focus on the relational nature of communication. This is crucial, since in ideal intercultural encounters, communicators show signs of close relationships such as relational ability, personal commitment, and interpersonal knowledge (Gudykunst & Kim, 2003; Spitzberg, 1994). Thus, the concept of relational competence makes unique contributions to ITA training. It was also mentioned several times by the participants in this study. For instance, research has shown that some undergraduate students have more negative attitudes towards ITAs to begin with (Damron, 2000; Fitch & Morgan, 2003; Gravois, 2005). These studies suggest strongly that communication in the classroom is a two-way street involving both teachers and students. In other words, just improving an ITA's overall communicative competence does not take the undergraduate students' preconceived attitudes and beliefs into account. As a result, undergraduate students should also be included in intercultural sensitivity training.

Suggestions for ITA support personnel. Departments should provide ITAs the opportunity to engage with U.S. undergraduate and graduate students outside the classroom, during informal "conversation corners" or "coffee talks." Consequently, the ITAs can learn about their potential students and become more comfortable interacting with them, and vice versa.

Taking into account ITAs' suggestions on communicative competence. The components of communicative competence have long guided ESL specialists' work with ITAs. Nonetheless, I further suggest that those who do research on ITAs and those who work with ITAs "on the ground" should also take into account what ITAs themselves say they need in the context of communicative competence. What aspects of communicative competence do ITAs consider to be challenging, or most needed? The current study attempts to explore this.

Acculturation. Apart from communicative competence, acculturation processes are also important in how well ITAs adjust to their lives in the U.S. Many international students have been academically successful in their native countries. Once they enter the U.S. educational system, however, they have to deal with a variety of new academic and social challenges, and often a new language as well. In the case of ITAs, the role of teacher needs to be added. Balancing these multiple roles can be very challenging and can lead to psychological and physiological symptoms of stress among international students (Mori, 2000; Pederson, 1991). As a consequence, it is crucial to know how ITAs adapt to and cope with the multiple challenges facing them.

Models of acculturation processes. Over the past decades, several models have been proposed to explain acculturation processes. In

1955, Lysgaard (1955) suggested that the cross-cultural adjustment of sojourners resembles the shape of a U-curve. He found that feelings of euphoria and optimism were followed by times of disorientation and crisis, and eventually feelings of integration into the host community. A decade later, Gullahorn and Gullahorn (1963) proposed a W-curve hypothesis which added the re-entry phase into the sojourner's native culture. The criticism of these early acculturation models is that they did not take into account the personal characteristics of the sojourners.

Since the latter part of the 20th century, researchers have proposed more nuanced models of acculturation processes. Berry's studies (1980, 1992, 2003) on acculturation are widely known. Berry was the first researcher who noted that a sojourner's identification with his or her home or host culture also influences the acculturation process. Thus, sojourners can either integrate or assimilate into the host culture, or separate or marginalize themselves. In other words, if an ITA maintains his or her cultural identity and, at the same time, tries to learn and adopt the rules and expectations of a U.S. classroom, he or she integrates in the U.S. educational system. If, on the other hand, the ITA identifies rigidly with his or her cultural identity and only applies rules learned in his or her educational system at home to the U.S. American classroom while rejecting U.S. standards, the ITA engages in a separatist strategy. These categories suggest that ITAs who engage in integration or assimilation strategies are likely going to be seen as more competent instructors as they try to adapt to their students' expectations. One can argue that by using an integrative or assimilative approach, ITAs are more likely going to develop more appropriate grammatical, sociolinguistic, discourse, and strategic competencies in order to fulfill the role of ITA effectively.

Purpose of the Study

The goal of this qualitative study was to describe and analyze the lived experiences of ITAs at a university in the Midwest in order to gain their perspectives and give voice to this international student and teacher population. Over the course of two semesters, I collected narratives from and conducted interviews with 15 ITAs in order to answer the following research question: What suggestions do ITAs themselves have for improving ITA training programs in order to improve teaching outcomes?

Method

Participants

ITAs. Eight of the participants were female and seven were male. They were in their early 20s to early 40s. The research participants came from: Bulgaria (1), China (1), Germany (2), India (5), Indonesia (1), Sudan (1), Taiwan (2), Thailand (1), and Tunisia (1). Eight were obtaining Ph.D. degrees and six were seeking master's degrees. Two research participants were classified as exchange students since they were not studying towards a degree in the U.S. The participants represented a wide variety of academic disciplines: Business (2), Chemistry (1), Economics (1), English (4), Linguistics (1), Mechanical Engineering (2), Microbiology (1), Psychology (1), Communication Studies (1), and Teaching English to Speakers of Other Languages (1).

Three of the participants were teaching for the first time in the U.S., seven were teaching their second semester, and five had taught for more than two semesters in the U.S. They were teaching small and large lecture courses, laboratory sections, and small discussion groups. Their classroom duties ranged from developing activities for new courses and choosing their own textbooks, to teaching assigned classroom materials and assisting a professor.

The researcher. Being a former international student from Germany and having studied at Midwestern University for seven years, I am very familiar with the campus and requirements for international students. As an ITA, I attended ITA training workshops and took the ITA proficiency test in order to be certified to teach. Because I was fortunate to hold teaching assistantships throughout my graduate studies, I am also deeply familiar with the challenges ITAs face. My experiences as an ITA mentor further contributed to my knowledge of ITAs' concerns and successes. These personal experiences as an ITA and ITA mentor influenced my decision to pursue an academic career in intercultural communication.

Materials

This study employed what Patton (2002) refers to as an unstructured interview with an interview guide approach. Since I did not have any preconceived categories of data that I might find, following Kvale's (1996) underlying assumptions of qualitative interview studies, an unstructured interview approach was especially appropriate in this research study. Additionally, unstructured interviews with interview guides are open-ended so that the participants have initial guidance with the research questions, but still have the chance to contribute their own thoughts and ideas.

According to Gerson and Horowitz (2002), conducting successful interview studies "depends on the prior construction of a theoretically and user-friendly interview schedule" (p. 205). To develop such an interview guide with open-ended, yet relevant questions, I thought about my personal experiences as an ITA and what I learned about being an ITA while teaching at the university. Additionally, I decided to pay close attention to the conversations during the university's ITA training workshops in which I had participated as an ITA mentor, speaking to incoming ITAs about my experiences and co-conducting several workshops with American ITA specialists. I tried to identify what kinds of topics the ITAs who participated in the workshops and who had just arrived in the U.S. were especially interested in, and sometimes worried about when thinking about their lives in a new country and as teachers in a new cultural setting. Among these topics were:

1. Not knowing what a TA is
2. Having difficulties understanding colloquial English
3. Not being respected in the classroom
4. Not knowing which class they were going to teach
5. Being overwhelmed with information related to immigration as well as university and departmental regulations and procedures
6. Managing time.

Based on these personal observations, I created a list of questions which I then discussed with an American ITA specialist. The two of us then re-grouped the questions into themes in order to have the interviews run more smoothly. See the Appendix for the instrument.

Following Kvale's (1996) suggestions for creating interview guides, I first asked questions about the participants' personal background, about their majors, about the courses they were teaching, and about previous teaching experiences in their home countries, because I assumed that these kinds of topics would not produce much anxiety. Depending on the participants' responses, I then turned to other topics, such as their experiences in U.S. classrooms, undergraduate student behavior, and differences and similarities between the U.S. and their home countries' educational systems. Towards the end of the interview, I turned to issues related to the participants' experiences with ITA training. Following this sequence was apparently effective since all research participants were very cooperative, and freely volunteered their opinions and ideas on their teaching and ITA training experiences at the university.

Procedure

In order to identify potential participants for this study, I contacted the university's ESL center where ITA courses were offered. Using criterion sampling, I visited several ITA training sessions and then introduced the study and asked for volunteers. A call inviting ITAs to participate was also sent via the university's ITA listserv. These methods yielded 15 research participants. Each of the 15 interviews, which lasted about 55 minutes on average, followed the same procedure. I met with each participant at the designated location, introduced the study again, answered any questions the participants had, and gave an overview of the topics that would be covered. Once each participant had signed a consent form, the interview was audio-recorded. After the interviews, each participant chose a pseudonym to ensure anonymity.

Analysis

The interviews were transcribed in detail, and in their entirety. Transcriptions included the frequent repetitions, pauses, laughter, and major emphases in intonation which are typical features of natural speech. Further, these kinds of verbal and nonverbal cues would help me with subsequent analysis of the data. After I completed the transcription of an interview, an American colleague working with ITAs on a regular basis listened to the recording while reading the transcript in order to clarify difficult-to-understand passages.

The transcribed interviews were then analyzed following Creswell's (2003) steps for qualitative data analysis and interpretation. First, the entire data set was read through in order to get an overall sense of its meaning, and to write down general thoughts. Second, a more thorough analysis was done using a coding procedure which was aimed at identifying major topics. In the case of this specific study, themes related to communicative competence and acculturation, foregrounded in the literature review, were focused on. Third, these overall themes were then used to break up the transcripts into smaller categories and "chunks," similar to Stewart and Shamdasani's (1990) "cut-and-paste" technique. Fourth, the transcriptions were cut apart and the data relevant to a particular topic were pasted together. Another ITA trainer and I, independently from each other, read through the document to identify patterns and connections between the various themes. Finally, we met in order to discuss the overall themes we had identified in the data. After reviewing these themes it became clear that the study participants focused on several issues related to acculturation (e.g., how to become an effective teacher; how ITA training--or the lack thereof--helped or hindered their teaching skills) and communicative competence (e.g., giving feedback on assignments, learning colloquial expressions). A context for these themes was provided in the literature review of this study, and will be further discussed in the Results section.

Results

During the interviews, all of the ITAs/research participants talked at length about the difficulties they were facing in their respective classrooms. The most persistent topic of interest was the role of ITA training and guidance, or lack thereof, at both the university and departmental levels. These could be organized into four main themes: 1. TA and ITA pre-teaching workshops, 2. guidance in academic departments, 3. advice from ITAs for new ITAs, and 4. recounting learning processes for classroom management.

TA and ITA pre-teaching workshops. In order to be able to teach at the university where this study took place, all TAs, both domestic and international, are required to attend a mandatory workshop either offered through the Graduate School or their respective departments before the beginning of their first teaching assignment. Since most of the departmental workshops are rather brief, most TAs attend a combination of Graduate School and departmental sessions.

Positive points. The ITAs' opinions on these workshops differed widely. Most of the ITAs found the training workshops prior to the beginning of the semester somewhat useful. Adam from India and Natapon from Thailand, for instance, pointed out that they learned a lot from the Graduate School speakers on how to deal with challenges in the classroom. Jiaxin from China and Sandra from Germany talked specifically about the sexual harassment training. Anna (Bulgaria), Guru (Indonesia), and Manoj (India) appreciated the lectures on effective classroom management and teaching methodology, but asked for more of these sessions. Additionally, Hadmin, also from India, liked his department's training on safety instructions in the labs.

Negative points. At the same time, many of the ITAs were not sure what the objectives of these workshops were and why they had to attend them. As Hadmin pointed out, "when I was told that I had to attend this workshop I didn't like it [...] because already I'm so much busy and then this thing comes up." MeiMei (Taiwan) admitted that she did not understand the purpose of many of the sessions since "they all seemed confusing." She added that most of the sessions in her departmental workshop were "not useful cause it's like we are just talking talk, talking theory but while you are trying to put them into practice then you will know what the problem is so I really feel the workshop is useless." In a similar vein, Jiaxin argued that there was so much information to digest that she felt tired and that "you can only understand something after you have experienced it." Thus, the latter two ITAs suggested that a training workshop prior to the beginning of the semester is less effective than one that is being conducted simultaneously to their first teaching assignment. Cyma, an ITA from India teaching science lab sections, stated:

> It was no help to me because I just need this program because I'm not an American student because I'm an international TA. [...] there's no point in telling me of what happens in the schools, that did not apply to me. That has nothing to do with the lab there and working in a lab [...] is definitely different so that thing was useless.

Cyma's comment is interesting since she also argued that she needed to learn more about her students' backgrounds and high school curricula in order to teach more effectively. Since the ITA training workshop attempts to give a brief overview on these issues, it seems as if Cyma was not capable prior to the semester of understanding the importance of the information she was given.

Guidance in academic departments. Judging from the ITAs' comments, receiving guidance and support throughout the semester was much more crucial than any of the general pre-semester training workshops. When given, departmental training helped the ITAs tremendously in coping with their teaching assignments. With regard to training and guidance given in academic departments throughout the semester, the 15 ITAs could be separated into four groups. These groups relate to Berry's (1980, 1992, 2003) categories of acculturation which will be explained in detail in the Discussion section.

ITAs without departmental support. Adam, Ahmed, and Natapon were the three ITAs who, apart from the required Graduate School workshops, had no training through their departments and no guidance while teaching. Natapon described this experience as thinking she was "fighting on her own." Adam pointed out that he did not get any teaching resources or help in developing his materials. Similarly, Ahmed from Sudan argued that his department "did not provide enough help. They just said, go teach, that's basically what they did." All of these three ITAs stated that they had to teach themselves how to become effective instructors and learn how to cope with their teaching assignments.

ITAs with programmed departmental support. Jiaxin and MeiMei were the two ITAs whose departments had an extensive training workshop; however, neither of them understood the objective of the workshop. They also did not feel welcomed within their department (i.e., they were not comfortable asking for help or advice), and thus felt they did not have any guidance. Jiaxin and MeiMei were the most unhappy ITAs; however, since it was their first semester teaching at the time of the interview, they were very likely still coping with their recent arrival in the U.S.

ITAs with informal departmental support. Apart from the Graduate School workshops, Anna (Bulgaria), Cyma, Guru (Indonesia), Manoj, Sandra, and Slouma (Tunisia) had not received any significant amount of training from their respective departments. However, they knew they were supported by their academic units. For example, Sandra and Guru knew that they could always approach their supervisors with questions and concerns. They were also appreciative that their supervisors shared their syllabi with them. Cyma and Manoj spoke very positively about the weekly TA meetings in their departments which helped them prepare for their classes. And Slouma and Anna felt supported by their friendly colleagues.

ITAs with programmed and informal departmental support. Ananya (India), Hadmin, Jan-Jakub (Germany), and Su-Ling (Taiwan) received both extensive training and guidance through their departments. All of these ITAs had to attend weekly meetings, either in the form of a credit-bearing course in their graduate program, or informal TA meetings, in order to discuss upcoming class assignments or challenges they were facing in their courses. Hadmin and Su-Ling were especially grateful for the mentoring they experienced in their departments. They both were observed by more experienced TAs as well as professors, and thus received feedback on their teaching methods. Ananya and Jan-Jakub felt their departments were very supportive and helped them whenever necessary. See Table 1 for a summary and comments from TAs, along with proposed interpretations (the results of the study).

Table 1. Summary and Comments on ITA Training and Support at the Departmental Level

Type of Departmental Support Provided	Sample ITA Comments and Proposed Interpretations
No departmental support No pre-semester workshop No guidance during semester	"I was fighting on my own." "No help in getting any teaching resources." "They just said, go teach, that's basically what they did." These ITAs felt overwhelmed and frustrated because they had to learn how to become effective instructors on their own without any help from mentors or their respective departments.
Programmed departmental support Extensive pre-semester workshop No guidance throughout semester	"They [the workshops] all seemed confusing." "You can only understand something once you have experienced it." "Not useful cause it's like we are just talking talk, talking theory." These ITAs received extensive training (e.g., teaching methodology, university/dept. rules and regulations, classroom management) which they were not able to comprehend prior to their teaching assignments. They also felt left alone during the semester because they were not comfortable approaching their departments with questions or concerns.

Informal departmental support No pre-semester workshop Guidance throughout the semester	"She [the faculty mentor] is always there for me." "I spoke to the chair and he gave me syllabi and teaching stuff to share." "This course has been going on for a very long time so everything has been decided. All the details are available, all the homeworks are available, all handouts are there. So it's pretty easy." Although these ITAs did not receive any pre-semester training, they felt comfortable in the classroom because of the departmental teaching support throughout the semester (e.g., weekly TA meetings, faculty/TA mentors, shared lesson plans or syllabi).
Programmed and informal departmental support Extensive pre-semester workshop Guidance throughout the semester	"But I'm very lucky because in my department we have one course for all new TAs, he [the instructor] invited different guest speakers and we learned about the conflict center and the writing center, that was helpful." "A mentor so he is around with us for four weeks, we watch how the procedures [in the Chemistry lab] is done. They help us." "I really have great colleagues in the Department so we try to prepare together the lesson plans for the week and share our workload. And also exchange ideas about what we do." These ITAs were the most comfortable teachers since they received extensive training and support throughout their teaching assignments.

Advice from ITAs for new ITAs. The research participants also had several suggestions for new ITAs which illustrates how they acculturated into the U.S. educational system, and show how they became effective international instructors. Among these were getting advice, learning about their students' backgrounds, being prepared for teaching, and taking care of their own health.

Getting advice. Most of the ITAs mentioned that getting advice from as many people as possible was the most crucial way for dealing with their teaching assignments, as well as their lives as graduate students. In this context, Ahmed and Slouma pointed out that it was important to ask different people such as professors, other TAs, and also friends and students about their thoughts and opinions about specific courses.

Learning about students' backgrounds. Adam said that having basic knowledge about U.S. classrooms such as knowing that students might be eating or drinking in class reduces "that sort of cultural shock [which is] something that international students need to be prepared for." Additionally, Natapon argued that it took her several semesters to understand that "the [U.S.] students have issues that are different from students in Thailand so sometimes I have to have compassion for things that we don't understand." Other ITAs were trying to understand why their undergraduate students were lacking basic math, computing, or writing skills. Yet others were surprised to learn about their students' workloads and other responsibilities outside the classroom.

Being prepared for teaching. The ITAs also suggested that new ITAs should be well-prepared for teaching. Ananya stated that with a detailed lesson plan, "other issues that might arise in the classroom are manageable [since] students pick up that you are prepared." Jiaxin even suggested that ITAs should prepare themselves for their teaching assignments prior to coming to the U.S. In her opinion, having a basic understanding of the concepts the ITAs are going to teach in their courses reduces the level of anxiety and thus increases an ITA's self-esteem as a teacher. Although Jiaxin's suggestion is well taken, it would be difficult to achieve if the academic units do not inform ITAs earlier about their specific teaching assignments; i.e., prior to their arrival in the U.S. A possible solution to this predicament might be virtual ITA training with which some universities have started experimenting (Zha & McCrory, 2006). In the case of virtual training, ITAs could engage with experienced TAs, ITA specialists, or department members prior to their arrival in the U.S. For example, incoming ITAs could join social networking sites with experienced TAs/ITAs and thus learn about potential challenges in the classroom.

Taking care of health. ITAs such as Anna, Guru, Jan-Jakub, and Su-Ling, who had full responsibility for a course including creating teaching materials, exams, and grading, were exhausted because of their time-consuming teaching preparation and taking their own graduate courses. Several ITAs including Ahmed and Sandra admitted that they put too much effort and time into their teaching duties during their first semester and thus felt overwhelmed. As a result, learning how to balance their workload and thus having more personal time seemed to be one of the learning processes that ITAs had to go through in order to cope with their teaching assignments and thus to become more efficient teachers in the U.S. ITAs' summarized suggestions are given in Table 2.

Table 2. ITAs' Suggestions for New ITAs

Get advice	Talk to as many professors, TAs, friends, and students to learn about U.S. classrooms and culture.
Learn about students' backgrounds	Know that students might be eating or drinking in class. Be aware that students have other responsibilities outside the classroom. Know that students might be underprepared for college
Be prepared for teaching	Prepare well-developed lesson plans. Learn about the course you are teaching.
Take care of your health	Learn how to balance your workload. Take some personal time.

Recounting learning processes for classroom management. When asked about their adjustment processes, all of the ITAs first pointed out that there were still many things they wanted to improve. Among the topics they wanted to improve were classroom management skills (i.e., having more interaction with students, giving better feedback on grading, improving lesson plans and assignments, and using more technology in the classroom), cultural knowledge (i.e., learning about the students' cultural background and U.S. culture in general), and communicative competence (i.e., improving pronunciation, speaking more fluently, familiarizing themselves with slang terms). However, the returning ITAs also pointed out that having taught for at least one semester helped them better understand how to become a more effective TA by changing their standards (e.g., teaching basic math skills in labs or grading differently) and strategies (e.g., using interactive teaching skills versus a lecture format), and by adjusting to some cultural differences (e.g., different student behavior). These adjustments lead to an increase in self-confidence as an international teacher.

Becoming reflective and flexible. Many of the ITAs were trying to become better teachers by being more self-reflective. Anna explained her new approach to teaching as follows:

> When I got to the classroom, I don't think about myself any more. I think about the students, how can I teach this material in a more

comprehensible way. When I [...] finish my class, I think about myself. What did I do wrong, how can I improve my teaching, how can I explain these things [...] so that the students can get it.

Ahmed, Guru, Jan-Jakub, Sandra, and Su-Ling also self-identified as self-reflective teachers who also listened to advice from colleagues and students. Based on the feedback they got, they made changes to the materials and teaching activities they used in class. For example, they discussed making homework assignments more relevant to students' needs and interests, incorporating more presentations and group work, using more technology in general and video clips in particular, changing strict attendance policies to accommodate student needs (e.g., student athletes), and explaining basic concepts in more details in order to help especially those students who lacked basic academic skills.

Apart from these strategies, many of the ITAs also reduced the amount of content or chapters to be covered in their courses and changed their standards in grading. For instance, in her next semester teaching the same course, Cyma wanted to change the amount of materials covered because "there is always a time constraint." She added "less materials are covered more intense [since] this class [an introductory science lab] needs to know the basics first." Natapon also reduced class content because she noticed that her U.S. colleagues were covering fewer chapters in other sections of the same course.

Several ITAs, including Ahmed, Ananya, MeiMei, and Natapon, pointed out that they tried to adjust to different grade expectations. As Ahmed stated,

The grades that I gave in the first semester, they were really, really strict. I think I [...] could have tried to be more easy. [...] I wish I wasn't that strict because they couldn't understand because I think the students whom I taught the first semester suffered a lot in the course, meaning I didn't [...] make it easy for them in terms of resources, in terms of making the grading policy clear, in terms of me teaching the course. [...] Now I keep changing the syllabus and the materials.

Apart from a change in his grading approach, Ahmed's statement further suggests an increase in his self-confidence as a teacher. He understood that teaching was a learning process and that he needed to revise his materials and policies in order to become a more effective instructor.

Adjusting to cultural differences. In addition to changing their strategies in the classroom, several ITAs also discussed that adjusting to cultural differences helped them become better teachers. In this context, they mainly referred to the "unusual" or "weird" student behavior they were encountering in their own classes at times. At the same time, the ITAs tried to see and interpret this undergraduate student behavior in a U.S. context instead of only basing it on their experiences in their home countries. Su-Ling explained this approach by saying:

> So I don't understand what's students' behavior, how rude it would be considered from American standards because I don't think I should not use my Asian idea to do that. [...] I should combine both -- Asian idea and American idea -- to help me make a decision.

Jan-Jakub stated, "I was surprised between the college in Germany and here in the United States. [...] Undergraduate college does not resemble university life in Germany but it's more of a high school so they [new ITAs from Germany] can be more prepared that they are like teaching high school students." Once he understood these differences between a more formal, lecture-style approach in Germany and the more student-centered classrooms in the U.S., Jan-Jakub was able to incorporate interactive strategies into his own teaching approach.

Desire for greater communicative competence. The ITAs also mentioned issues related to communicative competence. Hadmin, Jiaxin, and MeiMei mentioned that they needed to learn more idioms and slang terms in order to understand their students better. Slouma pointed to another interesting aspect of language use in the U.S.:

> When I came here, when I said "How are you?", I expected "I'm good" and then talk for a while like at least for one minute or two, but people when they say "Hey" it means "hello, how are you, and I'm leaving." [...] The most amazing thing here is, you know, I love this topic, people don't stop so when I say "Hello", and then I stop, you know people just keep on walking, [...] and I'm all by myself.

Slouma further explained that it took him some time to understand that these kinds of greetings were typical U.S. behavior and not a sign of disrespect towards him. He is now able to laugh about his initial encounters with greetings in the U.S. See Table 3 for ITAs' summarized comments on their adjustments to teaching in the U.S.

Table 3. ITAs' Adjustments to Teaching in the U.S.

Classroom management	• Have more interaction with students • Give better feedback on grading • Improve lesson plans and assignments; for example, by making them more relevant to students' needs • Use more technology in the classroom • Adjust classroom standards and policies as necessary • Use interactive teaching skills
Cultural knowledge	• Learn about students' backgrounds • Learn about U.S. culture • Adjust to different student behavior
Communicative competence	• Improve pronunciation • Speak more fluently and slower • Learn slang terms and colloquial expressions

Discussion

Despite the variety in their linguistic backgrounds and in the courses they were teaching, the ITAs went through similar experiences when adjusting to their new educational environments. The question in this context then is: If the ITAs' experiences are so similar, why are some ITAs able to handle their teaching assignments more effectively than others? Based on Berry's (1980, 1992, 2003) research on acculturation, ITAs who try to integrate or assimilate into the U.S. educational system would be more successful as international teachers, whereas ITAs who separate themselves or reject U.S. standards would be less capable of adjusting to their new educational environments. These projections based on Berry's research could be seen in the interview data, and the research participants could be divided into integrative, assimilative, and separatist categories.

Integration. Ananya, Cyma, Guru, and Su-Ling seemed to have integrated well into the U.S. educational system. They still experienced occasional doubts with regard to their English language ability and classroom management skills, but were quite confident about teaching in the U.S. These four ITAs tried to combine things they learned in their home countries with their new teaching environment. After understanding that her students needed additional help in solving the lab experiments, Cyma, for instance, started teaching basic math lessons in her labs, but kept stricter classroom policies, which she was used to in India. Ananya and Su-Ling incorporated examples from India and Taiwan in their courses. All of these ITAs tried to integrate educational aspects from their home cultures into the U.S. classroom, which has previously been linked to improved student recall and learning (Gorsuch, 2003; Smith & Simpson, 1993).

Assimilation. Ahmed, Hadmin, and Manoj tried to assimilate into the U.S. educational system and mainly used U.S. standards, strategies, and assignments in their classrooms. As opposed to Berry's paradigm, these ITAs did keep strong ties with their native countries. Contrary to the above-discussed group, however, they did not report any influences of their native cultures on their teaching styles in the U.S.

Separation. Jiaxin and MeiMei, on the other hand, had strong cultural links to China and Taiwan, respectively, and were still struggling with U.S. classroom standards, and thus could have been engaging in separatist strategies. Jiaxin, for example, kept on questioning the use of activities such as peer discussions and peer reviews since she did not see any value in these exercises and repeatedly mentioned that they were not used in China. MeiMei was mainly trying to make sense of the U.S. grading policy since she thought that U.S. students were graded too easily. Since these two ITAs had only been in the U.S. for about two months at the time of the interview, they were still at the beginning of their adjustment processes and thus might have been unconsciously engaging in these separatist behaviors.

The importance of departmental support and guidance, as opposed to just training. When looking closer at the ITAs in these three categories, it becomes clear that their cultural, educational, or linguistic background did not determine what kind of acculturation strategies these ITAs engaged in. Although likely an important factor, length of stay in the U.S. did not seem to be the most influential issue either since Hadmin also had been in the U.S. for about two months at the time of the interview, but responded differently to his new teaching environment, as opposed to Jiaxin or MeiMei. Not all of the ITAs who were coping well with their teaching assignments had received extensive ITA or TA training prior to their first teaching assignments. This group includes Ahmed, Cyma, Guru, Manoj, and Natapon. Jiaxin and MeiMei, on the other hand, had attended a lengthy departmental TA workshop, but were not coping well with their teaching assignments. Instead, the level of *perceived* support and feelings of being welcomed, especially at the departmental level, seemed to be the most potent factors in determining the research participants' perceived success as ITAs. For example, four of the 15 ITAs received both extensive training and guidance through the university and their departments. Although not always comfortable in doing so, these ITAs approached their professors, supervisors, or colleagues with questions or concerns. Six of the ITAs had only attended university-wide ITA and TA workshops and received no additional training through their academic units prior to the semester. They nevertheless felt supported by their departments, either through weekly TA meetings, a colleague's support, or an assigned mentor, and thus felt it was easier for them to cope with their teaching assignments. In contrast, two of the ITAs who had received the most extensive training through their departments prior to their first teaching assignment did not feel supported by their academic units and thus felt they could not ask for help and guidance and as a result were struggling with their teaching. This seems to suggest that an ITA's level of real as well as perceived support and guidance at the departmental level is crucial in helping the ITA adjust more effectively to their teaching assignments in the U.S.

Communication as a two-way street. A significant finding was a major discrepancy between the perceptions of the 15 ITAs in this study and the perceptions of undergraduate students as discussed in the literature review. As discussed previously, Spitzberg and Cupach's (1984) relational model of communicative competence states that competent communicators try to meet their interlocutor's needs by adapting to each other's expectations. In the context of ITAs and undergraduate students, this would mean that both sides should actively adjust to each other's level of speaking skills and classroom expectations. With the exception of Guru, the ITA from Indonesia, the research participants barely mentioned classroom challenges related to pronunciation issues and intonation patterns, but instead focused on educational and cultural challenges such as not understanding the role of a teaching assistant and facing stereotypes and sometimes even racial/ethnic discrimination in and outside the classroom. It might be argued that the prevailing view is that ITAs have sole responsibility for improving classroom communication. In contrast, the ITAs in this study saw communicative competence as a two-way street. They argued that, although English language skills are important for teachers, both ITAs and American undergraduate students should share the responsibility for creating effective communication in their classrooms. Both sides should be tolerant and accepting of each other's needs, accents, and speaking skills.

Implications for ITA Training

These findings have several implications for ITA training and mentoring (see Table 4). First, ITAs should receive contextualized and ongoing training throughout their teaching assignments since many research participants were not able to understand the information they were given in ITA training sessions prior to their first teaching assignment. For instance, Jiaxin did not understand why some sessions in her departmental training were focusing on students' attention spans and on keeping students engaged. Only during her first semester of teaching did she comprehend that U.S. students "were socializing a lot in class" and thus understood the necessity for such a training session. This suggests that ITAs, compared to pre-semester workshops alone, would benefit more from ongoing training simultaneously to their first teaching assignments since they would be able to apply the theoretical concepts more easily when put into context.

Second, the research participants focused on the importance of communicative competence as a two-way street. In order to improve their communicative competence, they wanted to have more direct interaction with American students and people in general. From the ITAs' perspective, meeting U.S. undergraduate students during their training would expose them to some of the cultural and social rules the undergraduate students would expect from their teachers. Additionally, since ITA training is a less formal setting than a credit-bearing course, a friendlier and more welcoming atmosphere for open discussion would exist too. I would further recommend assigning undergraduate and graduate mentors to incoming ITAs since this provides further contact between ITAs and U.S. students. ITAs could thus learn more about their students' backgrounds and expectations which is one of the areas ITAs wanted to learn more about. As a result, educators working with ITAs should provide them with an opportunity to interact with undergraduate students, mentors, and potentially host families in and outside the classroom.

A third implication relates to the level of *perceived departmental support*. This finding suggests that an ITA's level of real as well as perceived support and guidance at the departmental level is crucial in helping ITAs adjust more effectively to their lives as international instructors in the U.S. This points to the importance of mentoring ITAs throughout their teaching assignments. Apart from mentors' efforts, departments could offer weekly meetings to review course content and require ITAs to observe other successful teachers in their respective departments. On a university-wide level, ongoing courses in effective classroom management skills should be offered because theoretical concepts about teaching are difficult to grasp without any teaching experience prior to the semester. Similarly, while trying to understand American classrooms, and student and teacher roles, the ITAs also referred to the importance of departmental guidance and support. They discussed the importance of mentors, friends, or colleagues since being able to discuss their experiences with others helped the ITAs adjust faster to the U.S. educational system. Additionally, many of them also pointed out that they learned how to teach effectively thorough observations of more experienced instructors which again points to the importance of required observations. Table 4 summarizes the implications of the study's findings, with additional specific ideas for departmental-level support.

Table 4. Summary of Implications

Implication	Rationale
Contextualized and ongoing training throughout the ITAs' teaching assignments	Several ITAs lacked discourse competence. Offering ongoing guidance and training throughout the ITAs' teaching assignments helps the ITAs apply the theoretical concepts more easily. Thus, they can move from a passive to an active understanding of classroom discourse.
Communicative competence as a two-way street	Effective classroom communication involves both teachers and students. Interacting directly with undergraduate students, both in and outside the classroom, allows ITAs to learn more about their students and what they expect from TAs. Additionally, undergraduate students learn more about their international instructors, thus making communication a two-way street.

Support and guidance at the departmental level	The ITAs adjusted faster and were able to cope with their teaching assignments when they received departmental support. Providing guidance in the form of mentors, syllabi, teaching materials, observations of experienced TAs or faculty is important. Additionally, just listening to an ITA's concerns and questions is crucial too in making them feel welcomed and supported. Specific ideas for departmental-level support: • Make ITAs feel welcomed. • Offer a credit-bearing teaching course for all TAs (domestic and international). • Have weekly domestic and international TA meetings. • Have all TAs share lesson plans and challenges/successes. • Provide intensive mentoring for the first four weeks of classes. • Provide ITAs with sample syllabi, lesson plans, homework assignments. • Require ITAs to observe experienced TAs, ITAs, faculty members. • Offer mini-workshops throughout the semester on classroom management skills, teaching methodology, and TA-student interaction keyed to specific departmental concerns such as safety in science labs, writing lab reports, or grading essays. • Have ITAs present mini-lessons which can then be critiqued by an ITA or TA mentor, or experienced faculty member. • Organize informal conversation hours with U.S. undergraduates to discuss U.S. culture or to engage in role plays. • Consider using *The Intercultural Sensitizer*, which uses critical incidents focusing on misunderstandings between two or more people from different cultures (Cushner & Landis, 1996).

New Research Ideas

Additional research on ITAs' experiences from the ITAs' points of view is necessary. First, scholars could engage in studies on the effectiveness of ITA training workshops and courses. By interviewing ITAs before, during and after a workshop, we can learn more about which specific concepts or theories presented during the training sessions are difficult to grasp. This, in turn, can inform necessary changes in ITA training programs since challenging concepts could be repeated throughout the first semesters of teaching.

Second, in order to compare ITAs across different cultural backgrounds, similar studies should be conducted with more research participants. In this context, ITA scholars could interview several ITAs with similar linguistic and cultural backgrounds and analyze their experiences in the U.S. educational system and then compare them to other groups. Additionally, instead of focusing on the linguistic or cultural background of an ITA, a study could compare the experiences of ITAs who have full responsibility for a course versus those who are assisting a professor or who are in charge of a lab session.

Finally, ITA scholars could also engage in longitudinal studies focusing on the effectiveness of intercultural training programs for both ITAs as well as undergraduate students. For example, after implementing an intercultural training program involving undergraduate students, researchers could try to identify whether such a program has any effect on the relationship between ITAs and their undergraduate students. Through these kinds of studies, ITA researchers and trainers could analyze whether, after attending intercultural training sessions, U.S. undergraduate students increased their intercultural awareness on the one side and whether ITAs gained more knowledge about U.S. culture and students on the other.

Conclusion

This study provided additional information to ITA researchers, trainers, and mentors since it did not focus on the American perspective, but concentrated on the ITAs' points of view, including their perceptions of ITA training programs. To conclude, I want to quote Su-Ling: "ITAs are not dumb or stupid. We cannot speak English as fluent, but we [...] have something to offer." I agree with Su-Ling. ITAs are able to bring cultural diversity to U.S. campuses and play a significant role in exposing their U.S. students, faculty, and staff to diverse cultures and languages they might have otherwise had no opportunity to experience.

In a Nutshell

1. With higher numbers of international students in graduate programs, the number of ITAs has also increased.
2. The existing literature on ITAs focuses on challenges in the classroom based on numerous definitions of communicative competence, on creating effective ITA training programs and workshops, and on improving teaching and cross-cultural

skills in the classroom. Only a few studies focus on the ITAs' perceptions.
3. In order to strengthen the current best practices in ITA training, the ITAs' perceptions on ITA workshops need to be researched too.
4. Using an interview guide, I interviewed 15 ITAs to find out what suggestions the ITAs themselves have for enhancing ITA training programs in order to improve teaching outcomes.
5. In order to improve teaching outcomes, the ITAs suggested the following: weekly TA meetings, assigned mentors, shared syllabi, course assignments and lesson plans, required observations, ongoing workshops, critiquing of mini-lessons, including undergraduate students in ITA training, and establishing departmental and university-wide networking opportunities for all ITAs/TAs.
6. I found that the ITAs went through similar experiences when adjusting to their teaching assignments despite their differences in linguistic, academic, and cultural backgrounds.
7. Although receiving extensive training and guidance seems to be ideal for ITAs, the ITAs' comments suggest that receiving guidance and support throughout the semester is much more important than pre-semester training since most of them were not able to comprehend the information they were given prior to their first teaching assignment.
8. Academic departments should be strongly supported in their efforts to provide ongoing ITA training in addition to pre-semester ITA workshops. Specific suggestions are given in Table 4.

References

Axelson, E.R., & Madden, C.G. (1994). Discourse strategies for ITAs across instructional contexts. In C.G. Madden & C.L. Myers (Eds.), *Discourse and performance of international teaching assistants* (pp. 153-185). Alexandria, VA: Teachers of English to Speakers of Other Languages, Inc.

Bailey, K.M. (1982). Teaching in a second language: The communicative competence of non-native speaking teaching assistants. *Dissertation Abstracts International*, 43(10), 3305A.

Berry, J.W. (1980). Acculturation as varieties of adaptation. In A. Padilla (Ed.), *Acculturation: Theory, models and some new findings* (pp. 9-25). Boulder, CO: Westview.

Berry, J.W. (1992). Psychology of acculturation: Understanding individuals moving between cultures. In R.W. Brislin (Ed.), *Applied cross-cultural psychology* (pp. 232-253). Newbury Park, CA: Sage.

Berry, J.W. (2003). Conceptual approaches to acculturation. In K.M. Chun, P.B. Organista, & G. Marín (Eds.), *Acculturation: Advances in theory, measurement, and applied research* (pp. 17-37). Washington, D.C.: American Psychological Association.

Bresnahan, M.I., & Cai, D.H. (2000). From the other side of the desk: Conversations with international students about teaching in the U.S. *Qualitative Research Reports in Communication*, *1*(4), 65-75.

Briggs, S. L. (1994). Using performance assessment methods to screen ITAs. In C.G. Madden & C.L. Myers (Eds.), *Discourse and performance of international teaching assistants* (pp. 63-80). Alexandria, VA: TESOL.

Canale, M. (1983). From communicative competence to communicative language pedagogy. In J.C. Richards & R.W. Schmidt (Eds.), *Language and communication* (pp. 2-27). New York: Longman.

Canale, M., & Swain, M. (1980). Theoretical bases of communicative approaches to second language teaching and testing. *Applied Linguistics, 1*(1), 1-47.

Chomsky, N. (1965). *Aspects of the theory of syntax.* Cambridge, MA: MIT Press.

Christofi, V., & Thompson, C.L. (2007). You cannot go home again: A phenomenological investigation of returning to the sojourn country after studying abroad. *Journal of Counseling and Development, 85*(1), 53-63.

Cushner, K., & Landis, D. (1996). The intercultural sensitizer. In D. Landis, & R. S. Bhagat (Eds.), *Handbook of intercultural training* (2nd ed., pp. 185-202). Thousand Oaks, CA: Sage.

Creswell, J.W. (2003). *Research design: Qualitative, quantitative, and mixed methods approaches* (2nd ed.). Thousand Oaks, CA: Sage.

Damron, J.A. (2000). *Chinese 101, a prerequisite to math 100? A look at undergraduate students' beliefs about their role in communication with international teaching assistants.* Unpublished doctoral dissertation. West Lafayette, IN, Purdue University. (UMI No. 3018186).

Fitch, F., & Morgan, S.E. (2003). "Not a lick of English": Constructing the ITA identity through student narratives. *Communication Education, 52*(3-4), 297-310.

Gerson, K., & Horowitz, R. (2002). Observation and interviewing: Options and choices in qualitative research. In T. May (Ed.), *Qualitative research in action* (pp. 199-224). Thousand Oaks, CA: Sage.

Gorsuch, G.J. (2003). The educational cultures of international teaching assistants and U.S. universities. *TESL-EJ, 7*(3), A-1.

Gorsuch, G.J. & Sokolowski, J. (2007). International teaching assistants and summative and formative student evaluation. *Journal of Faculty Development, 21*(2), 117-136.

Gravois, J. (2005, April 5). Teach impediment: When the student can't understand the instructor, who is to blame? *The Chronicle of Higher Education, 51*(31), A 10.

Grimshaw, A.D. (1973). Rules, social interaction, and language behavior. *TESOL Quarterly, 7*(2), 99-117.

Gudykunst, W.B., & Kim, Y.Y. (2003). *Communicating with strangers* (4th ed.). Boston, MA: McGraw Hill.

Gullahorn, J.T., & Gullahorn, J.E. (1963). An extension of the U-curve hypothesis. *Journal of Social Issues, 19*, 23-47.

Hoekje, B., & Linnell, K. (1994). "Authenticity" in language testing: Evaluating spoken language tests for international teaching assistants. *TESOL Quarterly, 28*(1), 103-126.

Hoekje, B., & Williams, J. (1992). Communicative competence and the dilemma of international teaching assistant education. *TESOL Quarterly, 26*(2), 243-269.

Hoekje, B., & Williams, J. (1994). Communicative competence as a theoretical framework for ITA education. In C.G. Madden & C.L. Myers (Eds.), *Discourse and performance of international teaching assistants* (pp. 11-26). Alexandria, VA: TESOL.

Hymes, D. (1974). *Foundations in sociolinguistics: An ethnographic approach*. Philadelphia, PA: University of Pennsylvania Press.

Institute of International Education. (2014a). *Open doors data*. Retrieved from http://www.iie.org/Research-and-Publications/Open-Doors/Data

Institute of International Education. (2014b). *Fast facts open doors 2013*. Retrieved from http://www.iie.org/en/Research-and-Publications/Open-Doors

Kvale, S. (1996). *InterViews: An introduction to qualitative research interviewing*. Thousand Oaks, CA: Sage.

LaRocco, M.J. (2012). Chinese international teaching assistants and the essence of intercultural competence in university contexts. In G. Gorsuch (Ed.), *Working theories for teaching assistant development* (pp. 609-653). Stillwater, OK: New Forums Press Inc.

Lysgaard, S. (1955). Adjustment in a foreign society: Norwegian Fulbright grantees visiting the United States. *International Social Science Bulletin, 7*, 45-51.

Meesuwan, P. (1992). The exploration of international teaching assistants' perspectives on their work. *Dissertation Abstracts International, 53*(12), 4227A.

Mori, S. (2000). Addressing the mental health concerns of international students. *Journal of Counseling and Development, 78*(2), 137-144.

Neves, J. S., & Sanyal, R.N. (1991). Classroom communication and teaching effectiveness: The foreign-born instructor. *Journal of Education for Business, 66*(5), 304-309.

Patton, M.Q. (2002). *Qualitative research and evaluation methods* (3rd ed.). Thousand Oaks, CA: Sage Publications.

Pederson, P. (1991). Counseling international students. *The Counseling Psychologist, 19*(1), 10-58.

Plakans, B.S. (1995). Undergraduate experiences with and attitudes toward international teaching assistants. *Dissertation Abstracts International, 56*, 0474A.

Plakans, B.S. (1997). Undergraduates' experiences with and attitudes toward international teaching assistants. *TESOL Quarterly, 31*(1), 95-117.

Ross, P.G., & Krider, D.S. (1992). Off the plane and into the classroom: A phenomenological explication of international teachings assistants' experiences in the American classroom. *International Journal of Intercultural Relations, 16,* 277-293.

Rubin, D.L. (1992). Nonlanguage factors affecting undergraduates' judgements of nonnative English-speaking teaching assistants. *Research in Higher Education, 33*(4), 511-531.

Rubin, D.L., & Smith, K.A. (1990). Effects of accent, ethnicity, and lecture topic on undergraduates' perceptions of nonnative English-speaking teaching assistants. *International Journal of Intercultural Relations, 14,* 337-353.

Savignon, S. (1997). *Communicative competence: Theory and classroom practice* (2nd ed.). New York: McGraw-Hill.

Spencer-Rodgers, J. (2001). Consensual and individual stereotypic beliefs about internationalstudents among American host nationals. *International Journal of Intercultural Relations, 25*(6), 639-657.

Spencer-Rodgers, J. (2000). The vocational situation and country of orientation of international students. *Journal of Multicultural Counseling and Development, 28*(1), 32-49.

Skow, L.M., & Stephan, L. (2000). Intercultural Communication in the university classroom. In L.A. Samovar & R.E. Porter (Eds.), *Intercultural communication: A reader* (9th ed., pp. 355-370). Belmont, CA: Wadsworth Publishing.

Smith, C. (2012). The instructional discourse of domestic and international teaching assistants. InG. Gorsuch (Ed.), *Working theories for teaching assistant development* (pp. 483-528). Stillwater, OK: New Forums Press Inc.

Smith, K.S., & Simpson, R.D. (1993). Becoming successful as an international teaching assistant. *The Review of Higher Education, 16*(4), 483-497.

Smith, R.M., Byrd, P., Nelson, G.L., Barrett, R.P., Constantinides, J. (1992). *Crossing pedagogical oceans: International teaching assistants in U.S. undergraduate education.* ASHE-ERIC Higher Education Report No. 8. Washington, DC: The George Washington University, School of Education and Human Development.

Spitzberg, B. H. (1994). A model of intercultural communicative competence. In L. Samovar & R. Porter (Eds.), *Intercultural communication: A reader* (pp. 347-359). Belmont, CA: Wadsworth.

Spitzberg, B.H., & Cupach, W.R. (1984). *Interpersonal communication competence.* Beverly Hills, CA: Sage.

Stevenson, I., & Jenkins, S. (1994). Journal writing in the training of international teaching assistants. *Journal of Second Language Writing, 3*(2), 97-120.

Stewart, D.W., & Shamdasani, P.N. (1990). *Focus groups: Theory and practice.* Thousand Oaks, CA: Sage.

Tang, L., & Sandell, K. (2000). Going beyond the basic communication issues: New pedagogical training of international TAs in SMET fields at two Ohio universities. *Journal of Graduate Teaching Assistant Development, 7*(3), 163-172.

Tavana, S. (2005). Attitudes and beliefs of international teaching assistants regarding teaching practice: A case study. *Dissertation Abstracts International, 66*(3), 965A.

Thomas, C., & Monoson, P. (1991). Issues related to state-mandates English language proficiency requirements. In J. Nyquist, R.D. Abbott, D.H. Wulff, & J. Sprague (Eds.), *Preparing the professoriate of tomorrow to teach* (pp. 382-392). Dubuque, IA: Kendall/Hunt Publishing Company.

Yook, E.L., & Albert, R.D. (1999). Perceptions of international teaching assistants: The interrelatedness of intercultural training, cognition, and emotion. *Communication Education, 48*(1), 1-17.

Zha, S., & McCrory, M. (2006, March). *Virtual ITA preparation.* Paper presented at the 40th International Teaching English to Speakers of Other Languages conference, Tampa, FL.

Appendix

Final ITA Interview Guide

Personal Information:
1. Name:_____
2. Nationality:_____
   a. Did you grow up in (country) or not?
   b. If not, where did you grow up?
3. Native Language(s):_____
4. Knowledge of other languages:_____
5. Major:_____ Degree sought: MA PhD
6. Gender: Female   Male

Departmental Information:
7. Please specify the department you have been working for:_____
   a. Which courses did you teach/are you teaching?
   b. What are/were your specific responsibilities?
   c. How long have you been teaching at this university?

Previous Teaching Experience:
8. Have you had teaching experience before coming here? If so,
   a. Where did you teach (country, institution)?
   b. How long did you teach (time, semesters, etc.)?
   c. How would you describe your students (gender, background, etc.)?

Proficiency in English:
9. How do you feel about communicating in English?
10. How do you feel about your proficiency in English?

Teaching Experience:
11. In your opinion, what was your first impression of a U.S. American college classroom?
12. What are the differences and/or similarities between teaching in the U.S. and your home country/place you grew up?
13. What do you enjoy most about working with (teaching) U.S. American students?
14. Have you faced any difficulties or challenging situations in the classroom?
    a. If so, what kind of difficulties or challenging situations have you faced?

b. If so, have you solved these difficulties alone or have you sought help? From whom?
15. Why do you think these problems and challenging situations occurred?
16. What do you expect from your U.S. American undergraduate students?
17. How do you prepare for your teaching? Do you have enough time?
18. a. What specific teaching behaviors or techniques do you use in your classrooms?
    b. How do you approach teaching?
    c. How do students address you in your classroom? (first name, last name, etc.)
19. What are some aspects of your teaching that you especially like?
20. What are some aspects of your teaching that need further development?
21. If you are teaching this course again next semester, will you make any changes in your teaching approach? If so, which ones? If not, why not?
22. If you were teaching the same course in your native language, would it be different? How?
23. What kind of characteristics does a "good" or "competent" TA have?

Other Relevant Information:
24. What are your personal goals for teaching in the U.S.?
25. Do you have any advice for new ITAs coming from your country?
26. How does your department/university help you to prepare for teaching in the U.S.?
27. Are there things that your department/university could have done to help you teach more effectively? What are they?
28. Is there anything that you learned during your teaching experience here that you would have liked to know before starting to teach in the U.S.?
29. Do U.S. American students approach international instructors differently than they would approach U.S. American teachers?
30. How are ITAs perceived by U.S. American undergraduate students on this campus?
31. Is there anything else that you think is important for new (or returning) ITAs that has not been covered in this interview? If so, please explain.

A Study of International Teaching Assistant Recruitment Practices in Academic Departments

By Dale T. Griffee[1] and Greta Gorsuch, Texas Tech University

The number of international teaching assistants (ITAs) teaching undergraduate labs and classes has generally increased in the last decade. Many universities are expanding their undergraduate enrollments, thus increasing the demand for more classes and more instructors. To the extent U.S. universities continue the practice of employing graduate students to teach, and to the extent that ITAs continue to arrive, universities, and faculty and staff charged with supporting ITAs need to better understand the recruitment practices of departments. This is especially true for English as a Second Language (ESL) specialists. It is not necessarily the case that department recruiters look carefully at prospective ITAs' English proficiency scores used for the purpose of applying for graduate study. Thus, ITA candidates as a group may come to a university with widely varying levels of spoken English ability. ITA candidates with low spoken ability may require one or more semesters of ESL classes to be able to teach. This policy report is based on interviews with 56 ITA candidates, 8 department recruiters, and on a survey of 62 ITAs' English proficiency test scores used for application for graduate school. It was found that recruiters have multiple priorities when admitting ITA candidates. Looking carefully at prospective students' English proficiency scores for the purpose of teaching is not a high priority. Suggested cut scores are offered, not for the purpose of denying

---
1. Author contact: dale.griffee@ttu.edu

admittance, but for recruiter and ITA support planning purposes. ITA candidates arriving with lower English speaking ability scores ought not to be expected to be approved to teach upon arrival.

Although there has long been a tradition of international students studying in the U.S., recently their numbers have dramatically increased. As reported in the popular press, in 2011 the number of international students increased by 6% to 764,495 with much of the increase coming from China and Saudi Arabia (Marklein, 2012). At the same time many American universities are seeking to upgrade their status. For example, Texas Tech University (TTU), our institution, is one of several schools in Texas striving to become a national research university, and one of its stated goals to reach this status is increased enrollment (Texas Tech University Strategic Planning Council, 2010).

One of the implications of this desired upgrade in status is higher undergraduate student enrollment and a need for an increased number of classes to accommodate them. In the last several years, TTU has set undergraduate enrollment records each year (Wilson, 2013). These undergraduate students have needed to take the normal array of science labs and lower division introductory classes, and thus more sections of these courses are required. The role of international teaching assistants (ITAs) is likely to become more important because ITAs, who are international graduate students supported by the university, will be needed to staff the classes. In Fall, 2013, one undergraduate chemistry course at TTU offered 17 lab sections, 100% of which were taught by ITAs. A math course had 16 sections, 94% of which were taught by ITAs. And a physics lab offered 16 sections, 63% of which were taught by ITAs (Gorsuch, 2014). Many ITAs are non-native speakers of English, who come from countries where English is learned only as academic content, and not as a knowledge base to use for communication.

Literature Review

ITA programs and ITA program inputs. Since the 1980s, many universities, in response to perceived shortcomings and complaints about ITAs' English language use, established ITA preparation programs (Gorsuch, forthcoming; Hoekje & Linnell, 1994). Those charged with ITA preparation and support were, and still are, English as a Second Language (ESL) specialists, who view ITA candidates not only as early-career teachers, but also as second language learners. Even though ITA programs have an established presence on university campuses, and their missions remain essential to universities' successful delivery of instruction, there is a sense that ITA programs remain under-funded. The organizational logic behind TTU's own ITA summer workshop is somewhat a result of finding a cash-efficient way to prepare as many ITAs as possible in one fell swoop for their work in classrooms. If ITA programs are fortunate enough to continue to be funded at their current levels, and if the enrollments of ITA candidates continues to increase, ITA programs will be hard pressed to provide sufficient support for the second language learning of ITA candidates. Second language learning processes are slow (TESOL, 2010), and the broad-yet-deep skills needed to teach in a second language are hard to improve.

It makes sense for ITA educators, and the faculty members and staff who recruit international graduate students, to know more about prospective students' English ability, as estimated by English proficiency test scores used by international students to gain admittance to an academic department. For ITA programs, like any other academic unit charged to meet fairly rigid outcomes, it matters a great deal in terms of "what goes in" to a program ("inputs"). In other words, in what kind of shape are newly arriving students, in terms of their spoken English ability? This may make a difference in how ITA programs present their continuing worth to a university, as well as to plan resource allocation.

Why examine department recruitment practices? It is currently unclear what international graduate student recruitment practices are used by various academic departments. Even less known is whether, or how, academic departments consult prospective international graduate students' English proficiency scores, which are required to be admitted to the university. To the extent that departments' recruitment efforts result in ITA candidates coming to the university, needing support services, it is essential that ITA support personnel and departments examine recruitment processes. This is an important issue because ITA candidates admitted with low English language proficiency may take two or more semesters of preparation courses to achieve a level of language skill that enables them to communicate with and teach undergraduates.

Language proficiency is a process that will not be hurried, and the lower the spoken language ability of an incoming ITA candidate, the longer the process will be. This idea is expressed in Figure 1.

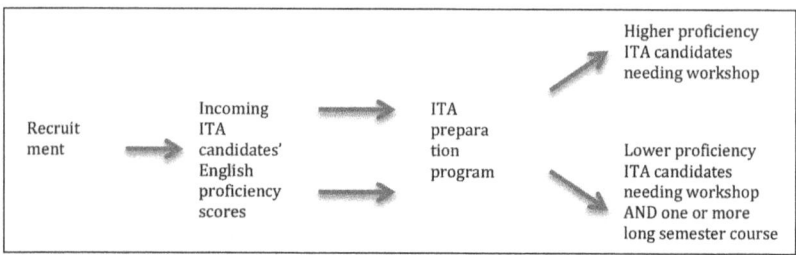

Figure 1. The relationship between international graduate student recruitment, English language proficiency, ITA preparation programs, and approval to teach.

Study Purpose

The purpose of this study is to describe ITA recruitment practices in academic departments at a university from the point of view of ESL specialists who are responsible for supporting ITA candidates. There is a need to understand the implications of academic departments' recruitment practices on the English communication ability of incoming graduate students who may go into ITA programs. Despite the fact that English proficiency scores on tests such as the TOEFL (ETS, 2014a) are required for admission, it is hypothesized that departments are recruiting ITA candidates with little attention to, or understanding of, their English ability. This results in incoming ITA candidates having widely varying levels of spoken English. Some ITA candidates who are accepted for study at the university may have low levels of spoken ability, and cannot be approved to teach upon arrival. Two questions focus the study:
- Research Question #1: How are ITA candidates recruited by academic departments?
- Research Question #2: What ITA candidate admission scores on a commonly used, standardized English proficiency test, best predict the likelihood of ITA candidates being approved to teach?

Stated another way, RQ #2 asks: What do academic department recruiters do, according to their own priorities, and what do they need to know about English proficiency test scores if one of their priorities is to recruit graduate students who can teach a lab or class upon arrival? To better understand the terms used in this report, here are some key definitions.

- *Approved to teach* means an ITA candidate passes three tests: The SPEAK test (Wikipedia, 2012) administered in a language lab, a listening test, and a teaching simulation performance test administered in the classroom.
- An *International Teaching Assistant* (ITA) is an international student, often a doctoral-level student, selected by their department to be a TA. ITAs typically teach labs, special tutoring classes, and occasionally lecture courses.
- An *ITA candidate* is an international student nominated by his or her department, but is not yet approved to teach.
- *ESL 5310* is a graduate level ESL course offered at Texas Tech dedicated to enable an ITA candidate to pass the three tests necessary to be approved to teach. This course meets during a regular "long" semester (not in the summer).
- *GPTI* is a graduate part-time instructor, essentially a TA assigned to a course, but as an instructor of record.
- *TA* is a teaching assistant, a loosely used term for a graduate student who assists a faculty member who is teaching a large class, or teaches a lab or class, but is supervised and not considered an instructor of record (a GPTI).
- *TOEFL* (ETS, 2014a), is a standardized English proficiency test, typically used by non-native English speaking international students for the purpose of university entrance in the U.S. and elsewhere. TOEFL reports contain five scores: Reading, writing, listening, speaking, and a total score.

The audience for this article is ITA support personnel, academic department recruiters, academic advisors, and other staff and faculty involved with international graduate students nominated by their departments to be GPTIs or TAs.

Method

This is descriptive research, which means no research design was used to ascribe cause and effect. Qualitative interview data were gathered from department recruiters and ITA candidates, and analyzed following a recursive and inductive theme identification technique (Glaser & Strauss, 1967) and operationalized in Griffee (2012). As part of this technique we also used a memo system of introspection as illustrated in Miles & Huberman (1994). A memo is simply a word processing document which acts as a diary of a data collection project, in which a researcher notes information, re-reads his or her own accounts, and introspects based on collected impressions and experiences.

Quantitative TOEFL test score data were gathered from ITA candidates/participants in an intensive ITA preparation summer workshop, and their test scores on the listening subtest, speaking subtest, and total test were correlated with whether ITA candidates were approved to teach or not approved to teach at the end of the workshop. We hypothesized that the listening and speaking subtests were the most likely measures to have predictive power for ITA candidates' English communication ability. At the same time, we hypothesized that when department recruiters look at test scores, they most likely consult the total scores. It is on the basis of total scores on the TOEFL (and other tests) that the graduate school makes an initial acceptance decision. More details on the admissions process are given below.

Participants

There were three groups of participants: academic department recruiters, ITA candidates enrolled in ESL 5310, and ITA candidates in a summer workshop. Data from the academic department recruiters and ITA candidates in ESL 5310 were used to answer RQ #1. Data from the ITA candidates in the summer workshop were used to answer RQ #2.

Academic department recruiters. Three recruiters from the foreign language department were initially interviewed to develop and refine interview questions (see Table 1). Eight additional academic department recruiters from Applied Linguistics, German, Math, and Spanish, were subsequently interviewed.

ITA candidates in ESL 5310. These were ITA candidates who were not approved to teach upon arrival at the school. They were enrolled in ESL 5310 by their departments, who wanted them to be approved to teach. ITA candidates from two sections of ESL 5310, with enrollments of 15 and 13, were interviewed for this study in

2013. ITA candidates from a later ESL 5310 course, held in Spring, 2014, were also interviewed. A total of 56 ITA candidates in ESL 5310 were interviewed.

ITA candidates in the summer workshop. Slightly over one hundred international students were registered by their departments for the three-week workshop, held in July and August, 2014. Of these, 91 attended the final day events and were asked to sign a consent form giving access to their entrance scores, as stipulated by the school's Internal Review Board (IRB) office. Eight candidates declined to consent, and twenty-one did not have did not have TOEFL scores or had no scores of any kind on record. This left 62 students who gave consent and had the full range of TOEFL scores (total score, and listening and speaking subtests) needed for the analysis. Workshop participants came from most university departments, but predominately from math, languages, science, and engineering.

Materials

There were three sources of data in this study: The department recruiter interview, the ITA candidate interview, and ITA candidates' TOEFL scores.

The department recruiter interview. Pilot interview protocols were developed following an inductive, recursive method (e.g., Griffee, 2012). Three department recruiters, all of them faculty members in modern languages, were interviewed using an ethnographic open-style procedure to create more focused interview items to be used later. In the first interview with the French section recruiter, one of the authors asked how she recruited graduate students (ITA candidates) for her language section, took notes on her responses, and asked follow- up questions. From this initial interview six items emerged, which were used in the second interview with the Spanish section recruiters. During the second round of interviews, two additional questions emerged. The eight-question interview protocol was then used in the third interview with the German section recruiter. These items, then, became the basis of the interview protocol. They are presented in Table 1. Only four of the items appear here, as the four other items were not germane to this study, and are being used in a different study.

Table 1. Partial List of Interview Protocol Items

1. Did the department give you any training, orientation, instructions?
2. What is your recruitment strategy?
3. How do you determine the English level of language of candidates?
4. Has a candidate you recruited ever had trouble being approved to teach?

The ITA candidate (ESL 5310) interview. A pilot study ($n = 10$) was conducted to develop interview items that would capture how prospective graduate students, who were eventually nominated by their departments to be TAs and GPTIs, came to be at TTU in the first place. One of the authors began by searching out any graduate student in his department, and conducting an open-ended interview. Sample open-ended questions were: How did they decide to come to TTU? Were they searching on their own to find TTU? Or, were they contacted by someone at TTU? And, if they were contacted, what happened? As a result of these pilot interviews, four categories emerged: 1. They searched the internet and found TTU; 2. Texas TTU was recommended by a person at their undergraduate institution with some connection to Texas Tech, such as a graduate or a friend; 3. Somebody from TTU visited their school and contacted them; or 4. another way. See Table 2 for the ITA candidate interview items.

Table 2. ITA Candidate Recruitment Group Interview Items

Introduction: I am conducting a survey into the way that ITA candidates come to Texas Tech University. I would like to ask you how you decided to come to TTU.

How did you first learn about Texas Tech University?

_____ I searched on the Internet and found TTU.

_____ TTU was recommended by someone at my school.
         (Did that person have a connection with TTU?)

_____ Someone from TTU visited my campus and talked to me.

_____ There was another way. Please write what it was.

Test scores provided in application dossier. Probably like many U.S. universities, prospective students applying to TTU build an electronic dossier on an online system. Thus, once we had the ITA candidates' consent, we searched for any standardized test scores they used to gain admission. At TTU, once the graduate school accepts students on the basis of their test scores and other criteria, students' dossiers are sent to the academic departments to make final decisions on admission to the department, and financial aid to be awarded in the form of a teaching assistantship or scholarship. Thus recruiters in academic departments have final say on admissions decisions. Recruiters have access to the electronic dossier with prospective students' test scores.

When the ITA candidates' scores were examined, it became apparent that multiple types of test scores were used in admissions decisions. One ITA candidate had GMAT scores (Graduate Management Admissions Council, 2002-2014), seven offered GRE scores (ETS, 2014c) and four had IELTS scores (IELTS, 2009-2013). Another nine had no test scores on record. Finally, the single largest group of 62 ITA candidates offered TOEFL scores, including the total score, and the listening and speaking subtest scores (ETS, 2014a). As a result of this patchwork of test scores offered for admission, and hence the difficulty of equating them on one scale for predictive purposes, only the TOEFL scores are considered in this report. With one exception, the TOEFL test was the only standardized test mentioned by department recruiters in interviews.

Summer workshop outcomes. The outcomes for the 62 participants for whom we had TOEFL scores were retrieved from the workshop records. The outcomes were dichotomous, meaning "approved to teach" or "not approved to teach."

Procedure

To answer RQ #1 dealing with how ITA candidates are recruited, interviews were conducted with departmental recruiters. Interviews took place in the recruiters' offices, and recruiters' comments to the interview items were recorded either in note form, or were recorded and later transcribed. Using the four categories distilled from the pilot with the ESL 5310 students (see Materials section), ITA candidates who were then-currently enrolled in an ITA preparation course were asked how they became aware of TTU and how they decided to apply.

In 2013 one of the authors conducted whole class interviews by handing out forms (see Table 2) and in 2014 wrote the four options on the board, asking students in the class to select an appropriate answer. This resulted in 28 responses from the Fall, 2013 class, and another 28 responses from the Spring, 2014 class ($N = 56$). ITA candidates' responses to the four answer choices were tabulated.

To answer RQ #2 about what ITA candidate admission scores best predict the likelihood of ITA candidates' approval to teach, TOEFL total and listening and speaking subtest scores from $n = 62$ ITA candidates were retrieved from the university database and entered into a statistical program. The total TOEFL scores, the listening subtest scores, and the speaking subtest scores were treated separately and arranged in ascending order so as to see the full range of scores on all three measures, and also to see the frequency of scores. Descriptive statistics were calculated for each of the three score sets. Point biserial correlations were calculated three times: Once with the total TOEFL scores (a continuous variable) and workshop outcome (a dichotomous variable); a second time with the listening subtest scores and workshop outcome, and a third time with the speaking subtest scores and workshop outcome. The higher the point biserial correlation coeffiecient, the better predictor a set of test scores will be of whether an ITA candidate will be approved to teach.

Results

RQ #1. How ITA candidates are recruited. International graduate student recruitment, it turns out, is a two-way street. Not only do departments search for and recruit prospective graduate students (who will become ITA candidates), but prospective students also actively search for schools to apply to.

The story from academic recruiters: Schools search for students. Most of the department recruiters interviewed for this report had been recruiting for about two years. They were unanimous in saying that they received no training, orientation, or instructions from their departments. They were tossed into the deep end of the recruitment "pool" and told to learn how to swim. Although they recognized the importance of what they were doing, they noted that recruiting takes effort and time. As one faculty member/recruiter said:

> It does because you are not only recruiting, you are also the person in charge of admissions into the program so you not only

have to read all the dossiers you have to be in contact with all the potential students constantly asking questions, you have to do the interviews, verify their CVs check their letters of recommendation so there is a lot of paperwork you have to do. It is not only contacting people and promote the program, answering questions here and there, that's generally what you do in the fall, once the spring semester goes in full force that's when you start doing all the other stuff you need to do, not only recruiting because you are still answering questions but you are also in charge of the whole process of admissions as well and that can take a lot of time.

Six recruiting strategies. Recruiters commented on their strategies. Six strategies emerged:

1. Contact other schools. Send emails and brochures to other schools. If recruiting for a doctoral program, make sure the target schools have MA programs but no doctoral program in the recruiting department's area. Give information about faculty members and other relevant details. Decide if any geographic area would be appropriate to target, for example the three or four states close to the recruiter's school.

2. A quick call as follow-up. One recruiter said that as soon as her department's clerical support staff reports someone has applied, she goes into the staff person's office, looks at the folder of the applicant, and then calls them. Another recruiter mentioned "the minute we receive any show of interest from a student, we make a friendly phone call noting that they are at the beginning of their application process and asking if they have any questions."

3. Exploit personal contacts. Another recruiter reported contacting anyone who has traveled abroad, asking them if they had met anyone over the summer who might be interested in coming to her program. She also reported contacting other faculty members who have not necessarily been travelling, but asking them the same question. She reported contacting former students in their home countries.

4. Create and maintain a web page. One recruiter noted: "There are many students throughout the world with whom we have had no previous contact with who search for programs they can apply to." She concluded that a departmental web page should have a clear description of the graduate program, the faculty, and the application process.

5. Recruit at conferences. Several recruiters mentioned that many professional conferences have recruitment centers, where

attending faculty members/recruiters can reserve spots for interviews. One recruiter reported preparing materials for such conferences, including computer power-point presentations. These presentation materials were made available to all faculty members attending conferences.

6. Develop in-country contacts. This was, surprisingly, a major recruitment strategy. It is a more complex strategy because it relies as much on other persons as it does on the recruiter, but it can be highly effective. In-country contacts named were graduates of the school who has returned with positive memories of your program, or a person befriended by a faculty member who visited the school in the country of interest. In some cases it was reported that the in-country contact not only supply names of potential students, but also selected and vetted the students. One recruiter noted always visiting the in-country contact when travelling abroad. As one recruiter said, "When I go on study abroad programs to (city in which the university is located) which is my hometown, I always make it a point to meet with the in-country contact and prospective students, and to go over our expectations so there is no ambiguity when they talk to various professors here on Skype interviews."

ITA candidates search for schools. Using the ITA recruitment interview form as shown in Table 2, ITAs representing various departments from two sections of ESL 5310 ($N = 56$) were interviewed as a group. The researcher wrote the four options on the board, and asked students in the class to select an appropriate answer. As can be seen in Table 3, the majority of these ITA candidates (59%) reported they were recruited by someone from their local schools in their home countries. In some cases this person could be considered an in-country contact for TTU, but in other cases the person was not informally or formally affiliated with TTU.

Table 3. How ITA Candidates Search for a Graduate Program

	2013	2014	Totals	%
Searched the internet	9	12	21	.37
Recommended	19	14	33	.59
Recruited by university	01	01	01	.02
Other	00	01	01	.02
Totals	28	28	56	

37% of the ITA candidates interviewed reported that they searched the internet for schools, and then applied to those schools that fit their qualifications and requirements. Only 2% (one student) noted that he or she had been recruited directly by TTU, and another 2% (again, one student) simply indicated "other" as a means of knowing about and applying to TTU. This student reported that when he took the GMAT test, the test program gave him TTU as a possible school to attend, based on his score.

Department advisors' priorities and treatment of prospective students' English ability. Once a prospective student has been accepted by the graduate school, department advisors need to make their own decisions about acceptance. Interviews revealed that recruiters had multifaceted priorities, and that they were not necessarily looking closely at prospective students' English ability. One commonly cited priority was pressure from department administration to increase graduate student enrollments, while another cited priority was getting the "best" applicants in a given field, such as math or languages. Recruiters mentioned they were competing with other schools for students who had the most "complete" (desirable) applications. Also, TTU's TA/GPTI stipend was seen as only comparable to that of other schools, or lower than that of other schools. As one math recruiter noted: "even though our math program is a better quality program than [other school's name] program…financially these students don't care about that." Recruiters were under pressure to recruit a certain number of students for the coming year, either to ensure viability of their graduate program with large-enough graduate classes, or to fulfill the department's need for TAs/GPTIs. Two recruiters expressed concern that the prospective students' stated interests matched those of faculty members in the department. The recruiters wanted to make sure that the department could offer the kinds of courses that would address students' academic and research interests.

Recruiters mentioned a number of ways they checked prospective students' English ability, in anticipation of students becoming ITAs/GPTIs. One recruiter mentioned asking for a writing sample in English, while another conducted Skype interviews. Four of the recruiters mentioned looking at TOEFL scores, and three of them mentioned only looking at the total scores. In contrast, the fourth recruiter mentioned becoming more interested in the TOEFL subtest scores, although even then: "we looked at it (TOEFL sub-scores) a little bit but our primary goal is to get the best [subject name] students and if we have to prop them up with training…then we will do that."

RQ #2. The relationship of English proficiency scores used to apply to the school and approval to teach. See Table 4 for the three score sets listed in ascending order, and then juxtaposed with whether the individual getting that score was approved to teach ("Yes") or not approved to teach ("No") at the end of the summer workshop. The range of possible scores on the TOEFL are 0 – 30 on any of the four subtests, adding up to 0 = 120 for a total score (ETS, 2014b). Note that the score sets have been treated separately, meaning that the person getting a score of 7 on the listening subtest was not the person to the right who got a score of 13 on the speaking subtest, nor the person getting a score of 59 on the total test. In other words, the three lists of scores are ranked independently, which means they cannot be read across because they are not scores from the same candidate. These columns must be read vertically.

Table 4. TOEFL Listening, Speaking, and Total Scores Ranked from Low to High Independently

Listening subtest scores	Workshop result compared with listening subtest scores	Speaking subtest scores	Workshop result compared with speaking subtest scores	Total scores	Workshop result compared with total scores
7	No	13	No	59	No
13	No	14	No	71	No
14	No	15	No	76	Yes
16	No	15	No	77	No
16	Yes	17	No	78	No
17	No	17	No	78	Yes
17	No	17	No	80	No
17	Yes	17	No	81	No
17	No	17	No	81	No
17	Yes	17	Yes	81	No
17	No	17	No	82	No
18	No	18	No	82	No
19	No	18	No	82	No
19	Yes	18	No	82	No
20	No	19	No	83	No

Listening subtest scores	Workshop result compared with listening subtest scores	Speaking subtest scores	Workshop result compared with speaking subtest scores	Total scores	Workshop result compared with total scores
20	No	19	No	83	Yes
20	No	19	No	83	No
20	Yes	19	No	83	No
22	No	19	No	84	No
22	No	19	No	84	Yes
22	Yes	19	No	85	No
22	No	19	No	85	No
22	Yes	19	No	87	Yes
22	No	19	Yes	88	No
23	Yes	20	No	88	Yes
23	Yes	20	Yes	88	No
23	Yes	20	Yes	88	No
23	Yes	20	No	90	No
23	No	20	Yes	91	Yes
23	Yes	20	Yes	92	Yes
23	Yes	20	Yes	92	No
24	No	22	No	92	Yes
24	Yes	22	Yes	92	No
24	No	22	No	92	Yes
24	No	22	Yes	93	No
24	No	22	Yes	93	Yes
24	Yes	22	Yes	94	Yes
25	Yes	22	Yes	95	Yes
25	Yes	22	Yes	95	No
25	Yes	22	Yes	95	Yes
25	Yes	22	Yes	96	Yes
26	No	22	Yes	96	Yes
26	No	23	Yes	97	Yes
26	No	23	Yes	98	Yes
26	No	23	No	98	Yes
26	Yes	23	No	98	Yes
26	Yes	23	No	99	No
26	Yes	23	Yes	100	No
27	Yes	23	Yes	100	Yes
27	No	23	Yes	100	Yes
27	Yes	24	No	101	No
28	No	24	No	101	Yes
28	Yes	24	Yes	102	No
28	No	24	Yes	103	Yes

Listening subtest scores	Workshop result compared with listening subtest scores	Speaking subtest scores	Workshop result compared with speaking subtest scores	Total scores	Workshop result compared with total scores
28	Yes	26	Yes	104	Yes
28	Yes	26	Yes	104	Yes
28	Yes	26	Yes	105	Yes
28	Yes	27	Yes	105	Yes
29	Yes	27	Yes	105	Yes
29	Yes	28	Yes	113	Yes
29	No	29	Yes	113	Yes
29	Yes	30	Yes	114	Yes

Notes. Listening subtest, speaking subtest and total refer to TOEFL scores. "Yes" means an ITA candidate getting a particular score on the listening subtest or speaking subtest or total score was approved to teach upon completion of the ITA preparation workshop. "No" means the ITA candidate who received a particular score was not approved to teach.

Note that generally as scores on any of the subtests or total scores increase, so does the likelihood of an ITA candidate being approved to teach ("Yes"). See Table 5 for descriptive statistics for the three sets of scores, including Fisher's skewness and kurtosis coefficients which follow the formula in Pett (1997).

Table 5. Descriptive Statistics for TOEFL Listening Scores, Speaking Scores, and Total Scores

	Listening subtest	Speaking subtest	Total
N	62	62	62
Mean	22.84	20.98	91.24
Median	23.50	21.00	92.00
Min	07	13	59
Max	29	30	114
SD	4.623.	60	10.64
Skewness	-.927	.257	-.159
Kurtosis	.963 .	001	.336
Fisher's skewness coefficient	-3.109	.845	-.052
Fisher's kurtosis coefficient	1.60.001	.560	

TOEFL test candidates can score up to 30 on any of the subtests (ETS, 2014b), and thus the M of 22.84 and M of 20.98 on the listening and speaking subtests, respectively, suggests that as a group, the ITA candidates scored somewhat high on the subtests. The same was true with the total TOEFL score, where ITA candidates got an M of 91.24 out of a possible score of 120. The ITA candidates were, after all, graduate students seeking admission to universities in the U.S. to gain an advanced degree.

In terms of variance, there is more ambiguity on the listening subtest score with an SD of 4.62 and a significant skewness coefficient of -.927 (-3.099 Fisher's), suggesting students "bunching up" towards the higher end of the *max* score of 29 for the group. The listening subtest scores were not normally distributed. In contrast, the speaking subtest and total score sets were normally distributed, with non-significant skewness coefficients. The speaking subtest score had a relatively small SD (3.60), with no significant skew. A median score of 21 and a mode score of 22 suggested that the group was slightly constrained at the upper end. If one arbitrarily chose a score of 25 (out of 30) as resoundingly "good," fully 25 ITA candidates qualified for this label on the listening subtest. Only eight ITA candidates qualified as "good" on the speaking subtest using our arbitrary cut score (see Table 4). Whether lower speaking skills are an effect of many countries in the world having limited educational resources to develop English speaking skills (Gorsuch, 2011), or is an indication of the type of students who tend to apply to Texas Tech, is not clear. In contrast, the total TOEFL scores had an SD of 10.64. On a test with 120 possible points, this was a reasonably small SD. The *max* score for the group was 114, suggesting less constraint at the upper end of the scores, unlike the speaking subtest scores.

Point-biserial correlation (r_{pbi}), a special case of the Pearson correlation, is the correlation of a continuous scale (the subtests and total TOEFL scores) and a nominal scale (approved to teach or not approved to teach), and is one way of showing the level of prediction of test scores and summer workshop outcomes. The higher the point-biserial correlation coefficient is, the better a test score predicts approval and non-approval to teach. See Table 6.

Table 6. Point-biserial Correlation Coefficients

	Listening subtest	Speaking subtest	Total score
Point-biserial	.33*	.59*	.52*

Notes. *significant at $p < .01$ (two tailed test).

The listening test was somewhat predictive of approval to teach, but most predictive was the speaking subtest, followed by the total scores on the TOEFL test. Intuitively, it makes sense that the speaking subtest score is most predictive, as two of the three workshop measures used to decide approval to teach are speaking performance tests. ITA education has traditionally focused on speaking skills somewhat to the exclusion of other areas of instruction, such as English grammar and vocabulary (Gorsuch, forthcoming). Nonetheless, the r_{pbi} correlation for the speaking subtest was only .59, suggesting plenty of variance unaccounted for. This also makes sense, intuitively. The TOEFL iBT speaking test has test candidates answering a series of prompts on the computer with recorded speech samples being scored by human raters (ETS, 2014a). In order to be approved to teach, ITA candidates at Texas Tech have to pass a test similar to the speaking subtest, but *also* must pass a ten-minute teaching simulation performance test viewed live by two trained raters. Answering oral prompts is not the same as teaching content, where a speaker is working to get interaction with the audience, and fielding questions. Still, as a means by which to predict success in being approved to teach upon arrival, the TOEFL speaking subtest seems relatively useful.

Discussion

Priorities of department recruiters and second language learning of ITA candidates. As the number of ITAs increase, academic departments at U.S. universities will have to pay attention to international graduate student recruiting practices because ITA language proficiency will play an important role in their being approved to teach. What was learned from this report was that academic recruiters, who are often faculty members with limited time, have a broad range of priorities, including the viability of their own graduate programs. Recruiters are also concerned that prospective students' research interests complement their programs. While some recruiters do check prospective students' English proficiency scores, not all recruiters have it in mind to prioritize students being approved to teach upon arrival. This is not unreasonable, given the constraints posed by competing schools with better stipends, or given demands from various levels of administration to increase graduate enrollments. In any event, recruiters may still not know to check the speaking subtest of the TOEFL. They may not know how slow second language acquisition processes are. Simply being in the U.S. is not guaranteed to improve international students' communication ability in English (Gorsuch, 2013; Gorsuch, forthcoming). It is likely that most ITA preparation programs lack sufficient intensity to quickly change ITA candidates' communication ability (Gorsuch, 2012).

Department recruiters' strategies and knowledge are ephemeral. There was one unexpected realization that department recruiters, who are often juggling a heavy service burden along with ordinary research and teaching demands, are untrained. They receive little support or guidance from their departments. Whatever strategies or skills they have learned are effective, are also transitory and ephemeral, and likely lost when the recruiters move on. Recruitment duties are taken up by someone else who will then have to re-invent the wheel (again). It was partly for this reason we included the descriptions of the six successful recruitment strategies.

We add a concern of our own, which is directly applicable to ESL specialists/ITA educators who are charged with preparing ITA candidates to teach. To the extent that ITA educators have contact with recruiters, it may be difficult to build up a shared knowledge of the relationship between English proficiency scores used for admission and ITAs' likelihood of being approved to teach upon arrival. Any shared knowledge might be lost when a department recruiter moves on. This is one reason language test cut scores need to be researched, carefully developed, and subjected to periodic re-analysis based on local data. Test scores may be a useful focal point upon which ITA educators and new department recruiters can build further understandings of each others' roles, priorities, and realities.

Suggested cut scores. We are prepared to offer test cut scores based on our data (see Table 4). We do not intend to tell department recruiters or graduate school admissions specialists to exclude all potential students with lower test scores than one might like. Thus, when we say "cut scores" we do not mean that all students below a certain score threshold should not be admitted by a department. What we really mean is something more like a "decision point" score where department recruiters will need to think carefully about whether a low-scoring prospective student can be supported as test graders or research assistants until they are approved to teach. And there is much to recommend such students.

There are many international students with perhaps shaky spoken English, but who have the research interests, and previous experience and education that will complement those of the departments they apply to. For a graduate program to be viable, the best talent available is needed. If a department has an active research agenda on bat conservation, and the best potential researchers in bats are from Indonesia, or Costa Rica, then that is where prospective students must come from. While these countries are linguistically diverse, neither of them claim English as an official language. What we *do* intend to say is if prospective students are admitted with lower-than-liked speaking subtest scores on the TOEFL, do not expect these students to be approved to teach immediately. It may take one or more semesters of preparation courses and intense effort on the part of the students, before teaching approval can realistically be granted.

A cut score determining the point at which it is likely a candidate is approved to teach was ascertained by visual inspection of the data in Table 4. The listening subtest scores were judged to reveal no obvious cut score. ITA candidates getting higher scores relative to the group mean were not approved to teach. With a low point biserial correction of $r_{pbi} = .33$, it would be difficult to claim the listening subtest score could predict likelihood of approval to teach.

Because the speaking subtest score was more predictive when viewing the crude implicational scale found in Table 4 and the point-biserial coefficient ($r_{pbi} = .59$), a cut score of 19 is suggested for the speaking subtest scores. Stated in probabilistic terms, at a cut score of 19 or lower, an ITA candidate has a 92% chance of not being approved to teach, but at 20 or higher an ITA candidate has a 76% chance of being approved. The total TOEFL score also has only moderately predictive power ($r_{pbi} = .52$), yet is still more accurate than the TOEFL listening subtest score. We offer a cut score based on ITA candidates' total TOEFL score of 94. At a cut score of 94 or lower for total scores, a candidate has a 68% chance of not being approved, but with a total score of 95 or higher a candidate has an 80% chance of being approved to teach.

There are, of course, exceptions. The implicational scale based on our data is not perfectly predictive, which underscores the importance of adopting, adapting, or creating locally administered assessments to incoming ITA candidates. One surprising exception involved an ITA candidate with a listening subtest score of 28, a speaking subtest score of 22, and a total score of 102. By all accounts this individual should have been approved to teach during the summer workshop. But this individual was not approved to teach. Could it be that the workshop assessments used to determine approval were invalid or inaccurate? Unless an ITA candidate who was not approved to teach enrolls in ESL 5310, it is difficult to follow up on such cases. However, this ITA candidate did attend the ESL 5310 class one of the authors taught. The instructor confirmed, after several weeks, that the ITA candidate should not have been approved, and showed substantial weaknesses in spoken English. This raised the uncomfortable possibility of test fraud during the application process.

Conclusion

It was found that department recruiters have multiple priorities when admitting ITA candidates. Looking carefully at prospective international graduate students' English proficiency scores for the purposes of teaching is not necessarily a high priority. Provisional suggested cut scores on the TOEFL speaking subtest, and the total TOEFL score scale are offered, but not for the purpose of denying admittance. ITAs, like any other group of talented prospective graduate students, bring with them previous experiences and education that make graduate programs more complete, and viable. The suggested cut scores are offered for department recruiter and ITA program planning purposes. ITA candidates arriving with lower English speaking ability scores ought not to be expected to be approved to teach upon arrival. Recruiters, departments, and ITAs themselves should not underestimate the slowness of second language learning processes, nor the intensive effort that will be required for ITAs to take their places as teachers in higher education.

In a Nutshell

1. It is likely that international teaching assistants (ITAs) will play an increasingly important role in U.S. higher education.
2. As the number of ITAs increase, academic departments will have to pay attention to recruiting practices because ITAs' language proficiency will play an important role in their being approved to teach.
3. Faculty recruiters are untrained by their departments, and when they move on the recruitment strategies they used may be lost. In other words, any study of department recruiters is a "moving target."
4. To the extent that ITA educators have direct contact with recruiters, it may be difficult to build up a shared knowledge of the relationship between English proficiency scores used for admission and ITAs' likelihood of being approved to teach upon arrival.
5. As a glimpse of what department recruiter do, and what their priorities are, several successful recruiting strategies, gained through interviews, are outlined.
6. The speaking subtest score of the TOEFL is the best indicator of approval to teach. It is, however, unlikely most faculty recruiters are aware of the TOEFL subtest score or the importance of the speaking score.
7. We offer cut scores based on the speaking subtest score of the TOEFL (19 and below) and on the total TOEFL score (94 and below).
8. The cut scores should not be used to exclude ITA candidates from being admitted. Many prospective students with moderate or low English communication ability have talents and experience that complement those of an academic department and its faculty members.
9. Rather, department recruiters should plan ahead and understand that ITA candidates with low scores on the speaking subtest will need to invest at least one or two semesters in language training to achieve communication ability sufficient to ensure adequate undergraduate learning in classrooms.

References

ETS (2014a). *About the TOEFL iBT® test.* Retrieved September 26, 2014 from: http://www.ets.org/toefl/ibt/about

ETS (2014b). *TOEFL iBT test scores.* Retrieved September 26, 2014 from: http://www.ets.org/toefl/ibt/scores/

ETS (2014c). *GRE.* Retrieved September 26, 2014 from: http://www.ets.org/gre

Glaser, B, G., & Strauss, A. J. (1967). *The discovery of grounded theory: Strategies for qualitative research.* Chicago: Aldine.

Gorsuch, G.J. (2011). Exporting English pronunciation from China: The communication needs of young Chinese scientists as teachers in higher education abroad. *Forum on Public Policy, 2011*(3). Available: http://forumonpublicpolicy.com/vol2011no3/archive/gorsuch.pdf

Gorsuch, G.J. (2012). The roles of teacher theory and domain theory in materials and research in international teaching assistant education. In G. Gorsuch (Ed.), *Working theories for teaching assistant development: Time-tested & robust theories, frameworks, & models for TA & ITA learning* (pp. 421-474). Stillwater, OK: New Forums Press.

Gorsuch, G. (2013). Helping international teaching assistants acquire discourse intonation: Explicit and implicit L2 knowledge. *Journal of Teaching English for Specific and Academic Purposes, 1*(2), 67-92. Available: http://espeap.junis.ni.ac.rs/index.php/espeap/issue/view/2

Gorsuch, G. (2014, January). *International teaching assistants at Texas Tech University.* Presentation given at the Olsher Life Long Learning Institute. Lubbock, Texas.

Gorsuch, G. (forthcoming). International teaching assistants at universities: A research agenda. *Language Teaching.*

Graduate Management Admissions Council (2002-2014). *The official website of GMAT).* Retrieved September 28, 2014 from: http://www.mba.com/us/the-gmat-exam.aspx

Griffee, D. T. (2012). Using grounded theory to develop emergent explanations on how second and foreign language TAs construct their teacher theory. In G. Gorsuch (Ed.), *Working theories for teaching assistant development: Time-tested & robust theories, frameworks, & models for TA & ITA Learning* (pp. 201-230). Stillwater, OK: New Forums Press.

Griffee, D.T., Gorsuch, G., Britton, D., & Clardy, C. (2008). Intensive second language instruction for international teaching assistants: How much and what kind is effective? In. G. Ollington (ed.), *Teachers and teaching strategies* (pp. 187-205). NY: Nova Science Publishers, Inc.

Hoekje, B., & Linnell, K. (1994). "Authenticity" in language testing: Evaluating spoken language tests for international teaching assistants. *TESOL Quarterly, 28*(1), 103-126.

IELTS (2009-2013). *IELTS.* Retrieved September 28, 2014 from: http://www.ielts.org/

Marklein, M. B. (2012, November 12). Record number of foreign students in U.S. *USA Today*, pp. 5A.

Miles, M. B., & Huberman, A. M. (1994). *Qualitative Data Analysis* (2nd ed.). Thousand Oaks, CA: Sage.

Pett, M.A. (1997). *Nonparametric statistics for health care research: Statistics for small samples and unusual distributions.* Thousand Oaks, CA: Sage.

Teachers of English to Speakers of Other Languages (2010). *Position statement on the acquisition of academic proficiency in English at the postsecondary level.* Alexandria, VA: Author. Available: http://www.tesol.org/docs/pdf/13489.pdf?sfvrsn=0

Texas Tech University Strategic Planning Council. *2010-2020 Strategic Plan.* Lubbock, Texas: Author.

Wikipedia (2012). *SPEAK (test)*. Retrieved September 27, 2014 from: http://en.wikipedia.org/wiki/SPEAK_%28test%29

Wilson, C. (2013, September 26). Tech nears 40,000 enrollment goal. *The Daily Toreador*, pp. 1A.

Working with International Graduate Students as New Instructors in a Chemistry Department During a Department-specific Summer Orientation

by Matthew Miller,[1] Ronald Hirko, Kevin Sackreiter, and Madelyn Francis, South Dakota State University

International graduate students (IGSs) are an important workforce in support of departmental research and teaching at universities. Investments have been made to prepare these students for these responsibilities. We have developed multiple components in a summer orientation program to emphasize the use of dialogue to prepare all graduate students (GSs) for their assignments, but also to help international graduate students (IGSs) enhance their verbal English skills. The components of this orientation include laboratory preparation, teaching pedagogy, and English as a second language (ESL) instruction. An assessment plan was initiated to identify the efficacy of the orientation. Interviews were conducted to obtain the perceptions of IGSs. The interviews revealed that most believed the opportunities for dialogue were important, not only for enhancing verbal English skills, but to prepare them for work in graduate school. A second assessment utilized

---

1. Author contact: matt.miller@sdstate.edu

a pre- and post-program evaluation of IGSs' English-speaking skills to determine future program-level strategies for the improvement in IGSs' verbal English skills.

The mission statement for the National Foundation for American Policy (NFAP) includes a description of the importance of immigration and education with respect to national interest (NFAP, 2015a). That aspect of policy discusses the number of graduate students attending American institutions of higher learning, specifically in science, technology, engineering, and mathematics (STEM). In a policy brief (Anderson, 2013), the NFAP argues that:

> [International graduate students] provide a key source of talent for U.S. employers and are crucial to enhancing the ability of U.S. universities to conduct research and offer high quality academic programs to U.S. students. International students also provide cultural and foreign policy benefits to the United States and are an important and inexpensive way to promote American ideas and values abroad.

Additionally, in the NFAP's Project on Global Talent and Competitiveness (NFAP, 2015b), it is stated that the need exists to attract students with an interest in STEM fields:

> America's openness and dynamic character is one of its greatest strengths. Allowing talented individuals to study and work in the United States is part of that strength. Today, it is clear that free trade in services is as important as the free flow of goods. To compete in the global economy of the 21st century, U.S. companies need access to skilled international professionals who can research, innovate, and grow businesses and key sectors of the economy.

Therefore, the number of international graduate students (IGSs) entering the United States to obtain higher degrees in STEM is a vital concern. Economists refer to the value of the education, training, and medical care for these students as human capital (Becker, 1975). This human capital, once recruited and trained, may have a major impact on the economic success of a country.

Recently the number of IGSs seeking advanced chemistry degrees across the United States was approximately 40% of the total graduate student (GS) population (National Science Foundation,

2010). In comparison to these national statistics, the Department of Chemistry and Biochemistry at South Dakota State University, where this study took place, has enrolled 80 total GSs since 2006 with 36 (45%) being IGSs. Because IGSs are an important source for teaching assistants in the department, an investment in human capital is necessary to properly prepare these students for teaching assignments in the department. All GSs (both domestic and international) arrive early in the summer prior to their initial year to participate in a departmental orientation program, which includes three components: 1. Laboratory instruction specific to their future teaching assignments, 2. A course on teaching chemistry in higher education, and 3. An English as a second language (ESL) class. In these components the emphasis is on getting all GSs to become more confident in their ability to verbalize their thoughts about science.

Learning to talk about science. In her book *Talking Their Way Into Science*, Gallas (1995) presents data suggesting that children gain a sense of importance for a topic when they must discuss topics verbally. Through that opportunity to verbalize their ideas, children gain confidence and excitement about science. Our philosophy for the orientation program is similar. When new GSs are involved in the orientation program, they are expected to talk about the science. Through this process they become more engaged and participate in conversations about science at a deeper level. The result is that GSs, including IGSs, engage in discussions that not only examine their knowledge about science, but also compel them to engage in a dialogue with others. We hypothesize that the resulting dialogue positively impacts the spoken English skills of IGSs. Therefore we have emphasized creating dialogues in the various components of the orientation program to enhance impact on the English speaking skills of the IGSs. During all three of these summer orientation components, all incoming GSs, including the IGSs, are required to verbalize their thoughts in an effort to improve discipline-specific communication. Thus, our goal is to improve GAs' and IGAs' communication while teaching undergraduate students.

This program description and evaluation report will provide detailed information about the methods we use during our summer orientation program and how we have evaluated the success of these methods. We will introduce the pedagogical methods we use to engage our new graduate students in three specific components of the orientation: Laboratory instruction, teaching chemistry in higher education, and English as a second language for the teaching assistant. Feedback from new graduate students will be presented to document the efficacy of these methods. Finally, a method for evaluating the English skills of IGSs will be outlined, and we will further describe data that speaks to the success of our program at enhancing those English skills.

The Summer Orientation

Component 1: Laboratory instruction. In the laboratory instruction component, GSs gain knowledge in what needs to be communicated when they are the teaching assistants of a laboratory course. During the summer, newly enrolled GSs must complete the entire series of laboratory experiments taught in both the large enrollment sequences of first-year undergraduate chemistry courses to gain an understanding of the topics and skills taught during these courses. These large enrollment courses are for science and allied health majors. Prior to the physical completion of each lab, GSs practice giving laboratory kickoffs. In this department of chemistry and biochemistry, the term "laboratory kickoff" refers to the typical way in which information is communicated from the teaching assistant to the students at the beginning of the laboratory period. Teaching assistants in these labs have a choice of what pedagogical method they would prefer to use during the kickoff (see discussion of Component 2 below), but regardless of the pedagogical method chosen, there are verbal communications of knowledge that must occur.

Each GS is expected to conduct at minimum three practice kickoffs during the summer orientation program. Peer and faculty feedback follow each of these practice sessions. In addition, the orientation director, for whom one of the fall and spring teaching assignments is that of undergraduate laboratory director, observes and gives feedback during these sessions. The practice kickoffs are a form of "talking science" (Gallas, 1995), and just like allowing elementary school students the opportunity to express personal concepts about science topics, the GSs are likely involved in their first opportunity to extend their thoughts as an instructor in such a way as to help others learn. This is a key first step in the development of an instructor--the consideration of how concepts can be presented to help students construct personal knowledge of the concepts.

Verbal feedback on concepts and on talk. Feedback during these teaching exercises touches on how new GSs are providing information on science concepts and more specifically, on how the GSs are conveying their messages verbally. Feedback from peers and faculty informs the new GS about how others perceive their verbal attributes as a teacher. For example, students receive feedback about eye contact, volume, and enunciation. These non-verbal and verbal characteristics are essential, especially for the IGSs as they prepare for teaching in labs. Performance and practice are extended into the first fall semester: All new GSs are video recorded while presenting an actual laboratory kickoff during the fall semester, and the video is peer reviewed during a follow-up orientation meeting. GSs again receive feedback regarding their talk. In addition, each student must submit a self-evaluation of his or her kickoff by viewing the videotape alone. As part of the evaluation, each GS must answer the following questions: 1. *If I were in this class, would I have been happy with how the information provided by the teaching assistant was presented?* 2. *Did I provide the opportunity for undergraduate students to gain the necessary information during the kickoff to complete the laboratory in an efficient and effective manner?*

Component 2: Teaching chemistry in higher education. The second component of the summer orientation is designed to prepare GSs for teaching in the classroom through enrolling in a graduate-level course. This course, "Chemistry Instruction in Higher Education," is currently a required core course for both the M.S. and Ph.D. chemistry degree candidates. Using primarily group work to engage GSs in discussions about teaching, the course is designed along two main themes: 1. tools and resources for teaching and 2. teacher attitudes. See Table 1.

Table 1. Topics and Readings for "Chemistry Instruction in Higher Education"

Session (90 minutes each)	Teaching tools: Topics and readings	Teaching attitude: Topics and readings
	Survival Handbook for the New Chemistry Instructor (Bunce & Muzzi, 2003)	*Becoming a Person of Influence: How to Positively Impact the Lives of Others* (Maxwell & Dornan, 1997) *Teach Like a Pirate: Increase Student Engagement, Boost your Creativity, and Transform your Life as an Educator* (Burgess, 2012)
Session 1	Initial meeting – set permanent dates, times, meeting place; Discuss syllabus and What is the role of higher education? Reading "The purposes of higher education" (Kahlenberg, 2011)	
Session 2	What is it like to teach in higher education? Chapter 1 & 2 in *Survival*, pages 2-18	Do we influence other people when we are instructors? Introduction of *Influence*
Session 3	How do you construct a syllabus? Chapter 4 *Survival*	How is integrity important to influence? Chapter 1 *Influence*
Session 4	What is the outline of the course? What resources should be used? Chapters 5 & 6 *Survival* plus textbook of choice	
Session 5	What materials should be made available as resources for students? Textbook of choice, Online methods (Day, Botch, Hixson, Lillya, Vining, & Gross, 2014)	How does nurturing cause influence? Chapter 2 *Influence* Hook 1
Session 6	How do we help students construct knowledge? Chapter 13 *Survival*, Formative assessment	How does faith cause influence? Chapter 3 *Influence* Hook 2
Session 7	How does teaching style (what is teaching style?) impact learners? Chapter 3 *Survival*	How does listening cause influence? Chapter 4 *Influence* Hook 3
Session 8	How can we motivate students to help them overcome apprehension? Chapter 7 *Survival*	How can we understand students and cause influence? Chapter 5 *Influence* Hook 4

Session 9	How do students learn chemistry? What are examples of learning strategies and solving problems? Chapters 8 & Chapter 9 *Survival* and "Teaching Science to Every Child" 5E learning cycle (Eisenkraft, 2003)	Hook 5
Session 10	What works and what doesn't? Innovations: Technology, course management systems, interactive media Read chapters 9 & 10 *Survival*	How can we enlarge people and cause influence? Read Chapter 6 *Influence* Hook 6
Session 11	What works and what doesn't? Innovations: POGIL (2012-2014)	How we help people navigate builds influence. Chapter 7 *Influence* Hook 7
Session 12	What works and what doesn't? Innovations: Cooperative learning Chapters 11 & 12 *Survival*	How we connect with people builds influence Chapter 8 *Influence*
Session 13	Mini-teaching experience	
Session 14	What works and what doesn't? Innovations: Demonstrations, simulations, internet courses "Where is the Science" (Penick, 1991)	How we empower people builds influence Chapter 9 *Influence*
Session 15	Mini-teaching experience	
Session 16	How do we learn more? Professional development Chapter 19 *Survival*	How can we reproduce people of influence? Chapter 10 *Influence*

    The teaching tools for chemistry include pedagogical methods such as group and individual techniques, and on-line instruction. GSs do not enter their graduate careers with strong knowledge about teaching. What they do know about teaching has been gained from their experience as students and is, of course, fragmented. The course about teaching provides them an initial opportunity to study ideas about teaching from the perspective of how they as the instructor would decide how to present topics in chemistry and biochemistry. The required textbook (Bunce & Muzzi, 2003) provides students with resources about multiple pedagogical methods used by chemistry instructors. The goal is for new GSs to gain fundamental knowledge about some of the best practices in chemistry teaching. Some examples of the best practices on which GSs focus in the course are now provided.

Current best chemistry teaching practices exploration. One best teaching practice in chemistry is Process Oriented Guided Inquiry Learning (POGIL)(2012-2014). POGIL was developed in college chemistry departments with the support of the National Science Foundation, and now is a widely used instructional method in colleges and high schools across the country (Farrell, Moog, Spencer, & Spencer, 1999). The POGIL website provides many curricular resources designed to support group work projects to enhance students' understanding of difficult chemistry topics (POGIL, 2012-2014). After studying the steps of POGIL technique, GSs are provided the opportunity to practice a POGIL activity.

Another best practices pedagogical approach studied is the use of computer simulations in the classroom. Specifically, students of chemistry examine Physics Educational Technology (PHET) (University of Colorado, 2015), which is a website developed at the University of Colorado to provide computer simulations on a variety of science topics (University of Colorado, 2015). College and high school chemistry instructors can use the simulations to engage students (University of Colorado, 2015). After reviewing initial simulations and discussing how they might be used in a course, GSs/IGSs are assigned the task of finding a simulation of interest and presenting about that simulation.

The last example of a best practices approach to teaching discussed is learning about "hooks" GSs could use to increase their students' interest in learning. These hooks were presented in another required book about how to engage learners and increase teachers' creativity (Burgess, 2012). Hooks are a series of motivational steps such as "the kinesthetic hook," "the costume hook," and "the mystery bag hook." GSs were organized into groups to study, present, and give an example of how they would use specific hooks in the classroom.

Finally, the theme on teacher attitudes (personal characteristics that instructors need to emulate) includes readings from a third required book on how to influence people (Maxwell & Dornan, 1997). In the class GSs discuss how we as instructors have tremendous influence over students, and that the attitudes we bring to the classroom greatly influence the outcome of the course for students.

Personal characteristics such as integrity, faith in others, and listening, help to influence, enlarge, and empower others. These personal character themes are interwoven with the topics of teaching to help the GSs to realize that teaching is not a focus only on the content, but a focus on the development of individuals.

How our verbalization goals are achieved in the course. Our ultimate goal of verbalization is accomplished in this course several ways. First, as previously mentioned, students engage with one another through group work to discuss the main topic of the course session. Group work in the course can involve small one-on-one discussions, or activities such as jigsaw sessions (Aronson, 2005; Aronson & Patnoe, 1997) and fish bowl discussions (Chien, 2004; Dutt, 1997). During the course we engage GSs in each of these activities to model the pedagogy. GSs therefore have the opportunity to consider what they might do as an instructor in their classroom. We urge GSs, as novice teachers, to use their laboratory classrooms to explore the variety of teaching techniques available to them, and not just to lecture. While one goal is for GSs to experience various pedagogical methods of group work, the overarching goal is to engage GSs/IGSs verbally in conversations about teaching science. We hypothesize this will result in two outcomes: 1. All GSs will learn alternative methods for teaching and, 2. IGSs will improve in their verbal English skills.

Final teaching project. For a final project in the course, GSs/IGSs are randomly assigned a general chemistry topic. They then plan a lesson, and then teach a 15-minute lesson. This assignment is peer-reviewed for content and presentation style (talk). Each summer, GSs construct an evaluation rubric for the purpose of evaluating both the science taught in the practice session, but also the presentation of the session. The creation of the rubric offers an opportunity for discussion, and is another example of learning how to teach through developing a teaching assessment strategy (Stevens & Levi, 2005). GSs are expected to meet specific standards for verbal communication during their presentation based on the rubric created by the individuals in the course. The process of self-designing the rubric helps GSs consider the important characteristics of talk and quality of content necessary for an effective classroom session. Again, the philosophy behind this teaching project is to engage GSs (including IGSs), in verbal challenges that require them to say scientific terminology and present that information in a logical manner. In this way students learn about aspects of teaching but also are practicing communication skills.

Component 3: English as a Second Language. The final component of the summer orientation requires IGSs to participate in an English as a second language (ESL) course. The goal is to help IGSs improve their enunciation of English in preparation for the instructional laboratory. The department recognizes the difficulty of chemistry and biochemistry as a topic of study for both undergraduate and graduate students. Improving the verbal ability of IGSs is a simple investment in human capital, and will serve two purposes: 1. Improve IGSs' communication in their graduate level courses and within their research groups, and 2. Improve instruction at the undergraduate level. Undergraduate students struggle with chemistry, and when an instructor also has a communication issue, these students can experience increased difficulty in understanding the topic. For that reason, the department decided that all IGSs would be involved in the ESL program to help develop their English communication skills.

Our ESL instructor uses the textbook: *Clear Speech: Pronunciation and Listening Comprehension in North American English* (Gilbert, 2012). The following is the textbook author's stated objectives (p. x):

> *Clear Speech*, Fourth Edition, concentrates on rhythm, stress, and intonation because improvement in these aspects of pronunciation can do the most good in improving both listening comprehension and clarity of speech. Individual speech sounds, however, are also significant, and are therefore covered throughout the book.

The book includes listening and speaking tests, pair work activities, taking dictation tasks, rhythm practice, and listening activities. As the instructor teaches the ESL class, pair work activities are used, which helps IGSs to become aware of their accents and enunciation issues. They have to work to listen to each other, and also make themselves understood. Further, the ESL instructor identifies intonation and speech rhythm patterns during an initial assessment to determine useful approaches for individual IGSs in the ESL component. *Clear Speech* (Gilbert, 2012) emphasizes the focus stress and intonation patterns at the sentence level, which is supported by the research of Hahn (2004) and Levis, Muller Levis, and Slater (2012). We believe that American prosodic patterns are best learned at the fundamental level of vowels, syllables, and word stress patterns. Our 8-week ESL course begins there and then moves on to the prosody of sentences, where IGSs are taught how to emphasize content words, de-emphasize structure words, choose the focus word for primary stress, and determine when to emphasize structure words. The last sections focus on correct consonant production, dialogues, and the prosody associated with thought groups in sentences.

To assess progress in this component, we developed a procedure to initially assess IGSs, plan a strategy for their speech development in the course, and then evaluate IGSs several times for speech intelligibility to evaluate the success of the strategy. The process involves the following steps:

1. Record an IGS reading a scripted passage from *Clear Speech* (Gilbert, 2012)(see Table 4 below).
   a. The ESL instructor evaluates the recording to identify how IGSs produce the speech sounds, whether they use appropriate intonation and rhythm patterns, and to create a plan for helping IGSs to improve English skills.

2. Assess the impact of the improvement plan by establishing an intelligibility number (IN) for the IGSs using a three-minute monologue on a topic of their choice.
   a. Record the monologue, and then an external rater listens to the recording and counts all the words not understood.
   b. Determine an IN (understood words/total spoken words) for individual IGSs.
   c. Repeat steps 2a and 2b for a total of three assessments (initial, middle, final) during the 8 week ESL program.

IN is the number of understood words divided by the total number of words spoken on the tape, and thus is a percentage. This method is based on the concept of word identification as described by Schiavetti (1992, p. 28):

> Word identification tests produce a metric of speech intelligibility that is more readily usable by the researcher or clinician in a form that can be communicated to other professionals and to

laypersons. The word identification score is typically calculated as a percentage of words correctly heard or as a proportion that can be easily converted to a percentage. Indexing speech intelligibility with a percentage makes a certain degree of intuitive sense for informing someone of the degree to which they can expect to understand the speech produced by a disordered speaker.

To date, we have only piloted this process. In 2014, out of the four IGSs we tested, our personal, anecdotal perceptions of the ability of IGS speakers matched the test results. Table 2 contains three IN values for the four IGSs at three stages in the ESL course, and the predictive perceptions of intelligibility by the orientation director and laboratory coordinator as a joint anecdotal assessment.

Table 2. Intelligibility Number (IN) Data for IGSs During the 2014 Orientation

International graduate student ID	Intelligibility number (IN) $$IN = \frac{\text{\# of understood words}}{\text{\# of words spoken}} \times 100$$			Predicted intelligibility (anecdotal perceptions of orientation faculty members)
	Initial evaluation (3- minute free speech)	Middle evaluation (3- minute free speech)	Final evaluation (3- minute free speech)	
IGS 1	95.1% (291/306)	96.4% (268/278)	97.7% (298/305)	Very intelligible
IGS 2	93.0% (279/300)	95.8% (275/287)	95.0% (283/298)	Some intelligibility issues
IGS 3	92.8% (258/278)	93.9% (216/230)	96.6% (288/298)	Difficult to follow
IGS 4	82.0% (173/211)	88.2% (187/212)	91.9% (251/273)	Very difficult to follow

As can be observed, IGSs scored relatively high on the IN evaluations throughout the eight-week ESL program. Comparing the IN values to the anecdotal prediction of intelligibility, these values corresponded to the orientation faculty members' predictions of intelligibility. The upward changes in IN values for each student suggests that IGSs improved in their ability to enunciate words in extemporaneous monologic speech, an important step for improving spoken language. However, it would seem that the IN values are not as representative as we might like of the levels of intelligibility of two of the four IGSs. Although IGS 3 and IGS 4 scored seemingly high on the IN values, they were difficult to understand on an anecdotal level. We hypothesize that IN measures the ability of the listener to recognize words, but not necessarily understand sentences. Therefore although the two lower-level IGSs were enunciating individual words in a way recognizable by the listener, they may still lack the intonation and rhythm necessary for intelligibility. Hahn (2004) suggests that how intonation and rhythm is used in sentences is crucial to intelligibility. Therefore this initial data supports the findings that improved enunciation is not enough. IGSs must improve in their use of rhythm and intonation patterns that native English speakers are more familiar with, if they wish to be more intelligible.

Summer Orientation Evaluation Methodology

We now describe the method and results of our evaluation of the summer orientation. As this work primarily was done to assess the impact the orientation had on IGSs, only the international students were invited to participate. 21 IGSs entering the Chemistry & Biochemistry graduate program from 2009 - 2013 were invited to participate in providing feedback through interviews. The interviews were completed during the spring of 2014. IN values obtained as previously described were used to evaluate changes in four IGS's English speaking skills (see Table 2).

Post-orientation interviews. IGSs in the department were asked to participate in an interview to collect their perceptions of the impact of the components of the orientation program. Of the 21 IGSs invited to participate, 6 IGSs participated in the interview sessions. The interview protocol is in Table 3.

Table 3. Interview Protocol for IGS Feedback Regarding Verbal English Skills

Question Themes	Questions Capturing the Theme
Perceptions of IGSs about verbal English skills	1. Do you believe that your skills in verbal English communication have improved as a result of training efforts within the department/university at SDSU? 2. Please provide some specific examples of where you have seen improvement in your verbal English communication skills. 3. Please share where you feel you have received the most assistance in improving your verbal English communication skills.
Laboratory instruction component	4. Were there activities that you feel improved your verbal English communication skills in the Lab Instructional Training Program of the Chemistry/Biochemistry Department? 5. Specifically what impact did the practice lab kick-offs of the Lab Instructional Training Program have on your verbal English communication? 6. Do you feel the activities of the Lab Instructional Training Program were intended to improve your verbal English communication skills?
Chemistry Instruction in Higher Education component (CHEM 715)	7. Were there activities that you feel improved your verbal English communication skills in the CHEM 715 course offered by the Chemistry/Biochemistry Department? 8. Specifically what impact did the Teaching Practice Section of CHEM 715 (15 minute teaching session) have on your verbal English communication? 9. Do you feel the activities of CHEM 715 were intended to improve your verbal English communication skills?
English as a second language instruction component	10. Were there activities that you feel improved your verbal English communication skills in the ESL Instruction provided by the Chemistry/Biochemistry Department? 11. Specifically what impact did the use of workbooks and the peer conversations in the ESL Instruction have on your verbal English communication? 12. Do you feel the activities of the ESL Instruction were intended to improve your verbal English communication skills?
Current practice methods in English	13. When you started your program in Chemistry/Biochemistry did you use your native language or English in social situations? 14. Currently do you use your native language or English in social situations? 15. What can be done by the Chemistry/Biochemistry Department/University to better assist you in developing your verbal English communication skills?

The protocol consisted of questions across five main themes connected to IGSs' verbal skills in English, as we believe they intersected with the orientation: 1. Perceptions of the orientation, 2. The laboratory instruction component, 3. The Chemistry Instruction in Higher

Education course, 4. English as a second language instruction, and 5. IGSs' current methods used to practice English on their own. Our goal was to collect information from the IGSs for the purpose of identifying any components not successfully accomplishing the goal of enhancing verbal English skills from the IGSs' point of view. Based on this information, the orientation components could be changed to more effectively enhance IGSs' verbal skills and prepare them for their instructional assignments.

The third author, the director of the Center for Enhancement of Teaching & Learning at the university, conducted the interviews. Participants had previous contact with this individual through teaching development workshops and university orientation sessions. We believed the IGSs would be more likely to provide accurate feedback with him, as opposed to individuals in the Chemistry department in charge of the orientation. All six IGS statements were recorded and transcribed, but only the third author had knowledge of the identity of the participants. Analysis of the de-identified data was conducted by the first author, who is the director of the department of chemistry's orientation program. These procedures are consistent with Kvale's (2007) description of the interviewer as a kind of traveller. The interviewer/analyst sought the perceptions of the IGSs' experiences in the program. The resulting information would describe the lived experiences of these IGSs, but could also change the view of the interviewer/analyst. Following Patton (2002) the transcripts were analyzed in search of emerging themes regarding the experiences of IGSs during the orientation, and their perceptions on how their English language skills were impacted by the experience.

Pre- and post-test speaking and pronunciation assessment. The fourth author is the ESL instructor hired by the department of chemistry, and is responsible for conducting the verbal assessment. As described earlier the verbal assessment was a pilot. Early in the ESL program, the ESL instructor recorded four IGSs reading a short manuscript aloud (see Table 4). This information was used to develop a course of action for each student to improve English-speaking skills. Then, three separate analyses of progress (initial, middle, and final) were made of that work by measuring the IN value described earlier. The three successive speech samples of four ITGs were short extemporaneous monologic talks (Table 2).

Table 4. The Clear Speaking Test Read-Aloud Text from Clear Speech

	Two University Students Meet
A:	Excuse me. Where's the library?
B:	It's on the corner of Main Street and Selling Road.
A:	Sorry, did you say Selling or Ceiling?
B:	Selling. It's directly ahead of you, about 2 blocks.
A:	Thanks. I need to buy some books for my classes.
B:	Oh, then you need the bookstore. You can't buy books at the library. You can only borrow them there.
A:	I guess I confused the words. They're different in my language.
B:	I know how it is. I get mixed up with Spanish words that sound like English words, but have different meanings.
A:	Are you studying Spanish?
B:	Yes, it's going to be my major. What are you studying?
A:	I'm studying English now, but my major will be economics.
B:	Really? My brother wanted to study economics. He took the entrance exam for that department just last week.
A:	Did he succeed?
B:	No, quite the opposite. He failed.
A:	That's too bad.
B:	Oh, it's OK. He would've had to study statistics, and he hated that idea. Anyway, he changed his mind, and now he plans to study music.
A:	That's great! Does he want to compose or perform?
B:	Both. He wants to compose and perform. He arranges programs for musicians, but he also plays classical guitar.
A:	Well, I wish him a lot of luck. And good luck to you, too. It was nice talking.

Note. Source of text: (Gilbert, 2012, p. 74)

Interview Results and Discussion

The interviews were conducted in the spring of 2014 with six IGSs who attended the orientation program in the two prior summers. Table 5 contains a summary of IGSs' perceptions of the orientation based on the questions from the interview.

Table 5. Summary of IGS Interviews

Themes	Summary of IGSs' Responses
Improved English due to orientation	✓ 4/6 IGSs indicated no. Reasons for the negative perception include: - Learning English takes personal time - Important to talk with others - It takes time
Specific situational areas of English improvement	✓ Three IGSs listed communication in the research lab with advisor or other students. ✓ Two IGSs listed teaching experiences both in orientation and actual teaching assistant appointments.
What aspects of the orientation provided the most assistance in English	✓ Five IGSs mentioned teaching experiences both in practice situations and actual teaching assistant appointments. ✓ Three of these IGSs mentioned specifically practicing giving kickoffs during the lab instruction component of the orientation.
Laboratory instruction component	✓ Five IGSs specifically mentioned the practice kickoffs as being very important, and two believed not enough time was given for the kickoffs.
Chemistry Instruction in Higher Education component (CHEM 715)	✓ All six IGSs mentioned the importance of teaching the topic in chemistry to their peers. ✓ One IGS mentioned the two books used for the class and indicated a continued use of the motivational book (Maxwell & Dornan, 1997) ✓ One IGS mentioned that the class involved too much philosophy and not enough teaching opportunities.
English as a second language instruction component	✓ Four of the IGSs indicated that the ESL was not necessary for them. ✓ Five IGSs indicated the importance of focusing on interactions between peers as important. ✓ Five IGSs indicated the importance of the focus on intonation, enunciation, and reduction of accents.
Current practice methods in English	✓ IGSs indicated a decrease in the use of English in social settings, as they tended to socialize with students from their own countries and therefore reverted to their native language outside the department.

What can the department do better?	✓ Promote the university programs in the Teaching & Learning Center to IGSs.
	✓ Provide more opportunities to conduct kickoffs and more time to think about how to give kickoffs.
	✓ Make more time to verbalize across the department (discussions with peers).
	✓ Need more time to verbalize with supervisors.
	✓ Need better assessment of the impact of the orientation.

IGSs indicated the need for more time to verbalize during all components of the orientation. In the laboratory instruction component, IGSs stated that the practice kickoffs were extremely important and believed that it would be helpful if all students had the chance to prepare a kickoff during the summer for all laboratory experiments. The extra opportunities for verbalizations allowed IGSs more practice while helping each prepare for the experiments during the first year of their GS career.

In the Chemistry Instruction in Higher Education component, students frequently mentioned the teaching exercise, which involved students teaching a random topic to peers, as an important opportunity. IGSs believed the project provided the opportunity to practice verbalizing chemistry terminology. One issue brought up by several IGSs was the topics were too broad and it was difficult to decide what to teach in the limited time given for the presentation. On the other hand, students suggested this helped them to organize their thoughts about that topic. We believe this is an extremely important step for new instructors in higher education, whether GSs or IGSs. The decision on what and how to teach along with the length of time to allocate for that instruction is a very important concept that each instructor must struggle with as they begin teaching. For the ESL component, several students mentioned the focus on intonation and enunciation. Although the majority stated the ESL work did not help their English speaking skills in the form used during the orientation, some suggested that a longer version of this component would be valuable.

IGSs' perceptions of the orientation program as being helpful toward improving their English speaking skills were mixed. Although the majority of IGSs, when directly asked their opinion of the efficacy of the program, stated they did not believe it had helped them to improve their English skills, most commented that specific verbalization exercises would be successful given more time. Specifically, the practice kickoffs, teaching general chemistry topics, and peer activity discussions were mentioned by multiple IGSs. One theme common across most interviews was the statement that time assigned to these activities was a key factor in how successful an activity was in improving English language skills. Limited time for verbalizations was given as the major reason IGSs believed the orientation program was not successful in improving their skills. This may explain participants' comments that long-term interactions with research advisors and colleagues were more likely to impact their English language skills.

Decisions based on feedback. Based on this feedback, the orientation directors plan to increase the opportunities for students to express verbally their ideas in chemistry and teaching. Additionally, peer collaborators (experienced GSs) will be assigned to the orientation program to increase interaction time. During the laboratory component, three experienced GSs will join the team to help new GSs to learn about teaching assignments. During each session in future orientations, experienced GSs will take the lead in helping students to learn about the experiments, providing peer interactions that we believe will enhance verbal interactions. If time permits, we plan to an increase the number of assigned practice kickoff sessions.

Feedback from the interviews indicated that the Chemistry Instruction in Higher Education (CHEM 715) course might have been too theoretical. The instructor of the course plans to continue to expose students to the teaching methods raised in the course, but will increase practice opportunities. An experienced GS will also be assigned to the Chemistry Instruction in Higher Education (CHEM 715) course. The role of this experienced GS will be to provide alternative interactions, beyond those offered by the instructor, to allow new GSs to express concepts and teaching ideas. This will allow for increased feedback on assignments, specifically from a peer. We believe this will encourage new GSs to be more expressive, and will allow for increased opportunities for the faculty and experienced GSs to comment on verbal English communication issues.

The ESL component will continue to have limited sessions due to budget constraints. However, after considering the interview data and discussions with the ESL instructor, we will focus on verbal English skills early in the orientation so that IGSs will be made aware of intonation and rhythm issues early and have additional time to focus on these intelligibility issues. We will continue to schedule many of the ESL sessions during the IGSs' first three weeks on campus. Once the focus has been established, the co-directors of the orientation and teaching assistants will maintain that focus by reminding students of critical points made by the ESL instructor. This will be done at critical moments during the components (practice kickoff sessions, practice teaching exercise) to refocus IGSs on their verbal attributes while they are practicing as course instructors. Finally, it has been proposed that IGSs be linked with an experienced GS for weekly conversations, again to increase the verbalizations of IGSs. Through this type of practice, we hope the intelligibility of IGSs will be increased to a level where undergraduate complaints are reduced.

Speaking Assessment Discussion and Decisions

The assessment developed by the Department of Chemistry & Biochemistry has been unfocused. More organized attempts at increasing the intelligibility of IGSs are needed. The method used to develop a strategic plan for each IGS is based on examining their intonation and rhythm patterns of the scripted passage read by IGSs from *Clear Speech* (Gilbert, 2012). Activities from *Clear Speech* then focus IGSs on these issues during the remainder of the 8-week orientation. It is likely we need to subsume the fundamentals of these activities into the interactions and verbalizations that occur during all components of the orientation, not just the activities within the ESL component. We plan to more carefully integrate these activities during the 2015 summer orientation program to enhance the potential outcome for IGSs.

We believe the IN values from the three-minute free speech sessions have some use as measures of intelligibility. All faculty involved in the orientation agreed that IGS #4 (Table 2) was very difficult to understand during orientation presentations, and the IN value for IGS #4 was correspondingly lower. We can use these values to provide evidence of the need for these students to continue to seek additional help, potentially enrolling in speech or theatre classes to engage in more verbal activities.

We did find the IN values likely do not measure the prosody of IGS speech, but likely provided some measure of intelligibility at the word level. We therefore think that an alternative means of measuring primary stress in IGSs' talk be developed for comparison with the IN values system. We will continue to develop various measures so that intelligibility of new IGSs can be better measured and appropriate remedial tactics applied based off these measures. It is also possible we need to change the speaking assessment task. This could be recording a variety of IGSs' verbalizations done during different components of the orientation. The lab kickoff is the most salient contact IGSs will have with U.S. undergraduates so we will consider using these practice sessions as replacements for the three-minute extemporaneous speeches we used earlier.

Conclusion: The Need for Time for Skills Development

We believe our approach emphasizing increased verbalization through the philosophy of Talking Science (Gallas, 1995) across the activities of the orientation while focusing on word and sentence prosody and vowel and consonant production during the ESL program has been validated. We believe our emphasis on verbalization in the orientation program is a good first step toward improving IGSs' intelligibility. These students specifically indicated that verbalization opportunities specific to chemistry and biochemistry as part of the orientation program were important toward their English-speaking development.

We further conclude that IGSs must be rewarded in some way for their efforts to enhance intelligibility. Currently, an environment in the orientation exists that may be described as more adversarial which may explain some negative responses in during interviews. Clearly, IGSs need to feel more of a buy-in for the orientation. The summer orientation organizers must work with experienced IGSs already in the department to develop a system that rewards new IGSs students for their participation in this critically important support program.

Successful communication between native English-speaking undergraduates and IGSs in the teaching laboratory has several implications. To return to our first theme in this report, IGSs are an important source of human capital, and all effort to improve their skills will have an impact not only on their careers but also on the national economy. IGSs represent a vital component toward growth in scientific production and therefore enhanced abilities to communicate will increase IGSs' chances for productive scientific careers. And, IGSs have a major impact on the success of the laboratory experience and therefore on the potential for the continuation of undergraduates in a STEM career.

In a Nutshell

1. An investment in human capital is necessary to properly prepare graduate students for teaching assignments in the department of chemistry to enhance learning outcomes for all students taking courses through the department.
2. "Science talk" (*Talking Their Way Into Science*, Gallas, 1995) is an effective method for developing a deeper understanding of science and an ability to convey that knowledge.
3. A rich summer orientation program can provide the environment to use science talk in various components with the goal of helping international graduate students to increase their English verbal skills.
4. Interviews with six international graduate students indicated that the components of the summer orientation were beneficial but not long enough to impact their verbal English skills.
5. International graduate students' perceptions indicated the need for more interactions with experienced graduate students and more opportunities to practice talking science.
6. Future orientations will add experienced graduate students to the instructional team with the goal of increasing verbal interactions.
7. Using a pre-assessment consisting of a read-aloud text, and a series of post-assessment, three-minute extemporaneous speeches, we were able to create an individualized strategy, based on *Clear Speech* (Gilbert, 2012), to enhance IGSs' English skills and provide grounds for planning improvements to ESL instruction in all aspects of the summer orientation.

References

Anderson, S. (2013). The importance of international students to America. National Foundation for American Policy. Available: http://www.nfap.com/pdf/New%20NFAP%20Policy%20Brief%20The%20Importance%20of%20International%20Students%20to%20America,%20July%202013.pdf

Aronson, E. (2000-2015). *The jigsaw classroom.* Social Sciences Network. Available: www.jigsaw.org

Aronson, E. & Patnoe S. (1997). *The jigsaw classroom: Building cooperation in the classroom.* New York: Addison Wesley Longman.

Becker, G.S. (1975). *Human capital: A theoretical and empirical analysis* (2nd ed.). New York: Columbia University Press.

Bunce, D. & Muzzi, C. (Eds). (2003). *Survival handbook for the new chemistry instructor.* Upper Saddle River, NJ: Pearson Prentice Hall.

Burgess, D. (2012). *Teach like a pirate: Increase student engagement, boost your creativity, and transform your life as an educator.* San Diego, CA: Dave Burgess Consulting, Inc.

Chien, A. (2004). *Generic fishbowl activity for the science classroom.* Available: http://www.scienceteacherprogram.org/genscience/Chien04.html

Dutt, K. M. (1997). The fishbowl motivates students to participate. *College Teaching, 45,* 143-148.

Eisenkraft, A. (2003). Expanding the 5E Model: A proposed 7E model emphasizes "transfer of learning" and the importance of eliciting prior understanding. *The Science Teacher,* 70, (6), 56-59.

Farrell, J.J., Moog, R.S., & Spencer, J.N. (1999). A guided inquiry chemistry course. *Journal of Chemical Education,* 76, 570-574.

Gallas, K. (1995). *Talking their way into science: Hearing children's questions and theories, responding with curricula.* New York, NY: Teachers College Press.

Gilbert, J. (2012). *Clear speech: Pronunciation and listening comprehension in North American English* (4th ed.). New York: Cambridge University Press.

Hahn, L.D. (2004). Primary stress and intelligibility: Research to motivate the teaching of suprasegmentals. *TESOL Quarterly, 38* (2), 201-223.

Kahlenberg, R.D. (2011, September 1). The purposes of higher education. *Chronicle of Higher Education.* Available: http://chronicle.com/blogs/innovations/the-purposes-of-higher-education/30258

Kvale, S. (2007). Doing interviews. In U. Flick (Ed.), *The SAGE qualitative research kit* (pp. 1-154). Thousand Oaks, CA: SAGE Publications Inc.

Levis, J., Muller Levis, G., & Slater, T. (2012). Written English into spoken: A functional discourse analysis of American, Indian, and Chinese TA presentations. In G. Gorsuch (Ed.), *Working theories for teaching assistant development* (pp. 529-573). Stillwater, OK: New Forums Press.

Maxwell, J. & Dornan, J. (1997). *Becoming a person of influence: How to positively impact the lives of others.* Nashville, TN: Thomas Nelson, Inc.

National Foundation for American Policy (2015a). *Mission statement.* Available: http://nfap.com/about-us/mission-statement/

National Foundation for American Policy (2015b). *Key projects.* Available: http://nfap.com/about-us/key-projects/

National Science Foundation (2010). *Survey of graduate students and postdoctorates* in science and engineering. Available: https://ncsesdata.nsf.gov/webcaspar/

Day, R., Botch, B., Hixson, S., Lillya, P. Vining, W., & Gross, D. (2014). *OWL online web learning.* Cengage Learning, Inc. Available: http://www.cengage.com/owl/

Patton, M.Q. (2002). *Qualitative Research and Evaluation Methods* (3rd ed). Thousand Oaks, CA: Sage Publications.

Penick, J.E. (1991). Where's the Science? *The Science Teacher 58, (5),* 26-29.

The POGIL Project (2012-2014). *Process oriented guided inquiry learning* (POGIL). Available: https://pogil.org/

Schiavetti, N. (1992). Scaling procedures for the measurement of speech intelligibility. In R. Kent (Ed.), *Intelligibility in speech disorders: Theory, measurement and management* (pp. 11-34). Philadelphia, NJ: John Benjamins Publishing Company.

Stevens, D.D. & Levi, A.J. (2005). *Introduction to rubrics: An assessment tool to save grading time, convey effective feedback, and promote student learning.* Sterling, VA: Stylus Publishing, LLC.

University of Colorado (2015). *Physics education technology (PHET) interactive simulations (2015).* Available: http://phet.colorado.edu/

Supporting International Teaching Assistants: A Benchmarking Study of Administrative and Organizational Structures

by Karen E. Brinkley-Etzkorn, Ferlin G. McGaskey,[1] & Taimi A. Olsen, University of Tennessee, Knoxville

More international graduate students are taking on the role of international teaching assistants (ITAs) in U.S. classrooms. With this has come increased interest in their preparation and training to enter the classroom as well as ongoing development of their language and communication skills, pedagogical skills, and cultural awareness and transition. Of the many factors that have been considered as potentially influencing ITAs' development, one that has not been adequately addressed is the administrative and organizational structures of the institutions to which they belong. This report focuses specifically on examining the ways in which these structures shape the provision of services and support designed for, and targeted to, ITAs. Findings suggest that an institution's organizational structures do impact ITA development, particularly with regard to the ways in which the supporting units coordinate their efforts.

As the number of international teaching assistants grows in the United States, there is increased interest in their professional development (Bengu, 2009; Gorsuch, 2003, 2012; LaRocco, 2011). Scholars have suggested that institutional leaders should

---
1. Author contact: fmcgaske@utk.edu

conceptualize ITA teacher training to meet three key areas of need: language, pedagogy, and culture (Smith, Byrd, Barrett, & Constantinides, 1992). That is, institutions should develop and provide training that addresses these areas to ensure that ITAs acquire the necessary communication knowledge, instructional skills, and cultural awareness. Higher education institutions have diverse offices and units on their campuses which, based on their expertise, are responsible for training ITAs in these subjects. However, scholars suggest looking to specialized services is not sufficient. Specifically, researchers have called for institutions, when considering the necessary services and support needed for ITA development (e.g. the needs of graduate students, availability of resources, and the units and offices to be involved), to also consider the administrative and organizational structures already in place and how services work as a whole (Ard, 1989; Smith et al, 1992).

This chapter examines the ways in which the organizational structures of universities may influence how ITAs develop their instructional communication skills. Specifically, the goal of this study is to understand the ways in which ITA programming is distributed and supervised at these universities, and how the universities' organizational structures affect the coordination, collaboration, and flow of information regarding ITA services and policies. This goal is addressed by examining the organizational structures of 20 institutions as they relate to international teaching assistant (ITA) services and resources. The following research questions guided this study:

1. What are the training and support services available to support ITAs in their language, cultural transition, and pedagogy?
2. What are the administrative and organizational structures of public research institutions as they relate to ITAs?
3. What is the level of collaboration and communication that takes place between organizational units providing ITA support services within these institutions?

Figure 1, below, illustrates the components outlined in these research questions. In the center, the administrative and organizational structures oversee and provide training, services, and support for ITAs, which influences not only the *components* of the training and support in place (left), but also the level and type of coordination that occurs in the provision of these services and support (right).

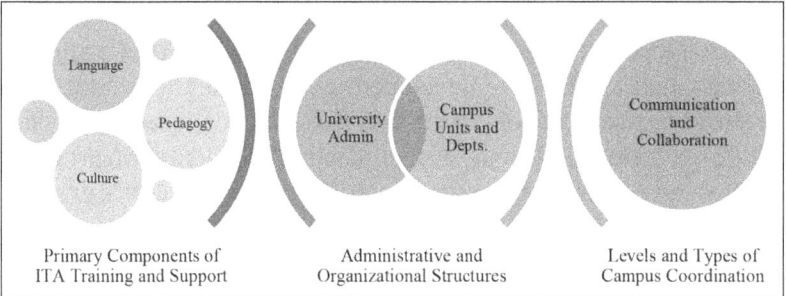

Figure 1. Institutional influences on training, services, and supports of ITAs.

Literature Review

Language, pedagogy, and culture. The literature on ITAs' needs for training and support in terms of language, pedagogy and culture is an important backdrop for the present study, which investigates the organization of these services. There are several noteworthy points concerning past work in this area. First, ITA training and support has focused historically on the development of English language fluency (Clayton & Monoson, 1993; Hoekje & Williams; 1992). Second, as other researchers began to point to the potential value of teaching and pedagogical techniques, an emphasis was placed on the practices related to ITA-student interactions such as asking questions in the classroom (Tanner, 1991), giving directives (Reinhardt, Thorne, & Golombek, 2007), office-hour interactions (Chiang, 2011), and general classroom management (Archer, 1994).

Other researchers have indicated that culture and cultural norms are important for ITAs to explore and understand as well (Gorsuch, 2003; Zhou, 2009). Cultural environments that are particularly important for ITAs to comprehend are those of the classroom, discipline, and institution (Bengu, 2009; Jenkins, 2000; Kuhn, 1996; LaRocco, 2011; Osa, 2010; Papajohn, Alsberg, Bair, & Willenborg, 2002; Trebing 2007; see also contribution by Trebing in this volume). For example, research in this area has investigated how ITAs might negotiate cross-cultural differences and misunderstandings (Jenkins, 2000; Williams, 2011), and managing intercultural communication anxiety (Roach & Bolanle, 2001). Overall, language, pedagogy, and culture have been combined and addressed in various ways as ITA programming has developed.

Development and provision of ITA services and support. Various institutions have developed programming that addresses the three critical areas of ITA training. For instance, Jia and Bergeson (2008) describes a campus-wide intensive ITA orientation program at a Research 1-level university which incorporated cultural orientation, training in presentation and teaching skills, and a "crash session" on pronunciation. Gorsuch (2006) examines a discipline-specific semester-length practicum in which participants who were part of an ESL class focusing on ITA classroom language skills also worked as pre-service ITAs in classes with discipline-specific mentors. The design of the program, she argues, "potentially combines the best of both approaches...academic departments [that] help ITAs learn how to teach within their disciplines and a university-wide ESL program... committed to developing ITAs' classroom skills" (p. 92).

While these and other programs like them are somewhat successful, both researchers and participants raise concerns regarding the level of coordination and communication among offices, units, and departments that are and should be involved. Jia and Bergeson (2008) noted that the program they studied lacked departmental input; thus, discipline specific needs were not addressed. Gorsuch (2006) suggested that the program in her study would have been enhanced with more discussions between ITA support staff and academic departments housing ITAs. International students in Zhai's study (2002) suggested that they would be better served if their academic programs coordinated with the Office of International Education.

These examples highlight the lack of full coordination and collaboration often encountered when executing ITA development programs. Given the complexity and importance of supporting ITAs, who in turn provide educational instruction in undergraduate general education programs, formal and regular communication and planning across offices, units, and departments could be highly beneficial. Thus, it seems that much can be gained from understanding how organizational structures of institutions as a whole might facilitate or, alternatively, create barriers to coordinated effort. It is for this reason we undertook this study and apply an organizational structure framework to understand the phenomenon.

Organizational structure. Organizational structure theory is used as the framework to guide the study. Organizational structure has been defined as the way in which an enterprise coordinates its employees and the tasks to be accomplished in order to meet the organization's objectives (Aiken, Bacharach, & French, 1980; James & Jones, 1976; Kim, 1980). How an enterprise organizes itself shapes communication between units and employees (Hull & Hage, 1982) and, ultimately, determines who develops plans and how these plans are executed for the production of goods or services. The present study focuses specifically on three aspects of organizational structure mentioned in the literature: centralization, hierarchical levels, and functional differentiation.

Centralization. First, centralization identifies where in organizational decision-making resides (Damanpour & Gopalakrishnan, 1998). Highly centralized organizations are characterized by top-level personnel or administrators making decisions. Decentralized organizations, on the other hand, yield some decision-making power to employees at lower levels who may have a more direct connection to issues or concerns. In applying this conceptualization to ITA development and education, a centralized structure would be one in which offices such as international student services had no authority to make decisions about ITA programming and would instead defer to a senior level central administrator to determine what services should be provided to ITAs. A centralized structure reduces the autonomy of employees, although it allows for greater continuity and consistency in communication.

Hierarchical levels. Second, hierarchical levels in organizational structure theory refer to the layers of administration that exist within the organization. "Flat structures" have relatively few levels and one manager may supervise several individuals (Dalton, Todor, Spendolini, Fielding, & Porter, 1980). However, managers may not be able to adequately supervise all parties at the next level down, as there may be less frequent interactions between supervisors and supervisees and more uncertainty regarding job expectations. Conversely, "tall structures" reflect an organization that has several levels of supervision or management between entry-level employees and the top manager. Because the manager at each level may only supervise a few individuals, tall structures allow for greater supervision and communication at each level. An example of a flat structure would be one in which the assistant vice provost is the direct reporting office for a group of units such as the international scholars office and the teaching and learning center. There may be, for example, monthly meetings during which the assistant vice provost asks questions and makes recommendations but offers little interference, trusting that each entity will fulfill its responsibility.

Departmentalization. Third, departmentalization describes the way in which the organization is arranged into units (Damanpour & Gopalakrishnan, 1998). In one type, referred to as functional structures, the organization is arranged by similarities in their purpose or function or along the lines of specialized knowledge or skills. Most academic offices and centers fall into this category. In a divisional structure, however, the institution is organized internally according to the products or services it provides. If this structure is followed, there may be a division composed of all the units involved in addressing a particular need or service, despite having differing purposes. An example of divisional structure would be one in which the university has a division of ITA development composed of all the offices involved in the support of ITAs.

Study Purpose

As the literature reviewed here suggests, the work of supporting ITAs is complex and perhaps can only be fully achieved through a coordinated effort of agents in many units of the university. Yet, there is little discussion in the literature of exactly how these programs and efforts within institutions come together to develop, provide, and improve ITA services and support. Much can be gained from understanding how organizational structures of institutions as a whole might facilitate or, alternatively, create barriers to such coordinated efforts. Because the goal of this study is to understand how the organizational structures influence ITA-serving units, organizational structure theory was an appropriate framework to guide this research. As defined, the framework explains how certain structures might facilitate or inhibit communication and collaboration within an organization and thus allow us to address the central questions of this paper.

Method

Research Approach

This study employs a benchmarking approach, which is a common and longstanding process in higher education (Epper, 1999). The process begins with an examination of the internal work procedures at one's home institution and is then followed by the identification of practices in other organizations. This particular approach to research and data collection provides several key benefits as laid out by Epper (1999). First, benchmarking serves as a model for action, not just data collection. That is, by reviewing the practices of other institutions and *how* these practices are employed, one's own performance can be improved. Second, the practice of benchmarking helps to distinguish between innovation and reputation by focusing on real practices that can be tracked and reported. Third, this approach can encourage new ways of thinking by challenging traditional or long-held assumptions about what is effective. Fourth, benchmarking promotes learning that translates into "levers for change" (p. 31). By employing this approach, these benefits can be achieved and extended to others via findings, conclusions, and recommendations to aid in decisions that optimize campus resources and improve services for, in this case, ITAs.

Sample Identification

Given that large populations of ITAs are found at Research 1-level universities, our study utilizes that category of institution. In order to identify public, high-research institutions, the Carnegie classification online sorting feature was employed, which yielded an initial list of 75 schools (Carnegie Foundation, 2014). Next, information obtained via institutional websites was used to calculate the number and percentage of international graduate students and total student populations for each school. From the initial list of seventy-five institutions, this number was reduced by eliminating "outlier" schools with extremely low or high total student populations. Institutions with extremely small or large international populations were removed as well. Of interest to this study was tracking the characteristics and practices at schools falling within the middle range that could then be matched across the two categories. Only institutions falling within the middle fifty percent in terms of *both* total student and international populations were included. Thus, a set of schools was identified that included those with a "typical" range of services for institutions with total and international student populations closest to the median in both areas.

Data Collection and Procedures

Two types of data were used to answer the three research questions for this study. First, information and data was gathered via a web-based benchmarking approach about institutional characteristics, administrative and organizational structures, available courses and training for international teaching assistants, social and/or cultural programs, and other forms of ITA support. This data collection process included the following sources of information: annual reports and fact books, "quick-facts" pages, other data made available by the school's office of institutional research, and other institutional webpages such as The Graduate School, Teaching and Learning Center/Faculty Development Office, Office for International Students and/or Scholars, English Language Departments and/or Institutes, and other units providing support for international instructors. This information aided the identification of administrative and organizational structures related to ITA services, as well as the nature of specific courses, workshops, orientations, and other programs and training provided to support ITAs in the areas of communication, pedagogy, and culture. Data collected during this phase of the research was used to answer RQs #1 and #2.

Second, interviews were conducted with institutional stakeholders and representatives from 11 of the 20 schools included in the benchmarking. In order to identify individuals for these interviews, an initial review was conducted of all twenty-one schools and participants were identified across each of the following areas for each institution: (1) provost or head administrator, (2) head of the graduate school, (3) director or administrator of the internationally-focused office, (4) director or administrator of the teaching and learning center or faculty development office, and (5) the head of English language office *or* the office responsible for testing and oral proficiency.

While the roles of these participants varied across institutions, all were associated with an office or unit previously identified as offering services or assistance to ITAs. In all, six of the participants were administrators (either for the university or for a unit) and five were other staff positions working in the area of ITA services and support. Interviews were semi-structured in that they all followed an established protocol, were conducted one-on-one by telephone, and were audio recorded. Interview items were designed to investigate information falling under four broad areas about the participant's institution: (1) the individual's role in working with ITAs, (2) the participant's general opinions about ITAs and ITA-services, (3) the interaction and coordination of ITA services, and (4) predictions or expectations about the future of ITA services. This process was used to address the third research question. Table 1 provides an overview of the individuals who participated in these interviews.

Table 1. Overview of Interview Participants

	Area of Focus	Employee Level	Job Description / Notes	Total Participants
11 Participants, 11 Institutions	Communication and Language	Administrator	Director, English Language Proficiency	2
		Other personnel	ESL instructor	1
	Cultural and Social	Administrator	-	-
		Other personnel	Coordinator, ITA Culture & Language	1
	Pedagogy and Teaching Focus	Administrator	Director, Teaching & Learning Center	2
		Other personnel	Program Coordinator, Grad Teaching	1
	Other	Administrator	Graduate School dean	2
		Other personnel	Director, ITA Program	2
			Total	11

Data Analysis

Information collected via the web-based benchmark was entered into a spreadsheet and tracked to identify the various administrative and organizational structures, units, practices, programs, and services that are in place to aid international teaching assistants.

Given the small sample size in this study, detailed information on the types, focus, and nature of these components could be tracked as well. The methods of data analysis were to (1) conduct counts of commonly-identified approaches, units, courses, programs, and services, (2) identify themes that emerged from their descriptions, and (3) locate trends and patterns among the institutions' administrative and organizational structures. In the next phase of analysis, interviews collected via the eleven participant interviews were fully transcribed. Second, the transcripts were read multiple times to identify an initial set of themes. They were then coded using key words and phrases that corresponded to both the research questions as well as the emergent themes that were initially identified. To ensure trustworthiness of the qualitative data analysis, two members of the research team independently coded the interview data using an inductive coding approach. One employed *Nvivo* software (Richards, 1999) and the other coded by hand. Themes derived by each party were compared and reconciled by the third member of the research team.

Results

Following a review of the benchmarking and interview data, three key findings emerged. First, the institutions studied here offer a wide variety of training and support services directed at ITA development. Second, while multiple campus units are involved in these programs and services, there are certain aspects of the organizational structure that impact these services at the time of this study. Lastly, approaches to cross-unit collaboration are varied as well, and units tend to operate autonomously and independent from one another.

Research question 1: Available training and support services. The first research question for this study asked, "What are the training and support services available to support ITAs in their language, cultural transition, and pedagogy?" A review of the data revealed that the twenty universities benchmarked in this study offer a variety of courses, workshops, and other support services to enhance the needed instructional communication skills of ITAs. These courses and services can be classified into two broad areas. The first is formal support, which is typically more structured and includes a facilitator. This category includes courses, workshops, training institutes, and other similar programs. The second is informal support, which is typically less structured and tailored to the individual. This category includes mentoring, conversation groups, or buddy programs. Table 2 depicts the formal and informal support services that directly support the particular needs of ITAs.

Table 2. Formal and Informal Support Services for ITAs

Type of Support	Examples of Support	# Benchmarked
Formal support: More structured, typically includes a facilitator, and targets multiple individuals	Courses and seminars	17
	Workshops	9
	Orientation training	10
	Speech clinics	3
	Web tutorials	2
	Advanced/Intensive institute	11
Informal support: Less structured, usually lacks a formal facilitator, and typically tailored to the individual	Conversation groups/circles	7
	Mentoring/Individual coaching	2
	Buddy programs	15

While there was a broad range of services and programs available to ITAs, English proficiency courses and seminars were by far the most common, while conversation circles and advanced instructional development programs were the least common.

Several interview participants (and this is also supported in the web-based data) indicated that the first formal training that ITAs receive is via an orientation or introductory workshop. While some orientation programs were available to all teaching assistants on a campus, most were targeted for ITAs specifically. Orientations were offered by various units within the organization including academic departments, the Graduate School, and teaching and learning centers. Regardless of whether they targeted all teaching assistants or only ITAs, orientations were nearly always offered (and, at times, required) prior to a graduate student ever entering a college classroom. The ITA-tailored workshops among the schools in this sample lasted from a half day to four days and consisted of targeted activities designed to prepare international teaching assistants for their unique challenges in the classroom. For example, one institution reported using trained facilitators who listen to international students and according to one participant, "give English language feedback and then [suggest] other opportunities for them to get English language support."

Some units from the schools in this study conduct workshops or seminars on topics such as the American classroom, indicating they do provide some information designed specifically for ITAs. Two of the twenty institutions offer ITA training online. Another institution offers a "workshop series [which covers] not only for how international teaching assistants prepare for American students but how American students prepare for their international students."

As confirmed through both web-based data and participant interviews, units within the institution such as English Language Institutes, departments of ESL and Linguistics, and other language-related units often offer training as it pertains to oral proficiency, although many of these do not exclusively serve ITAs and their unique needs. Rather, these programs are open to all international students and, in some cases, the spouses of students. The same can be said of conversation groups and friendship/buddy arrangements. Institutions with programs designed specifically for ITAs generally offer seminars or courses designed to help students increase their oral proficiency. Since most schools have minimum passing scores on standardized and/or in-house English language assessments, these courses are designed to either help these students become full ITAs or to support them concurrently as they take on more limited ITA roles such as a lab assistant. Even after completing the courses, however, graduate students may be required to obtain an authorization to teach, which might be granted by the ITA course instructor or the department/program graduate teaching assistant coordinator, or by attaining the required score on a subsequent oral English language proficiency test. As one participant clarified, "Courses are not an alternative to passing; they still have to pass the test."

This study also identified several instances of units offering additional workshops and seminars designed to further develop ITA's instructional communication abilities. For example, one teaching and learning center offers a two-part workshop series, with one targeting accent reduction and the other addressing the culture of the American classroom and pedagogical responses in the classroom context. Among the institutions benchmarked, there were several examples of informal support programs typically offered as additional resources for international students. In three instances, language clinics were offered as separate activities specifically for ITAs. Additionally, conversation circles were widely available to ITAs.

Research question 2: Organizational structures. The second research question for this study asked, "What are the administrative and organizational structures of public research institutions as they relate to ITA support? While only eleven organizational structure charts could be identified, these revealed a wide array of offices and units involved in the programs and support services available to ITAs. Overall, the analysis of this data revealed three aspects of organizational structure that seem to affect the potential interactions between offices that provide ITA services.

The first aspect concerns the hierarchical structure of the organization. The examination of organizational charts revealed that in many cases ITA-related offices or units typically reported to one of the many vice provosts or associate vice provosts in the system. These vice- and associate provosts in turn reported to the university provost. Among all institutions reviewed in this study, at least four vice provosts reported directly to the provost, who supervised diverse areas including faculty affairs, undergraduate academic affairs, and international programs. There was also considerable variation in the number and composition of the units that each vice provost supervised. While some vice provosts supervised very few units (in some cases, only one), others had a larger number (5+) of offices, centers, and programs to supervise. This structure is generally considered a flat structure (Dalton, Todor, Spendolini, Fielding, & Porter, 1980).

The second aspect refers to the level of departmentalization that existed within institutions. We found that not all ITA-serving offices reported to the same vice/assistant/associate provost. In only two cases did the same senior-level supervisor oversee all the units that provided ITA support. Thus in the other nine cases, offices that provided ITA support were in different reporting lines. This seemed to be a function of the units' knowledge or expertise in a given area. For example, at one institution, all ITA-serving offices that facilitated instructional staffs' development of new pedagogical skills reported to the vice provost of *academic affairs*, while those units serving ITAs as international students reported to the vice provost of *student affairs*. Finally, those entities that focus on developing oral proficiency directly reported to the dean in their particular college. Organizational theorists would state that this is an example of functional departmentalization (Damanpour & Gopalakrishnan, 1998).

Finally, the third aspect of organizational structure that existed among the institutions was the general level of autonomy that offices had in order to make decisions. Universities have commonly been characterized as decentralized. Academic units and offices are generally composed of individuals who have developed knowledge in their field. Given that they are seen as the experts, staff personnel are given power to make decisions about effective programming. For example, participants spoke of having "autonomy" and units "having their (own) way of doing things." One participant described her institution as follows: "It is a very decentralized campus in general."

In total, these three aspects of the organizational structure shape the potential likelihood and level of interactions between offices and units that serve ITAs. A flat structure suggests that an ITA-serving office might be one of many, sometimes unrelated, units that report to a senior level administrator. Thus, the unit might not have an opportunity to interact with others who also serve ITAs. In a functional structural form, units are organized by their expertise rather than who they serve. Therefore, if a teaching and learning office includes instructional technology, then this arrangement could lead to ITA's pedagogical needs being met separately from their linguistic and cultural needs. Finally, the decentralized nature of organization might encourage independent decision-making without seeking out collaborative opportunities. Understanding how the organizational structure of institutions actually influences the coordination and collaboration between offices is important. We now turn our attention to addressing this question.

Research question 3: Coordination and communication. The third research question for this study asked, "What is the level of coordination and communication that takes places between organizational units providing ITA support services within these institutions?" While those interviewed indicated a desire to collaborate and interact more with others at their institution involved with ITAs, the offices, units, and departments generally acted as unrelated entities with only superficial contact with other offices. While there were some examples of communication and collaboration among offices, the communication overall tended to be informal and collaboration was not the norm. Ultimately, while the overarching organizational structure did not necessarily contribute to the kind of ITA services and programming that was available, it did seem to contribute to the lack of communication and collaboration between parties that work on behalf of ITAs. For example, one participant stated he couldn't think of any offices with whom his group collaborated, as they were "self-sufficient;" nevertheless, he stated, "I try to stay in touch with people across campus [and] communicate with departments, but we don't do joint projects together."

When asked specifically about collaboration, another participant explained, "It's somewhat haphazard. I would say we have really good coordination with [the offices in the same building] but [the others] are all doing their own thing. Another noted, "Our campus is pretty notorious for departments not talk[ing] to each other; they call it silos, so it seems like there's not a lot of contact between different departments and so, when I contacted [another office], I think that was one of the first times anyone had tried anything like that." Most of the interaction between units was in terms of referring international teaching assistants to resources that may be beneficial to them. One participant noted, "A lot of people refer students to the writing center," while another stated, "I always recommend that [ITAs] get a graduate teaching certificate because that's just a great way for them to continue their professionalization as a TA." It is important to note that these services, while helpful to ITAs, were not specifically designed with them in mind and may not fully meet their unique needs.

Among the institutions, there were some examples of individuals and units maintaining ongoing and active relationships with other offices that ultimately led to collaboration. Participants at two institutions described informal collaborations between centers for English language study, teaching and learning centers, and centers for international studies. One participant stated, "We're quite cooperative with all the programs at our university [and] they know that we are here." Another interviewee explained, "Our collaboration is informal, working between staff who've worked here a long time and what the resources are, and staff who purposefully go out and attend things where they can learn about more resources."

A common theme regarding collaboration that emerged was a willingness to work with others, coupled with a sense of being unable to do so due to time constraints and responsibilities of the position. Said one participant, "I would very much welcome that kind of collaboration, but with a university this size, we are…in silos." Another stated," I think we have friendly relations, but I don't think we partner much; we all have our hands full. A third explained, "I think there's a lot of good will among various offices [and] a lot of individuals that would like to work together more often, but…there is so much happening that it's hard to structure regular meetings for people to get together."

Discussion

The purpose of this study was to understand the organizational structures that exist regarding the provision of ITA services at a sample of public, high-research universities in the United States. To address this topic, a benchmark approach was employed to examine the kinds of services these campuses provided specifically for ITAs, which units provided these services, and the levels of collaboration and communication that existed between ITA-serving entities. Through this research, three important conclusions may be extrapolated.

Resources available. First, institutions make many services and resources available that are specifically designed to facilitate the development of ITAs and to improve their instructional communication. These services are provided by a variety of offices, schools, centers, units, enterprises, programs, and departments. While some are mandatory, such as general TA orientations or departmental seminars, the majority are *optional*. The extent to which ITAs develop their instructional communication skills is placed largely in their own hands and subject to external forces such as advisors' opinions about the value of teaching and/or time constraints.

Decentralized, flat organization structure. Second, the general pattern of administrative and organizational structure was consistent with what Mintzberg (1993) termed "professional bureaucracies," which are decentralized, hierarchically flat, and are structured to be both functional (due to specialized knowledge and skills) and divisional (having a single product to produce or constituency to serve). Individuals who work within this organizational structure type have specialized skills that those to whom they report may not have. Thus, they are free to make decisions in their own interests within their budgetary guidelines. In the case of units providing ITA services, they may determine the kind of programming that they will provide as along as it serves ITAs in some capacity.

Lack of coordination. Third, although there was a desire for greater coordination for many of the participants, they did not experience notable opportunities to engage in these actions. This seemed to be a function of the organizational structure which, along with a high level of specialized knowledge and skills, resulted in a considerable degree of autonomy. This autonomy, in turn, allowed many offices to remain "siloed," resulting in an environment where communication, collaboration, and coordination, while valued by some, were not valued by everyone. Other researchers have found this condition to exist in a wide variety of organizations (Kanter, 1994; Senge, 1990). While this level of independence might be valued, there are drawbacks such as obstructing innovation. The development of new activities or programs would require communication and collaboration, especially if one is considering including an aspect that is outside his/her specialty (Mintzberg, 1993). If one is not willing to do this, innovation will be slow to occur, if at all.

ITAs not adequately supported in all areas of need. Taken as a whole, the findings of this study suggest that ITAs are, in many cases, not adequately supported in the areas of communication, pedagogy, and cultural knowledge needed to be successful in the classroom. A contributing factor to this situation is that the organizational structures of their institutions make it difficult for those who work on behalf of ITAs to connect with others who have the same objective, and who may have complementary expertise. Empirical research, such as this study and others that will follow, can help administrators and practitioners address and overcome barriers that exist to more meaningful coordination across offices and units. This study breaks new ground in identifying factors that influence the development of ITAs. The administrative and organizational structures in place throughout higher education can create significant barriers that prevent the kind of coordination across ITA-serving units that can result in better meeting the needs of students. Further, the organizational structure of the university may indirectly influence programming and, ultimately, ITA development, through its effect on communication, collaboration, and coordination among various units. There are few formal, sanctioned, and regular interactions between those individuals in different units who work on behalf of ITAs, which likely has an effect on the rate at which students participate in various activities or events, the content that is included in these activities, and the type of ITA development plan that exists.

Limitations and Areas of Future Research

Several limitations to this study should be acknowledged. First, the number of institutions investigated was limited to 20. While this sample size is acceptable in benchmarking studies (Stapenhurst 2009), expanding the number might have revealed patterns and findings that did not emerge here. Second, only public institutions were included in this study. ITAs are also employed at private institutions and how they are prepared for their role at these universities is important to understand as well. Finally, the study is cross-sectional, examining only the current actions, programming, and services offered. A longitudinal or historical case study approach that examines one or more schools over time might allow for greater insight into how institutions came to be organized as they are and what factors contributed to the development and expansion of programming and services.

Recommendations

Develop a campus-wide ITA development interest group. It is recommended that schools create an ITA development interest group. In the case of an ITA-targeted group, representatives could include, but not be limited to: ESL specialists, individuals from the international office, graduate school officials, those charged with assessment oral proficiency, teaching and learning experts, and a senior level administrator who is in a position to forward recommendations to appropriate parties. By engaging in regular information sharing, brainstorming, and review of their services with each other, such a group can overcome the some issues that occur among offices and units in organizations structured as "professional bureaucracies", naming coordination and innovation. For example, such a group could be useful in the redesign of programming such as orientations and certification programs. Specifically, if the graduate school regularly conducted ITA orientation, they may not be as aware of the emerging literature on brain science and how this influences teaching as those in instructional development. Additionally, they may not be as aware of changes in the educational cultures as those in international education. Collaborating with both of these groups in redeveloping the orientation will likely lead to a more relevant learning experience for the participant. In developing an ITA teaching certification program, an instructional development office might consider including the English language institute as well as the international education office to insure that the language and cultural needs of the participants are considered and adequately addressed within the program in addition to pedagogical training.

Establish more centralized knowledge on ITAs. It is recommended that information should be centralized or linked to improve dissemination of knowledge on the campus. To aid both those who work with ITAs and ITAs themselves, it could be useful for all the information related to ITA development to be located centrally or linked across various departments, offices, and units. For one of the institutions in this study the graduate school served as the coordinating site for all information, although each individual office contributes their particular program information. Such a site also conveys the message that these are important professional development opportunities for all students to experience.

Create an ITA services project manager. Third, it is recommended that a position for Coordinator or Project Manager of ITA services be created. As many of our participants communicated, time and knowledge about other ITA-related programs are constraints to their coordination and collaboration with one another. In order to create a more unified approach to supporting ITAs, it might be worth investing in a coordinator or project manager position for ITA development. Responsibilities of this role may include: Facilitating communication between the parties that work with ITAs, identifying and supporting opportunities for collaboration between offices, aiding units in creating a plan for ITA training and ongoing development, and reporting to the designated administrators about the joint projects and work of the units. Such a person could be charged with helping departments and programs access campus resources to support and develop their ITAs, provide joint consultation for ITAs with other offices, and serve in an advocacy role for ITAs. Given the current budgetary constraints faced by many institutions, this responsibility may be taken on by someone who already works in one of the units that provide ITA support, given some job restructuring.

Conclusion

Our findings suggest that ITAs are in many cases not being adequately supported in all the areas of they need to be successful in the classroom. Contributing to this are the organizational structures of their institutions that make it difficult for those who work diligently on behalf of ITAs from making necessary connections with others who have the same commitment. Empirical research such as this, and that which comes after it, can only help administrators and practitioners think more explicitly about the barriers that exist to communication, collaboration, and cooperation across offices and units and how best to overcome them.

Those who work with ITAs understand the unique challenges these instructors face in their goal to effectively communicate interpersonally and academically with their students in the face of limited pedagogical knowledge, differences in cultural norms, and language. If we want to ensure that these student instructors have more successful teaching and learning experiences in the classroom, we must be willing to examine what we currently do in hopes of improving. This requires developing mechanisms within our organizational structures to facilitate the discussions, interactions, and planning. It is hoped that the findings here will aid institutions in creating those necessary processes to generate important and useful action on behalf of ITAs.

In a Nutshell

1. There is ongoing interest in the factors that might influence the services specifically designed for ITAs to develop and support their instructional communication skills.
2. Several researchers (Ard, 1989; Matsuda, 2006; and Smith et al, 1992) have suggested that institutional structure should be considered when developing ITA programs.

3. The appeared to be little research that expressly examined the role organizational structure plays in the kind of services that are provided to ITAs related to language, pedagogy and culture.
4. Using a benchmarking approach and semi-structured interviews, we examined the twenty institutions to determine the services they offered, their organizational structure, and how this influenced collaboration and coordination between the offices and units that serve ITAs.
5. We found that while it had no influence on the kind and location of ITA services, organizational structures did have an negative influence on communication, collaboration, and coordination between units
6. We believe this state of affairs hinders ITA's ability to take advantage of all available services.
7. We also believe this hinders the development of ITA programming that addresses concerns related to language, pedagogy, and culture not singly, but in combination.

References

Aiken, M., Bacharach, S.B., & French, J.L. (1980). Organizational structure, work process, and proposal making in administrative bureaucracies. Academy of management journal, 23(4), 631-652.

Archer, C. (1994). Managing a multicultural classroom. In G. Althen (Ed.), Learning across cultures. NAFSA/Intercultural Press. Available: http://www.culture-bump.com/Classroom.pdf.

Ard, J. (1989). Grounding an ITA curriculum: Theoretical and practical concerns. English for Specific Purposes, 8, 125-138.

Bengu, E. (2009). Adapting to a new role as an International Teaching Assistant: Influence of communicative competence in this adaptation process (Electronic Dissertation). Available: https://etd.ohiolink.edu/

Carnegie Foundation for the Advancement of Teaching. (2014). Carnegie classification of institutions of higher education (Data file). Available: http://classifications.carnegiefoundation.org/

Chiang, S.Y. (2011). Pursuing a response in office hour interactions between U.S. college students and international teaching assistants. Journal of Pragmatics, 43(14), 3316–3330.

Clayton, F.T. & Monoson, P.K. (1993). Oral English language proficiency of ITAs: Policy, implementation, and contributing factors. Innovative Higher Education, 17(3): 195-209.

Dalton, D.R., Todor, W.D., Spendolini, M.J., Fielding, G.J., & Porter, L.W. (1980). Organization structure and performance: A critical review. Academy of Management Review, 5(1), 49-64.

Damanpour, F., & Gopalakrishnan, S. (1998). Theories of organizational structure and innovation adoption: The role of environmental change. Journal of Engineering and Technology Management, 15(1), 1-24.

Epper, R.M. (1999). Applying benchmarking to higher education: Some practices to improve quality. Change, 31(6), 24-31.

Gorsuch, G. (2003). The educational cultures of international teaching assistants and U.S. universities. TESL-EJ, 7(3), 1-17 [On-line]. Available: http://www.tesl-ej.org/wordpress/issues/volume7/ej27/ej27a1/.

Gorsuch, G. (2006). Discipline-specific practica for international teaching assistants. English for Specific Purposes, 25(1), 90-108.

Gorsuch, G. (2012). International teaching assistants' experiences in educational cultures and their teaching beliefs. TESL-EJ, 16(1), 1-26.

Hoekje, B. & Williams, J. (1992). Communicative competence and the dilemma of international teaching assistant education. TESOL Quarterly, 26(2): 243-269.

Hull, F., & Hage, J. (1982). Organizing for innovation: Beyond Burns and Stalker's organic type. Sociology, 16(4), 564-577.

James, L.R., & Jones, A.P. (1976). Organizational structure: A review of structural dimensions and their conceptual relationships with individual attitudes and behavior. Organizational Behavior and Human Performance, 16(1), 74-113.

Jenkins S. (2000) Cultural and linguistic miscues: A case study of international teaching assistant and academic faculty miscommunication. International Journal of Intercultural Relations, 24, 477-501.

Jia, C.L. & Bergerson, A.A. (2008). Understanding the International Teaching Assistant Training Program: A Case Study at a Northwestern Research University. International Education, 37(2), 77–98.

Kanter, R.M. (1994). Collaborative advantage: The art of alliances. Harvard Business Review 4, 96-108.

Kim, L. (1980). Organizational innovation and structure. Journal of Business Research, 8(2), 225-245.

Kuhn, E. (1996). Cross-cultural stumbling blocks for international teachers. College Teaching 44(3), 96-99.

LaRocco, M.J.F. (2011). International teaching assistants and the essence of the development of intercultural competence" (2011). (Electronic Dissertation). Available: http://digitalcommons.ric.edu/etd/40

Matsuda, P.K. (2006). The myth of linguistic homogeneity in U.S. college composition. College English, 68 (6), 637-651.

Mintzberg, H. (1993). Structure in fives: Designing effective organizations. Englewood Cliffs, N.J.: Prentice-Hall, Inc.

Osa, O. (2010). "What works in one culture may not work in another:" Teaching mistakes in the college classroom. Faculty focus: Magna. Available: http://www.

jsums.edu/jsuoaa/resources/Teaching%20Mistakes%20from%20the%20College%20Classroom.pdf

Papajohn, D., Alsberg, J., Bair, B., & Willenborg, B. (2002). An ESP program for international teaching assistants. In T. Orr (Ed.). English for specific purposes (pp. 89-101). Alexandria, VA: Teachers of English to Speakers of Other Languages, Inc.

Reinhardt, J., Thorne, S., & Golombek, P. (2007). A Corpus-informed pedagogical innovation for ITAs. Available: http://www.ita-is.org/seattle07/2185RTGH.pdf

Richards, L. (1999). Using Nvivo in qualitative research. London, England: Sage.

Roach, D. & Bolanle, A.O. (2001) Intercultural willingness to communicate and communication anxiety in international teaching assistants. Communication Research Reports, 18(1), 26–35.

Senge, P. (1990). The fifth discipline. New York, NY: Doubleday.

Smith, R., Byrd, P., Nelson, G., Barrett, R., Constantinides, J. (1992). Crossing pedagogical oceans: International teaching assistants in U.S. undergraduate education. Washington, D.C.: ERIC Clearinghouse on Higher Education.

Stapenhurst, T. (2009). The benchmarking book: A how-to-guide to best practice for Managers and practitioners. Oxford, England: Elsevier Ltd.

Tanner, M. (1991). Incorporating research on question asking into ITA training. In J. Nyquist, R. Abbott, D.Wulff, & J. Sprague (Eds.), Preparing the professoriate of tomorrow to teach (pp. 375–381). Dubuque, IA:Kendall/Hunt Publishing Company.

Trebing, D. (2007) International teaching assistants' attitudes toward teaching and understanding of United States American undergraduate students (Unpublished Dissertation). Southern Illinois University at Carbondale, ProQuest, UMI Dissertations Publishing. 3284710.

Williams, G. M. (2011). Examining classroom negotiation strategies of international teaching assistants, International Journal for the Scholarship of Teaching and Learning. http://www.georgiasouthern.edu/ijsotl 5(1), 1–16.

Zhai, L. (2002). Studying international students: Adjustment issues and social support. Washington, D.C.: ERIC Clearinghouse on Higher Education.

Zhou, J. (2009). What is missing in international teaching assistants' training curriculum? Journal of Faculty Development, 23(2), 19-14.

Part Three

ITAs, Tests, and Language Politics

Native and Non-native English Speaking ITA Performance Test Raters: Do They Rate ITA Candidates Differently?

by Jeremy Ray Gevara,[1] *Pennsylvania State University; Greta Gorsuch, Hasan Almekdash, Texas Tech University; and Wei Jiang, Texas A & M*

This study investigates whether differential item functioning (DIF) is occurring among international teaching assistant (ITA) performance test raters, who are both native and non-native speakers of English. DIF refers to the detection of different test item responses between two groups. DIF is an important tool to detect rater biases that test administrators would like to control through rater training and other means. This study also addresses a second, sensitive, question: Is it appropriate for trained, highly proficient non-native English speaking raters to rate other, less proficient non-native English speaking candidates on a high-stakes test? This can be an explosive issue when viewed in the context of current ITA programs in North America. Such programs may be subject to local negative politics where both faculty members and ITA candidates themselves complain that non-native English speaker raters are being employed. To examine this issue, each of 80 ITA candidates were rated on an established, ten-criteria teaching performance test by three raters: Two of them native English speakers, and one a non-native English speaker. Two additional variables were modeled, based on the literature: Raters' level of experience teaching and rating ITA

---

1. Author contact: jrg351@psu.edu

populations; and raters who had completed a graduate degree in language, literature, or applied linguistics, or who were still in-progress with their graduate work. The results underscored the importance of using caution when attributing rater bias to a single variable such as native speaker or non-native speaker status. We hope this study will be useful to faculty members in academic departments as they navigate their own doubts about an ITA or ESL (English as a second language) program at their school that may hire non-native speakers of English as instructors or test raters. This study may also be useful for faculty members who need to mediate complaints from their own international students who have participated in ITA or ESL programs.

Current language testing research and practice has revised tests to be better predictors of language use in specific contexts by measuring both general language knowledge and modeling language performance for professional or academic purposes. This has resulted in more reliable and valid performance tests. In the International Teaching Assistant (ITA) education field, these are often teaching simulation tests (Gorsuch, 2006; Smith, 1994; see also Smith, Myers, & Burkhalter, 1992 for an early and established example). One result of this testing shift is the increased need for human raters to grade these performance tests.

Globally, non-native speakers of English outnumber native speakers of the language (Graddol, 2006, 2014), and this shift is reflected in increasing numbers of non-native English speaking students attending applied linguistics and TESOL graduate programs in the U.S. There are robust numbers of non-native speaker teachers of English in the world (Meadows & Muramatsu, 2007; Moussu, 2006; Wu, 2010). ITA programs employ highly proficient non-native English speakers as instructors and TAs, and they presumably participate fully in these programs to prepare ITAs for their future duties and to assess their teaching-specific English ability. In some institutions questions have arisen as to whether these non-native English instructors and TAs can be recruited as teaching simulation test raters. While stakeholders in some educational institutions may be reluctant to use non-native English speaking test raters, there have been recent shifts in major testing companies to hire highly English-proficient raters (e.g., Johnson & Lim, 2009), and also speakers of Indian varieties of English as raters (e.g., Xi & Molluan, 2011).

The current study seeks to detect if there are significant differences between native English speaker raters, and trained, highly proficient non-native English speaker raters on ten criteria on an oral-based performance test of 80 ITAs. In this study, two statistical procedures will be used to measure Differential Item Functioning (DIF), namely the Mantel-Haenszel Method (MH) and Logistic Regression (LR). The referent groups and focal groups for this study will be native English speaker raters *versus* non-native speaker raters, raters with experience teaching and rating ITAs *versus* non-experienced raters, and graduate degree awarded *versus* graduate degree in progress. The MH method will be used to determine uniform DIF, an indication of difference between two given groups, considering only one comparison such as "teaching experience," at a time. Then, the Logistic Regression method will be used to determine non-uniform DIF, an indication of difference between rater groups where all three variables (language background, teaching experience, and education level) can be included into a single, best-fit predictive model which shows their impact on likelihood of whether test candidates will pass or fail.

The results of uniform and non-uniform DIF analyses will be given, and will be discussed within the context of potentially charged institutional discussions about the appropriateness and fairness of employing non-native English speakers for ITA rating. For instance, what do the findings mean for ITA candidates who are concerned their raters do not have sufficient skill to rate them? Or that the non-native English speaking raters will be *tougher* on them? What will the findings mean for ITA program directors who wish to employ experienced, fluent, non-native English speakers as raters? Finally, what will the findings mean for faculty members in academic departments who have their own doubts about an ITA program employing non-native English speakers for test rating, or who may need to mediate complaints from their own international students who are participating in ITA programs?

Literature Review

In the following literature review, we examine past literature on issues we think are relevant to the politics and realities of hiring non-native speakers of any language to be test raters. These issues include: 1. Attitudes of language learners toward non-native speaker teachers, 2. Hiring patterns of native and non-native speaker teachers in second language programs, and 3. Empirical evidence concerning rater factors which influence how test raters go about assessing second language learners' writing and speech.

Attitudes of students toward non-native speaker teachers. There are robust numbers of non-native English speaker teachers of English in the world (Meadows & Muramatsu, 2007; Moussu, 2006; Wu, 2010). The same is presumably true for any modern foreign language. There are likely many high schools and universities globally offering foreign language classes in Russian, German, Arabic, or Chinese, etc. where the instructors are non-native speakers (Meadows & Muramatsu, 2007). At the university where this study took place, between 30% and 56% of American Sign Language, French, and German undergraduate classes were taught by non-native signers/speakers of those languages. Because students are stakeholders in the second and foreign language classes they are taking, their perspectives have been taken into account in past empirical studies.

Using survey research designs with samples of convenience ranging from 37 to 422 student respondents, past commentators have found that students do differentiate between native speaker and non-native speaker teachers. Studies have found that non-native speaker teachers are more *highly* regarded than native speaker teachers in terms of their perceived ability to teach grammar (Benke & Medgyes, 2005; Lasagabaster & Sierra, 2005; Mahboob, 2004), and also reading and writing (Mahboob, 2004). Learners also perceived non-native speaker teachers as more successful in their ability to answer questions about the language (Benke & Medgyes, 2005; Mahboob, 2004). Non-native speaker teachers were prized by students for their teaching methodology (Mahboob, 2004; Pacek, 2005). Finally, non-native speaker teachers were appreciated as role models of successful second language learners, where the teachers were seen as being empathetic to learners' struggles (Lasagabaster & Sierra, 2005; Mahboob, 2004; Pacek, 2005), and on the same "wavelength" (Benke & Medgyes, 2005).

In the same studies, native speaker teachers were valued by students for their native-like pronunciation and speech (Benke & Medgyes, 2005; Lasagabaster & Sierra, 2005; Mahboob, 2004; Pacek, 2005). One commentator speculated that globally, students wishing to study in higher education in the U.S. or U.K. would prefer native English speaker teachers. International students at a university in the U.K. "hope to dramatically improve their English language ability by studying through the medium of English," (Pacek, 2005, p. 245) hence the assumption that while in the U.K., they will be taught by native speakers of English. However, when the issue of learners' perceptions of native speaker and non-native speaker teachers was explored empirically, it was found that the majority of learners being taught by a non-native speaker teacher at the university ended up with "either positive or mixed reaction[s]" with "few entirely negative ones" (Pacek, 2005, p. 260).

In contrast, one study focused on four Chinese graduate students teaching English composition in the U.S., finding that while half of their American students praised their non-native speaker teachers' ability to teach from "unique perspectives" and their apparent dedication, the other half criticized their teachers (Liu, 2005, p. 169). The criticisms focused on students' disappointment they were not being taught by a professor (as opposed to a graduate student), and dismay at their "problems of miscommunication" with their TAs (p. 171).

Summary. In sum, the literature suggests that language learners hold complex attitudes toward both native and non-native speaker teachers. We can imagine that similar attitudes may negatively color some ITA candidates' perceptions of the qualities and contributions of non-native English speaker teachers employed by an ITA program. Since many ITA instructors are also hired to rate ITA candidates on teaching simulation tests, some ITA candidates may feel that non-native English speaker raters are somehow "in the wrong place" for the specific task of assessing their spoken abilities. This discussion thus establishes native-speaker status as a rater factor (a variable) in our design.

Hiring patterns of native and non-native language teachers. As Mahboob, Uhrig, Newman, and Hartford (2004) point out, enrollments in graduate foreign language education programs in the U.S. and elsewhere are swelling with international students (see also Liu, 2005). At the school where this study took place, 22 out of 35 M.A. students in applied linguistics are international students (63%). Even though many of them are being supported as teaching assistants (TAs) in their native languages such as Arabic or Spanish, many also take an optional qualification in the form of an ESL graduate certificate. Students have stated that this qualification would enable them to teach English in their home countries and elsewhere. But the question remains, how many non-native speakers of English are hired to be English teachers in the U.S. or in other countries in which English is the dominant, established language?

Mahboob et al (2004) surveyed 122 intensive English programs (IEPs) in the U.S., finding that only 3.8% of full-time IEP instructors were non-native speakers of English (p. 105). They also found that 9% of part-time instructors and 21% of graduate TAs were non-native speakers of English. At the institution where this study took place, 33% of ESL TAs are non-native speakers of English. These percentages seem small compared to the percentages of non-native English speaking graduate students being prepared as English teachers in the U.S. (63% at the school where this study took place, and 70% reported by Kamhi-Stein, 1999 at another institution).

While Mahboob et al (2004) made a case of hiring bias against non-native speakers of English, there may be other reasons for this discrepancy. Not all international students wish to stay in the U.S. or wherever they earned their degree. Their family members want them back, and job opportunities for English teachers with advanced degrees might be better in their home countries or elsewhere in the world. As in the U.K. (Clark, Paran, & Clark, 2007), full-time ESL teaching positions are difficult to find in the U.S. And, unfortunately, ESL teachers in North America may not be respected. In a recent blind review from a reputable journal, ITA programs and the ESL instructors in them were described as "politically incorrect" and "a travesty." Finally, ESL teachers in the U.S. may become enmeshed in politically volatile issues such as the provision of basic adult education services to immigrants (TESOL, 2013).

It may be useful to focus on what administrators of IEPs and other institutions say are their hiring qualifications for instructors. A combined total of 208 administrators surveyed in both Clark et al (2007) and Mahboob et al (2004) cited teaching qualifications, experience, good recommendations, and education as their top priorities. Native-speakerness or "accent" followed with lower mean rankings, but with mode scores of 5 ("very important") and 4 ("important"), respectively, in both studies. Clark et al explained they did not define the term "native English speaker" for the questionnaire respondents for fear of drawing too much attention to this linguistically ambiguous term. For example, what of Singaporeans or Indians who speak English well, but speak a variety of English with a different accent or different usage than is used in countries such as the U.S. or Australia (Xi & Molluan, 2011)? Yet language appears to be of concern to administrators and thus their apparent conceptions of "language" need to be examined.

In open-ended comments made to Clark et al, administrators revealed they wanted applicants to have "language competence and awareness," "native-like proficiency," and the ability to write a letter of application using "standard written English" with a "general level of professionalism" (2007, p. 37). In an advocacy position paper, a professional organization for ESL teachers decried proposed legislation in Arizona they felt would discriminate against ESL teachers who were perceived to speak "heavily accented or ungrammatical" English (TESOL, 2010, p. 1). The statement goes on to say that "all English language educators should be proficient in English...but English language proficiency should be viewed as only one criterion in evaluating a teacher's qualifications" (p. 1).

From this variety of direct and indirect statements it may be surmised that administrators do not wish an instructor's spoken or written English to be an issue with students or other stakeholders. "Issues" with language may be construed as a perceived lack of fluency, a lack of accurate and appropriate use, and a strong accent (e.g., Lev-Ari & Keysar, 2010). It may be argued that for legal, cultural, and professional reasons, no administrator is going to openly admit to discriminating against non-native speakers of English (nonetheless, see TESOL, 2010). Yet the empirical evidence provided by Clark et al (2007) and Mahboob et al (2004) suggest that to the extent non-native English speakers apply for IEP jobs, *and* to the extent to which their English ability is judged proficient, *and* to the extent they have the desired experience and education, *and* to the extent teaching jobs are available, then, evidently, non-native English speakers are hired as ESL instructors in the U.S. and the U.K.

Summary. To summarize, non-native English speaker teachers are hired at rather lower rates in the U.S. and the U.K. than might be suggested by high enrollments of non-native speaker international students in English teacher preparation programs. However, there may be a number of reasons for this that are unrelated to the native-speaker status of job applicants. When considering "language," administrators seem interested in some threshold of fluent and competent use when hiring IEP instructors. Whatever is considered a "heavy" accent, however poorly defined, may be problematic. This discussion establishes teacher experience and education as two more rater factors (variables) in our design.

Empirical evidence concerning raters with different backgrounds. There has been an increase of research interest in how second language test raters arrive at their ratings. In other words, do rater factors like language background, amount and type of education or teaching experience, amount of rater training on specific tests, or other cognitive factors influence how raters assess the writing or speaking of second language learners? We offer this model as a way to visualize how we think rater factors may work. See Figure 1.

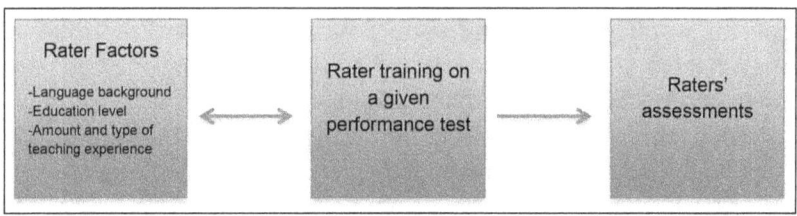

Figure 1. Rater factors, rater training, and raters' assessments.

We posit that rater factors such as language background do have an effect on how raters assess test candidates, hence the arrow going right from "rater factors," eventually to "raters' assessments." However, we also posit that "rater training" likely mediates the effect of rater factors on raters' assessments. We further hypothesize that rater training may have an effect on raters themselves, hence the bi-directional arrow going left from rater training to rater factors. We believe that principled rater training, based on theoretically-derived and well-articulated rater criteria, may be a source of education and learning for raters. In essence, what every test administrator aims for is fair and internally consistent ratings from all raters for all test candidates. Judicious rater selection and then training are seen as the best means for achieving this.

Native speaker and non-native speaker test raters. Some of the literature comparing these two groups is focused on rater bias. In other words, are native speaker or non-native speaker raters likely to grade more harshly or more easily on test candidates' speaking or writing because of an interaction between their own language background and the language background of the test candidates? The answer is mixed. Hamp-Lyons and Zhang (2001) found that Chinese English teacher raters graded more leniently a composition written by an English language learner who used Chinese rhetorical patterns. However, Johnson & Lim (2009) found no evidence of rater bias based on language background on a large-scale English writing test (N = 7,400 test candidates), where ratings of fifteen native English speaker raters and four non-native speaker raters were analyzed. Similarly, Kim (2009) found no evidence of rater bias of Korean English teacher raters being more lenient with Korean speakers using English on three oral response tasks. Kim (2009) raises an intriguing point that the native speaker raters in his study commented more on learners' vocabulary, pronunciation, fluency, and grammar use than the non-native speaker raters. Reflecting a common thread in other rater factor research, the two groups in Kim's study drew on slightly different criteria on which to base their assessments of test candidates' speaking. Of even greater interest to test administrators, Kim (2009) found evidence suggesting that the two rater groups in his study came to the same conclusion for each test candidate and would have assigned the same final score.

Teaching experience of raters. In the studies cited above, nearly all of the raters, whether native or non-native speakers, were second language teachers and had some minimum of experience and education in the field. There is evidence that teaching experience is also a significant rater factor. Chalhoub-Deville (1995) compared native speaker raters of Arabic who were also Arabic language teachers, and native speakers of Arabic who were not language teachers. Raters with teaching experience focused on creativity first and then grammar in Arabic learners' spoken samples, while raters without teaching experience focused primarily on learners' grammar mistakes. Thus, not all native speakers of a language are created equal when it comes to assessing learners of that language. The two different groups drew on different primary criteria to do their ratings.

Education of raters. Educational background and level have also been demonstrated as a significant rater factor. Chalhoub-Deville and Wigglesworth (2005) compared four groups of native speaker English teachers from Canada, the United Kingdom, Australia, and the United States. When judging the speech of English language learners, the teachers from the United Kingdom were significantly harsher than the teachers from the United States. This suggests differences, by country, in the type of education English language teachers receive. And, this again underscores the notion that native speakers of a language will not rate learners of that language in the same way. Finally, Kobayashi (1992) compared 145 native speakers and 124 non-native speakers of English with varying levels of education ranging from undergraduate students, to college professors. The participants were invited to indicate the number of grammar mistakes in two compositions by undergraduate learners of English. The native speaker raters as a group indicated more grammatical errors than the non-native speaker raters. However, as the education level of the non-native speaker raters increased, they indicated more errors in the compositions. For Kobayashi, a writing teacher, this was a positive indication in that students in writing classes need to receive corrective feedback.

Rating training on specific tests. Finally, there is evidence that training on rating specific tests is a significant rater factor. Some of this literature reflects a concern to identify how different raters seem to use different criteria to complete their assessments (e.g., Kim, 2009). Brown, Iwashita, and McNamara (2005) found that raters, when left to their own devices while assessing the speech of English language learners, seem to reliably pay attention to grammar, vocabulary, pronunciation, fluency, and learners' use of discourse markers. Raters seem to rate much less reliably on a "fulfilling a spoken task" criterion. In other words, if a test task calls upon learners to give directions on a map, some of the raters do not take into account whether the learner actually succeeds in giving directions. Finally, Pollitt and Murray (1996) found that without training on a specific test, raters assessing lower-level learners' speech samples focus on grammar. The same raters, when assessing high-level learners' speech samples, focus on sociolinguistic competence (whether what test candidates said was socially appropriate).

Summary. There are a number of rater factors that influence how raters judge the speech or writing of second language learners, including teaching experience, education level, and rater training. While native or non-native speaker status may be a rater factor, only mixed evidence was found. It is of course important to hire raters who have appropriate professional credentials, as the literature suggests. But native-speaker status should not be the only consideration. As a research issue, how rater factors influence raters' work comprises an important agenda. As a related practical issue, then, additional research is needed that focuses on the extent to which rater differences, in combination, may contribute to the likelihood of pass/fail decisions of test candidates.

Motivation for the Current Study and Research Questions

The motivation for the current study is to investigate the influence of three established rater factors on pass/fail decisions made. See Table 1 for a description of how "rater factors" and "rater groups" are related to each other in practical terms.

Table 1. Rater Factors and Rater Groups in this Study

Rater factor	Rater groups	
Language background	Native English speakers	Non-native English speakers
Teaching experience	Experience teaching ITAs	No experience teaching ITAs
Education level	Graduate study completed	Graduate study not completed

One way to investigate is through differential item functioning (DIF). DIF examines whether members of two groups have different probabilities of giving a certain response on a specific test item. In our case, the raters were the ones who were seen as giving certain responses on the ten criteria of the ITA Performance Test. We ran two different DIF analyses on all ten criteria, oriented to our three rater factors (native speaker *versus* non-native speaker, experience teaching ITAs *versus* no experience, graduate study completed *versus* not-completed). The practical importance of this is that in using DIF analyses *for each criterion*, it is possible for us to make inferences about which criteria are contributing to the likelihood of ITAs passing or failing, by rater group.

In order to guide our DIF investigations we first conducted rater group comparisons that would indicate differences in raters' decisions, by rater factor, on whether ITA candidates overall would have passed or failed the ITA Performance Test. Hence research question #1:

RQ #1: Do the rater factors of language background, teaching experience with ITAs, or education level contribute to a difference in passing or failing ITA Performance Test scores?

Based on the results of RQ #1, we then investigated *uniform DIF* in our data set. We wanted to find out if membership in different rater groups could significantly predict raters' likelihood to pass an ITA candidate with reference to each of the ten criteria of the ITA Performance Test. In this type of analysis, significant results can be interpreted as members of two groups (e.g., native speaker *versus* non-native speaker) as behaving differently, but systematically, on a specific test criterion. Further, that difference can be directly related to raters' perceptions of whether an ITA candidate should pass or fail the test with reference to only one test criterion at time. This is analogous to studies cited above which used different methods to determine that raters as members of defined groups seem to draw from different primary criteria to form overall judgments of learners' performances. In terms of our study, for example, we wanted to know if experienced teachers of ITAs were systematically giving more credence to a particular test criterion than raters with no ITA teaching experience. We posed this research question:

RQ #2: Do the rater factors of language background, teaching experience with ITAs, or education, analyzed in turn, contribute to a difference in perceiving a passing ITA candidate amongst the ten criteria of the performance test?

Finally, we wanted to find out if the three rater factors interact to significantly predict the likelihood of a rater with complex rater group memberships passing a candidate. Table 2 provides the information as to why we needed to investigate possible predictive differences among the three factors.

Table 2. How Nine Individual Raters were Distributed into Rater Groups

Rater factor	Rater groups	
Language background	Native English speakers 6 are native English speakers	Non-native English speakers 3 are non-native speakers
	3 have experience teaching ITAs, 3 do not	2 have experience teaching ITAs, 1 does not
	5 have completed a graduate degree, 1 has not	3 have not completed a graduate degree
Teaching experience	Experience teaching ITAs 5 have experience teaching ITAs	No experience teaching ITAs 4 do not have experience teaching ITAs
	3 are native speakers of English and 2 are non-native speakers	3 are native speakers of English and 1 is a non-native speaker
	3 have completed a graduate degree and 2 have not	3 have completed a graduate degree and 1 has not
Education level	Graduate study completed 5 have completed a graduate degree	Graduate study not completed 4 have not completed a graduate degree
	5 are native speakers of English	1 is a native speaker of English and 3 are non-native speakers
	2 have experience teaching ITAs and 3 do not	3 have experience teaching ITAs and 1 does not

Note that the rater groups are not exclusive between rater factors such as language background and teaching experience. Some native speakers of English have *no* experience teaching ITAs, while some non-native speakers *do* have experience teaching ITAs, and so on. The *non-uniform DIF* procedure using logistic regression will allow us to determine if these three factors significantly predict the likelihood of passing a candidate. This statistical method, unlike the method that must be used to detect uniform DIF, allows us to understand how each rater factor contributes, as an indicator, to the overall model of passing an ITA candidate. Results would allow us to observe how inclusion of all three factors impacts raters' judgments. Our third research question is:

RQ3: Do any rater factors of language background, teaching experience with ITAs, or education taken altogether contribute to a difference in perceiving a passing ITA candidate amongst the ten criteria of the performance test?

Method

Participants

ITAs. The data set that was used for this study's analyses was 240 sets of test scores taken from a combination of 80 ITA candidates who were rated each by three raters (80 X 3 = 240). There where three test examination rooms being used concurrently and each room had three raters (two native English speaker raters, and one non-native English speaker rater). The 80 ITA candidates were the participants in an annual summer workshop that certifies them to teach undergraduate classes and labs in their departments. The ITA candidates came from a variety of disciplines, such as chemistry, economics, engineering, etc., and also language backgrounds, such as Chinese, Korean, Arabic, etc. The ITAs' performance test ratings were the result of regularly scheduled, routine test administrations.

Test raters. The nine raters were six instructors, who were all native speakers of English. Three of the six instructors were male, and three were female. Five had completed graduate degrees in applied linguistics, French, or Classics, and one was halfway through a graduate degree in applied linguistics. Only three of the instructors had experience teaching ITAs, while the other three had been instructors of French and Latin undergraduate classes. All three of the teaching assistants (TAs) were highly proficient non-native English speakers. Two had experience teaching ITAs and the third had taught Arabic in the U.S. and also English as a second language in his home country. All three were halfway through their graduate degrees in applied linguistics. See also Table 2 above. While the ratings of the TAs were not used to make decisions about ITA candidates, TAs routinely rate

ITA candidates' performance tests alongside instructors for their own enrichment and education as applied linguists.

Materials

The ITA Performance Test version 9.0 accompanies the *English Communication for International Teaching Assistants* textbook (Gorsuch, Meyers, Pickering, & Griffee, 2013). The performance test consists of ten rating criteria that are operational definitions of Bachman and Palmer's (1996) language ability model, including criteria such as "ITA uses word stress," "ITA uses transitional phrases," and "ITA uses thought groups." Each of the ten criteria is given a score from 1 ("low") to 5 ("high") with a score of 4 being required to "pass" each criteria. In order to pass the performance test, ITA candidates must score a 4 or higher on at least nine criteria. Stated in terms of total scores, the passing score is 39 or above. The minimum score possible is 10 and the maximum score possible is 50. See the Appendix. Instructors and TAs who teach in the "long semester" ITA courses have weekly meetings where, among other things, rating on the ITA Performance Test is discussed. The test is also routinely used in class to give students feedback on their presentations. Instructors who teach only in the summer workshop get two days of general training, including rater training on the ITA Performance Test.

The test is a teaching simulation test, which also classifies the test as a Target Language Use task (Bachman & Palmer, 1996). An ITA candidate must give an eight-minute presentation in which he or she defines a term or explains a process in their field. The ITA candidate must also respond to audience questions. While the ITA candidate is presenting, two to three raters (workshop instructors) rate the presentation and ITA candidates' responses to audience questions. Validation evidence for this performance test can be found in Gorsuch et al (2013); Gorsuch (2006); and Griffee, Gorsuch, Britton and Clardy (2008).

Procedure

The ITA Performance Test was administered as described in the Materials section. On the day of the test, ITA candidates were randomly assigned to a test examination room in groups of six for a one-hour block. Three raters (two instructors and one TA) completed the rating sheet (Appendix) as they listened to the presentations, and the question and answer session. The scores of the two instructors in each examination room were used for achievement decisions.

Data Analyses

The data analyses for answering all three research questions was done using *SPSS* version 21. A program called *R* can also be used for analyzing both DIF methods, and is free to download (R Core Team, 2013). To answer RQ #1, we analyzed the data using first parametric, then non-parametric measures. Our three parametric independent samples *t*-tests indicated the data were not normally distributed. We were not surprised to find non-normality, in that the rater factor groups were not equally represented in the dataset. As illustration, for the native speaker versus non-native speaker comparison, 149 score sets were completed by native speakers and only 91 by non-native speakers. So, we ran three non-parametric Mann-Whitney U tests to compare the different rater groups' ratings on ITAs' total performance test scores. The total scores were obtained by adding up numbers for each criterion the raters circled. For each group comparison of interest, the total scores were added up and averaged within each group.

To answer RQ #2, we analyzed the data using the Mantel-Haenszel (MH) method, which is appropriate when the assumption of non-normality is not met, and when sample sizes are smaller. Previous studies have used the MH method to analyze differences between language (Uiterwijk & Vallen, 2005; Harding, 2011) and gender (Pae, 2012). Used for estimating uniform DIF (Narayanan & Swaminathan, 1996), the MH method is a 2 X 2 contingency table statistic that compares two levels of an independent variable (e.g., native speaker *versus* non-native speaker) to two possible outcomes (pass or fail)(Camilli & Shepard, 1994). Thus we ran the analysis three times, once for each rater factor (language background, teaching experience, and education) for each of the ten ITA Performance Test criteria. The two values calculated for the MH method are the odds-ratio and a Chi-Square Test of Association. Both values will be given in the results, but the odds-ratio will be used for interpretation, because it is also one of the outputs of the Logistic Regression (LR) method, which we use for RQ #3.

Uniform DIF can be viewed as two groups understanding different test candidate ability levels as meeting the threshold for passing. Figure 1 shows a graphical depiction of uniform DIF.

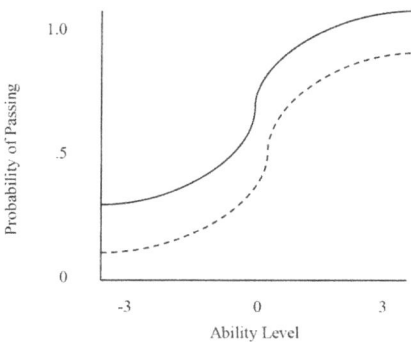

Figure 2. Graphical depiction of uniform DIF between two groups.

In Figure 2, the solid line represents one group (called a referent group) while the dashed line represents a second group (called a focal group). The figure can be interpreted as the referent group passing a candidate at a lower ability level than the focal group, hence the "higher" position of the solid line representing the reference group. Note the leftmost end of the line is positioned higher on the "probability of passing" axis, which means at a low learner ability level (-3 on the Y axis), the referent group is being more lenient in grading. What most test administrators want is a figure showing non-significant uniform DIF, where the two lines are nearly indistinguishable from each other (no difference between the two rater groups). A significant DIF would show up as it does in Figure 2 where the two lines are clearly distinguishable from each other. Based on our reading of the literature, we anticipated the possibility that on some performance test criteria, we might find significant uniform DIF, but that on others, we would not.

To answer RQ #3, we used the logistic regression (LR) method for each of the ten criteria of the ITA Performance Test. LR allowed us to add multiple rater factors (predictors), as can be seen denoted by b_1, b_2, etc. in Figure 3:

$$p(U = 1) = \frac{e^{(b_0+b_1x_1+b_2x_2+\cdots b_kx_k+\varepsilon)}}{1 + e^{(b_0+b_1x_1+b_2x_2+\cdots b_kx_k+\varepsilon)}}$$

Figure 3. Logistic regression equation.

The focus of interpretation for the LR method is on the change in slope of the curves (see Figure 4) as more predictors (rater comparisons) are added to the equation:

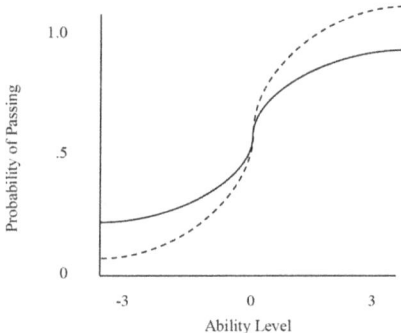

Figure 4. Graphical representation of non-uniform DIF.

Figure 4 represents significant non-uniform DIF. Note that the referent group curve (solid line) crosses the focal group curve (dashed line), suggesting an interaction in the lines predicting rater group behavior. If we were looking only at one rater factor, we would interpret this as the referent group being more likely to pass lower ability students on a given test criterion than the focal group, but *less likely* to pass *higher ability* students on the same criterion than the focal group. Because LR allows us to put all three rater factors into one analysis, we can better interpret the influences of rater factors by raters with complex group memberships (see Table 2). For interpretation, we focused on the odds-ratio figure provided from the calculation, which is an indication of two rater groups behaving differently, or not. An odds-ratio value of 1.0 suggests that both rater groups behaved similarly, with similar likelihoods of passing test candidates on a given test criterion. Negative or positive values diverging from 1.0 suggest different rater group behavior.

Results

RQ #1. Descriptive statistics for the total scores of the 240 ratings were $M = 38.73$, $SD = 2.362$, a minimum score of 30, and a maximum score of 46. Recall the cut score is 39. Table 3 shows the results of the Mann-Whitney U for the three rater group comparisons of the total test scores.

Table 3. Mann-Whitney U Results Using Total Score Ranks

Rater Characteristic	N	Z-score	Significance
Language (NS vs. NNS)	NNS = 91 NS = 149	-1.519	.129
Experience teaching ITAs (No vs. Yes)	No = 91 Yes = 149	-3.123	.002*
Graduate education (Working vs. Completed)	Working = 89 Completed = 151	-0.564	.573

Note. * means statistically significant.

Only the ITA teaching experience rater factor was significant. The negative z-score value suggests that as a group, raters with experience teaching ITAs were more likely to fail ITAs ($M = 38.38$) than raters without experience teaching ITAs ($M = 39.27$). The rater factors of language background and graduate education were not significant.

RQ #2. Table 4 shows the results of the MH method for two rater factors on all ten items of the ITA Performance Test. The rater factor of education level was not significant on any test criteria, suggesting that raters with completed graduate study and raters with graduate study in progress did not draw upon any of the test criteria in different ways in order to arrive at their overall assessments of passing or failing test candidate performances.

Table 4. Mantel-Haenszel Results for Language Background and Teaching Experience Rater Factors

	Language		Experience	
	X^2 (p-value)	Odds-Ratio	X^2 (p-value)	Odds-Ratio
Criterion 1 (word level pronunciation)	2.465 (.116)	NS	.046 (.829)	NS
Criterion 2 (word stress)	4.646 (.031*)	2.828	4.646 (.031*)	2.828
Criterion 3 (thought groups)	.034 (.853)	NS	1.753 (.186)	NS
Criterion 4 (sentence-level grammar)	.181 (.670)	NS	.181 (.670)	NS
Criterion 5 (transitional phrases)	1.130 (.288)	NS	.240 (.625)	NS
Criterion 6 (examples)	.829 (.362)	NS	.015 (.903)	NS
Criterion 7 (prominence)	13.689 (<.001*)	2.998	5.571 (.018*)	.464
Criterion 8 (comprehension checks)	.038 (.846)	NS	2.318 (.128)	NS
Criterion 9 (tone choices)	.883 (.347)	NS	.429 (.512)	NS
Criterion 10 (Q and A)	2.650 (.104)	NS	.206 (.650)	NS

Note. NS means not statistically significant. * means statistically significant.

Significant results from the language background supported a difference between native English speaking raters and non-native English speaking raters on both criterion 2 on word stress, and criterion 7 on prominence (sentence-level stress used to establish information structure). The two same criteria were also lightning rods for the teaching experience rater factor with significant results supporting a difference between raters with previous experience teaching ITAs and raters with no previous experience. An odds-ratio of 1.00 is a null hypothesis, meaning that both groups of raters are equally likely to endorse a passing score with reference to a given test criterion. For the word stress criterion, native speakers of English were three times (2.828) more likely to pass test candidates than non-native speaker raters. Raters with experience teaching ITAs were also three times (2.998) more likely to pass test candidates than raters with no experience. For the criterion on prominence, native speaker raters were three times (2.828) more likely to pass test candidates than non-native speakers. Native English speaker raters seemed to feel that ITAs' use of prominence contributed more to a pass decision. However, raters with experience teaching ITAs were 50% (.464) more likely to *fail* test candidates on the same criterion.

RQ 3. Results for the LR method analysis are shown in Table 4.

Table 5. Logistic Regression Results with Three Predictor Variables

	Overall	Language		Experience		Education	
	X² (Sig.)	B (Sig.)	Exp(B)	B (Sig.)	Exp(B)	B (Sig.)	Exp(B)
Criterion 1 (word level pronunciation)	70.673 (<.001)*	1.125 (<.001)	3.079	.625 (.002)*	1.868	-.555 (.067)	NS
Criterion 2 (word stress)	44.403 (<.001)*	-.128 (.724)	NS	.584 (.043)*	1.792	.897 (.018)	2.453
Criterion. 3 (thought groups)	135.281 (<.001)*	1.470 (.001)*	4.350	1.047 (.001)*	2.850	-.277 (.501)	NS
Criterion 4 (sentence-level grammar)	14.351 (.026)*	.166 (.627)	NS	-.108 (.731)	NS	.446 (.245)	NS
Criterion 5 (transitional phrases)	58.198 (<.001)*	-.137 (.806)	NS	1.475 (.004)*	4.370	.598 (.285)	NS
Criterion 6 (examples)	17.036 (.009)*	.716 (.162)	NS	.432 (.287)	NS	-.176 (.727)	NS
Criterion 7 (prominence)	151.315 (<.001)*	1.076 (.012)*	2.934	.851 (.001)*	2.341	.304 (.447)	NS
Criterion 8	19.621 (.003)*	.060 (.846)	NS	-.004 (.988)	NS	.917 (.009)*	2.501
Criterion 9 (tone choices)	123.680 (<.001)*	1.068 (.008)*	2.911	1.006 (<.001)*	2.734	-.093 (.811)	NS
Criterion 10 (Q and A)	66.917 (<.001)*	.160 (.486)	NS	.492 (.003)*	1.636	.439 (.057)	NS

Note. NS means not statistically significant. * means statistically significant. Exp(B) means odds-ratio.

The Exp(B) column in Table 5 provides the odds-ratio variable for every predictor (rater factor) that is significantly different from the null model (1.0). For the word pronunciation criterion, native speaking raters were three times (3.079) more likely to pass an ITA candidate. Accounting for experience, however, showed that experienced raters are nearly twice (1.868) as likely to pass ITAs. For the word stress criterion, raters who had experience teaching ITAs were nearly three times (1.792) more likely to pass ITAs than raters without ITA teaching experience. This ratio changed slightly (2.453) when education was taken into account. For the criterion of thought groups, native speakers of English were four times (4.350) more likely to pass a candidate. This odds-ratio changed to nearly three times (2.850) likely to pass when experience was taken into account. On the transitional phrases criterion, experienced raters were over four times (4.37) as likely to pass candidates. On the prominence criterion, native English speaker raters were nearly three times (2.934) more likely to pass an ITA than a non-native English speaker. However, raters with experience teaching ITAs were nearly just as likely (2.341) for passing an ITA. For the criterion of comprehension checks, raters with completed Master's degrees were 2.5 times more likely to pass candidates than raters still completing their Master's degrees. On the criterion of tone choice, native speakers of English were nearly three times (2.911) more likely to pass candidates than non-native speakers. The odd-ratio is similar for the rater factor of experience, nearly three times (2.734). Finally, the odds ratio of passing an ITA candidate for the Q & A criterion are over 1.5 times (1.636) when experience is taken in account. The Cox & Snell R square values (effects sizes) for the previously discussed criteria were .255, .169, .431, .215, .468, .079, .403, and .243, respectively. Effect sizes for all regression models range from small, $\leq .16$, to large, $\leq .36$ (Cohen, 1988).

Discussion

Research question 1: Significant differences between rater characteristics on total performance test scores. Results from the Mann-Whitney U test support rejecting the null hypothesis, and suggests that raters with previous ITA teaching experience rate test candidates significantly differently from raters who do not have previous experience (Table 3). Experienced ITA teachers are less likely to pass ITA candidates. And, at first blush, we might conclude that native English speaker raters are more likely to fail ITAs on the performance test, and that as a group, they are simply harder graders. But we suggest that the other rater factor z-scores from Table 3 offer a more nuanced interpretation, which points to the reason we used DIF analyses. All three z-scores for each of the three rater factors are negative. According to this, native English speaker raters *and* raters with prior experience teaching ITAs *and* raters with completed degrees are all more likely to fail ITA candidates. Yet according to Table 2, some native English speaker raters (more harsh raters?) have no experience teaching ITAs (more lenient raters?). Rater group membership is tangled, just as tangled as the literature we reviewed on rater factors. Thus we need to look to the DIF results for RQs #2 and #3 to tease these effects apart using a best-fit, best-predictive model.

Research question 2: Uniform DIF, Word stress, language background, and teaching experience. In terms of uniform DIF, the MH method identified two test criteria, word stress and prominence, that were scored significantly differently by rater groups with different language backgrounds and with different teaching experience. On word stress, the native English speaker raters, and raters with prior experience teaching ITAs, were nearly three times more likely to pass an ITA candidate. These two rater groups associated good word stress with passing ITAs on the performance test (Table 4). We could speculate that native English speaker raters may be more sensitive to word stress patterns than their non-native rater counterparts. This sensitivity can be duplicated, however, with non-native English speaker raters ($n = 2$) who had guided, supported experience teaching and rating ITAs.

Research question 2: Uniform DIF, Prominence, and language background and teaching experience. On prominence (stressing of key words in utterances), the results were not as symmetrical. Native English speaker raters were *more* likely to pass an ITA candidate with reference to this criterion, but raters with prior experience teaching ITAs were *less* likely to pass a candidate (Table 4). One reason for this non-symmetrical shift may be that this particular ITA program places much emphasis on hearing and saying prominence as a key resource for expressing information structure in teaching talk. ITA candidates are asked, throughout the semester courses and the summer workshop, to work on emphasizing key words. A rater with previous experience teaching and rating ITAs in this program (3 native speakers, and 2 non-native speakers) might be more sensitive to identifying key words, and then be critical (more likely to fail) when lower-ability ITA candidates do not use prominence, or overuse it by putting prominence on every word without regard to intended meaning. An ITA may do this if they are overgeneralizing what they learned about prominence in ITA classes. This utterance, spoken in a complete monotone: *this is today's topic we are talking about exothermic reactions* would be hard to process, just as the same utterance would be spoken with prominent words without regard to the information structure: *THIS IS TODAY'S TOPIC WE ARE TALKING ABOUT EXOTHERMIC REACTIONS*. Compare the two utterances with *this is toDAY's TOpic we are talking about exoTHERmic reActions.*

We wonder, however, if native English speaker raters (3 with experience teaching ITAs, but 3 without) may be better equipped to listen for the linguistic and acoustic cues associated with prominence without necessarily paying close attention to the content of the lecture. Alternatively, we wonder whether native speaker raters are perhaps more likely to impose, through their own expectations of what words *should* receive prominence, a perception that prominence has been used. Are they perhaps, in their own way, overgeneralizing? The results from the MH method are suggestive of interpretation, but the raters as human beings with complex pasts do not belong solely in one of three distinct rater factor categories (see Table 2). It is evident, however, that one or both rater groups lack clarity on the construct of prominence.

Research question 3: Presence of non-uniform DIF on the word stress criterion. Because the three rater factors were not nominal categories with exclusive membership, LR was better able to examine group differences as additive factors of raters. In other words, LR helped better explain which rater factor or factors accounted for the most variance on given test criterion. On the word stress criterion (#2), we found that only the teaching experience rater factor accounted for rater group differences (Table 5), not language background or teaching experience rater factors as was suggested by the MH method (Table 4). In other words, teaching experience trumps language background. This result supports the previous interpretation that guided, supported teaching experience with ITAs in the program gave non-native English speaker raters the opportunity to better understand the construct being measured (word stress in continuous spoken utterances). We would further argue that native speaker raters were just as likely supported, through teaching experience with ITAs, to better understand the word stress construct. It would be wrong to suggest that non-native speaker raters must somehow be "refurbished" to be more like native speaker raters. Guided, supported teaching experience, which in our program includes rater training, has the potential to change anyone.

Research question 3: Presence of non-uniform DIF on the prominence criterion. In the LR analysis, all three rater factors contributed to explaining the variance evident in raters' behavior on this criterion (Table 5). Language background accounted for most of the variance, with native English speaker raters nearly four and a half times more likely to pass ITA candidates with reference to prominence. At the same time, raters with experience teaching ITAs were 50% more likely to *fail* ITAs, and raters who had completed their graduate education were 44% more likely to *fail* ITAs with reference to the prominence criterion. This particular model took into account the tangled rater group memberships (Table 2) and thus we can underscore two somewhat competing hypotheses that we proposed in the discussion on RQ #2. We can argue that: 1. Native speaker raters of English have more linguistic resources for hearing prominence. It can also be argued that because prominence is so expected in talk, native English speaker raters have assigned great importance to this criterion. When they feel an ITA candidate is using or not using prominence, they strongly consider this criterion in passing or failing a candidate. However, we can also argue that: 2. Native English speaker raters may be perhaps more likely to impose what prominence they *think* they should be hearing, because they have the on-line, real-time linguistic resources to do so. This does not mean, however, that the ITA candidate is actually using that much prominence, or is using it appropriately and consistently. If an ITA is not speaking entirely in a monotone, and is using *some* prominence in their talk, even if the placement is illogical, it may be just enough to give the impression that they "have" prominence and are capable of using it consistently in such a way as to clearly mark information structure.

We offer evidence that experience teaching ITAs and completion of a graduate degree somewhat reduce the "native speaker" effect on this criterion. It is worth considering why. Perhaps this means that while the native English speaker raters can hear prominence better and assign it greater importance, experience and education may reduce a tendency to over-assign ITAs' use of prominence. A trained and experienced native English speaker rater will always be preferred to an untrained and inexperienced native English speaker rater. In the end, we have no real evidence for either hypothesis. See our comments about this issue under Research Ideas. With an effect size estimate of 0.104, we are concerned about this discrepancy between rater groups. We want to revise our rater training to take into account both native and non-native English speaker raters' possible lack of clarity on this construct, particularly when a rater from either group comes to us without prior experience teaching ITAs.

Research question 3: Presence of non-uniform DIF on the transitional phrase criterion. The LR analysis revealed an additional criterion on which different rater groups behaved in significantly different ways (Table 5). Transitional phrases, like prominence, are important for signaling information structure in teaching talk. Native English speaker raters were nearly four times more likely to pass ITAs than non-native speaker raters with reference to this criterion, and this rater factor explained the lion's share of variance. Raters with experience teaching ITAs were around 18% more likely to *fail* ITAs with reference to this criterion. It is true that transitional phrases and prominence have discoursal functions in common. It may be argued, also, that when transitional phrases are given prominence by a speaker, the information structure of the talk is probably enhanced. However, we wonder whether the ability to *hear and rate* transitional phrases is as challenging to non-native English raters (or native speaker raters, really), as hearing and rating prominence is. Surely the frequency of prominence would be greater in any naturally occurring talk than actual, formal, transitional phrases? We wonder if, for linguistic or cultural reasons, native English speaker raters value the use of transitional phrases more than non-native speaker raters do?

Research Ideas

To test the hypothesis that native speakers of English may be overestimating test candidates' use of prominence, versus a hypothesis that non-native speakers lack the linguistic resources to adequately focus on the prominence construct, we suggest the following: Both native and non-native speaker raters with varying degrees of experience, etc., could mark a transcript of an ITA talk predicting prominence. Then, after a suitable period of time, they could mark a new, unmarked transcript for what prominence they hear in an audio recording of the ITA giving the talk. Then machine measures of the actual prominence used in the audio file could be compared again against what both rater groups think they should hear, and what they thought they heard. To more firmly fix causality for rater training, in which we place so much store, additional research could look at conducting a DIF analysis of raters before and after participating in rater training.

Comments on the Utility of MH and LR Analyses

From a test data-and-analysis standpoint, we are pleased with the information the MH and LR analyses afforded us. This shows two methodologies that are capable of getting information from a test in more fine detail than a composite score. Recent research in language testing has focused on DIF analysis associated with Item Response Theory (Beglar, 2010; Aryadoust, 2012; Winke, Gass, & Myford, 2012). One limitation of using IRT is that model convergence requires a relatively large sample size (Suen, 1990), likely a minimum of 120 participants per category. The advantage of using the MH and LR methods is that they are capable of producing significant results with a sample size minimum of 30 participants per category. For many working testing programs with limited sample sizes, and a concomitant need to investigate systematic differences in behavior between rater groups in a timely fashion, the MH and LR analyses are a significant resource.

Conclusions

This study investigated whether differential item functioning (DIF) was occurring among international teaching assistant (ITA) performance test raters. Given the literature, we focused on three rater factors: language background, teaching experience, and education level. We found that three out of ten test criteria were being rated differently by some rater groups. On two of the criteria which concerned how information structure is marked in teaching talk, native English speaker rater versus non-native speaker rater differences explained most of the variance. However, on one criterion, that of word stress, rater teaching experience explained most of the variance. We wanted to explore raters' work on a high stakes performance test in the context of local hiring politics with an eye to illuminating possible variables we, as applied linguists, felt were at play. We also wanted to have this discussion against the backdrop of global discussions on native speakers and non-native speakers of a language, and the second language teaching profession.

In the final analysis, the purpose of DIF studies is to identify sources of DIF that are not desired, and to help guide rater training. The results from the MH and LR analyses in this study could be interpreted as support for the training program being conducted, as seven of the test criteria showed no DIF. We persist in believing that rater training (Figure 1), and experience teaching and rating ITAs, are the best ways to ensure that all ITA candidates are rated fairly by all raters, whether native English speakers, or fluent non-native speakers.

In a Nutshell

1. The literature suggests that second language learners hold complex attitudes toward both native and non-native speaker teachers.
2. Some ITA candidates, as second language learners, may feel that non-native English speaker teachers and raters in an ITA program are somehow "in the wrong place" for the task of assessing their spoken abilities.
3. Administrators in second language programs seem interested in some threshold of fluent and competent language use when hiring instructors. Whatever is considered a "heavy" accent may be problematic.
4. We tested whether native or non-native English speaker raters were harsher or easier graders on a teaching simulation test, and whether either group might lack clarity on the ten constructs being assessed.
5. We found one construct that both native English speaker and non-native raters may be unclear about, but for dif-

ferent reasons. It can be resolved through revised rater training.
6. Our results strongly suggest that an ITA instructor or test rater should never be hired entirely on the basis they are native speakers of English. Without prior experience teaching ITAs, and with inadequate rater training, native English speaker test raters may not be entirely competent. (We would also claim this of non-native English speaker raters—they must have appropriate experience and education, and rater training, to do the job competently.)
7. Hiring decisions for ITA programs should be based on job candidates' English language ability, *and* experience and education relevant to the job.

References

Aryadoust, V. (2012). Differential item functioning in while-listening performance tests: The case of the International English Language Testing System (IELTS listening module. *The International Journal of Listening, 26*, 40-60.

Bachman, L., & Palmer, A. (1996). *Language testing in practice: Designing and developing useful language tests.* Oxford: Oxford University Press.

Beglar, D. (2010). A Rasch-based validation of the Vocabulary Size Test. *Language Testing, 27*(1), 101-118.

Benke, E. & Medgyes, P. (2005). Differences in teaching behavior between native and non-native speaker teachers: As seen by the learners. In E. Llurda (Ed.), *Non-native language teachers* (pp. 195-210). New York: Springer.

Brown, A., Iwashita, N., & McNamara, T. (2005). An examination of rater orientations and test-taker performance on English-for-Academic-Purposes speaking tasks. *Research Report-Educational Testing Service, 5*.

Camilli, G., & Shepard, L. A. (1994). *MMSS: Methods for Identifying Biased Test Items.* Thousand Oaks, CA: Sage Publications.

Chalhoub-Deville, M. (1995). Deriving oral assessment scales across different tests and rater groups. *Language Testing, 12*(1), 16-33.

Chalhoub-Deville, M., & Wigglesworth, G. (2005). Rater judgment and English language speaking proficiency. *World Englishes, 24*(3), 383-391.

Clark, E., Paran, A., & Clark, W. (2007). The employability of non-native speaker teachers of EFL: A U.K. survey. *System, 35*(4), 1-47.

Cohen, J. (1988). *Statistical power analysis for the behavioral sciences.* (2nd ed.). Hillsdale, NJ: Lawrence Erlbaum Associates.

Gorsuch, G. (2006). Classic challenges in international teaching assistant assessment. In D. Kaufmann & B. Brownworth (Eds.), *Professional development of international teaching assistants* (pp. 69-80). Alexandria, VA: Teachers of English to Speakers of Other Languages, Inc.

Gorsuch, G., Meyers, C. M., Pickering, L., & Griffee, D. T. (2013). *English communication for international teaching assistants.* (2nd ed.). Long Grove, IL: Waveland Press, Inc.

Graddol, D. (2006). *English next.* The British Council.

Graddol, D. (2014). Five megatrends shaping the future of TESOL. James A. Alatis Plenary Session, Teacher of English to Speakers of Other Languages Convention, March 27, Portland, Oregon.

Griffee, D. T., Gorsuch, G. J., Britton, D., & Clardy, C. (2008). Intensive second language instruction for international teaching assistants: How much and what kind is effective? In G. F. Ollington (Ed.). *Teachers and teaching: Strategies, innovations, a problem solving* (pp. 187-205). Hauppage, NY: Nova Science.

Hamp-Lyons, L., & Zhang, W. X. (2001). World Englishes: Issues in and from academic writing assessment. *English for academic purposes: Research perspectives*, 101-116.

Harding, L. (2011). Accent, listening assessment and the potential for a shared-L1 advantage: A DIF perspective. *Language Testing, 29*(2), 163-180.

Johnson, J. S., & Lim, G. S. (2009). The influence of rater language background on writing performance assessment. *Language Testing, 26*(4), 485-505.

Kamhi-Stein, L. (1999). Preparing non-native professionals in TESOL: Implications for teacher education programs. In G. Braine (Ed.), *Non-native educators in English language teaching* (pp. 145-158). Mahwah, NJ: Erlbaum.

Kim, Y. H. (2009). An investigation into native and non-native teachers' judgments of oral English performance: A mixed methods approach. *Language Testing, 26*(2), 187-217.

Kobayashi, T. (1992). Native and nonnative reactions to ESL compositions. *TESOL Quarterly, 26*(1), 81-112.

Lasagabaster, D. & Sierra, J. (2005). What do students think about the pros and cons of having a native speaker teacher? In E. Llurda (Ed.), *Non-native language teachers* (pp. 217-241). New York: Springer.

Lev-Ari, S., & Keysar, B. (2010). Why don't we believe non-native speakers? The influence of accent on credibility. *Journal of Experimental Social Psychology, 46*(6), 1093-1096.

Liu, J. (2005). Chinese graduate teaching assistants teaching freshman composition to native English speaking students. In E. Llurda (Ed.), *Non-native language teachers* (pp. 155-177). New York: Springer.

Mahboob, A. (2004). Native or nonnative: What do students enrolled in an intensive English program think? In L.D. Kamhi-Stein (Ed.), *Learning and teaching from experience* (pp. 121-147). Ann Arbor, MI: The University of Michigan Press.

Mahboob, A., Uhrig, K., Newman, K., & Hartford, B. (2004). Children of a lesser English: Status on nonnative English speakers as college-level English as a second language teachers in the United States. In L.D. Kamhi-Stein (Ed.), *Learning and teaching from experience* (pp. 100-120). Ann Arbor, MI: The University of Michigan Press.

Meadows, B. & Muramatsu, Y. (2007). Native speaker or non-native speaker teacher?: A report of student preferences in four different foreign language classrooms. *Arizona Working Papers in SLA & Teaching, 14,* 95-109.

Moussu, L. (2006). *Native and nonnative English-speaking English as a second language teachers: Student attitudes, teacher self-perceptions, and intensive English administrator beliefs and practices.* Unpublished doctoral dissertation, Purdue University, West Lafayette, Indiana.

Narayanan, P., & Swaminathan, H. (1996). Identification of items that show non-uniform DIF. *Applied Psychological Measurement, 20*(3), 257-274.

Pacek, D. (2005). "Personality not nationality": Foreign students' perceptions of a non-native lecturer of English as a British university. In E. Llurda (Ed.), *Non-native language teachers* (pp. 243-262). New York: Springer.

Pae, T. (2012). Causes of gender DIF on an EFL language test: A multiple-data analysis over nine years. *Language Testing, 29*(4), 533-554.

Pollitt, A., & Murray, N. L. (1996). What raters really pay attention to. In *Performance testing, cognition and assessment: Selected papers from the 15th Language Testing Research Colloquium (LTRC), Cambridge and Arnhem* (Vol. 3, pp. 74-91).

R Core Team (2013). R: A language and environment for statistical computing (Version 3.0.2) [software]. Available: http://www.R-project.org.

Smith, J. (1994). Enhancing curricula for teaching assistant development. In C.G. Madden & C.L. Myers (Eds.), *Discourse and performance of international teaching assistants* (pp. 52-80). Alexandria, VA: Teachers of English to Speakers of Other Languages, Inc.

Smith, J., Meyers, C., & Burkhalter, A. (1992). *Communicate: Strategies for international teaching assistants.* Englewood Cliffs, NJ: Regents/Prentice Hall.

Suen, H. K. (1990). *Principles of Test Theories.* Hillsdale, NJ: Lawrence Erlbaum Associates, Inc.

Teachers of English to Speakers of Other Languages (2010). Joint statement on the teacher English fluency initiative in Arizona. Retrieved February 24, 2014 from: http://www.tesol.org/docs/pdf/13248.pdf?sfvrsn=2

Teachers of English to Speakers of Other Languages (2013). TESOL comments on the Workforce Investment Act of 2013. Retrieved February 24, 2014 from: http://www.tesol.org/docs/default-source/advocacy/tesolcommentss1356-final.pdf?sfvrsn=4

Uiterwijk, H., & Vallen, T. (2005). Linguistic sources of item bias for second generation immigrants in Dutch tests. *Language Testing, 22*(2), 211-234.

Winke, P., Gass, S., & Myford, C. (2012). Raters' L2 background as a potential source of bias in rating oral performance. *Language Testing, 30*(2), 231-252.

Wu, A. (2010). Editor's remarks. *NNEST News, 12*(1). Retrieved November 10, 2013 from http://www.tesol.org/read-and-publish/newsletters-other-publications/interest-section-newsletters/nnest-newsletter/2011/10/27/nnest-news-volume-12-1-(june-2010)

Xi, X. & Molluan, P. (2011). Using raters from India to score a large-scale speaking test. *Language Learning, 61*(4), 1222-1255.

Appendix

ITA Performance Test V. 9.0

Grammatical competence
1. The ITA candidate pronounces sounds clearly enough at the word level that the listener can understand what word is intended.
1   2   3   4   5   Occasional difficulty, but usually understandable.
Low   *   High

2. ITA uses word stress (*expectation, similar*) and does not add or drop syllables.
1   2   3   4   5   Multisyllabic words usually understandable.
Low   *   High

3. ITA candidates uses thought groups effectively.
1   2   3   4   5   Generally listeners not aware of whether thought groups used.
Low   *   High

Textual competence
4. ITA uses grammatical structures effectively.
1   2   3   4   5   Listener not confused by ungrammatical propositions.
Low   *   High

5. ITA uses transitional phrases effectively to provide cohesion to the content (*First, second, Ok, my next point is…*).
1   2   3   4   5   Listeners can follow the logic of the talk.
Low   *   High

6. ITA gives clear definitions and examples based on audience awareness.
1   2   3   4   5   Candidate frequently inserts definitions and examples.
Low   *   High

Sociolinguistic competence
7. ITA uses prominence.
1   2   3   4   5   Listeners are aware of important words.
Low   *   High

8. ITA aware of listener non-comprehension by techniques such as eye-contact, wait time, and checking for comprehension. (*Does everybody understand so far?*)
1   2   3   4   5   Does at least two of the above.
Low   *   High

9. ITA varies tone choice so as to produce a variety of rising and falling tones; not a monotone.
1   2   3   4   5   Not all rising tones, not all falling tones.
Low   *   High

Functional competence
10. Candidate expands beyond audience questions by acknowledging the question, confirming understanding by repeating or paraphrasing the question, answering the question, and checking back to confirm question has been answered.
1   2   3   4   5   Candidate accomplishes at least 3 of the 4
                                    techniques.
Low   *   High

Recommendations for the future that the candidate can work on:

Index

A

Academic departments, xvii
   developing conditions for ITA
      spoken language development,
      x - xviii
   faculty members in, viii – xix, 249
      - 250
   ITA orientations in, x – xi, 265
   lack of support for ITAs, 218 - 220
   numbers of ITAs in, 265
   ongoing support from, 218 – 220
   recruiters
      knowledge of second language
         learning processes, 257
      priorities of, 241 – 242, 248 –
         249, 251 – 252, 256 - 257
      strategies of, 249 - 250
      transitory knowledge base of,
         257
   relationship to ITA programs, 241
   staff members in, viii – xix
   teaching practices in, x, 265 - 266
Acculturation, 211
   integration or assimilative strategies, 211, 225 - 226
   models of, 212
   separatist strategies, 211, 226

C

Coherence
   definition of, 142 – 143
Cohesion
   description of, 144
Cohesive ties
   classes of, 151, 153 - 157
   distance from referent, 146 - 147
   examples of, 144
   functions of, 143
   ideas for instruction of, 159 - 162
   ITAs' use of by proficiency level, 152
   need for instruction in, 159
   previous research on, 146
   teaching materials for, 161 - 162
College instructors
   concerns of, xix, 279
   host instructors for ITAs, xix - xx
   learning of, viii
   classroom management, 222 - 223
   of undergraduates, vii - xvii
   team teaching, xix
College courses
   embedding intercultural contact
      activities in, 192 – 194
   need for evaluation of, 195
Communication
   between ITAs and undergraduates,
      46 – 48, 56 – 58, 77, 84, 98 – 99
   published research on, 76
   between teachers and students, 44
   in chemistry labs, 266 - 270
      description of, 44 – 48, 56 - 66
      topics discussed in, 40
   in physics labs, 85 – 86
   in STEM education, 77 - 78
   judgments of success of, 44
   learning to do in science, 265 - 266
   patterns in science labs, 45
   role of learner questions, 44, 55, 67
Communicative Competence, xi
   components of, 142, 208 - 209
   definition of, 141 – 142
   international teaching assistants'
      perspectives on, 290 - 211
   suggestions for development of, 209 - 211
   used as basis for ITA support program curricula, 141, 208
Comprehensibility
   factors detracting from, 147, 157
Contact Hypothesis, 175
   application of in undergraduate
      courses, 177
   published research on treatments
      based on, 175 - 176

Conversation Analysis, 77
   specialists in, x

D

Data collection methods
   Benchmarking approach, 293 – 294
   websearches in, 294
   concurrent verbal report (think-aloud report), 115 – 116, 133
   concurrent verbal report training video, 118
   interviews, 40 – 43, 244
      analysis of data, 215 – 216
      development of, 245 - 246
      methods for, 214 – 215
      piloting, 245 - 246
      sample of, 237 – 238, 275
      sampling method for, 294 - 295
      semi-structured, 41 - 43
      unstructured, 213 – 241
   memos, 244
   observations
      in chemistry labs, 44 – 48
   recorded and transcribed oral proficiency test responses, 150
   performance test scores, 327 – 328
      differential item functioning analysis, 328 - 330
   questionnaires, 181 – 182
      constructs of, 182 – 184
      example of, 200 - 201
      sample items, 184
   speech samples, 181 - 182
Declarative knowledge (see propositional knowledge)
Discourse competence
   definition of, 142
   examples for, 141 - 142
Discourse markers
   functions of, 78, 80 – 83, 87 - 98
   in ITA lectures, 78 – 79
   previous research on, 146 - 147
   uses in ITA preparation, 99
   uses in mentoring ITAs, 99 - 100

E

English as a Second Language
   learners, xii - xiii
   programs, xvi
   teachers, vii – xiii
      attitudes towards native speaker teachers, 316 - 317
      attitudes towards non-native speaker teachers, 316, 317
      hiring patterns of, 317 - 317
ESL (see English as a second language)

F

Faculty members
   perspectives on communication success, 51 – 52, 265 – 266

G

Graduate Schools
   admissions process, 247
   standardized test scores used for, 247, 251

H

Higher education
   changes in student enrollments, 240

I

Information structure
   role of parentheticals, 7, 29
Instructional discourse
   parentheticals in, 17, 28 – 29
Intelligibility
   definition of, 110
   effect of overall proficiency on, 128 - 130
   listeners' judgments of, 110, 114
   using discourse contexts for, 113 - 114

Interaction
    ITA and undergraduate, 77
    transcriptions of, 87 - 98
    transcriptions of used for instruction, 104 - 108
Interaction analysis
    coding of interactions, 39 - 40
    turn-taking, 56 - 58
    unit of analysis, 39
Interactional competence, 87
Intercultural communication
    cultural differences and, xi
    specialists in, x - xii
Intercultural competence, xiii
    role of second language in, xiv
International graduate students, vii
    attitudes of, 177 – 178
    attitudes towards undergraduates, 190 - 191
    numbers of, ix, 204, 265
    strategies for finding schools to apply to, 250 - 251
International Teaching Assistants
    adjustments to teaching in the U.S., 225
    as contributors to ITA programs, 212
    as international sojourners, 204
    as second language learners, xi
    assessment of, viii – x
    challenges for, 207
    communication skills of, 33
    comparison with American TAs, 20 - 27, 35
    complaints about, 240 - 241
    comprehensibility of, 140
    controversies about, 33, 170 - 171
    description of, vii
    diversity of, 204 – 206
    English proficiency scores of, 241
        relationship with approval to teach, 241 - 242
    experiences teaching undergraduates, 205
    inadequate support for, 303 - 304
    in-classroom research on, 34
    mentors of, xiv – xx
        suggestions for, 134
    need for, 204
    numbers of, 204 – 206, 287
    perspectives on communication success, 51 - 53
    need for feedback, xii - xx
    numbers of, ix
    rate of speech by proficiency level, 158
    relationship with undergraduates, 27 - 28
    research on, xii, 6, 34
    research agenda on, 34 – 35, 207
    roles of, 206
    speaking tests for Clear Speech test, 277
        pre- and post-tests with, 277
        scoring intelligibility with, 264
        Oral English Speaking Proficiency Test, 149 - 150
    spoken proficiency of, 115, 119 – 120
    state mandated testing of, 207
    support personnel for, xiv
    support programs, x, 288, 303 - 304
    use of parentheticals, 6, 27 – 28
    worth to universities, 258
International Teaching Assistant programs, ix
    as an established presence on campuses, 241
    coffee talks, 211
    conversation corners, 211
    curriculum of, x – xx, 77, 79, 100, 266 – 272, 287 – 290
    descriptions from national sample of, 297
    evaluation of, 275 – 283
        results of, 279 – 282, 284
    fragmented within institutions, 291
    graduate student recruitment and implications for, 241
    importance to the institution, 241
    in academic departments, 209, 216, 218 – 220, 266 - 282
    inputs, 241
    institutional influences on, 289,

299 – 300, 302 - 303
ITAs' suggestions for, 216 – 217, 228 – 230, 280
intra-campus communication, 300 - 301
origins of, ix, 206
professional interest groups, ix
recommendations for improvement, 304 - 306
relationships with academic departments, viii - xx
seen as an obstacle to timely graduation, viii
shortcomings of, 257
static funding for, 241
summer orientations, vii-viii, 265 - 282
TA and ITA pre-teaching workshops, 216 - 217
theoretical underpinnings of, xi
ITAs (see International Teaching Assistants)

L

Linguistic stereotyping, 172 – 173
   causes of, 196
   contact activities for amelioration, 184 – 186

O

Organizational Structure Theory, 291 - 292

P

Parentheticals
   definitions of, 4, 5, 6, 7
   functions of, 4, 5, 14, 15, 16, 17, 18
   informationally marked
      pronouns used in, 19, 27
      vocabulary used in, 20, 21
   prosodically marked, 5, 8, 13
      content-connecting, 11, 16, 28
      interpersonal, 11, 13, 18, 28
      regulatory, 11, 12

   teacher use of, 5, 27
Performance tests, 314, 327
   criteria, 332 – 333
   needing more rater training on, 335 - 338
   raters of, 314, 323
      education level, 322, 325
      native speakers, 314, 321, 325
      non-native speakers, 314, 321, 325
      teaching experience, 321, 325
   rater training
      evaluation of, 334 - 338
      on specific tests, 322
   rater training model, 320
   teaching simulations, viii – xii, 327
Practice
   de Keyser, xv - xvi
   opportunities for in academic departments, xvii - xx
   second language learning and, xv
   teaching, xix
Procedural knowledge
   encouraging development of, ix - xiii, xvii
   ITA programs and, viii - xviii
   role of language in developing, xiii
   second language use, x - xvi
Proceduralization
   second language, xv – xvi
Pronunciation
   curriculum for, 111, 114, 134 - 135
   goals of instruction in, 110
   intelligibility, 110 – 111
   published research on, 112
   segmental aspects of, 111 – 113
   suprasegmental aspects of, 111 - 113
Propositional knowledge
   ITA programs and, xiv - xviii
   second language learning and, xvi
Prosody
   analysis of, 8, 11, 17
   functions of, 7

S

Science, Technology, Engineering, and Mathematics (STEM)
  teaching in, 4
  need to recruit international graduate students, 264
  role of graduate students in U.S. economy, 264
Second language learning
  role of talk within disciplines, 265
  role of practice, xviii
  slowness of, viii – xiii, 257, 259
  spoken fluency, xix – xx
Segmentals
  arguments for focus on, 111 - 112
  and intelligibility, 131 - 133
  which affect listener's ability to understand, 121 - 128
Self efficacy
  role of experience in, xiv - xviii
  role of mentor, xv
  second language use and, xiv
Systemic functional linguistics
  definition of, 8
  logico-semantic relationships in (projection, expansion), 9
  metafunctions in (ideational, interpersonal, textual), 8

T

TEACH, 116 – 117, 134 – 135
Teaching and Learning Centers ITA support programs in, x, 295
Teaching assistants, definition of, 243
Test of Spoken English (TSE), 149

TOEFL test, 117, 149, 242 – 245
  description of, 243
  ITAs' widely varying scores on, 254
  listening subtest, 244, 248
    as predictor of approval to teach, 244, 252 - 256
  SPEAK test (retired versions of Test of Spoken English—TSE)
  speaking subtest scores, 244, 248
    as predictor of approval to teach, 244, 252 – 256
    cut score caveats and proper use, 259
    suggested cut scores, 258 - 259
    use of by recruiters, 251 - 252

U

U.S. undergraduates
  background characteristics of, 37
  questionnaire for, 72
  effects on international teaching assistants, 171
  improveming intercultural sensitivity of, 174, 194 - 195
  judgments of ITA communication success, 51 – 55
  judgments of non-native speech, 188 - 189
  linguistic stereotyping done by, 172 - 173

www.ingramcontent.com/pod-product-compliance
Lightning Source LLC
Chambersburg PA
CBHW061422300426
44114CB00014B/1496